The Awakening of
Modern Japanese Fiction

The Awakening of Modern Japanese Fiction

Path Literature and an Interpretation of Buddhism

Michihiro Ama

Artwork on the cover by artist Atsuko Kubota.

Publication of this book was supported by a gift from Taikō Hamaji, President, Hamaji Corporation (Japan).

Published by State University of New York Press, Albany

© 2021 State University of New York

All rights reserved

Printed in the United States of America

No part of this book may be used or reproduced in any manner whatsoever without written permission. No part of this book may be stored in a retrieval system or transmitted in any form or by any means including electronic, electrostatic, magnetic tape, mechanical, photocopying, recording, or otherwise without the prior permission in writing of the publisher.

For information, contact State University of New York Press, Albany, NY
www.sunypress.edu

Library of Congress Cataloging-in-Publication Data

Names: Ama, Michihiro, author.
Title: The awakening of modern Japanese fiction : path literature and an interpretation of Buddhism / Michihiro Ama.
Description: Albany : State University of New York, 2021. | Includes bibliographical references and index.
Identifiers: LCCN 2020023297 (print) | LCCN 2020023298 (ebook) | ISBN 9781438481418 (hardcover : alk. paper) | ISBN 9781438481425 (pbk. : alk. paper) | ISBN 9781438481432 (ebook)
Subjects: LCSH: Japanese fiction—Taishō period, 1912–1926—History and criticism. | Buddhist literature—History and criticism. | Buddhism in literature. | Buddhism and literature—Japan.
Classification: LCC PL747.63.B8 A43 2021 (print) | LCC PL747.63.B8 (ebook) | DDC 895.63/609382—dc23
LC record available at https://lccn.loc.gov/2020023297
LC ebook record available at https://lccn.loc.gov/2020023298

10 9 8 7 6 5 4 3 2 1

To Tomoko

Contents

Acknowledgments ix

Notes about Japanese Names xi

Introduction 1

Chapter 1 A Disciplinary Divide and the Conceptual Framework of the Present Study 11

Part 1
Writing Personal Fiction as a Confessional and Religious Practice

Chapter 2 Modern Japanese Writers as Lay Buddhist Practitioners 35

Chapter 3 *Ari no mama* as Literary and Buddhist Discourse 61

Chapter 4 Shin Buddhist Confession and Literary Practice 89

Chapter 5 A Shin Buddhist Historical Novel 121

Part 2
The Buddhist Reading of Personal Fiction

Chapter 6 Buddhist Words and Buddhist Symbols in Personal Novels 147

Chapter 7 Buddhist Attainment and Mystical Experience 171

Chapter 8   Literary Representations of Buddhist Funerals   191

Conclusion   215

Appendix 1   Translation of the Preface to *Before and after My Rebirth*
by Akegarasu Haya   225

Appendix 2   Translation of the Preface to *Guardians of the
Dharma Castle* by Matsuoka Yuzuru   247

Notes   263

Bibliography   315

Index   333

Acknowledgments

I received support from so many people in writing this book that it is easier for me to recollect and thank them by putting them into categories. Please forgive me if I failed to recall individuals who guided me graciously during a period of more than ten years of research.

First and foremost, I would like to thank David Stahl for reading the entire draft manuscript on two separate occasions and for giving me valuable feedback. My learning curve in the study of modern Japanese literature was steep, and without his guidance, I would have been unable to move away from just the biographical criticism with which I had been primarily occupied until then.

The second group of scholars read draft manuscripts (either in their entirety or in part) at various stages of my research. I would like to thank my former PhD advisors affiliated (or once affiliated) with the University of California Irvine—Susan Klein, Edward Fowler, Anne Walthall, and Duncan Williams. They did not have to read this second book manuscript, but continued to support my research. I am also grateful to Michael Cronin, who improved my book proposal. Brian Dowdle, Robert Tuck, Marty Marton, and Ashby Kinch kindly participated in my manuscript workshop at the University of Montana, while Eric Schluessel helped fund the workshop.

The third group of scholars to whom I am so indebted are affiliated with Japanese universities and invited me to their research institutes. Tomoe Moriya of Hannan University funded my research in Japan in 2012. Takami Inoue and Michael Conway of Otani University Shin Buddhist Comprehensive Research Institute gave me the freedom to work on this book, while I was a short-term visiting fellow there in 2013, 2014, and 2015.

The fourth group of scholars introduced me to various articles and books of which I had not been aware. I thank Charles Hallisey (and Dennis Hirota who set up a meeting with Hallisey at the 2011 AAS annual conference in Honolulu), Steven Heine, Richard Payne, Mary Sheldon, and Kimberly Beek.

The fifth group of scholars supported my career in various ways. I thank Natasa Masanovic, Liz Ametsbichler, Mark Unno, James Dobbins, Mark Blum, Jessica Main, Susan Klein, and Duncan Williams. I would also like to thank Francisca Cho for reinitiating my contact with SUNY Press.

Various organizations funded my research. They include the Karashima Fund from the College of Humanities and Sciences at the University of Montana (UM), the Yamaguchi Opportunity Fund run by the UM Mansfield Center, the Faculty Development Grant from the University of Alaska-Anchorage (UAA), travel grants provided by the UAA College of Arts and Sciences, and the UAA Montgomery Dickson Center for Japanese Language and Culture.

Publication of this book was supported by many people. I would like to thank the Humanities Institute of the College of Humanities and Sciences at UM for the Baldridge Book Subvention Fund. Ranko Hamaji offered me a place to work in Japan and "fed" my wife and me, and graciously contributed to the book cover jacket in the name of Taikō Hamaji, president of Hamaji Corporation. Atsuko Kubota designed the book cover artwork. Special thanks goes to Ken'ichi Yokogawa. He tirelessly edited numerous draft manuscripts, helped me balance between academic and ordinary jargon, and polished my translations. I am grateful to Rachel Smith, Emi Okitsu, and Allison Grigonis for proofreading the manuscript. I am indebted to anonymous reviewers, Christopher Ahn (former acquisition editor at SUNY Press), James Peltz (co-director of SUNY Press), and other staff members of SUNY Press. I thank Teruo Akegarasu and Mariko Handō for giving me permission to publish partial translations of *Before and after My Rebirth* and *Guardians of the Dharma Castle*, respectively. Tadatoshi Miyamori helped me connect with Akegarasu, while resident priest of Honkakuji helped me connect with Handō.

Finally, I could not have completed this work without my wife Tomoko. I thank her for her patience and understanding—she supported my career and moved from Los Angeles to Anchorage and from there to Missoula with me—and I dedicate this book to her. I also thank Ayami Haruno for her kindness.

Michihiro Ama

Notes about Japanese Names

In this book, Japanese names appear in Japanese order: family name and then given name. In citations of scholarly works of Japanese authors who published articles and books in English, however, names appear in English order: given name and then family name. For scholarly works of Japanese authors translated into English, authors' names appear in order of family name and given name. However, names of the translators who rendered Japanese articles and books into English appear in English order. Natsume Sōseki is referred to as Sōseki and Tayama Katai as Katai because Sōseki and Katai are pen names.

Introduction

> The time of snow
> Closes in on Mount Hiei . . .
> Bleak days
> Of ultimate loneliness;
> My path never ends.[1]
>
> —Yukawa Hideki (1907–1981)

Japan's first Nobel laureate, Yukawa Hideki, wrote the above *waka* poem during December 1945, just months after Japan's unconditional surrender, which ended the Pacific War. With this first defeat as a modern nation state in Japanese history, Japanese society was completely devastated. It was during this bleak period that Yukawa seems to have identified his feeling of loss as a Japanese with the cold of winter on Mount Hiei, which he looked up to as the cradle of Japanese Buddhism. What connects his sense of loneliness, the severe cold, and Buddhism is the process of following a path toward an only dimly sensed goal—perhaps the recovery of Japan in general and a new world of physics in particular. Yukawa's idea of an "endless path"[2] is derived from Japanese literary tradition. He was fond of medieval and early modern Japanese literature, including *The Tale of Genji* (*Genji monogatari*), Saigyō's *Mountain Home Anthology* (*Sankashū*), and Bashō's *haikai*, as well as Chinese classics, especially *Zhuangzi* and *Laozi*. Yukawa represents a broad range of modern Japanese intellectuals who do not consider themselves to be religious but maintain an interest in literary expressions of Buddhism.

Buddhism is one of the dominant forces that shaped Japanese culture. Western scholars have discussed Japan's Buddhist art, Buddhist architecture, and performing art influenced by Buddhism, as well as Buddhism's impact on medieval Japanese literature; however, they have done so by considering

Buddhism to be incidental to modern Japanese literary studies. On the other hand, Japanese scholars have studied the representation of Buddhism in modern Japanese literature mostly through a denominational doctrinal lens. *The Awakening of Modern Japanese Fiction* introduces to the Western academic world the significance of Buddhism in modern Japanese literature by extracting unrecognized Buddhist elements from the disciplinary divide between literary and Buddhist studies through the notion of "path." It also corrects the dominant perception in which the Christian practice of confession has been accepted as the primary informing source of modern Japanese prose literature.

This book features prose works created during the first three decades of the twentieth century both by literary figures—Natsume Sōseki 夏目漱石 (1867–1916), Tayama Katai 田山花袋 (1872–1930), Shiga Naoya 志賀直哉 (1883–1971), and Matsuoka Yuzuru 松岡譲 (1891–1969)—and Buddhist priests, such as Kiyozawa Manshi 清沢満之 (1863–1903) and Akegarasu Haya 暁烏敏 (1877–1954). Their works are approached from a Buddhist point of view more than a literary point of view and analyzed in terms of the Buddhist narrative structure of "ground, path, and goal." In Buddhism, path is a metaphor for spiritual growth that leads to the attainment of Buddhist realization. The Buddhist notion of path is not only useful for analyzing the structure of personal fiction that features the spiritual growth of the main character but is also helpful in the allegorical reading of such texts from a Buddhist perspective.

The Awakening demonstrates two types of textual study. First, it presents textual study that is inseparable from analyzing the writer's interiority. When Sōseki, Katai, and Shiga are considered in light of the lay Buddhist movement, they had their own spiritual training that was comparable to Buddhist practice. Although they did not intend to write religious novels, for these writers—and for Kiyozawa and Akegarasu—writing can be considered a path and a narrative is a medium of self-reflection that triggers self-transformation. Second, this book uncovers the meaning of a work—a meaning defined by an unlimited number of contexts—rather than explaining the authorial intent of the work.[3] It demonstrates a way of reading in which Buddhist imagery and symbols are interpreted on subtextual levels to reveal their connections to the main characters' spiritual impasse, self-realization, and Buddhist awakening. Allegorical readings of the texts, underpinned by the Buddhist notion of path, are, to some extent, inseparable from the writers' Buddhist experiences. Their Buddhist engagement is evident in their works through their linguistic codifications and in their religio-philosophical choices. Those stories are neither doctrinal nor written from a Buddhist clergy's point of view, but represent how most Japanese, including the writers themselves, relate to Buddhism in their daily lives. *The Awakening* thus demonstrates the informing presence of Buddhism in the writers' engagement with Buddhism by writing personal fiction and in readings of personal novels.

For works that were formerly treated as I-novels (*shishōsetsu* 私小説), this book adopts the term "personal fiction." The I-novel is the most popular literary form of confession in modern Japan and is believed to present the author's life without mediation, whether in first- or third-person narration. The protagonist, or hero, and the author are, however, not identical, because I-novels are, after all, fiction. In *The Rhetoric of Confession*, Edward Fowler uses the term "autobiographical fiction" instead of I-novel, and defines it as a literary form that mediates between the experiences of a writer and the hero. Unlike Fowler, who questions the authenticity of self-referentiality in autobiographical fiction, Tomi Suzuki considers I-novels a retroactively constructed discourse and shifts the discussion of I-novels as a literary form to a Japanese cultural ideology. When Suzuki's argument is considered, the Buddhist sensibilities that appear in I-novels can be explained as part of the later ideological construction of I-novels, defined as traditional and uniquely Japanese. However, the practice of confession has always been a part of Buddhist culture. The Buddhism represented in I-novels is also contemporary and mirrors the modern development of Japanese Buddhism and the reinterpretation of traditional Buddhist values. This book focuses on the selected writers' Buddhist experiences as stories that are personally constructed and does not investigate the "nonfictional" (historical) development of modern Japanese Buddhist organizations. Personal fiction includes not only autobiographical fiction, which is confessional in nature, but also novels in which parts of the protagonists were modeled after the authors and novels in which main characters were based on people the authors knew, as well as diaries and documentary works.

Sōseki, Katai, Shiga, and Matsuoka had experiential contacts with Buddhism not only by reading Buddhist scriptures but also by participating in funerary Buddhism and interacting with Buddhist clergy. Although Confucian ethics had been the norm for modern Japanese intellectuals, this lived experience was significantly different from their experiences of other forms of East Asian religio-philosophical traditions, such as Confucianism and Taoism, with which they had become intellectually familiar by reading Chinese classics, including the *Analects of Confucius* and *Zhuangzi*. Buddhism, therefore, constitutes a key category for analyzing these writers' growing spirituality and serves as a point of reference for exploring their experiences of other religions, such as Christianity and Tenrikyō, as well as their perceptions of popular indigenous religious beliefs.

The form of Buddhism embraced by the literary authors and Buddhist priests examined in this book is both traditional and modern. Their works represent cultural forms that grew out of the exchange between Western European civilization and local traditions in non-Western countries after the nineteenth century. During the rise of Japan as a modern nation-state in competition with the West, the Japanese searched for a distinct national identity through a new form of writing. In this modernizing process, Japanese intellectuals reconfirmed and articulated traditional Buddhist ideas. They renewed their sense of impermanence when they experienced rapid social changes, which also altered human relationships, and new types of death caused by recent developments in their country concomitant with modern epidemics, warfare, mental breakdown, and growing poverty. Modern Japanese writers associated untimely death, loneliness, self-detachment, and the beauty of nature with the Buddhist sensibility of impermanence and Buddhist awakening. They did not accept the notion of karmic punishment, but projected their present on their past, incorporated various non-dual Buddhist images into their work, and adopted the Buddhist attitude of seeking the way.

At the same time, the Buddhism that modern Japanese writers experienced—and to which they contributed—is a modern construction. They accepted new discourses on Japanese Buddhism created by the Buddhist clergy, such as United Buddhism, as a trans-sectarian Buddhist movement, and Kamakura New Buddhism, as the pinnacle of Japanese Buddhist development. Lay Buddhist leaders invented methods of the unmediated inner religious experience and overlooked a wide range of long-standing "physical discipline and ritual competence," according to Robert Sharf.[4] This tendency coincides with the "myth of sincerity" that Fowler points out in the development of autobiographical fiction.[5] The Buddhist practice of seeing things *as they are* resonates with realism as a vision of reality, namely, describing what writers perceived exactly *as they are*, or *ari no mama* ありのまま. The ability to detach oneself from one's attachment was sought in both the Japanese literary establishment and the Buddhist world of modern Japan.

This book consists of eight chapters. Chapter 1 provides a background for two types of readers—specialists and students of Japanese Buddhism and Japanese literature. It highlights the problem of disciplinary boundaries that have prevented discussions of literary figures' interest in Buddhism within the categories of either literary studies or Buddhist studies and introduces previous discussions of Buddhism and literature in modern Japan by Japanese scholars. It then provides a survey of Japanese Buddhism, including discussions of basic Buddhist doctrines, major Mahayana sutras, and the formation of funerary

Buddhism. Chapter 1 also explains the overarching conceptual framework of the book—that is, modernism, personal fiction, and path literature.

The following chapters are divided into two parts. Part 1 consists of four chapters and considers the writing of personal fiction to be a Buddhist practice. Chapter 2 introduces Sōseki, Katai, and Shiga from the point of the lay Buddhist movement. They are known as great literary writers of modern Japan, but their Buddhist experiences are relatively unknown in the West. Although they considered themselves to be neither Buddhist practitioners nor religious thinkers, they expressed great interest in Buddhism. They were not interested in Buddhist sectarianism, but were drawn to Buddhist worldviews, Shakyamuni Buddha's teachings, and aesthetic conventions of Japanese culture through which evanescent sentiments are expressed. Further, Sōseki practiced sitting in meditation, wanderlust led Katai to seek a reclusive life, and Shiga took pleasure in viewing Buddhist art.

Chapter 3 focuses on the notion of *ari no mama*, which Sōseki, Katai, and Shiga considered crucial to the descriptions of realistic fiction, and analyzes the ways in which these authors articulated the relationship between literary art and Buddhism. While investigating the impact of realistic writing as developed in both Japan and the West on their personal fiction, this chapter demonstrates the relationship between the literary practice of observing and describing things as they are and the Buddhist practice of "right view" or seeing things as they are. For these writers, writing personal fiction—particularly autobiographical fiction that is confessional and highly self-reflective—was a form of spiritual practice that made them aware of who they were. They did not, however, write personal novels in order to gain spiritual comfort; rather, writing personal fiction helped them understand how their present conditions came to be by their conduct in the past. Sōseki's *Grass on the Wayside* (*Michikusa* 道草, 1915), Katai's *Remaining Snow* (*Zansetsu* 残雪, 1917–1918), and Shiga's "At Kinosaki" (*Kinosaki nite* 城の崎にて, 1917) are read as examples of the authors' paths and in light of their introspective practice that paralleled Buddhist practice. Although the notion of a self is negated in Buddhism, that does not mean the existence of a self is denied. Rather, the denial of the self leads to an awareness that the cause of suffering is self-attachment and the self is always in a state of change. Those who attain Buddhist realization develop non-dual perspectives and understand that life is interdependent.

Chapter 4 treats the confessional writings of Shin Buddhist clerics as variants of personal fiction. A close reading of the texts demonstrates that Shin Buddhism was part of a system of confession and served as one of the sources of modern Japanese literature. It thus replaces Karatani Kōjin's position that

Christianity's confessional mode was the primary "source of modern Japanese literature."[6] Shinran (1173–1263), the founder of Shin Buddhism, confessed how difficult it was for him to overcome his base passions, and since then, expressing the burden of karma and repentance became an established Shin Buddhist practice. For modern Shin Buddhist leaders such as Kiyozawa, who suffered from tuberculosis and a fear of death, and Akegarasu, who struggled with his carnal desires, confessional writing as a record of religious conversion and as reportage of a spiritual experiment was a method through which they examined their Buddhist path and questioned the limits of moral judgment.

Chapter 4 begins with an investigation of Kiyozawa's "The Nature of My Faith" (*Waga shinnen* 我信念, 1903) and continues to Akegarasu's sexuality as observed in *Before and after My Rebirth* (*Kōsei no zengo* 更生の前後, 1920). Unlike Kiyozawa, whose confession is rational and expository, Akegarasu, who was aware of the artistic effects of confessional writing, employed literary techniques and deliberately constructed his work to be read as literature. For him, confessional writing represents both traditional and modern Shin Buddhist practice. He was also interested in prose, poetry, and autobiographical fiction. The social standing of Kiyozawa and Akegarasu as Buddhist priests and their intentions to write about personal religious experiences, as well as those of their readers, have led their works to be distinguished from works of "literature." Akegarasu represents a writer excluded from the disciplinary boundary formed around modern Japanese literature. The difference in the personal novels of Akegarasu and the other literary authors examined in this book is that for Akegarasu, personal fiction served as a means of religious propagation—whereas for Sōseki, Katai, and Shiga, it did not—and that unlike Katai and Shiga, Akegarasu was not concerned with the transient beauty of nature.

Chapter 5 explores a personal novel that features the history of a contemporary Shin Buddhist denomination, its reform movement, and the lives of Shin priests and lay members. While *Guardians of the Dharma Castle* (*Hōjō o mamoru hitobito* 法城を護る人々, 1923–1926)—a best seller that contributed to the so-called Taishō Religious Boom—is Matsuoka Yuzuru's autobiographical fiction, its historical account is supported by his documentary work. This chapter analyzes the ways in which Matsuoka placed his hero in modern Shin Buddhist history. His documentary work became his religious practice and a path that led him to address a Buddhist reform by means of fiction. *Guardians* also represents two major Shin Buddhist events. Although Matsuoka wrote *Guardians* to question a Shin Buddhist organization, because it depicts the lives of ordinary clergy and laity from a Marxist perspective and shows Shin Buddhist history from the bottom up, it adds to the organization's institutional history that is created by its ministerial authority. Despite a recent surge of interest in modern versions of medieval Buddhist hagiographies, serious scholarly attention has not been given to modern Buddhist historical fiction. This chapter therefore contributes to a wider discussion of historical novels in modern Japan.

Part 2 consists of three chapters. It demonstrates allegorical Buddhist readings of personal novels created by Sōseki, Katai, and Shiga. Not all of the main characters and narrators studied in this section experience Buddhist awakening; however, because Buddhism deals with the nature of suffering, the Buddhist notion of path is helpful in exploring the ways in which main characters and narrators handle their problems, deepen their sense of being, reflect their conditions of selfhood on others, and gain self-realization. While Buddhist traditions are diverse, when the personal novels are read from the standpoint of path, the transformation of main characters or the development of the narrator's self-awareness is the common theme. These changes are brought about by their reflections on other characters, suffering, death, and nature, as well as through their interaction with Buddhists, Christians, and followers of other religions.

In chapter 6, the words and objects used in daily life in Sōseki's *The Three-Cornered World* (*Kusamakura* 草枕, 1906) and *The Gate* (*Mon* 門, 1910), as well as in Katai's *The Quilt* (*Futon* 蒲団, 1907), are examined as Buddhist allegories. Both secular meanings and religious messages are found in such words as *ōjō* 往生 (birth in the Pure Land) and *mondō* 問答 (dialogue). The word *futon*, sleeping mattress and cover, which has now become part of the English language, was used to refer to cushions for Buddhist meditation. Chapter 6 views those words and objects as Buddhist symbols and clarifies their implications by highlighting the non-dual nature of Buddhist symbolism. Through the system of Buddhist symbols, the characters' struggles against themselves, others, and society are seen as the beginning of their accepting self-limitation and base passions, which leads them to experience self-transformation.

The main characters analyzed in chapter 7 advance their spiritual inquiries and attain peace of mind. Katai's *The Miracle of a Buddhist Monk* (*Aru sō no kiseki* ある僧の奇蹟, 1917) and Shiga's *A Dark Night's Passing* (*An'ya kōro* 暗夜行路, 1921–1937) are treated as the stories of the main characters' "turning of the mind." Their experiences of Buddhist awakening are analyzed in terms of their experiences of mysticism, organized religion, and nature. The relationship between self and others and the impact of death on the main characters are also examined.

Chapter 8 investigates literary representations of funerary Buddhism. Funerals are Buddhist symbols that appear in personal fiction as rites of passage. During Buddhist funerals, the periods of transition in the lives of literary characters and new sensations regarding life and death are identified through the connection of the term "path" as a synonym for passage. In Sōseki's *Sanshirō* (*Sanshirō* 三四郎, 1908), Sanshirō comes across the funerary procession of a child and thinks deeply about the innocence of death, associating it with beauty of the woman he has fallen in love with. In Sōseki's *The Miner* (*Kōfu* 坑夫, 1908), after the protagonist and miners view the parade for a dead miner, which deviates from conventional Buddhist funerary processions, the barrier between the protagonist and the miners disappears. The Buddhist funeral of an Imperial Japanese army officer in northern China observed by the narrator of Katai's *The Diary of the Second Army Corps at War* (*Dainigun jūsei nikki* 第二軍従征日記, 1905) during the Russo-Japanese War evokes in him loneliness and a sense of displacement. Unlike those accounts of Buddhist funerals, characters in Katai's *Life* (*Sei* 生, 1908) and Sōseki's *To the Spring Equinox and Beyond* (*Higan sugimade* 彼岸過ぎ迄, 1912) lose loved ones. They find spiritual solace in a Shinto-Buddhist hybrid funeral and a Shin Buddhist funeral, respectively. Liminality is a key to exploring the spiritual growth of the characters in those novels and for examining both the unsettling and cathartic effects of Buddhist funerals as well as relating those discussions to analyzing the non-dual nature of Buddhist symbols.

Sōseki is the thread that binds the contexts of this book. This study initially began as an exploration of Sōseki and Buddhism, and then the scope of inquiry was expanded so as to bridge literary and Buddhist studies. Examination of Sōseki's Buddhist engagement led the research to delve into Buddhist experiences of other literary authors who also wanted to understand why they had been struggling against themselves. Although Katai was hostile to Sōseki, both writers considered nature to be the source of self-detachment. Shiga admired Sōseki's idea of "leaving oneself by becoming one with heaven" (*sokuten kyoshi* 則天去私) and entrusted himself to Mother Nature. Although Sōseki and Kiyozawa may never have met, Sōseki modeled the character "K" in *Kokoro* (*Kokoro* こころ, 1914) partly on Kiyozawa, who was attached to ascetic practice, ruined his health, and then entrusted himself to Amida Buddha's original vow. Matsuoka was one of Sōseki's students who interpreted *sokuten kyoshi* as Sōseki's determination to avoid a self-centered way of living.[7] Yukawa Hideki also became interested in Sōseki's work because Yukawa's father-in-law was the physician who treated Sōseki when Sōseki was hospitalized at his clinic in Osaka.[8]

In the appendices, the works of Akegarasu and Matsuoka, which the present study explores, are partially translated. While the personal fiction of Sōseki, Katai, and Shiga, as well as Kiyozawa's religious testament have been translated into English and studied by Western scholars, Akegarasu's confessional writing, which is treated as an adaptation to personal fiction in this book, and Matsuoka's *Guardians*, have been neglected.

Finally, caveats associated with this book must be noted. First, this book deals primarily with the Zen and Pure Land traditions as it builds on the analysis of Sōseki's Buddhist experience. Analyses of other forms of Buddhism in modern Japanese literature are omitted. Esoteric Buddhism is represented in Izumi Kyōka's *The Saint of Mt. Koya* (*Kōya hijiri* 高野聖, 1900), and Miyazawa Kenji, who wrote many children's stories, was influenced by the *Lotus Sutra*. Also, it is important to note that the personal novels of female writers, such as *Child's Play* (*Takekurabe* たけくらべ, 1895–1896) by Higuchi Ichiyō 樋口一葉, which includes episodes about the son of a Buddhist priest, are excluded from the present study, though they are touched on in the conclusion. Although many prominent literary writers during the postwar period, such as Takeda Taijun and Okamoto Kanoko, commented on the relationship between Buddhism and literature, this study focuses on the prewar era.[9]

Second, those who specialize in literary studies and those who are familiar with the works of Sōseki, Katai, and Shiga may find summaries of these authors' novels descriptive and lengthy. They may suggest that a summary of a work should be part of a textual analysis, rather than dividing summary and analysis in which portions of the summaries are reiterated. This book takes the form it does because of consideration for those who are not familiar with works of modern Japanese literature. Literary critics may also point out the lack of intertexual analysis in this book, especially concerning Sōseki's major works. The spiritual struggles and developments of the main characters in his so-called "trilogy" can be analyzed as one spectrum of the main characters' religious experiences, but such intertexual study is beyond the scope of this book.

Despite these shortcomings, *The Awakening of Modern Japanese Fiction* presents a more nuanced understanding of the role of Buddhism in the development of modern Japanese literature. A creative take on the title of the book is that it derives from *Treatise on the Awakening of Faith,* an English translation of *Dasheng qixin lun* (J. *Daijō kishinron* 大乗起信論). This Buddhist commentary, complied in China in the sixth century, is "one of the most influential treatises in all of East Asian Buddhism" and its author aims to "reconcile two of the dominant, if seemingly incompatible, strands in Mahayana Buddhism: *tathāgatagarbha* (embryo or womb of the buddhas) thought and the *ālaya-vijñāna* (storehouse consciousness) theory of consciousness."[10] *The Awakening* brings together Buddhist studies and literary studies, opens new vistas at the intersection of religion and literature, and brings Buddhism out of the shadows and interstices of early twentieth-century Japanese literature.[11]

CHAPTER ONE

A Disciplinary Divide and the Conceptual Framework of the Present Study

On another occasion, Dōgen instructed:

> Students of the Way should neither read the scriptures of other Buddhist teachings nor study non-Buddhist texts. If you do read, examine the writings of Zen. Other works should be put aside for a while.
>
> Zen monks are fond of literature these days, finding it an aid to writing verses and tracts. This is a mistake. Even if you cannot compose verse, just write what is in your heart. Grammatical niceties do not matter if you just express the teachings of the Buddha. Those who lack the mind that seeks the Way may complain that someone's writing is bad. Yet no matter how elegant their prose or how exquisite their poetry might be, they are merely toying with words and cannot gain the Truth. I have loved literature since I was young and even now recall beautiful phrases from non-Buddhist works. I have been tempted to take up such books as the *Wen-hsüan* [*Wenxuan* 文選], but I have come to feel that it would be a waste of time and am inclined to think that such reading should be cast aside completely.[1]

This chapter provides an overview of literature and Buddhism in modern Japan and helps readers prepare for the following chapters. First, the contours of literature and Buddhism in medieval and early modern Japan are delineated, and previous attempts by Japanese scholars to explain the relationship between literature and Buddhism are introduced. Second, a brief history of Japanese Buddhism is presented, including discussions of basic Buddhist doctrines, major Mahayana sutras, and the institutionalization of Japanese Buddhism—particularly the development of funerary Buddhism. Finally, the conceptual framework of *The Awakening of Modern Japanese Fiction* is explained.

Buddhism Overlooked in the Study of Modern Japanese Literature

Buddhist attainment and artistic achievement are two different activities; yet, in Japan, the boundary between Buddhist practice and literary pursuit is not as clear as what they suggest. William R. LaFleur states that "[e]ver since the publication of the *Man'yōshū* in the middle of the eighth century, the Japanese world of poetry had included a tradition of poems of passion and of gently handled eroticism. For Buddhist clerics who wished to be both traditional and spiritually serious, this obviously created a dilemma."[2] The poets expressed various emotions, including their attachments, whereas Buddhist monks considered the so-called "three poisons"—greed, anger, and ignorance—to be the causes of suffering and tried to contain their attachments. However, the nobility in medieval Japan—specifically, retired emperors and aristocrats in Kyoto—took refuge in Buddhism while pursuing literary activities. Despite emphasizing that literary and religious practices are separate pursuits, Zen master Dōgen (1200–1253) also composed poetry.[3]

During the late Heian and Kamakura periods, Japanese writers recognized the skillful means of worldly writings. They celebrated the concept of "floating phrases and fictive utterances" (*kyōgen kigo*) and wished for poetry and prose to become a conduit for Buddhist teaching.[4] Prominent poets, such as Fujiwara Shunzei (1114–1204) and Fujiwara Teika (1162–1241), related poetic composition to Buddhist meditation and explained it in terms of Buddhist philosophy.[5] Writers of popular prose-poetry works, such as tales (*monogatari*), diaries (*nikki*), and explanatory stories (*setsuwa*), wrote about miraculous works of Buddha and *kami*, introduced divine legends, and reinforced the idea of karmic retribution.[6]

In early modern Japan, or during the reign of the Tokugawa shogunate, also known as the Edo period (1603–1867), relative peace and commercial growth enabled people to develop more optimistic views on life. As they affirmed present life, and as the idea of a floating world (*ukiyo* 浮き世) prevailed, they generally lost interest in matters of the afterlife. Neo-Confucianism, which the government employed as its official study, and funerary Buddhism, which assured peace after one's death, contributed to the shift in the Japanese attitude toward religion—from the need for salvation in gaining access to the other world to the pursuit of practical benefits in this world. With the development of printing technology, popular literature transformed "the past into the present, the high into the low, and the sacred into the profane,"[7] as Haruo Shirane observes.

That does not, however, mean that Buddhist themes disappeared from the popular culture of early modern Japan. Ichikawa Danjūrō (1660–1704), a Kabuki actor and pioneer of the wild style (*aragoto*), modeled his famous posture after the images of *Niō* and *Fudōmyōō* (the guardians of Buddhism). He revered esoteric Buddhism (*shingon*) and mountain asceticism (*shugendō*).[8] In Chikamatsu Monzaemon's (1653–1724) *jōruri* (puppet theater) plays, couples commit a double suicide and long for birth in the Pure Land.[9] *Rakugo* ("the traditional Japanese art of storytelling"[10]) developed from popular Buddhist sermons.[11] Further, Matsuo Bashō (1644–1694) expressed the Buddhist ideas of impermanence in his *haikai* ("a form of poetry derived from the linked verse of medieval times"[12]), and *yomihon* (reading books) writers during the Bunka-Bunsei era (1804–1830) reproduced earlier Buddhist folktales and miraculous stories in their works.[13] The presence of Buddhism is therefore still strong in Edo literature.

Despite a number of studies that examine the role of Buddhism and its artistic expressions in medieval and early modern Japan, scholarship has neglected Buddhism's influence on modern Japanese literature.[14] The lack of scholarship was caused by historical and institutional conditions specific to the modern era. First, in modern Japan, Buddhism, which had shaped the minds of medieval Japanese, was no longer the dominant religious discourse. The Meiji government suppressed Buddhism as an institution of foreign origin that had ruined Japan through its "evil" customs and rituals, removed its influence from Shinto shrines and political organizations, and redefined and promoted Shinto as the imperial institution by which Meiji ideologues connected emperor with commoners and Japan's mythological origin with the present.[15]

Second, the modern disciplinary divide between "literature" and "religion" has caused the study of literary Buddhism to be excluded from academic inquiry.[16] During the Meiji period (1868–1912), the concept of literature, or *bungaku* 文学, was modeled after the Western notion of literature and defined as a literary art, including poetry, the novel, and drama. (For what is translated as "literature" in the epigraph, Dōgen used the term *bunpitsu* 文筆, which referred to Chinese literary work.) The term *shūkyō* 宗教 (literally, the teaching of a [Buddhist, or religious] sect) was coined to translate the Western notion of organized "religion." According to Shirane, by the second half of the Meiji period the scope of *bungaku* had become limited to imaginative writing, with the novel being the primary literary form, excluding other types of writings such as historiographical, philosophical, and religious texts.[17] The boundary of "literature" was then reinforced by literary writers, who identified themselves as novelists (*sakka*, or *shōsetsuka*) and distinguished themselves from authors of other types of writing, as well as by public perceptions of the novelists.[18]

It is therefore not surprising that scholars have not paid enough attention to Buddhism as a literary model of modern Japan. Japanese scholars of modern Japanese literature tend to discuss literary authors' interests in Buddhism seen through their works,[19] while Buddhist studies specialists have disregarded Buddhism in modern Japanese literature because it was not part of "canonical" studies.[20] On the other hand, novels about Japanese Christian experiences have raised scholar's interest as a new literary phenomenon.[21] In the West, Irmela Hijiya-Kirschnereit and Roy Starrs recognize Buddhism as part of the collective consciousness of modern Japanese writers, but only a handful of scholars have looked into the literary significance of modern Japanese Buddhism.[22] A few attempts made by Japanese critics to connect literary studies and modern Japanese Buddhist studies are introduced next.

An Overview of Previous Scholarship

Critics who have evaluated the role of Buddhism in modern Japanese literature can be categorized into three groups. First, cultural and literary critics tend to treat Buddhism as an undercurrent of Japanese culture running from medieval to modern times. They perceive Buddhism not from a doctrinal perspective but explain it in terms of Japanese sensibilities. Second, specialists trained in Buddhist studies tend to view literature as a vehicle for transmitting Buddhist teachings. The third group of scholars have questioned these approaches and proposed a different strategy in approaching the study of Buddhism and literature. They have not, however, fully developed their visions at present. Let us examine each position.

Japanese critics have long seen (and reinforced) the connection between aesthetic sensibilities and Buddhist principles in their cultural histories of Japan. Watsuji Tetsurō (1889–1960), a critic who was awarded the Order of Culture, perceives the impermanence of all things and reincarnation through the six worlds—that is, the belief that after a person dies, one's spirit transmigrates among the realms of hell, hungry ghosts, domesticated animals, warriors, human beings, and heavenly beings—as well as the realization of the state of emptiness to be part of the cultural forces that have shaped the contours of literary arts.[23] Kawabata Yasunari (1899–1972), winner of the Nobel Prize for Literature, traces the essence of Japanese poetry to the fleeting beauty of nature and Zen.[24] Umehara Takeshi (1925–2019), the first director-general of the International Research Center for Japanese Studies known as *Nichibunken*, recognizes the aesthetic dimension of death in Pure Land Buddhism and discusses the continuity of its literary expressions from the medieval to modern periods.[25] Nishida Masayoshi is perhaps the only literary critic who wrote a book on Buddhism and modern Japanese literature, and like Watsuji, he traces the development of Japanese impermanent sensibilities in the history of modern Japanese literature.[26]

Itō Sei (1905–1969) is a prominent literary critic who explored the place of Buddhism in modern Japanese literature.[27] In *Recognition by Means of the Novel* (*Shōsetsu no ninshiki*), he identifies two models—the harmonious and the escapist/destructive—and analyzes the impact of Buddhism in each archetype. In the first group, he lists literary writers, such as Natsume Sōseki, Mori Ōgai, and Shimazaki Tōson, together with Nishida Kitarō, a philosopher, and Uchimura Kanzō, a Christian leader. In order to come to terms with society, which was full of contradictions, Sōseki renounced the "self" by accepting the irrational existing order as something given, and sought a unity of self and other—known as *sokuten kyoshi*. Ōgai avoided confrontation and turned to literary production, which for him, was a "playful activity," under the pretense of pure objectivity. Tōson, who neither insisted on logical thinking nor accepted the traditional patriarchal system without questioning its authority, established a literary style based on the sense of ambiguity. Buddhist and Chinese thought played a significant role in Sōseki's and Ōgai's intellectual activities, while for Tōson, Christianity was as important as Buddhism.[28]

In the second group—the escapist/destructive model—Itō finds a strong Buddhist influence as well. Talented writers disliked government service and the business world, and made a career of writing autobiographical fiction. They welcomed misfortune and willingly destroyed their lives through a series of crises, which included illness, depression, and illicit love affairs; portrayed a breakdown of family life and the vicissitudes of their lives with a sense of impermanence; and lamented their societal behaviors but expressed pride in shunning careers in bureaucracy and not conforming to old social customs, even though they suffered from poverty as a consequence of their choices. When unable to find their places in society, they only had extreme choices—revolting against society or dying. Kawakami Bizan, Kitamura Tōkoku, Arishima Takeo, Akutagawa Ryūnosuke, and Dazai Osamu ended up committing suicide.[29] Their autobiographical fictional works were popular because readers perceived them as actors who lived an ideal lifestyle—that is, not submitting to authorities, not flattering, and not lying.

Not all of the writers classified as belonging to the escapist/destructive model took their lives, however. Itō uses the terms ascending and descending (*jōshōgata to kakōgata*) to distinguish those who survived from those who committed suicide. Both patterns are built on the perception of eternal life seen from the point of death or the notion of nothingness (*mu* 無), yet these writers rejected a one true God or a transcending spiritual authority as the foundation of life.

The ascending movement is driven by a writer's desire to elevate his quality of life. For such writers, all living beings appear to be beautiful by themselves—whether insects, grass, or even hateful persons. Those who gain peace of mind by renouncing the world are no longer concerned about describing mundane egotistic events, but rather are fascinated by the beauty of nature and liveliness of each individual life. For the ascending type, Itō lists Masaoka Shiki, Hori Tatsuo, Ozaki Kazuo, Shimaki Kensaku, Kajii Motojirō, and Hōjō Tamio—none of whom committed suicide, despite serious illnesses—as well as Shiga Naoya, who connected the notion of nothingness, which derived from Buddhism and Taoism, with a social science that originated in Western Europe. Itō considers Shiga, in particular, to be representative of modern Japanese intellectuals who denied organized religion but established a spiritual standpoint oriented toward the state of nothingness gained through his observation of nature. Other writers, such as Kanbayashi Akatsuki and Tonomura Shigeru, examined the meaning of life when they lost loved ones. Niwa Fumio and Nakayama Gishū deepened their understanding of life when a loved one became mad or self-destructive.[30]

While the realization of death made these writers spiritually strong, according to Itō, that realization simultaneously generated a different effect on the descending writers. They wished to taste the bitter experiences of those at the bottom of society even at the risk of destroying their own lives. These writers lost their families, but that loss led them to recognize the importance of ordinary life they once enjoyed. The regret enhanced their sense of nothingness and ironically contributed to improving their works. A negative cycle of a hands-on experience with the nitty-gritty of human life and writing autobiographical fiction eventually caused them to terminate their lives.[31]

Throughout his analysis, Itō defines death as a state of nothingness. He does not discuss the Buddhist concept of emptiness, but instead uses the term "consciousness of nothingness" (*mu no ishiki*) to point to a broader "oriental" (*toyōteki*) tradition. Nor does he illustrate the degree to which nihilism in the West affected the mentality of modern Japanese writers. By treating death and nothingness on the same level, Itō limits the implications of Buddhism in modern Japanese literature to the writers' perceptions of impermanence and representations of nature linked to traditional aesthetic principles. He is, in this respect, not too different from the critics mentioned previously.

In Itō's analogy, differences in the attainment of spiritual peace between the writers in the harmonious group and those of the ascending type in the escapist/destructive group are unclear. He neither discusses how Sōseki's state of *sokuten kyoshi* is similar to, yet different from, Shiga Naoya's admiration of nature, nor explains how Amida Buddha's compassion is important to Niwa Fumio and Tonomura Shigeru. Itō does not fully address the impact of Buddhist soteriology on these writers. Further, he ignores the modern discourse on Japanese Buddhism and does not take into account the impact of the lay Buddhist movement when discussing religious experiences of modern Japanese writers who were not members of Buddhist organizations.

Unlike Itō, scholars of Buddhist studies have often used a classification system that views literature rigidly through the lens of the Buddhist denomination. Biased by sectarian divisions, they have dogmatically applied Buddhist imagery and doctrine in their analyses of texts. Kenri Bunshū, for instance, separates "Buddhist literature" (*bukkyō bungaku* 仏教文学) and "Buddhist-like literature" (*bukkyōteki bungaku* 仏教的文学). The former suggests "literature in Buddhism" (*bukkyō ni okeru bungaku* 仏教における文学)—works that are written to protect and propagate Buddhism, whereas the latter implies "Buddhism in literature" (*bungaku ni okeru bukkyō* 文学における仏教)—works that represent the dialectical development of Buddhism and literature.[32]

Kenri organizes the Buddhist-like literature of modern Japan in three ways. First, he classifies the works of Buddhist-like literature according to the two lineages of Japanese Buddhism, that is, the traditions of self-power and other-power Buddhism. In the former category, he lists the writers interested in, and works dealing with, Dōgen, Ryōkan, and Ikkyū. In the latter category, he focuses on the lives and works of the writers who were interested in Shinran. Second, Kenri creates four categories: works based on the author's analysis of Buddhist history (such as Inoue Yasushi's *Dunhuang* [*Tonkō*, 1959] and *Roof Tile of Tenpyō* [*Tenpyō no iraka*, 1957]); works reflecting the author's background in Buddhist culture (including Mori Ōgai's *Hanshan and Shide* [*Kanzan jittoku*, 1916] and Mishima Yukio's *The Temple of the Golden Pavilion* [*Kinkakuji*, 1956]); works grounded on Buddhist doctrines and concepts (such as Kurata Hyakuzō's *The Priest and His Disciples* [*Shukke to sono deshi*, 1916]); and works based on the author's Buddhist experience (for instance, Niwa Fumio's *The Buddha Tree* [*Bodaiju*, 1955–1956]). Third, Kenri classifies the writers who had Buddhist experiences into three groups: those who were born into temple families, those who pursued a Buddhist way of life, and those who became resident temple priests. Kenri concludes that Buddhist-like literature is characterized by the ways in which a writer seeks the path and expresses his or her soteriological concerns through literary skills. As a provisional truth, Buddhist-like literature inquires into the foundation of human existence, brings various kinds of human attachment into relief, and seeks solutions to problems caused by attachment. In his opinion, however, there is no significant work of modern Japanese Buddhist-like literature that includes a discussion of Buddhist doctrine, and the influence of Buddhism in modern Japanese literature is limited to the depictions of a modern ego (*jiga* 自我) and the patriarchal household (*ie* 家),[33]—that is, "a quasi-kinship unit with a patriarchal head and members tied to him through real or symbolic blood relationship."[34]

Similarly, critics have examined the impact of particular Buddhist traditions on modern fiction. Many writers wrote biographical novels based on the lives of the so-called founders of "Kamakura Buddhism"—such as Hōnen (1133–1212), Shinran, Nichiren (1222–1282), and Dōgen—and incorporated the founders' doctrines into their works. Critics note that Hōnen's teaching is included in the writings of Satō Haruo; Shinran's thought is explicated in the works of Kinoshita Naoe, Kurata Hyakuzō, Niwa Fumio, Tonomura Shigeru, Kamei Katsuichirō, and Noma Hiroshi; Nichiren's doctrine is manifested in the works of Kōda Rohan, Takayama Chogyū, Tsubouchi Shōyō, Miyazawa Kenji, Mushanokōji Saneatsu, and Osaragi Jirō; and the influence of Zen is seen in the works of Natsume Sōseki, Mori Ōgai, and Shimazaki Tōson.[35] The exclusive focus on a single writer through a sectarian perspective is, however, not helpful for understanding eclectic elements of literary Buddhism.

Jean-Jacques Origas suggests that critics need to look at a writer's religious experience as a whole.[36] In his opinion, interpreting a writer's religious experience from a particular religious tradition is not useful; instead, scholars must bring together and systematize various spiritual elements that affected the writer's perspective. When approaching literary works that reflect popular religious beliefs, for instance, separating Buddhist and Shinto elements is not meaningful. Origas therefore offers a *longue durée* approach to the examination of the formation of a writer's religious character. For example, Shimazaki Tōson became a Christian but later abandoned his faith. This change does not suggest he became an atheist. Tōson remained strongly interested in religion, including

Buddhism. Works such as "Pilgrim's Song" (*Junrei no uta*) in *Chikuma River Sketches* (*Chikumagawa no suketchi*, 1912) express Tōson's religious sensibility.[37] Mori Ōgai was seemingly indifferent to religion at first, but later created "The Last Phrase" (*Saigo no ikku*, 1915),[38] which reveals the contradictions and strengths of believing, and *Hanshan and Shide*, which depicts an enigmatic and unrestrictive religious faith. Because a writer's spiritual needs vary from time to time, according to Origas, it is necessary to survey a longer period of his or her life, even though such a method can be exhausting for researchers.[39]

Origas's *longue durée* approach is useful with regard to biographical criticism, but his rejection of a single religious tradition as the basis of religious readings of the texts needs to be reconsidered. By the late Meiji era, the notion of organized religion had become established in Japan with categories of Buddhism and Christianity, together with a new religious movement. Shinto was excluded from the category of organized religion. All the writers examined in *The Awakening of Modern Japanese Fiction* were associated with Buddhism through institutions that distinguished Buddhism from other types of religion.

Making thematic connections with Buddhism is another approach in the study of modern Japanese literature. Hata Kōhei proposes to investigate ways in which writers express a sense of alienation, sexuality, and discrimination based on occupation, status, race and ethnicity, gender, and belief, as well as to analyze how Buddhism enables them to identify the causes of these problems and express their solutions. Tōson's *The Broken Commandment* (*Hakai*, 1906) and Akutagawa's "Hell of Loneliness" (*Kodoku jigoku*, 1916) seem to express these Buddhist motifs and concerns.[40] Hata did not, however, put his ideas into practice. To better understand the Japanese cultural practice associated with Buddhism and modern Japanese writers' Buddhist experiences, the institutional development of Buddhism is summarized next.

Buddhism as an Institution

Shakyamuni Buddha taught the Four Noble Truths. Like a doctor who diagnoses and prescribes medicine, the Buddha discussed the nature of suffering (the first truth); identified the three poisons—greed, hatred, and delusion—as the causes of suffering (the second truth); explained the cessation of suffering as nirvana (the third truth); and demonstrated the way to remove suffering by pursuing the eightfold path (the fourth truth)—that is, "right understanding, right thought, right speech, right action, right livelihood, right effort, right mindfulness, and right concentration."[41]

According to the Buddha, we suffer because we do not see things as they are. We fail to understand the nature of impermanence—all things are transitory, changing moment by moment—and cling to ourselves as if the self is permanent. The Buddha explained that the self comes into being through the interaction of the five aggregates (i.e., form, sensation, perception, mental formation, and consciousness) and through the process of dependent arising, "all things arise and pass away due to certain conditions."[42] The state where the dependent arising of a being ends is death (*parinirvāṇa*), the state of nirvana, which is the ultimate release from suffering. At the same time, nirvana generally refers to "the complete cessation of craving (thirst), letting it go, renouncing it, being free from it, detachment from it."[43] It is the state where suffering stops.

After Shakyamuni's death, groups of his followers spread throughout Asia and reinterpreted his teachings over a long period. Buddhists began using the word *Mahāyāna* in the first century BCE, and the Mahayana movement advanced from India to Tibet and Central Asia, and from there to East Asia, including China, Korea, and Japan.[44] The characteristics of Mahayana Buddhism include the following: emphasis on the Bodhisattva path, realization of emptiness (S. *śūnyatā*; J. *kū* 空), analysis of consciousness, and the use of skillful means (S. *upāya*; J. *hōben* 方便). In the Mahayanist's mind, pursuing only personal attainment of Buddhahood is selfish; hence, one needs to be altruistic and guide others to the cessation of suffering while seeking personal spiritual freedom. As a result, icons of Bodhisattva, such as *Avalokiteśvara* (J. *Kannon bosatsu*), *Samantabhadra* (J. *Fugen bosatsu*), and *Mañjuśrī* (J. *Monju bosatsu*) developed. Mahayanists also believe that, in addition to Shakyamuni Buddha, there are countless cosmic Buddhas, such as *Amitābha*, *Amitāyus*, or Amida Buddha (J. *Amida butsu*), and *Vairocana* or Sun Buddha (J. *Dainichi nyorai*), who guide sentient beings living after the time of Shakyamuni Buddha.

Mahayanists elaborate the idea of dependent arising through the notion of emptiness. That is, all things lack inherent existence because they "arise and pass away due to certain conditions."[45] For Mahayanists, the realization of emptiness is a higher wisdom that enables them to see things as they are. Simultaneously, Mahayanists analyze the mechanisms of conscious activities—how we conceptualize things, develop further mental formations, create attachments, and fail to see things as they are. Mahayana Buddhism thus developed through the doctrine of both the Madhyamaka school, which explains the nature of emptiness, and the Yogācāra school, which analyzes consciousness.[46] Dualistic thinking is identified as a cause of suffering and a schism between subject and object is bridged in a vision of oneness.

Mahayanists created their own scriptures, or sutras. Some of the earliest Mahayana sutras are the *Perfection of Wisdom Sutras*, written in the first century CE. The *Diamond Sutra* and the *Heart Sutra*, later versions, define the Bodhisattva path through the practice of six perfections—giving, observing precepts, enduring hardships, devoting to practice, meditating, and gaining wisdom. Other popular Mahayana sutras include the *Vimalakīrti Sutra*, which explains the story of Vimalakīrti, a layman of extraordinary wisdom surpassing even the renowned Bodhisattvas, and expounds the doctrine of emptiness; the *Lotus Sutra*, which reveals the eternal life of the Buddha, despite Shakyamuni Buddha's limited life, and the importance of skillful means to guide others to attain nirvana; and the *Larger Sutra of Immeasurable Life*, which illustrates the salvific power of Amida Buddha determined to bring all sentient beings who recite his name to the Land of Bliss, or Pure Land. These sutras have become extremely popular in East Asia.[47]

Buddhism was introduced to Japan from Korea and China, and became Japanized through the incorporation of its indigenous culture, while conversely shaping Japanese society, customs, and values. Over time, Japanese Buddhist sects developed their own organizations, doctrines, and liturgy. Buddhist sects and denominations (*shū* 宗) expanded their influence by the following means: establishing a head temple and enforcing a hierarchy within their organization; cultivating regional networks and subsuming local customs and practices; reinterpreting and compromising the founder's teachings with popular beliefs of the day; and negotiating with other denominations, religious groups, and political authorities.[48] By the Tokugawa period, Buddhist sects and denominations had become deeply politicized and had implemented a temple registration system (*terauke*) for all Japanese. In addition to acting as tax collector, the resident priest of each temple certified that people affiliated with his temple were not Christians—one way the Tokugawa government controlled Christianity.[49]

The practice of funerary Buddhism through the *danka* system (*danka seido*) was another popular Buddhist institution during the Tokugawa period. It refers to a collective ritual, officiated by a Buddhist priest and followed by temple members, which honored their loved ones and ancestors through vigils, funerary rites, and periodical memorial services. According to Nam-lin Hur,

> The danka system was never a monolithic or unilateral institution, but rather a socio-religious practice in which householders, temples, and the state were linked together and interacted with one another through the practice of funerary Buddhism—a practice that can be epitomized in the symbolic presence of a Buddhist household altar (*jibutsu* or *butsudan*) where tablets containing ancestral spirits were placed and to which rites of ancestral veneration were devoted.[50]

The *danka* system and funerary Buddhism kept households together, separated members of Buddhist temples from Christianity, enabled state regulation of individual subjects, and provided a stable economic foundation for Buddhist temples. Further, funerary Buddhism reinforced the notion of *ie*. In this patriarchal structure, the head of a family dominated women, fed his children, and worshipped his ancestors through funerary Buddhism rooted in the *danka* system.

Funerary Buddhism remained strong in modern Japan, despite the reform of Buddhist sects and denominations. In response to the Meiji government's persecution of Buddhism, Buddhist leaders used rationalism and science to repackage their tradition as a modern religion. They reformed their organizations, compiled new collections of core Buddhist texts, and created the modern discipline of Buddhist studies; represented the ethos of conformity to the Japanese state apparatus; and competed with Christians, followers of other Asian Buddhist traditions, and Euro-American Buddhologists who imagined and constructed the original form of Buddhism. In the midst of this Buddhist reform, however, clergy and the Japanese populace continued to accept and practice funerary Buddhism. It was not uncommon for intellectuals to observe Buddhist funerals and memorial services of their loved ones and to honor their ancestors. Funerary Buddhism continued to provide resources for the modern development of Buddhist organizations and Buddhist studies in Japan.[51]

The emergence of lay Buddhist movements characterizes another aspect of modern Japanese Buddhism. Lay Buddhist leaders, such as Nishida Kitarō and Suzuki Daisetsu, cooperated with reformers of the Buddhist organizations and contributed to the revival of Buddhism in modern Japan, although they criticized established Buddhist organizations from time to time. As a result, various concepts emerged, forming new discourses on Japanese Buddhism, including United Buddhism as the trans-sectarian Buddhist front against Christianity, Eastern Buddhism as compared to original Buddhism, and Kamakura New Buddhism—featuring medieval Buddhist figures like Hōnen, Shinran, Ippen (1239–1289), Nichiren, Eisai or Yōsai (1141–1215), and Dōgen—as the pinnacle of Japanese Buddhist development.[52] To further examine the impact of the Buddhist revival in modern Japan and on Japanese literature, the concept of modernism is examined next.

Modernism, Art, and Religion

Thomas Tweed defines culture as the collective schemata of "meaning imbedded in language and symbols which orient individuals in the world. These frameworks include presuppositions, beliefs, values, attitudes, symbols, myths, and codes of conduct."[53] Religions are thus cultural products. He defines cultural forms that both consciously accept and reject particular sets of sociohistorical conditions that emerged in Western Europe during the sixteenth century and dominated the world after the nineteenth century as modernism.[54] For modern Japanese intellectuals, modernism is the simultaneous denial and reevaluation of tradition, parallel to both the adaptation to and the rejection of contemporary innovations derived primarily from Western Europe. They made these attempts in literature and film, painting and sculpture, music and theatrical performance, and architecture as well as in religion. For Japanese Buddhist leaders, Buddhist modernism suggested that Western experiences of ancient Buddhism be integrated into their discourse on Buddhism to reinterpret their tradition, and that Japanese Buddhism be introduced to Western Europe and North America as the superior form of Buddhism.[55]

Modernism in Asia is, however, more than a reappraisal of tradition. Iftikhar Dadi discusses a complex interplay of modernism, nationalism, cosmopolitanism, and tradition in terms of the experience of modern South Asian Muslim artists.[56] He defines modernism as "a range of artistic practices characterized above all by anti-illusionism, medium-specificity, and reflexivity"[57] and emphasizes its transnational character by quoting Andreas Huyssen's concept of modernism, that is, "crossnational cultural forms that emerge from the negotiation for the modern with the indigenous, the colonial, and the postcolonial in the 'non-Western' world."[58] Dadi employs the term "transnational modernism" and moves away from the dominant European model of art studies, which assumes "the centrality of Western art in specific geographic and cultural sites,"[59] and he considers a single nation state to be an inadequate unit for investigating Islamic artists' subjectivities in modern South Asia.[60]

The rise of nationalism against the British Empire in India led to the emergence of distinct identities defined by religion, ethnicity, and language. It enabled Indians to reinvigorate earlier Hindu and Buddhist practices. Muslims in India viewed themselves as a minority and formed a Pan-Islamic identity, reforming their religion and education. For major artists, such as Abdur Rahman Chughtai (1894–1975), the articulation of modern Islamic art includes Hindu and Buddhist iconography.[61]

For South Asian Muslim artists, tradition is, by nature, cosmopolitan, and transnational modernism continues to be multicultural. Cosmopolitanism implies imagined associations with other parts of the world without conforming to a particular political authority or affiliating with an institution. Dadi argues that these artists have acquired a cosmopolitan outlook by translating a variety of historical and cultural Muslim expressions created before the period of Western colonialism and by translating transnational modernism. He states that "twentieth-century artistic cosmopolitanism not only references earlier cosmopolitanisms but also negotiates the poles of commensurability and participation in transnational modernism in an attempt to secure its own fraught location and voice."[62] The modern development of South Asian Islamic art has been a complex process characterized by cultural politics and identity formation, national imaginary and belonging, transnational networks, a universal consciousness in the Islamic world, and negotiations with Western and non-Western aesthetics.

The concepts of modernism, nationalism, cosmopolitanism, and tradition discussed by Dadi serve as the background to the present study. Conditions of the modern nation state of Japan differ from those of India, and the collective experiences of modern Japanese writers are unlike those of Muslim artists in South Asia. However, with the rise of Japan as a modern nation state in competition with the West, all the writers examined in this book—whether as novelists (*shōsetsuka*) or Buddhist priests—searched for a distinct national identity through new forms of a popular medium (e.g., confessional writing) and engaged in self-reflection. They were rational thinkers who carefully described and analyzed the psychological development of an alter ego and contributed to the formation of modern literature in Japan through their local cultural practices, broader Asian perspectives, and Western influences.

For Sōseki, Katai, Shiga, and Matsuoka, tradition suggests reevaluating earlier literary conventions, arts, and religions. They read classical Chinese prose and poetry, medieval Japanese literature, including *waka* and *haikai*, and the writings of Ihara Saikaku and others during the Edo period;[63] enjoyed calligraphy, monochrome painting, *nanga* painting ("[Southern School] style of literati painting"[64] during the Edo period), Buddhist art and statues, and temple and shrine architecture; attended *yōkyoku* ("the sung portion of Nō"[65]) and *jōruri* performances; learned Buddhist doctrines, Confucian ethics, and Taoist worldviews; and experienced the yin-yang practice, sacred mountain worship, and congeries of popular religious practices that overlapped with the religious practice defined by organized religion. Particularly for Katai and Shiga, sensing impermanence became sensing sadness and the beauty of nature. The perception of changes in natural scenery and meditation on the transient beauty of nature was understood to offer an avenue to self-realization.[66]

At the same time, the writers examined in *The Awakening of Modern Japanese Fiction* received a great deal of foreign influence. Sōseki majored in English literature at Tokyo Imperial University and studied in London. He visited Manchuria and the Korean Peninsula in 1909, whereas Katai went to Manchuria as a member of a photography team during the Russo-Japanese War (1904–1905). Shiga first studied English and Japanese literature at Tokyo Imperial University and then joined Uchimura Kanzō's Christian group. He did not study abroad but praised Lafcadio Hearn's works, which he read in English, and interacted with Bernard H. Leach through the *Shirakaba-ha* group. Matsuoka majored in philosophy at Tokyo Imperial University and became Sōseki's student. His Buddhist upbringing helped expand his imagination with regard to Indian Buddhism and inspired him to pursue historical studies of Buddhism. He later fictionalized Shakyamuni Buddha's life and created a documentary of expeditions to Dunhuang led by Great Britain, France, and Japan during the early twentieth century. All these writers maintained associations with Asia and Western Europe through overseas travel and by studying world literature.

Two Shin Buddhist priests examined in chapter 4 had similar experiences vis-à-vis tradition and the modern. Kiyozawa Manshi learned classical Chinese and majored in philosophy at Tokyo Imperial University under Ernest Fenollosa. Kiyozawa is known as the first religious philosopher of modern Japan. He later had his *Skeleton of a Philosophy of Religion* (*Shūkyō tetsugaku gaikotsu*, 1893) translated into English and submitted it to the World's Parliament of Religions in Chicago in 1893. While studying Western philosophy, he rediscovered the importance of his Buddhist tradition. Kiyozawa considered the *Āgama Sutras* (early Buddhist scriptures), which he read in Chinese; *The Discourses of Epictetus*; and the *Passages Deploring Deviations of Faith* (*Tannishō*, a popular Shin Buddhist text written during the Kamakura period [1185–1333]) to be the foundation of his intellectual and spiritual life.

Akegarasu Haya, one of Kiyozawa's students, also revived Shin Buddhism. Unlike his teacher, who ignored popular literature, Akegarasu employed both his own story and other writers' novels as a means of propagation and used Christianity as a point of reference. He wrote a short story about the life of an old Buddhist priest based on a story he heard from a friend.[67] Between 1926 and 1929, Akegarasu traveled to India, Sri Lanka, Jerusalem, Greece, Hungary, Italy, France, Germany, Moscow, and northern Asia, as well as Hawaii and the North American continent. By going beyond Japan's national borders, he realized the place of Shin Buddhism in the world and proposed global propagation of his religion.[68]

For Kiyozawa and Akegarasu, tradition includes the much broader Asian Buddhist identity that Shinran had created. It refers to his teaching, which is built on the doctrines of the so-called Seven Pure Land Masters (Nāgārjuna and Vasubandhu of India; Tanluan, Daochuo, and Shandao of China; and

Genshin and Hōnen of Japan), morals and ethics derived from Confucianism, the hierarchy of their denomination and ritual protocols that originated in earlier times, and the Honganji's imperial connection and military propaganda. Akegarasu, especially, grew nationalistic and supported Japan's colonial expansion on the Asian continent.

Although the aim of writing for Shin Buddhist clergy is different from the goal of literary artists, works of both Buddhist and literary writers developed because of the "antinomies of self and society beyond formulaic positions," to borrow Dadi's words.[69] Both Buddhist priests and literary authors grappled with a society that was rapidly changing, and Kiyozawa and Akegarasu found a spiritual solution in a particular Buddhist teaching. The personal novels are records of personal struggles against social norms, authorities, and others, as well as documents of self-transformation.

Personal Fiction

In early twentieth-century Japan, a new literary genre, or form, known as *shishōsetsu* emerged. It was considered similar to the German *Ich-Roman*, commonly translated as "I-novel," and developed from the naturalist movement of modern Japan. The I-novel achieved its status as confessional literature "whose aesthetic value began to be judged according to the sincerity of the confession," according to Irmela Hijiya-Kirschnereit.[70]

Three scholars published works on the subject of I-novels in English.[71] In *Rituals of Self-Revelation: Shishōsetsu as Literary Genre and Socio-Cultural Phenomenon*, Hijiya-Kirschnereit treats I-novels as a literary genre and discusses their communicative functions. While exploring the interests of the author, hero, and reader, as well as examining their relationships, she finds that traditional concepts, such as *mujō* (impermanence) and *mono no aware* ("capacity to be moved by things," such as "the beauties of nature and the feelings of people"[72] that lead poets and writers to express aesthetic feelings), retain their importance. She recognizes those concepts as part of the cultural heritage of Japanese literature.[73]

Unlike Hijiya-Kirschnereit, in *The Rhetoric of Confession: Shishōsetsu in Early Twentieth-Century Japanese Fiction*, Edward Fowler defines I-novels as a literary form. He takes up the issue of the author's self-referentiality in the text and questions the "sincerity" of confession: "style is rhetoric, the literary equivalent of acting, the concealed art without which the honesty and sincerity could not be 'revealed.'"[74] Sincerity, in essence, derives from form, even though I-novel writers and Japanese critics have insisted on the unmediated experience of literary confession. As is the case for Hijiya-Kirschnereit, Fowler introduces the Japanese ideas of self-cultivation, such as *jiko tankyū* (search for a self) and *gudō* (seeking the way)—both of which come from the Buddhist tradition—as recurring themes of the I-novels.[75]

In *Narrating the Self: Fictions of Japanese Modernity*, Tomi Suzuki argues that I-novels need to be studied as a discourse—what she calls the "I-novel discourse" or the "I-novel meta-narrative." This discourse emerged when Japanese writers participated in the discussion of self and recognized the novel as a social medium influenced by the West. Suzuki states,

> From the 1920's the I-novel meta-narrative not only defined the modern Japanese novel as a form that directly transcribed the author's lived experience but also emphasized the confessional, self-exploratory, autobiographical nature of the "indigenous" Japanese literary tradition, describing classical literature with such highly Western, romantic terms and phrases as "immediacy," "directness," "lyricism," "spiritual search for the self," "unity with nature."[76]

According to Suzuki, the notion of I-novels was retroactively constructed and became the standard for Japanese writers and critics not only to further create and categorize I-novels but also to evaluate the status of Japanese literature as a whole. Unlike Hijiya-Kirschnereit and Fowler who recognize the impact of traditional Buddhist sensibilities on the development of autobiographical fiction, Suzuki seems to suggest that the connection between Buddhism and I-novels was made as part of the Japanese literary establishment's later justification to make I-novels uniquely Japanese. While Buddhism is a traditional component of I-novels, these critics do not explain how modern Japanese writers reinvented and adapted traditional Buddhist ideas in them. *The Awakening of Modern Japanese Fiction* thus employs the term "personal fiction" to disassociate its argument from their discussion of I-novels and explores the impact of both traditional sensibilities and the modern development of Buddhism on the Japanese writers' private sphere. The Buddhist notion of path is one example by which traditional Buddhist ideas were reconstructed in modern Japan.

Path in Buddhism, Narrative Structure of Buddhism, and Path Literature

Until the Western notion of Buddhism was introduced to Japan and translated as *bukkyō* 仏教 (literally, "teaching of the Buddha"), Japanese Buddhists used the word *butsudō* 仏道, meaning the way, or path, of the Buddha. While the term *bukkyō* implies the philosophical aspect of Buddhist teachings, *butsudō* suggests Buddhist praxis. The *dō* in *butsudō* even includes the sense of the way of life as suggested in *Laozi* and *Zhuangzi*.[77]

According to Robert Buswell and Robert Gimello, Buddhist schemes that integrate Buddhist doctrine and practice are known as the schemata of *mārga*, or path. They define path as "a valid model for religious endeavor in Buddhism only insofar as it poses a destination to be reached, and only to the extent that someone actively pursues that destination."[78] This model can serve as a "theory according to which certain methods of practice, certain prescribed patterns of religious behavior, have transformative power and will lead, somewhat necessarily, to religious goals."[79] In other words, the development of Buddhist insight is expressed as moving on a path. In the Four Noble Truths, nirvana, or the cessation of suffering, is defined as the third truth because the attainment of nirvana needs to be sought by a practitioner through specific forms of practice, such as the eightfold path (the fourth truth) and six perfections (*pāramitā*). In other words, nirvana is the ultimate goal, but seeking and moving on a path to nirvana is as important as attaining the goal—lest a practitioner becomes complacent after reaching the goal. As Dōgen would say, sitting in meditation, or *zazen*, is not "a means to an end," but "practice-realization."[80] For Zen practitioners, engaging in sitting in meditation is an endless path.

While in the history of Japanese Buddhism the "way of the Buddha," or *butsudō*, was a premodern concept, Buddhism and a notion of path played a significant role in the modern development of Japanese aesthetic sensibilities. According to Steve Odin, the "detached contemplation of beauty as a means to enlightenment was central in the Japanese Buddhist religio-aesthetic tradition of *geidō* 芸道: the *tao* (or way) of art." Referring to Japanese scholarship, he introduces words and concepts expressing a sense of "detached resignation"—such as "*aware* (melancholy beauty)," "*yūgen* (profound mystery)," "*ma* (negative space)," "*wabi* (rustic beauty)," "*sabi* (simplicity)," "*fūryū* (windblown elegance)," and "*iki* (chic)"—and discusses their Buddhist implications.[81] The set of aesthetic sensibilities expressed by these words is, at the same time, a modern construct. Overemphasizing the impact of Zen Buddhism on the high culture of Japan through the concept of "aesthetics," which was retroactively created by modern Japanese intellectuals, is ideological.[82] They appropriated the notion of path, or *dō*, for redefining, and even reducing, Japanese cultural practice. For instance, in *The Book of Tea* (1906), Tenshin Okakura introduced the way of tea, or *sadō*, to the West as an exemplary model of Japanese culture influenced by Buddhism and Taoism, and discussed its significance in terms of modern aesthetics and art.[83] In *Bushidō: The Soul of Japan* (1889), Inazō Nitobe introduced the way of the samurai, or *bushidō*, to the West as the moral and self-disciplinary system of Japan which, in his opinion, included a universal value.[84] With an emphasis on spiritual training, the word *bujutsu* or *bugei*, martial arts, was replaced with the word *budō*, the way of martial arts; thereafter the words *kendō*, *jūdō*, and *kyūdō* were created. In particular, Kanō Jigorō (1860–1938), the founder of *jūdō*, combined the scientific study of body and mind, which derived from the West, with the traditional concept of seeking the way as the basis for enhancing one's spiritual state.[85]

Modern Japanese writers who wrote personal novels also sought the way of literary art. Among them, the phrase "life is training" (*jinsei shugyō*) became popular, encouraging the writers to taste the bitterness of life. Suzuki Sadami considers the foundation of their view of life to be a combination of Western romanticism and social decadence with the Japanese tradition of seeking the way and the Buddhist attitude of leaving the world.[86] As Japanese writers appropriated the Buddhist concept of path for their making of modern literature, personal fiction began to acquire the quality of path literature.

For Buddhists, poetry and narratives are conduits of Dharma transmission. As Peter Skilling suggests, they are the means to celebrate the Buddha, Bodhisattvas, and deities; discuss Buddhist ontology, epistemology, and soteriology; explain monastic rules; and engage in dialogue with other religious systems.[87] Aśvaghoṣa (80?–150? CE), a prominent Indian Buddhist poet, said, "Seeing that the world generally holds the pleasure of sensory experience uppermost and is resistant to liberation, I, holding liberation to be paramount, have described the truth in the guise of poetry."[88] As mentioned earlier, in East Asia the notion of "floating phrases and fictive utterances," which is said to have been created by Bai Juyi (772–846) [J. Hakurakuten], helped reconcile the way of poetry and of the Buddha.[89] In medieval Japan, Buddhist writers rejected prose fiction but accepted storytelling in the form of parables as a skillful means to deliver higher truths.[90] The *Jātaka* tales, stories of the Buddha's former lives, represent one of the most popular narratives of Buddhism.

Scholars have investigated the relationships between narrative and religious experience. According to Bruce Hindmarsh, stories of religious conversion often take the form of autobiographical narratives. Conversion and narrative are similar in terms of their structures: "If narrative in its classical form is defined as a plot with a beginning, middle, an end—with sufficient magnitude, as Aristotle said, to allow for transformation—then all narratives are, in one sense, conversion narratives."[91] Autobiography is the narrative of both construction and discovery of a self.

Charles Hallisey and Anne Hansen recognize the transformative power of narrative in Buddhism and associate it with the role of religious ethics. They analyze three ways in which narrative defines moral life—"prefiguration (the effect of narratives in enlarging an agent's moral horizon), configuration (the power of narratives to expose the opaqueness of moral intention), or refiguration (the healing and transformative potential of narratives)."[92] As an example of refiguration, Hallisey and Hansen introduce the story of Paṭācārā, a female disciple of the Buddha who was born to a wealthy family. Paṭācārā runs away with a male servant and gives birth to two sons. Her lover, however, dies during her delivery. When she decides to return to her family, a hawk snatches one child away while the other falls into a river and dies. Upon her return, she discovers that the mansion in which she was raised has collapsed and that her parents have died. Paṭācārā becomes insane as a result and wanders around naked. After much more suffering and humiliation, she meets the Buddha and attains spiritual liberation.[93]

Hallisey and Hansen consider the oral tradition of Paṭācārā's story to be an example of "refiguration." When Paṭācārā washes her feet and meditates on short, medium, and long streams, she realizes the nature of death, which the tradition describes as the moment of her awakening. That is, all people, whether young or old, die someday.[94] Hallisey and Hansen conclude, "For Paṭācārā, that vision effects a personal conversion by refiguring her experience into something distant from herself and allowing her to become detached from the story in which she herself is the main character."[95] In Buddhist tradition, refiguration suggests a detachment from one's own past that is formulated as a story, through which one investigates the cause of suffering, develops insight into the nature of human life, and redirects one's life. The story of Paṭācārā shows a pattern of Buddhist realization structured as narrative in which basic Buddhist doctrine, such as the Four Noble Truths, is explained.

As is the case for the story of Paṭācārā, patterns of religious doctrine and practice are often converted into narratives in which a main character's religious experience is organized in a sequence. According to Richard Payne, a Buddhist notion of path "provides a narrative structure, in the sense that it is not only found as a topic in much Buddhist literature, but also gives structure for Buddhist thought." The idea of a path helps us understand narrative as a way to organize events into a "meaningful order" and in a "progressive sequence" where a "causal relation" is clarified.[96] Payne proposes a narrative pattern specific to Buddhist praxis:[97]

> The specific narrative structure that informs much of Buddhist praxis is the system known as "ground, path, goal," that is, a description of the ordinary human condition and its problematic nature (ground), the way in which one moves out of that condition (path), and the

nature of what one seeks to ultimately attain (goal). "Ground, path, goal" reveals the underlying narrative structure of Buddhist praxis in the sense of narrative as a temporally developing trajectory (i.e., causally coherent), in which change is reframed as meaningful.[98]

The narrative pattern of the ground, path, and goal includes reflections of ordinary human activities on doctrines, analyses of the effectiveness of practice at various stages, and discussions of the nature of self-realization and of Buddhahood.[99]

The structure of a path is not monolithic,[100] and not all the main characters analyzed in *The Awakening of Modern Japanese Fiction* attain their goals—in fact, some characters are not even aware of their goals. This book treats path as various kinds of spiritual activities triggered by the protagonist's sense of loneliness, displacement, loss, frustration, and other types of suffering. These activities develop further, as main characters seek self-detachment, the state of oneness, and a spiritual strength; make efforts to understand, overcome, and move away from the causes of suffering; and accept their past, engage with their present conditions, and come to terms with self and others. Despite these differences, realization and acceptance of suffering is the beginning of a path that leads them to self-realization, self-transformation, and Buddhist awakening. For some characters, self-transformation can be a goal, but for others, it can be an ongoing process. The paths of the main characters also intersect with the authors' paths and can be framed by ideology. Further, the developments of spiritual paths are related to the main characters' external activities, such as traveling (moving to or away from a city), wandering from one place to another, and observing Buddhist funerals and processions. *The Awakening of Modern Japanese Fiction* demonstrates the diversity of path literature through these variants. In the next chapter, the paths followed by these authors are investigated. Sōseki, Katai, and Shiga are treated as lay Buddhist practitioners and their Buddhist experiences are explored.

PART 1

Writing Personal Fiction as a Confessional and Religious Practice

CHAPTER TWO

Modern Japanese Writers as Lay Buddhist Practitioners

Although most modern Japanese writers would not consider themselves to be Buddhists, their connections to Buddhism cannot be underestimated. Natsume Sōseki, Tayama Katai, and Shiga Naoya had experiential contacts with Buddhism through reading Buddhist scriptures, participating in funerary Buddhism, and interacting with Buddhist clergy. Sōseki sat in Zen meditation, Katai traveled frequently and often participated in the lifestyle of wandering monks, and Shiga was a connoisseur of East Asian Buddhist arts. These practices associated with Buddhism helped them come to terms with troubles in their daily life. Although they dissociated themselves from organized religion, whose concept emerged as *shūkyō* in modern Japan and from sectarian Buddhism, they were interested in Buddhism as part of Japan's literary tradition and were influenced by the contemporary development of Japanese Buddhism. In this chapter, the three writers' Buddhist experiences and their attitudes toward other religions are discussed.

Natsume Sōseki (1867–1916): Death as Nirvana and Seeking the Way

Sōseki maintained an interest in Buddhism throughout his life. As early as 1891, when he was twenty-five, his teacher, James Main Dixon, asked him to translate into English Kamono Chōmei's (1155–1216) *Hōjōki* (*Records of Ten Feet Square*), which is characterized by the Buddhist sensibility of impermanence. Sōseki seems to have been inspired by the Pure Land and Zen Buddhist teachings. He idealized death as an ideal state equivalent to nirvana, and before his death, asked one of the two young Zen monks with whom he had interacted closely, to give the last Dharma Words (*indō*) at his funeral—although Shaku Sōen was the officiant of Sōseki's funeral. Sōseki's posthumous Buddhist name is *Sōseki koji*.[1] This section introduces Sōseki's Buddhist experiences in two periods, before and after his near-death experience known as the Shuzenji crisis (*shuzenji taikan* 修善寺大患).

Before the Shuzenji Crisis

Sōseki had a troubled childhood. He was born in 1867, the youngest child of Natsume Naokatsu (also known as Kohei) and Chie. His name at birth was Kinnosuke. Kohei had two daughters before marrying Chie, so including them, Sōseki had three elder sisters and four elder brothers. Kohei cared little for Kinnosuke and sent him away to be raised by foster parents—Shiobara Shōnosuke and his wife, Yasu. Kinnosuke, was, however, abandoned by his foster parents and returned to Kohei. He lost his eldest sister at the age of twelve and his beloved mother at fifteen.[2] These events affected young Sōseki's personality and raised issues of love and trust for him as he grew up.

Sōseki idealized death throughout his life. As early as 1889, he expressed a "weariness of life" to his friend Masaoka Shiki (1867–1902), showing "a deep-rooted dislike of life and a sympathy for death."[3] In 1891, about a year after he started studying at Tokyo Imperial University, Toyo, one of his sisters-in-law whom Sōseki respected, died. He had also lost two elder brothers, including Daisuke, whom Sōseki held in high esteem. Because his family was affiliated with a Shin Buddhist temple, Sōseki became familiar with Shin Buddhist rituals and scriptures as a result of attending funerals and memorial services.[4] A copy of *Sacred Texts of Shin Buddhism*, published in 1913, was also found in his library.[5]

Between October 1900 and January 1903, the Japanese government assigned Sōseki to study English literature in London. While this opportunity allowed him to learn much about Western literature, it affected his personality negatively and shaped his persona even to the point of madness, because of the racial discrimination, poverty, and loneliness he experienced in London.[6] All these events caused him to ponder the meaning of his life. In 1901, he wrote in "A Fragment" (*Danpen*): "Were we born, we must die—whence we come, whither we tend [sic]? Answer!"[7]

After returning from London, Sōseki taught at Tokyo Imperial University and began writing novels. He published *I Am a Cat* (*Wagahai wa neko de aru*, 1905–1906), *Tower of London* (*Londontō*, 1905), *Botchan* (1906), and *The Three-Cornered World* (1906). In 1907, he resigned from the university and became the "highest-paid staff writer" at the *Tokyo Asahi Shinbun* (Tokyo Morning Sun Newspaper).⁸ He then published *The Poppy* (*Gubijinsō*, 1907), *The Miner* (1908), *Ten Nights of Dreams* (*Yume jūya*, 1908), and a so-called trilogy—*Sanshirō* (1908), *And Then* (*Sorekara*, 1909), and *The Gate* (March–June, 1910)—as well as other works, including *Theory of Literature* (*Bungakuron*, 1907).⁹

Images of death persist in Sōseki's early writings. In *Ten Nights of Dreams*, for example, a woman is reincarnated as a white lily to meet her lover, who waits for her for a hundred years; a samurai is determined to attain *satori* in exchange for killing a Zen master or take his own life if he fails in meditation; a father carrying a blind son on his back realizes his past karma—he killed a blind man a hundred years ago; an old man unsuccessfully casts a spell to transform a hand towel into a snake, walks into a deep river, and is never seen again; a samurai captured by an enemy chooses to die, but because he wishes to see his lover one last time, she gallops to meet him but falls from her horse because of a devil's spell; a man who dislikes being on a ship filled with foreigners and does not believe in God decides to commit suicide, but after throwing himself into the dark sea, regrets his decision to take his life; and a young mother visits a shrine for a hundred days, praying for her husband's safe return without knowing he had died in action.¹⁰

According to Mizukawa Takao, another instance of Sōseki's concern with death can be found in *I Am a Cat* and *The Poppy*.¹¹ Although we should not treat Sōseki and the narrator as being identical, in these works the narrators idealize death as a state of ultimate peace. At the end of *I Am a Cat*, the two are connected: "I died. I died and am at peace. Peace cannot be had without dying, *namu amida butsu* 南無阿弥陀仏 [repeated six times], how thankful I am, how thankful I am, how thankful I am, how thankful I am."¹² Also, consider the beginning of *The Poppy*:

> Only silence remains. In silence, we are brought to realize that life is what we are entrusted with. My blood, which is related to both heaven and earth, was energized and circulated quietly and serenely (*jakujōri* 寂定裏), making no demands on my body. Being aware of life but not troubled by it is like the sky without its clouds, changing in the morning and evening. It is the spirit that transcends all kinds of attachment (*kōdei* 拘泥). If I cannot step into a world beyond this world, spanning east to west and emptying the three realms of

the past, present, and future, I would rather be a fossil—a black fossil—which absorbs red, blue, yellow, and purple, never returning to the original colors. If not, I wish to die. Death is the end of everything. But it is also the beginning of all things . . . Why do those of you with noble minds (*harukanaru kokoro*) not long for that far-off land of eternity (*harukanaru kuni*)?[13]

According to Miyazawa Masayori, the word *jakujōri* implies the Buddhist concept of "calm and concentration" derived from the *Longer Sukhāvatīvyūha Sutra* (known in Japanese as *Daimuryōjukyō*, or the *Larger Sutra on Amitāyus*).[14] The narrator's idealization of death also brings to mind another popular Pure Land Buddhist notion of "aversion to the impure world and aspiration for the Pure Land" (*onriedo gongujōdo* 厭離穢土、欣求浄土). The narrators of *The Poppy* and *I Am a Cat* express a popular Pure Land Buddhist belief and romanticize death as leading to the world of eternity. These descriptions do not suggest Sōseki himself believed in the "land of eternity," but rather demonstrate his familiarity with Pure Land Buddhism.

Yet Pure Land Buddhism brought Sōseki spiritual relief. According to Miyazawa, Sōseki's interest in Pure Land Buddhism can be found in his poetry. He interacted with Masaoka Shiki and Takahama Kyoshi (1874–1959), Shiki's student, and composed poems in the "style of gods and hermits" (*shinsentai*),[15] which included Amidist expressions such as *namu amida butsu* and "minding of Amida Buddha." In 1904, Sōseki wrote the following poem:

> Crawling under the covers,
> Trying to sleep, but unable to.
> [Reciting] *namu amida butsu* . . .
> Finally, to sleep without worries and dreams.[16]

What is represented in this poem may not be completely true, but Sōseki seemed to have recalled his childhood during which he suffered from nightmares and resorted to Amida Buddha. Sōseki's poem reflects a long-standing tradition of Japanese poetry that developed closely with Pure Land Buddhism.[17]

Despite his Amidist outlook, Sōseki was mostly interested in Zen. Between December 24 and January 7, 1894, at the age of twenty-nine—about a year after graduating from Tokyo Imperial University—Sōseki lived in Kigen-in in the Engakuji compound in Kamakura and practiced meditation for about two weeks. Sōseki was said to have suffered a nervous breakdown at the time and sought a spiritual practice to heal from it.[18] Through Suga Torao, Sōseki's good friend, who had been a disciple of Imakita Kōsen (1816–1892), Sōseki met Shaku Sōen (1860–1919) and learned Zen from him.[19] Imakita revitalized Zen during the 1870s and 1880s by improving the monastic education of the Rinzai sect, contributing to the emergence of a new group of Japanese Buddhists known as *koji*, or Zen for lay practitioners. Shaku Sōen was one of Kōsen's immediate disciples and presented the teachings of Japanese Buddhism at the 1893 World's Parliament of Religions in Chicago.[20] Janine Tasca Sawada points out that cultivation of the self became one of the central concerns among intellectuals and bureaucrats in Tokyo during the late nineteenth century. Groups of lay practitioners gathered at Engakuji in Kamakura, practicing Zen and Shingaku while maintaining Neo-Confucian ideals. Sōseki's *sanzen* (vising a temple for Zen instruction) experience at Engakuji in 1894 testifies to his association with that network.[21]

At Engakuji, Sōseki received a kōan 公案, or test of Zen understanding: "What was your original state before your parents were born?" He is said to have replied, "There is no mind apart from object and no object apart from mind." The master found his reply too intellectual and told him to "stop calculating with your reason" and "come up with something glittering."[22] Later, Sōseki received another kōan, "Does a dog have Buddha nature?" to which he could not respond satisfactorily.[23] He then quit Zen.

Sōseki's immediate response to Zen after leaving Engakuji was negative. He considered Zen a "magic trick" (*genjutsu*) and the kōan "an intoxicating play where questions and answers are further exchanged as though preparing for a dialogue (*mondō*), which is similar to exchanging opinions prior to a discussion."[24] Despite his negative experience at Engakuji, as we will see in chapter 6, Zen masters have an impact on the main characters in *The Three-Cornered World* and *The Gate*.

The Shuzenji Crisis and Afterward

Sōseki eventually came to face his own "death." After finishing *The Gate*, his health deteriorated rapidly. He was diagnosed with a gastric ulcer and hospitalized. At the end of July, he moved to a place called Shuzenji on the Izu Peninsula to convalesce. His condition worsened and on August 24, 1910 he vomited a large amount of blood. A subsequent attack, caused by cerebral anemia, almost killed him. According to his wife, Sōseki was "dead for thirty minutes."[25] This incident is usually referred to as the Shuzenji crisis.

The incident helped Sōseki confirm his understanding of death. In "Recollections" (*Omoidasu koto nado*, 1911)—a type of writing called *shōhin*, between a short story and an essay[26]—Sōseki wrote about his survival. He could not accept the relationship between life and death in either logical or mystical terms. For him, going back and forth between the realms of life and death was simply incomprehensible.[27] According to "Recollections," Sōseki accepted that neither his spirit nor his consciousness sustained an afterlife—he neither imagined himself turning into a ghost nor submitted to a transcendent authority. He disagreed with European spiritualism and rejected mysticism concerning death. For him, death was simply a matter of "just losing my personality and consciousness"[28]; hence, it could be neither conceptualized nor verbalized. Further, Sōseki wrote, "I died once and experienced that death *in the way I had always imagined*"[29] (emphasis added). In other words, for Sōseki, the Shuzenji crisis was a simulation of dying, which the narrators of *I Am a Cat* and *The Poppy* internalize as a state of ultimate peace. Sōseki reconfirmed their feelings that death is the supreme state.

During his convalescence after the Shuzenji crisis, Sōseki retreated from the world. He enjoyed composing poetry and reconnected with his family and friends. He found value in things that he thought trivial prior to his illness and praised them as rare things, which he would never again come across. According to "Recollections," Sōseki enjoyed reading *Biographies of Immortals*. As Maria Flutsch points out, Taoism and its poetic expressions "contained, for Sōseki, the most comforting and restorative views of the human being, not only because of their familiarity but also—and importantly—because of their respect for the emotional life of the human being."[30]

Sōseki was grateful to his wife, his doctors and nurses, his students, and his friends who came to visit him. He sensed humanity in their actions and was able to accept his life "as worth living for the first time."[31] Further, Sōseki wrote, "I came to thank my illness. I came to thank those who devoted so much time and energy on my behalf. These experiences made me *want to become a good person* (*negawakuwa zenryō na ningen ni naritaito kangaeta* 願わくは善良な人間になりたいと考えた) and to always maintain that feeling [of thankfulness]. I vowed that anyone who disturbed this feeling would forever be my enemy"[32] (emphasis added). Resurrected from the realm of death as it were, the Shuzenji crisis led Sōseki to change his attitude toward himself, others, and society as a whole.[33]

As death raises the issue of goodness, Sōseki's aspiration for becoming a good person implies a religious persona. The thought of death affects our speculations on moral judgment and the course of ethical conduct. According to Mark Johnston, who analyzes naturalists' accounts of surviving death, the "good person" can reevaluate one's past and one's connections to others. Johnston states,

> The good person is one who has undergone a kind of death of the self; as a result he or she lives a transformed life driven by entering imaginatively into the lives of others, anticipating their needs and true interest, and responding to these as far as is reasonable. *The good person is thus a caretaker of humanity, in himself just as in others. By living this way, the good person encounters himself objectively, as just another, but one with respect to which he has a special trust.*[34] (emphasis added)

A good person, for Johnston, is someone informed by the "best forms of Judaism, Christianity, and Buddhism" and by the Buddhist doctrine of *anatta*, or no-self, and the notion of *agape* in the New Testament.[35] In other words, a good person is aware of his egocentricity and has attained a certain level of self-realization, namely ethical and religious.

Sōseki resumed writing after his recovery. He produced five more novels before his death in December 1916: *To the Spring Equinox and Beyond* (1912), *The Wayfarer* (*Kōjin*, 1912–1913), *Kokoro* (1914), *Grass on the Wayside* (1915), and *Light and Darkness* (*Meian*, 1916), his last but incomplete work. He also created *shōhin*, kept diaries, jotted down fragmentary notes, and wrote many letters.

After the Shuzenji crisis, Sōseki continued to show his engagement with death, but did not wish to attain that state by his own hand. A few months after completion of *Kokoro*, in a letter addressed to Hayashihara Kōzō, dated November 14, 1914, Sōseki discussed his thoughts about death and suicide:

> I did not intend to state twice in a row that I selected death over life but unintentionally did so because of my mood then. But that's neither a lie nor making light of the matter. I really hope that after I die, everyone will gather before my coffin and send me off with a "Banzai!" I believe consciousness is all there is to life, and yet I cannot believe that the same consciousness is all there is of me. I believe something of me will remain even after I die, and further, that I will return to my original self when I die. *I do not look fondly on suicide at present, and very likely will try living to the fullest.* And while living, like most people, *I believe I will exhibit the*

weak points I was born with. That's because I believe that's what life is. What I dislike most of all, however, is while disliking life, forcibly moving from life to an exceedingly agonizing death. *That's why I have no desire to commit suicide.* Besides, selecting death means an aversion to this world (*enseikan* 厭世観) that is not the same as a pessimistic view of life (*hikan* 悲観). You understand the difference between them, don't you?[36] (emphasis added)

For Sōseki, who was influenced by William James's notion of a stream of consciousness, defining death as the end of physical and mental activities was a matter of course. He rejected the idea that his spirit would hover around in space. At the same time, he was hesitant to accept the disappearance of his spirit. Sōseki appears to have contradicted himself over his vision of the continuum between life and death; however, his statement indicates his thinking on death in terms of both phenomenon and noumenon.

Such a perception of death resonates with the traditional image of birth in the Pure Land—after one dies, one is born in Amida Buddha's Pure Land where one attains enlightenment. The Pure Land is the realm of nirvana, which can be neither verbalized nor conceptualized. Unlike the popular image of the Pure Land as a magnificent place, Sōseki neither glorified the realm of death nor visualized it as a utopia, but rather associated it with the absolute state and the "original self," which resonates with a kōan he grappled with while sitting in meditation in Kamakura.

Sōseki's interest in Zen increased in later life. When writing *Grass on the Wayside* and *Light and Darkness*, he used the term "path" or way (*dō* or *michi* 道) several times in letters describing his spiritual status. Examples of such expressions include, "I am on the point of entering the path," "intending a path," or "working at the path."[37] Although Sōseki's reference to path points to broader East Asian religious traditions, his path implies a Buddhist way of life. He communicated closely with two young Zen priests at that time—Tomizawa Keidō and Kimura Genjō. He found them simple and open-minded, yet ritualistic and appreciative. Sōseki even felt that their personalities were sacred[38] and considered them much nobler than his students.[39]

Sōseki's determination to seek a path is recorded in his personal writings. On November 15, 1916—about a month before his death, he wrote to Tomizawa Keidō, "This may seem strange to say but I am an 'ignorant thing' who, only after reaching the age of fifty, has become aware of aspiring to follow the Way. Considering when I will be able to devote myself to it, I am surprised at how great the distance is."[40] In "A Record of Understandings" (*Tentōroku*, 1916), which was written in the year Sōseki died, he wrote,

One cannot ultimately predict one's death, as one's length of life cannot be determined by oneself. Although having many kinds of illnesses, I am still ten years younger than when Zhaozhou raised the bodhi-mind. I shall not live for a hundred and twenty years, but I think that it is possible for me to make some kind of achievement if I try as hard as possible. Therefore, I am determined to exert myself by modeling myself on Zhaozhou.[41]

In the same way considering life from the point of death helped Sōseki objectify his process of thinking, sitting in meditation enabled him to neutralize his perspectives and contain expansion of the "modern ego."[42] Although Sōseki failed in solving kōans at Engakuji, he remained intrigued by Zen. He read classical books of Zen and was familiar with the sayings of Chinese and Japanese Zen masters. He composed a number of Chinese poems, which in essence are Zen poems, enjoyed Ryōkan's verses, and took pleasure in viewing classical Chinese paintings associated with Zen.[43]

Sōseki also maintained his interest in the masters of Pure Land Buddhism. He is said to have expressed a wish to write a historical novel about Hōnen, the founder of the Jōdoshū, a Pure Land sect of Buddhism.[44] In a lecture titled "Imitation and Independence" (*Mohō to dokuritsu*), given at First High School in December 1913, he considered Shinran, the founder of the Jōdo Shinshū—another Pure Land Buddhist sect known as Shin Buddhism in the West, who declared that he is neither a layman nor monk, to be a man of independent spirit in medieval Japan. Sōseki admired Shinran's lifestyle, in which he ate meat and married, both of which are against Buddhist precepts, and considered Shinran's activities revolutionary.[45] Considering Shinran to be the first Buddhist monk who publically announced his marriage is, however, a modern construct. Sōseki, who interacted with Shin Buddhist leaders, seemingly relied on their historical perspectives of Japanese Buddhism and accepted such an image of Shinran uncritically.[46]

Further, Sōseki speculated on the connection between Zen and Pure Land paths. In 1915 he wrote, "Because the absolute self and non-ego are really one, there is a correspondence between self-power [represented by Zen Buddhism] and other-power [associated with Pure Land Buddhism developed by Hōnen and Shinran]."[47] Although the nature of this note is uncertain, Sōseki might have taken a universalistic approach to Buddhism. He was intrigued by the Buddhist values of self-realization and death, rather than by the categorization of sectarian Buddhist teachings. Moreover, according to Matsuoka Yuzuru, if the attainment of self-realization is a goal of Christianity, Sōseki did not necessarily differentiate between Buddhism and Christianity.[48]

Sōseki's engagement with Zen and Pure Land Buddhism, as well as his attentiveness to universal elements of Buddhism, show lines of thought that his contemporary Japanese Buddhist leaders developed. First, the Meiji Buddhist leaders promoted the notion of a United Buddhism, or a form of trans-sectarian Buddhism, by identifying Shakyamuni Buddha's "original" teachings shared by all denominations. According to Jamese Ketelaar, this movement was not necessarily in disagreement with each denomination's efforts to emphasize its own doctrine and practice. He states that "The conception of a transcendent unity combined with an evolved sectarian particularity of a manifest teaching was useful to Meiji era Buddhists as they sought to locate their own positions vis-à-vis critiques of their institutional artificiality."[49] Second, parallel to the movement of seeking the "origins" of Buddhism, reformers of the established Buddhist organizations encouraged their followers to embrace the teachings of their founders in order to revitalize their sects and denominations. A wide range of lay intellectuals supported this movement. For instance, Tanaka Chigaku promoted Nichiren-ism (*Nichiren shugi*) which inspired Takayama Chogyū and Anezaki Masaharu, while Shinran-ism (*Shinran shugi*) encouraged Kurata Hyakuzō to write *The Priest and His Disciples*. Sōseki's perception of Shinran as a man of independence—and Tayama Katai's admiration of Nichiren—reflect such an intellectual climate of modern Japan.

Tayama Katai (1872–1930): A Naturalist Writer's Buddhist Experience

As was the case for Sōseki, Tayama Katai upheld a paradigm of self-power (*jiriki* 自力) Buddhism versus other-power (*tariki* 他力) Buddhism, and yet recognized their goals to be identical. While Sōseki sought to re-experience the state of no-self that he thought he had attained during the Shuzenji crisis, Katai retrospectively interpreted his experience of death, relationships with women, and the perception of impermanence from a Buddhist perspective. Scholars have pointed out an important shift in Katai's literary career from being a naturalist writer to one who incorporated religious elements and mysticism in his work.[50] It can be argued, however, that early on in life, Katai had developed awareness of loneliness and impermanence, which derived from Buddhism. His study of Buddhism in his forties only helped Katai reconfirm the pessimistic and self-detached position that he had previously held as a naturalist writer.

In this section, Katai's biography is presented, a short essay "From Naturalism to Buddhism" (*Naturalism kara Buddhism e*, 1918) is discussed, and then his sensibilities connected to Buddhism, which he gained when he was young, are analyzed. Although Katai said that his interest had changed from naturalism to Buddhism, the connection between a sense of alienation that he associated at the beginning of his career with Japanese naturalism and the traditional sense of impermanence later led him to understand his life from a Buddhist perspective and to incorporate Buddhist themes into his personal novels.

Katai as a Naturalist Writer

Katai was born in 1872 in present-day Gunma Prefecture as the fifth child of Tayama Shōjūrō and Tetsu. His name at birth was Tayama Rokuya. When Katai was five, his father fought on the side of the new Meiji government in the Seinan War of 1877 and was killed. This war was the last major rebellion led by a group of samurai in southern Kyūshū against the Meiji government, which took away the samurai's privileges as part of its efforts to modernize Japan.[51] After Katai lost his father, he lived in poverty and could not receive higher education. However, he studied *kanshi* and *kanbun* with Yoshida Rōken (1809–1886), a local Confucian scholar, and *waka* with Matsuura Tatsuo (1843–1909), who taught him ideas of "realistic tendency" and "mystic subtle profundity" (*shinpi yūgen*). At Matsuura's private school, Katai made friends with Yanagita Kunio (1875–1962) and Ōta Gyokumei (1871–1927). Ōta later became the resident priest of Kenfukuji—a temple affiliated with the Sōtō Zen sect and located in present-day Gyōda City (Saitama Prefecture)—and helped Katai understand Buddhist doctrine.[52]

In 1899, Katai joined Hakubunkan, a publishing company and married Ōta's younger sister, Risa. By this time, he had become more interested in prose than in poetry.[53] Katai wrote about his travels, and *The End of Jūemon* (*Jūemon no saigo*, 1902) is one such precursory work. The male protagonist appears as a traveler from Tokyo and interacts with people in Nagano, records their daily lives and incidents in which they are involved, and observes the beauty of nature with a sense of impermanence.[54]

By the time *The End of Jūemon* was published, Katai had become interested in a broad range of nineteenth-century European literature and contributed to the movement that was to become *shizen shugi*, or naturalism. Mori Ōgai first coined this term in 1889, but naturalism in Japan initially suggested the idea of objective and realistic descriptions that Japanese writers learned from the West. Katai, and other naturalists, advanced the movement by associating the term with the works of Emile Zola, Gustave Flaubert, Guy de Maupassant, the Goncourt brothers, Gerhart Hauptmann, and Hermann Sudermann. According to Irmela Hijiya-Kirschnereit, features of Japanese naturalism include references to the French, German, and Scandinavian naturalists together with Russian novelists, such as Tolstoy, Dostoyevsky, and Turgenev, and philosophers, such as Nietzsche and Rousseau; a shift from poetry-based romanticism to prose-centered realism; an early identification with and later rejection of Christianity; expressions of the dark side of humanity, pessimism, and alienation; proclamation of a new artistic activity and efforts to reinvigorate the prose tradition after the Russo-Japanese War; weak scientific analysis in narratives, despite accepting Darwin's theory of evolution; and the effort to emancipate the self from the problems of the modern nation state, feudalistic conventions, and social hierarchies, whose activities were, however, limited to the private sphere. Because Japanese writers perceived themselves to be readily available for objective examination, naturalistic novels became confessional, and naturalist writers contributed to the emergence of a new literary genre known as *shishōsetu* or the "I-novel."[55]

Katai produced many works during the height of the naturalist movement. Before *The Quilt*, he published "The Girl Watcher" (*Shōjobyō*, 1907), based on his fantasies concerning a schoolgirl he saw everyday on the train while commuting to work. After *The Quilt*, he produced a so-called trilogy, consisting of *Life* (1908), *Wife* (*Tsuma*, 1908–1909), and *Bond* (*En*, 1910). These autobiographical works of fiction are based on the lives of Katai's family members and his personal affairs. Katai then published "One Soldier" (*Ippeisotsu*, 1908) and other short stories, reflecting his experience in northern China between March and September of 1904 as a member of a photography team. In *The Diary of the Second Army Corps at War* (1905), he documented the activities of the Japanese Imperial Army fighting Russian forces. *Country Teacher* (*Inaka kyōshi*, 1909) is another work that describes the popular Japanese sentiment about the Russo-Japanese War.[56]

After Katai established himself as a successful writer, naturalism declined quickly as a result of an emerging literary movement initiated by the Shirakaba group that stood "in opposition to the pessimistic, dark outlook of the Naturalists."[57] In 1912, Katai was fired from Hakubunkan, where he had worked for thirteen years. His marriage was about to fall apart then because of Katai's extramarital relationship with Iida Yone, who had relationships with several other men at the same time. Critics, in general, agree that Katai began exploring religious ideas from his mid-forties.[58] He turned to Buddhism in order to reconcile the self with others, if not to bring man to terms with society.

Katai's Association with Buddhism

Katai admits that he developed an interest in Buddhism during the 1910s. In 1913, he visited Ōta Gyokumei and spent about half a year at Iōin, a Buddhist temple in Nikkō (Tochigi Prefecture), and imagined himself to be Durtal—one of Joris-Karl Huysmans's characters and his alter ego in *En Route* and *La Cathédrale* who moves from naturalism to decadence and from there to Catholicism.[59] Unlike Durtal, Katai read a number of Mahayana Buddhist scriptures at Ōta's temple, including the *Lotus Sutra*; the *Avataṃsaka Sutra*, which explains the mutual identity and the penetration of all things; the *Nirvana Sutra*, which expounds the Buddha's teachings immediately before his death; and the *Laṅkāvatāra Sutra*, which discusses the seed of Buddhahood embedded in the ordinary mind.[60] Katai traveled frequently during this period. Between 1913 and 1916, he visited hot springs in Gunma Prefecture and then journeyed to the Tōhoku, Hokuriku, and Chūgoku regions. He also went to Shikoku where he spent a month, and then to Shinshū, where he stayed in Suwa for three months.[61] These series of journeys helped restore his mental state and helped him better understand Buddhism.[62]

Based on his spiritual experiences and his travels, Katai realized that human beings are trivial when compared to the working of space and time. According to Kenneth Henshall, Katai developed the idea that humans and society are part of a larger whole, which Katai called the void (*kū* or *kūkan* 空観) based on the Buddhist notion of emptiness (S. *śūnyatā*). The void simultaneously negates and generates all phenomena.[63] Time is another concept that subsumes a set of opposite perspectives—time as infinite and time as finite.[64] Henshall summarizes Katai's view on the void and time: "One moment is to infinite time what one life is to infinite life. Infinite time and infinite life both derive from and help form the infinite matrix of the void, the void that is everything but nothing just as eternity is 'all time' but also 'timeless.'"[65]

Katai realized that there would be a state where subject and object, as well as the self and others, were unified. In an essay called "The Unity of Self and Others" (*Jita no yūgō*, 1916), he used the metaphor of milestones to explain the path to the state of unity:

> It is interesting to see what comes out when passing a milestone one after another. It is interesting to see what a traveler experiences when making a series of overnight stays at train stations. The more we pass milestones, the closer we get to the state of unity between the self and others.

> In Zen, there is what is called the path of realization (*godō* 悟道). To me, that is the degree to which one progresses and, therefore, is not absolute, although Zen monks may say otherwise. Probably I can never attain such state of unity. Only when I die will I be able to attain it. . . .
>
> I don't like discriminating and punishing others based on hierarchies. I wish to discover the entirety of a thing. I don't like to judge people based on whether they have power or not. If asked why, I say because bringing one's judgment to a stop is the only way to enter the state of unity between the self and others. . . . But in order to enter the state of non-distinction, first we have to understand the differences.[66]

For Katai, Buddhist realization needs to be a path, not just a goal. The path made him aware of his spiritual growth, moving from one stage to another.

Katai wrote a short essay, "From Naturalism to Buddhism" (1918), in which he discussed his interest in Buddhism. First, he found Buddhism attractive because it covers all of human psychology (*shinri*) and explains the causes of everyday experiences. Buddhism helped him better understand the causes of one's psychological development and mental changes according to biological rhythms as well as the principles of karmic retribution and the oneness of different emotions—such as laughter and anger, joy and sorrow.[67]

Second, Katai considered the mind to be inscrutable. According to him, the mind is inseparable from experience. As time passes and as a person accumulates experiences, that which is incubating within that person begins to appear. The way it appears differs depending on the individual, and as a result, some people turn out to be wise while others turn out to be foolish. It all depends on how the mind works. At the same time, there is an innate quality to the mind, so the question arises, Why are some people born with a sensible mind while others are not? Buddhism does not answer this question, but gives a didactic explanation by recognizing that past, present, and future lives are all connected by one's own karma. Katai found this explanation mystically compelling.[68]

Third, Buddhism helped Katai establish a standpoint—a "powerful mind" (*chikara no aru kokoro*). He liked the Buddhism of self-power because it helped improve his life; however, according to Katai, it is insignificant whether one believes in the Buddhism of self-power or in the Buddhism of other-power, as long as one can establish a spiritual standpoint—that is, maintaining a powerful mind, an undistracted and detached state, in the midst of disturbing events. In Buddhism, this state is called a "diamond-like mind," a state of "fearlessness," or a state of "birth without birth and death without death." Those who have attained it are neither reclusive nor destructive, but simultaneously spontaneous and aloof.[69]

Fourth, Buddhism enabled Katai to come to terms with death. Among various Mahayana sutras, Katai praised the *Lotus Sutra* and the *Nirvana Sutra*: the former is easy to understand because it explains the importance of Buddhist faith, while the latter is fascinating because it portrays Shakyamuni Buddha's death. Katai ended his essay with the Buddha's response to a disciple: "If you want to know about the afterlife, you must first question your inquiry [that is, why do I want to know about the afterlife]."[70] Although the essay is intriguing, it is sketchy and shows that Katai's study of Buddhist philosophy was still in progress.

As already mentioned, Katai began reading Mahayana Buddhist scriptures and gained knowledge of Buddhism after 1913; however, he had made specific references to Buddhism prior to that. In his essay "A New Theory of Fiction" (*Shōsetsu shinron*, 1911), he identified himself as a "practitioner of novels" (*shōsetsu shūgyōsha*), who must find "naturalness" (*shizen rashisa*) within himself and understand the working of nature as a true principle.[71] To accomplish this, Katai juxtaposed the mental state of an artist, who devotes himself to the discovery of naturalness in a phenomenon, with the spiritual state of a Buddhist monk who practices Zen or "cessation and meditation" (S. *śamatha-vipaśyanā*; J. *shikan*)[72] to point out the similarity between art and religion.[73] As Katai wrote, "A novelist is, therefore, a splendid philosopher (*tetsugakusha*) in one respect, a seeker (*tankyūsha*) of the truth in universe and life, and a brave practitioner (*gyōja*) who explores a mysterious cave without fear."[74] Using the rhetoric of practitioner, Katai likened the life of a novelist to that of a Buddhist trainee.

In "A New Theory of Fiction," Katai recalled reading *Hōjōki* and *Seashells in the Inlet* (*Ura no shiokai*) when he was young. He remembered discussing with a student who lodged at his house that Kamo no Chōmei's sense of impermanence was heightened by Chōmei's observation of the rise and fall of the Minamoto and Taira clans and that Chōmei's pessimism was rooted in the dissatisfaction of his life. Katai characterized impermanence in terms of relationships—dewdrops on a morning glory disappear and then the flower wilts in the morning sunlight, or the flower wilts first and dewdrops disappear before evening. *Seashells in the Inlet* is a collection of poems by Kumagai Naoyoshi, who devoted his life to the way of poetry and Zen during the Edo period. Katai was impressed with the expression of naturalness and Zen Buddhism that helped Kumagai perceive present moments as they are.[75]

Katai's familiarity with Buddhist sensibilities indicates his worldviews were favorable to Buddhism long before his reading of Mahayana Buddhist scriptures. His early activities must have inclined him in such a direction, including his study of poetry with Matsuura Tatsuo, who taught him the notion of the *yūgen*, or mystical and profound subtlety, and his close interaction with the Buddhist priest Ōta Gyokumei. *The Diary of the Second Army Corps at War* testifies to Katai's growing sense of loneliness and impermanence, as well as his recognition of suffering caused by irrational death, such as death in battle. As Hijiya-Kirschnereit points out, although Katai modeled his naturalism on the patterns of European literary conventions, that activity also led him to turn to the cultural and literary tradition of Japan.[76]

As his interest in Buddhism grew, Katai wrote personal fiction exploring Buddhist themes. His work ranges from *Remaining Snow* (1917–1918), an autobiographical novel that depicts Katai's reflection on Buddhist philosophy, to novellas and short stories that address the miraculous power of religious faith, such as *The Miracle of a Buddhist Monk* (1917) and "Death by Lightning on a Mountain Top" (*Sanjō no shinshi*, 1918). At the same time, Katai's literary treatment of religion was not limited to Buddhism, but his work also represented "a mysterious other-worldliness revered by all religions," to borrow Henshall's words.[77] Katai died in 1930, and his friend Shimazaki Tōson chose the posthumous Dharma name for Katai.[78]

Shiga Naoya (1883–1971): From Buddhism to Nature Worship

As with Sōseki and Katai, thoughts of death greatly disturbed Shiga Naoya, who is known as the "god of fiction" (*shōsetsu no kami sama*) in Japan. The way Shiga dealt with his spiritual crisis was, however, different from how Sōseki coped with his troubled self—that is, neutralizing his consciousness through composing Chinese poetry and sitting in Zen meditation—and the ways in which Katai turned to Buddhism. Shiga healed himself by reading Buddhist scriptures; viewing classical East Asian art, such as Buddhist statues and Buddhist paintings, and visiting old Buddhist temples; and by observing the beauty of nature. After a long struggle, he overcame his problems by identifying himself as part of Mother Nature. The name Shiga is used throughout this book, instead of Naoya, since, unlike Sōseki and Katai, Naoya is not a pen name.

Early Religious Influence

Shiga Naoya was born in 1883 as the second son of Shiga Naoharu, a banker of the First National Bank (*Daiichi ginkō*), and Gin. Shiga Naomichi (1826–1906), Naoya's grandfather, was a steward of the Sōma clan and one of Ninomiya Sontoku's students. After the Meiji Restoration, Naomichi served as the lieutenant governor of Fukushima Prefecture and developed the Ashio copper mine together with Furukawa Ichibei—founder of the Furukawa Zaibatsu. In other words, Naoya was born into a wealthy family.[79]

Unlike Sōseki and Katai, Shiga did not interact with Buddhist clergy and clearly kept away from organized religion, but the religious people he encountered in his youth were integral to his life. In 1901, Shiga joined a nondenominational Christian group organized by Uchimura Kanzō—whom he considered one of the three most influential men in his life—and stayed with that group for about seven years.[80] Shiga Naomichi was the second important individual who helped Naoya develop an interest in Zen. (The third important person was Mushanokōji Saneatsu.) Naomichi became a serious Zen practitioner in his later years. According to Naoya, his grandfather visited Vinaya Master Unshō, Nishiari Bokusan, Shimaji Mokurai, Murakami Senshō, and Ōuchi Seiran. Eventually, Naomichi became a student of Kitano Genpō of Seishōji (who later became the sixty-seventh abbot of Eiheiji) and hosted Genpō's Zen talk at his home. Naomichi began reading Buddhist scriptures and stopped hunting after that.[81]

In addition to Zen Buddhism, Shiga's familiarity with Pure Land Buddhism is evident as early as 1904. In his diary dated April 5—when Shiga and his friends visited Okitsu in present-day Shizuoka Prefecture—a series of poetry exchanges was noted:

> Tonight, we stayed at the same inn [as yesterday]. A guest wrote:
> Only in his appearance,
> Is found a distinction of ugliness and beauty,
> In his bones, however, is there neither emotion, color, nor distinction.
> [An unidentified individual] responded:
> "No-distinction" derives from the world of the Dharma.
> Life-and-Death and Beauty-and-Ugliness
> Is a matter of this brief world.
> The guest wrote back:
> The floating world of man is all about
> Chasing dogs of base passions,
> And being chased by the dogs [of base passions].

> [The same unidentified individual] responded:
> Because of the base passions,
> For the sake of human beings,
> [There is] Amida Buddha's Original Vow for us to attain Buddhahood.
> Speaking of the dogs [of base passions] and in reference to the popular saying of "even a dog bumps into a pole," there is a word-play of a Buddhist bonze.
> That is, even an octopus that tastes awful [and a bad bonze] is dissolved in acid,
> because base passions are part of the wondrous Dharmas.
> [The bonze should] know that his conditions
> Are formed by the Buddha's efficacy.
> Growing dark, scattering of the flowers,
> The base passions are instantly the Bodhi-mind
> Finally, the bonze surrendered.[82]

Although the nature of this poetic exchange—and whether or not Shiga composed any of the poems—is unknown, these poems demonstrate Shiga's knowledge of basic Pure Land Buddhist doctrine. He maintained his interest in Pure Land Buddhism and later wrote calligraphy of important Pure Land Buddhist words, such as *namu amida butsu* and *gongu jōdo*, and closely interacted with Yanagi Muneyoshi, who initiated the folk art movement (*mingei undō*) based on his understanding of Pure Land Buddhism. Although Shiga did not talk about Yanagi's Pure Land Buddhist influence on his literary activity, he highly praised Yanagi's achievements.[83]

Shiga's Crisis

Despite his interactions with religious people, Shiga was unable to overcome fear of death. His obsession with death began when he lost his mother in 1895 at the age of twelve, and it became worse. In his late sixties, Shiga recalled, "When I was twenty-four or -five, I was extremely afraid of death. Every night when I went to bed, the fear of death immediately came over me, generating inexplicable anxiety. I could feel it when the sun went down. There was a period when I became depressed and felt like entering into a place of infinite darkness."[84] His fear of death was partly caused by his anxiety about the end of the world. In the essay "Idle Ramblings of a Man of Leisure"

(*Kanjin mōgo*, 1950), he recollected how he reacted to Anatole France's "The Garden of Epicurus":

> Reading this, I was filled with great antagonism to the notion of man's eventual extinction. That might be the fate of the earth, but it need not be the fate of man. Before that time, before the earth became unsuited for the continuance of human progress, man would have developed sufficiently to separate his fate from that of the earth. This was a very practical way of thinking, one that would make it possible to live with almost any phenomenon. If one accepted such a long-range view of human accomplishment, it became possible to find meaning in even the most disturbing of earthly phenomena. Everything could be attributed to the movement of the Will of Mankind. . . . I entertained these illusions until I was thirty-two or thirty-three. I was often in a state of high excitement over them, but just as often I felt great anxiety and dread, as if I might find myself at any moment falling headfirst into a deep ravine.[85]

Experiencing the terror of death on both individual and collective levels, Shiga set out to understand the meaning of his life within the "Will of Mankind"; however, such attempts only made him neurotic.

Shiga faced a crisis point during the period between 1912 and 1917—from the age of twenty-nine to thirty-four. Francis Mathy summarizes a series of difficulties: "the continuing discord with his father, further aggravated by his marriage, the grave injury sustained in the streetcar accident; his wife's nervous condition; his continued inability to write; and the death of his first child."[86] Short stories produced during this period mirror Shiga's morbidity and ambivalence toward death. He wrote "Confused Head" (*Nigotta atama*, 1911) when he had a nervous breakdown and "Han's Crime" (*Han no hanzai*, 1913) after being hospitalized following a train accident. Each story depicts the ethical dilemma of a main character—Shiga's alter ego—about the crime of murder triggered by his instinctive desire that simultaneously denies violence.[87]

By referring to Shiga's own accounts, William Sibley introduces two more instances of dreadful coincidences that Shiga experienced. The first episode is associated with the short story "The Razor" (*Kamisori*, 1910), about a murder in a barbershop. Immediately after Shiga finished the work, he read in a newspaper that his next-door neighbor had taken his life using a razor the night Shiga had considered how the barber slashes a customer's throat with one in "The Razor." The second incident is related to "An Accident" (*Dekigoto*, 1913), a story about a small child almost killed by a streetcar. The day Shiga completed that work, he was struck by a train on the Yamate Line. From these two incidents, Sibley concludes that Shiga "still saw himself as both subject to and, at times, the active agent of some hidden, all determining Fate, a version of which was (in his earlier quoted words) 'not accessible under normal conditions of sanity.' "[88] Shiga called these kinds of incidents "coincidences" (*gūzen*),[89] but as Makoto Ueda suggests, they reinforced Shiga's idea that imaginary creation and actual facts were equally important for a work of fiction.[90] To separate Shiga Naoya and his literary representation, Sibley coined the term "Shiga hero," as he considered Shiga's method of projecting his consciousness onto a single character to be too direct.[91]

Buddhist Scriptures, Buddhist Arts, and the Beauty of Nature

Shiga's physical condition had improved greatly by 1917. After that, he began writing much-acclaimed autobiographical novels, such as "At Kinosaki" (*Kinosaki nite*, 1917) and *Reconciliation* (*Wakai*, 1917). In "At Kinosaki," the Shiga hero reflects on his survival after a fatal train incident and mulls over the nature of life and death. In *Reconciliation*, the Shiga hero meets his father on the twenty-third anniversary of his mother's passing, which he considers special, and lets the conversation take its own course. Just as it is represented by the Shiga hero, who restores his relationship with his father, Shiga's crisis ended.[92]

Mother Nature and Buddhist scriptures were sources of Shiga Naoya's spiritual inspiration. He seems to have had an unforgettable experience on Mount Daisen during the summer of 1914, which was similar to a religious conversion.[93] The Shiga hero reenacts this event in *A Dark Night's Passing* some twenty years later. Although the nature of Shiga's experience is unknown, part of an unpublished draft of *A Dark Night's Passing*, written in October 1914 with the working title "Tokitō Nobuyuki" (not the same as Tokitō Kensaku of *A Dark Night's Passing*), gives us a clue. Shiga wrote "Tokitō Nobuyuki" a few months after his trip to Mount Daisen. In it he wrote,

> I am extremely happy now. For about a year, or precisely for nine months, I suffered a great deal. The pain was not caused externally but created internally. An unfortunate incident deriving from my mind triggered it. In a nutshell, I was being punished. Something absolute was punishing me, though I don't think it was God. Now, I truly think I deserved that punishment. I cannot hold a grudge

against anybody. I, who am celebrating happiness at this moment, could not have come to this state without being punished.

I didn't know anything, yet I was arrogant. Or, rather, I tried to be arrogant. But I couldn't be conceited. I made myself neurotically arrogant, but anxiety immediately removed my arrogance. I wished to be a man of arrogance. How stupid. . . .

I really was stupid. I pretended to be pedantic. I did, in fact, know many things, but only partially. I had a capacity to understand, but I hadn't grasped the most important thing. But at least I think I'm at a point where I've discovered the ox's footsteps, as described in the *Ten Abiding Stages of the Mind* (*Jūjūshinron*). Or, perhaps, I've seen its tail. At any rate, I have a clue to what it is and that makes me happy.[94]

Tokitō Nobuyuki, the Shiga hero, recounts his spiritual breakthrough and the overcoming of his melancholic state. The narrator does, however, make a mistake in alluding to the *Ten Abiding Stages of the Mind According to the Secret Maṇḍala* rather than *The Ten Oxherding Pictures* (*Jūgyūzu*).[95]

The Ten Oxherding Pictures is about searching for one's "true" self, explained through ten stages. During the twelfth century, in China, the Zen master Kuo-an Shih-yuan (J. Kakuan Shion) drew ten pictures and attached a verse to each illustration. It is one of the so-called Four Zen texts, known as *The Four Records of the Zen Sect* (*Zenshū shiburoku*). A herdsman loses an ox and sets out on a journey to retrieve it. The discovery of the ox's footsteps that the Shiga hero mentions is the second stage of *The Ten Oxherding Pictures*, where one gains the understanding about the self by reading Buddhist sutras. Ultimately, one realizes that neither the self nor the ox is there because a self does not exist by itself, and that the self and the ox are the same. In order to come to this realization, however, one must first start searching for one's real identity.[96] Although Tokitō Nobuyuki and Shiga Naoya should not be treated as identical, Shiga's familiarity with *The Ten Oxherding Pictures* should be noted. Additionally, Shiga read *Lives of Eminent Priests* (*Kōsōden*) on Mount Daisen and was moved by the exchange between Kūya and Genshin in this work, in which Kūya tells Genshin that even an ignorant person can attain birth in the Pure Land if he detests samsara and sincerely longs for the Pure Land.[97]

Shiga also found traditional East Asian art (*tōyō no kobijutsu*) therapeutic. To relieve his anxiety, he viewed statues of Buddhas and bodhisattvas, monochrome paintings, and Buddhist calligraphy. In the preface to "A Treasure by

One's Side" (*Zauhō*, 1926), he recalls the cathartic effects that such artistic works had on him.

> I first felt drawn to Eastern art at a time when everything in my life was a source of pain and threat, when my spirit was restless and exhausted and I was searching desperately for a place of rest. I was naturally inclined toward contemplation [*sei* 静] rather than toward action [*dō* 動], and so I was drawn to things Eastern, which until then I had not paid much attention to.[98]

Shiga was initially interested in Western art, but later became more attracted to traditional East Asian arts. In 1912, he moved to Onomichi (in Hiroshima Prefecture) and later, during September 1914, to Kyoto. This gave him more opportunities to visit Buddhist temples and museums in Kyoto and Nara. Shiga felt an inexplicable sense of peace in the presence of traditional East Asian arts.[99]

The cathartic effect that Shiga experienced through art can be explained in religious terms. Western thinkers of his time, such as Rudolf Otto (1869–1937) and Clive Bell (1881–1964), attempted to form a link between religious and aesthetic experiences. According to Ernest Rubinstein, Otto applies the Kantian notion of schematization—knowledge produced as a result of a relationship between two different kinds of consciousness responding to particular feelings—and believes that the "feelings of the sublime" and "feelings of the numinous" can generate knowledge of the "holy" as "aesthetically religious holiness."[100] Similarly, Bell defines the notion of beauty as a "significant form in visible objects" which provokes an aesthetic emotion through the elements of "ecstasy" and "detachment." They are connected by *ecstasis*, being outside of ordinary interests. As a perceiving subject becomes independent from the matters of one's life, so does the perceived object, being "an end in itself."[101] The object is therefore a manifestation of "noumenon," "ultimate reality," "essential reality," and "the God in everything." Rubinstein concludes that Otto and Bell would agree that "art 'is a means to states of mind as holy as any that men are capable of experiencing.'"[102] Going back to Shiga, at one point, he actually equated religion and art. Shiga wrote, "If I were asked what my faith is, I would say it is art."[103]

In later life, however, Shiga stopped viewing traditional East Asian arts. According to Nanyan Guo, Shiga became unsatisfied with a Buddhist painting attributed to Genshin, *Amida Rising over the Mountain*, which he had admired in 1923, when he viewed natural scenery that was similar to the painting.[104] Together with other paintings of Amida Buddha descending from the Pure Land, this painting had reminded Shiga of Kūya's words spoken to Genshin and the beauty of scenery Shiga had seen before. It had further led him to think that art—including literary art—could be the source of spiritual inspiration.[105] Later, the beauty of nature, however, inspired Shiga more than a work of painting.[106]

In his essay "My Life Principles" (*Waga seikatsu shinjō*, 1949), Shiga wrote that only nature is beautiful and reliable. The aesthetic quality of man-made objects no longer appealed to him:

> I am still of the opinion that the one thing man can certainly depend on is "nature." There have been various literary and art movements, but I cannot think of any alternative other than to follow the trail of nature.[107]
>
> Whatever it is, if naturalness is missing in art, it cannot be considered beautiful.
>
> I do not believe in a materialized God. There is no such a thing. Although it depends on the meaning of God, I consider myself to be *mushinron-sha* [which implies atheist]. Being atheist does not necessarily mean to deny moral values as conveyed by the words of God. Buddhism, if it appears to be atheistic, may be close to my feelings. I don't know anything about Shinto. I know Confucianism, but I have not read its texts.
>
> [Because of the times in which we grew up] Confucianism is embedded in old people like me. It has provided me with moral values.[108]

For Shiga, naturalness meant spontaneity unregulated by rules. This principle applied not only to art but also to religion. Among various religious traditions, Shiga found Buddhism attractive because of the absence of an absolute figure, which reminded him of God that restrained man's natural growth, and he considered moral values of religion necessary for man's maturity.

Shiga's Attitude toward Superstitious Religious Practice

While recognizing the importance of religious morality, Shiga avoided religions that promoted worldly benefits and miraculous healing. He criticized Tenrikyō, which was founded by Nakayama Miki (1798–1887) and grew out of a new religious movement that developed before the Meiji Restoration. According to Saburō Morishita, Tenrikyō teaches that "humankind was created with the sole purpose of joyful living, and by realizing such a way of life, God [the Parent, *oyagami*], too, would share in that joy."[109] The place where humankind is said to have emerged is called *jiba*, or "earth place," and is located in the main worship hall of Tenrikyō in Tenri City, Nara Prefecture. At the beginning of the Meiji era, Tenrikyō, together with other new religious organizations, such as Konkōkyō and Kurozumikyō, promoted worldly benefits through faith, including healing, and evangelical spirituality.[110]

In "A Reply to the Tenrikyō Journal" (*Tenrikyō kikan zasshi e no henji*, 1937), Shiga discussed his understanding of religious practice as being opposed to Tenrikyō's religious activity. He disliked Tenrikyō partly because he did not trust any clergy. Here, Shiga directed his criticism at Tenrikyō leaders who seized illness as an opportunity to promote their religion. He wrote,

> I don't know anything about Tenrikyō, but one day while traveling, I met a minister associated with that religion. I asked him about the teaching, but all he talked about were cases of illnesses being cured, because of having faith in it, and I could not understand the teaching at all. I don't think all Tenrikyō teachers are like that, but I can't respect a teaching that is designed to promote healing effects to those in physical pain. I'm under the impression that Tenrikyō's teaching is not highly developed and its clergy takes advantage of human weakness.
>
> The real benefit of religion is to allow us to stay in peace and to not lose composure, even when facing death—a martyr stands still spiritually, though physically in pain. I think real religion gives a person such spiritual strength. Maeterlinck's *Intelligence and Fate* describes this point very well with concrete examples. I was very moved by it when I read it about twenty years ago.[111]

For Shiga, "real religion" should help people develop a spiritual capacity to deal with all of life's problems; therefore, seeking worldly benefits within a religion is an act of deception. One episode, recorded in 1915, shows how strongly he opposed superstitious practice. Shiga suffered from sciatica after returning from Mount Akagi. His wife took that as a sign of divine punishment because he had accidentally kicked over a Buddhist statue on the mountain and thrown a stone at it in anger. Shiga, however, discouraged her from contacting an exorcist because he firmly believed that acting on such superstitious beliefs was unhealthy. He recuperated from the illness several months later.[112]

Although Shiga was critical of religious organizations that promoted practical benefits, he expressed admiration at how Jesus, Confucius, and Shakyamuni had continued to inspire people throughout the world. In "Idle Ramblings of a Man of Leisure," Shiga recognized the perpetuity of man's spirit (*seishin*) as infinite aspiration, but not as spirits of the dead (*reikon*). He believed that a writer should nurture good intent and devote himself to writing, after which he should let the work take its own course. Because the work represents his spiritual activities, that is how a writer's spirit will remain permanently and how Shiga himself could find a connection with the world.[113] Earlier, in another essay, called "My Memoirs" (*Shinpenki*, 1937), Shiga considered the spirit of the Buddha to be truly perpetual.[114] Despite his inclination toward Buddhism, Shiga never chose to affiliate himself with a Buddhist denomination. His funeral was conducted in what he might have referred to as a nonsectarian, or nonreligious (*mushūkyō*), way.

Conclusion

Near-death experiences led Sōseki, Katai, and Shiga to seriously think about life and death and made them more susceptible to the Buddhist worldview. Sōseki believed that he entered the absolute realm during his Shuzenji crisis and attempted to recapture a higher spiritual state exemplified in Buddhism. Katai almost lost his life during the Russo-Japanese War as a member of a photography team. He went to a combat zone where bombshells were flying everywhere and later contracted typhoid. The observation of unnatural death urged him to view human life as irrational and subject to sudden change and disruption. After surviving a train accident, Shiga was able to look at life and death as a single organic process and conquered his fear of death. For him, self-realization took the form of a union with natural surroundings, and Buddhism facilitated that process. Their experiences of being on the verge of death helped these three writers to form a personal connection to Buddhism.

None of them, however, made commitments to Buddhist organizations or identified themselves as Buddhists. Although Sōseki, Katai, and Shiga admired various religious figures, they chose not to affiliate themselves with organized religion. Sōseki practiced sitting in meditation and interacted with young Zen monks, but did not become a member of a Zen sect. Katai also befriended a Buddhist priest and attempted to connect Buddhism and literary art, but at the same time he insisted on the separation of "art" (*geijutsu*) and "religion" (*shūkyō*).[115] Shiga defined himself as not religious, despite his inclination toward Buddhist art and his acceptance of Buddhist sensibilities. For these three individuals, "religion" meant organized religion.

Those three writers' classification of Buddhism based on the notions of self-power and other-power Buddhism and their participation in funerary Buddhism, however, suggest that their Buddhist experiences took place within the parameters of institutional Buddhism. Their connections to the modern development of Japanese Buddhism and their participation in the revival of Japanese Buddhist tradition illustrate the diversity of lay Buddhism (*zaike bukkyō* 在家仏教) in modern Japan. In the next chapter, their personal novels are analyzed as forms of spiritual practice and examined in terms of how the main characters' paths intersect with the authors' paths.

CHAPTER THREE

Ari no mama as Literary and Buddhist Discourse

This chapter explores the connections between the Buddhist practice of observing a phenomenon *as it is* and realistic depiction in autobiographical fiction on theoretical and practical levels. Both Sōseki and Katai commented on the relationship between the attainment of Buddhahood and the achievement of penmanship. Although Sōseki and Katai considered themselves to be different from each other, they shared a similar attitude toward writing, that is, they attempted to describe things realistically just as they are—*ari no mama* or *aru ga mama* in Japanese. This notion, which became widely shared among modern Japanese intellectuals as the basis of "experience," derived from multiple sources, such as realism, naturalism, and Buddhism. Significantly, the "right view" in Buddhist practice correlated to observation in realistic writing. For both Buddhist practitioners and literary writers, cultivating self-detachment was necessary for perceiving things as they are.

To more closely examine the idea that writing personal fiction is a self-reflective spiritual practice, Sōseki's *Grass on the Wayside*, Katai's *Remaining Snow*, and Shiga's "At Kinosaki" are analyzed. When *Grass on the Wayside* is read as a work of narrative memory, Sōseki becomes a subject who transforms traumatic memory into narrative memory. The novel can further be read as a work of the author's path literature when indications of "way," as in the "wayside," are considered, even though the story itself appears on the surface to have nothing to do with Buddhism. *Remaining Snow* includes Buddhist philosophical discussions, which cannot be separated from Katai's understanding of Buddhism, and its narrator discusses the importance of expressing Buddhism through literary art. In "At Kinosaki," the Shiga hero reflects on his narrow escape from death and realizes the oneness of life and death. When these texts are read as related to the writer's spiritual practice, differences between the author, narrator, and hero suggest that their relationship is interdependent. Further, personal fiction serves the writer as a medium of self-reflection that triggers self-transformation.

Sōseki's Attainment of Buddhahood by Writing

In "Imitation and Independence," Sōseki considers the value of writing to be of a higher order than moral and ethical considerations. According to him, the ultimate objective of writing can be compared to a writer's attainment of Buddhahood. Sōseki said,

> If robbers and killers can express their minds as it is when they committed crimes, and if they can impress others with those descriptions, there will be no crimes. The best medium, through which one can impress others are novels, well-written novels.[1]
>
> Suppose there is a person who can depict the true reality of things exactly as they are. Imagine further that this person has done things that are bad from whatever angle you look at them. *If this person succeeded in describing these things exactly as they are* (ari no mama), *without hiding or omitting anything, this person would be able to reach buddhahood precisely by the merits of that description.* For the law, he may have to go to prison but, in my opinion, his crimes are sufficiently purified by his descriptions. I firmly believe this.[2] (emphasis added)

Sōseki's expression, "reaching buddhahood," seems rhetorical, since he did not discuss its practical implications in detail; however, the philosophy of spiritual development in Japan was related to the modern development of Japanese prose writing and the modern interpretation of Buddhism. First, in terms of his phrase, "describing things as they are," Masaoka Shiki's impact on Sōseki's realistic writing needs to be considered. Shiki used the expression *ari no mama* in his discussion of prose writing. In *Descriptive Prose* (*Jojibun*, 1900), he states the following:

> When one sees a certain scene or human happening and thinks it interesting, and wants to put it into words which will make the

reader feel the same interest as oneself, one should not employ verbal decoration or exaggeration but should simply depict the thing itself as it is, as one sees it [*tada ari no mama mitaru mama*].³

According to Janine Beichman, Shiki, a well-known haiku poet, was influenced by contemporary Western-style Japanese painters and used the term "sketch from life" (*shasei*) together with "to depict as is" (*ari no mama ni utsusu*) and "reality" (*shajitsu*) to point out a method of realistic depiction. Some Japanese critics even suggest that modern Japanese writers' tendency toward realistic depiction began because of Shiki's influence, although Tsubouchi Shōyō and Futabatei Shimei introduced realistic novels prior to Shiki (and Tayama Katai made naturalist writing widely known after Shiki's death). Sōseki's early works, such as *I Am a Cat* and *The Three-Cornered World*, mirror Shiki's method of the sketching from life.⁴

At the same time, Sōseki's usage of *ari no mama* differs from Shiki's definition of realistic writing in that it indicates the cathartic effect of writing—that is, describing what a writer sees, hears, and feels without involving his judgment constitutes a form of redemption—and a state of detachment. According to Ōno Akihiko, however, Sōseki perhaps did not believe in a writer's ability to depict what he senses as it is. Rather, in Ōno's view, the aforementioned passages imply Sōseki's understanding that it is extremely difficult to describe things as they are and denote a writer's transformation as the subject of écriture in a way that is comparable to a religious conversion.⁵ Later in this chapter, Sōseki's *Grass on the Wayside* is read as his attempt to improve himself.

The term *ari no mama*, which Sōseki juxtaposes with the state of Buddhahood, is derived from the religio-aesthetic tradition in Japanese Buddhism known as artistic detachment. According to Steve Odin, psychic aloofness in aesthetics developed in China through the Confucian notion of "equilibrium" (*chung*), or detached observation; the Taoist concept of *wu wei*, which is translated as "nonaction," "naturalness," or "spontaneity"; and the Chan (Zen) concept of the "immediate experience of liberation in sudden enlightenment through 'no-mind' (*wu hsin*)."⁶ In Japan, *shikan* ("tranquility and insight") meditation practiced by Tendai Buddhist practitioners contributed to the formation of the so-called *shikan* aesthetic consciousness among *waka* poets, such as Shunzei and Teika, during the Heian and Kamakura periods. *Shikan* meditation led the practitioners to cultivate a "tranquil attitude of calm detachment free of mental perturbation" and to realize the middle path, neither affirming nor denying phenomena from the standpoint of emptiness.⁷

In Buddhism, developing an insight into the nature of things—or perceiving phenomena just as they are—is extremely important. As Zen master Dōgen says:

> I didn't go to many monasteries, but I happened to see my teacher and directly found that my eyes are horizontal and my nose is vertical. Then I was not to be fooled by anyone. So I came back [from China] with open hands. That is why I haven't got any Buddhism at all; I pass the time leaving it to the flow. Every morning the sun rises in the east, every night the moon sets in the west.[8]

Dōgen returned from China after realizing the nature of things and not necessarily after mastering complex Buddhist doctrines. He then taught "just sitting" to his disciples.

The Buddhist meditative practice gave rise to aesthetic contemplation with an attitude of detached observation. According to Odin, Zeami (1363?–1443?), a writer, theorist, and practitioner of Nō drama, discerned the "seeing from the standpoint of detached seeing" (*riken no ken* 離見の見) from the "seeing based on ego" (*gaken* 我見).[9] Matsuo Bashō, a major haikai master, spoke of "oneness of self and nature," while Yosa Buson (1716–1784), another haikai master and a leader of literati painting (*bunjinga*), whose style of poetry and haikai painting (*haiga*) influenced Shiki to form a method of sketching, expressed the "precise beauty of events with a clarity of impression as seen with the objectivity of a painter or poet."[10]

Lay Buddhist leaders of modern Japan reevaluated the tradition and came to believe that the state of *ari no mama* was cultivated through intuitive observation. In his discussion of "pure experience" (*junsui keiken*) in *Inquiry into the Good* (*Zen no kenkyū*, 1911), Nishida Kitarō defines "to experience" as "to know facts just as they are (*so no mama*), to know in accordance with facts by completely relinquishing one's own fabrications."[11] Pure experience refers to the intuitive experience that is "not the judging of the original consciousness by the later one, but simply knowledge of facts just as they are (*ari no mama*)."[12] Later, in 1928, in his discussion of religious consciousness, Nishida states, "When one truly becomes aware of absolute-nothingness, there is neither a self nor God. In absolute-nothingness, a mountain is perceived as just a mountain and water is perceived as just water. All things come to beings just as they are."[13]

Suzuki Daisetsu uses *ari no mama* in explaining the Buddhist notion of *prajñā*. In the essays "Zen in *Vajracchedikā-prajñāpāramitā Sutra*" (*Kongōkyō no zen*, 1944) and "Religion and Philosophy of *Prajñāpāramitā Sutra*" (*Hannyakyō no shūkyō to tetsugaku*, 1950), he defines Buddhist wisdom as "seeing things as appearance of suchness" (*nyo no sō ni oite* [*yathābhūtatā*] *mono o mirukoto*) and explains the "appearance of suchness" as "intrinsic qualities of the things just as they are" (*aruga mama* [*yathābhūtam*] *no mono no honshitsu*).[14] The attainment of Buddhist wisdom suggests setting aside a practitioner's personal interests and judgment, and seeing the totality of things.

Nishida and Suzuki invented the vision of *ari no mama*, which is attained through sitting in meditation, as unmediated experience. According to Robert Sharf, they integrated Western philosophy and rationalized Japanese Buddhism in order to "encounter the threat posed to Buddhism by modernization, secularization, and science." As a result, they defined *satori*, or enlightenment, phenomenologically—that is, as "discrete 'states of consciousness' experienced by Buddhist practitioners in the midst of their meditative practice." In this process of Buddhist awakening, disciplinary practices other than meditation—such as observing precepts and ritual practice, which are part of monastic training—and the importance of *sangha*, or Buddhist community, were overlooked.[15]

Scholars have explored the connection between Nishida's philosophy and Sōseki's thinking. They note that Sōseki and Nishida shared the same interest in East Asian philosophy, including Buddhist logical thinking, and Western philosophy, such as the works of William James and Henri Bergson. According to Ogihara Keiko, Nishida's notion of pure experience resonates with the unity of subject and object sought by Ichirō, the protagonist in *The Wayfarer*.[16] Nishida states that "[t]o say that we know a thing simply means that the self unites with it. When one sees a flower, the self has become the flower."[17] Ichirō looks at the lilies, woods, and ravines and says, "Those are mine."[18] In other words, Ichirō expresses the oneness of himself and his surroundings. Later in *The Wayfarer*, Ichirō's friend H speaks of Ichirō by saying, "After all, your brother's [Ichirō's] alleged desire to possess things would ultimately seem to mean being possessed by things, wouldn't it? Consequently, to be absolutely possessed by things, I think, is to possess things absolutely. Only then and there will your brother, who does not believe in God, find his peace of mind in this world."[19] If Ichirō had been able to internalize the unity of a self and the other, he would have been liberated.

In fact, Sōseki discussed the unity of two different realms on an ontological level. Sometime in 1915, the year he wrote *Grass on the Wayside*, he slightly modified his position concerning death. In an undated portion of "A Fragment" (*Danpen*), he wrote,

Death over life . . . but that implies disliking life and does not seem to integrate life and death. In order to be consistent about life and death (or transcend the two), one must accept that *phenomenon is existence* [*genshō soku jitsuzai*] and *relative is absolute* [*sōtai soku zettai*].

"That may be so logically."

"Perhaps."

"But can you reach [such a state] by merely thinking about it?"

"I just want to get there."[20]

Sōseki examined the correlation between the changeable and the unchangeable, and concluded that they were identical. Such an understanding allowed him to realize the oneness of life and death. The instant unity of the opposite realms was conceptualized by Suzuki Daisetsu and endorsed by philosophers of the Kyoto School as *sokuhi no ronri* 即非の論理, or the logic of "simultaneous acceptance of both is and is not as pertaining to the same thing," to borrow Robert Carter's translation.[21] While Sōseki's fragmentary note is abstract, *Grass on the Wayside* represents his effort to cast fair-minded views on his unhappy childhood and a period of life he abominated, when Sōseki had perceived things from the standpoint of him versus others.

Grass on the Wayside: A Pathless Path

Grass on the Wayside represents the period between Sōseki's return from England (in 1903) and 1909, when his troubled relationship with the man who adopted him ended, and compresses the events that occurred during those seven years into a narrative that covers a period of ten months.[22] Until his debut of *I Am a Cat* in 1905, Sōseki is said to have felt alienated from society and was insecure about his future. By 1909, he had begun working at the *Asahi Shinbun* and had written three novels. In *Grass on the Wayside*, Sōseki reenacted a period of his life that he detested so much that he even wanted to "destroy his body" and felt that "the entire society had gotten on his nerves."[23]

As discussed in chapter 2, Sōseki expressed his determination to "enter the path," when writing *Grass on the Wayside*, and the title of the book—*Michikusa* in Japanese—reinforces this idea. This word is often used negatively as part of a proverbial expression, *michikusa o kuu* 道草を食う, which implies delaying one's way to a destination (for example, a horse eating grass on the wayside). The word *michikusa* does not appear in the body of *Grass on the Wayside*, which is the literal meaning of this phrase, and Sōseki did not indicate how he conceived that title. This word can be associated with the sense of wasting time that Kenzō, his alter ego, feels because he cannot solve his problems immediately and ends up doing unnecessary things over and over, as well as with Kenzō's frustration over his inability to pursue his goal, for which he blames others.[24] At the same time, when the narrator analyzes Kenzō from a less self-serving point of view, Kenzō's unpleasant past does not appear to have been meaningless, because his past serves as an opportunity for him to learn about himself and others. After all, a person feels disturbed by a delay in his progress to a destination precisely because he has already taken that path. *Grass on the Wayside* is therefore written from the perspective of a person who gains the Buddhist insight and attains a high level of self-realization.

Sōseki's Buddhist attempt can be read as a linguistic choice: he gives the kanji compound 頓着 kana syllables that represent the traditional and Buddhist reading of the word. There are twelve places in *Grass on the Wayside* where the word 頓着 appears, and in all cases it is read *tonjaku* instead of *tonchaku*, which is the popular reading.[25] In earlier Buddhist texts, the word *tonjaku* appears as 貪着 or 貪著, which means "greed" or "attachment," and later as 頓着. In *Grass on the Wayside*, all twelve instances of 頓着 appear in nonreligious contexts and describe the behaviors of various characters, expressed as *mutonjaku* 無頓着 (not caring) or *tonjaku shinai* 頓着しない (not caring or not concerned)—for instance, "Shimada seemed quite *unconcerned*"[26] (emphasis added). By choosing the traditional reading over the popular reading, Sōseki seems to have valued the Buddhist indication of the kanji 頓着 in his work of autobiographical fiction.[27]

In *Grass on the Wayside*, Sōseki transformed traumatic memory into narrative memory by having Kenzō revisit his childhood and come to accept events which did not make sense to him in the past. Pierre Janet draws attention to the process of healing connected to the act of recalling. He states that "Memory is an action: essentially it is the action of telling a story."[28] When memory takes the form of narration—"narrative memory"—those who remember the traumatic event can share their horrible experience with others and the feelings associated with it. Remembering and narrating a traumatic event, therefore, slowly leads to recovery.[29] Writing *Grass on the Wayside* can thus be considered Sōseki's attempt to shed light on the mistreatment of his early years, to examine it by detaching himself from what he had felt then and realize what he had not understood in the past, and to accept the ways in which his past affects his present. In the following reading of *Grass on the Wayside*, the text is analyzed as a work of narrative memory, highlighting the narrator's growing awareness of interdependence, karmic connections, and the effects of causes and conditions that have shaped Kenzō's presence.

A Summary of Grass on the Wayside

After returning from a foreign country, Kenzō resettles in Tokyo. One day he notices Shimada, his foster father, whom he has not met for some sixteen years, looking at him. Kenzō learns from Onatsu, his elder sister, and her husband Hida that because Shimada is aging and has no one to look after him, Shimada has recently contacted Hida to see if it would be possible to bring Kenzō back into his family registry. Shimada's request is unreasonable and Kenzō could have easily rejected it. As a dutiful son, however, and despite his unhappy memories of Shimada, Kenzō feels obligated to do something for him.

Because he has been abandoned several times, Kenzō considers his childhood to have been cursed. His natural father sent him away to be raised by Shimada and his wife, Otsune. The couple initially took good care of him, but that soon changed when they began fighting about Shimada's affair with a woman named Ofuji. Shimada left home. Otsune soon began dating another man and returned Kenzō to Shimada, who then brought Kenzō back to his natural parents and wedded Ofuji. After that, Shimada and Otsune terminated their relationship.

While trying to make sense of his past and cope with Shimada, Kenzō reflects on his own conjugal relationship. Since the beginning of his marriage, Kenzō has made decisions by himself on matters important to his family. In this case too, he ignores his wife, Osumi, who suggests that he consult with his brother, Chōtarō, and avoid Shimada. Kenzō, however, decides to meet Shimada. Although Kenzō cares about Osumi in his own way, his quick temper and sarcastic behavior often causes her to suffer attacks of hysteria.

After Shimada's stepdaughter, Onui, dies, Shimada escalates his requests to Kenzō for financial help. Onui is Ofuji's daughter and the source of Shimada's income. Kenzō firmly rejects Shimada's request, but Shimada still has a memo that he had asked Kenzō to write when he returned him to his natural parents. Now he wants Kenzō to buy it back and sends a surrogate to negotiate the transaction. At the termination of the adoption, Kenzō wrote a few lines expressing the hope that Shimada and Kenzō "would not henceforth become strangers merely because their relationship had been altered."[30] The memo means nothing to Kenzō, but he reluctantly responds to Shimada's demand and asks Hida and Chōtarō to represent him. They get the note back from Shimada and Kenzō pays Shimada off.

Grass on the Wayside as a Work of Narrative Memory

Although Buddhism is hardly mentioned in *Grass on the Wayside*, the beginning of Kenzō's effort to recall his boyhood indicates his familiarity with "the buddha." In addition to a "large square house" and "a house with a red gate" where he lived with Shimada and Otsune, Kenzō remembers a large Buddhist statue:

> Right across the road a large bronze buddha sat cross-legged on a lotus. He held a staff and wore a broad-brimmed hat.
> From the dark front entrance with its earthen floor he [Kenzō] would cross the road where the horses passed and go down the stone steps to the buddha. Holding on to the staff Kenzō would stand on the trailing bottom folds of the ample cloak. He would edge his way around to the back and try to pull himself up onto the shoulders, but *always the brim of the hat stopped him*.[31] (emphasis added)

As a child, Kenzō alternated between the profane and sacred realms. His inability to climb to the top of the statue of the Buddha reminds him of his limitation at the time, but recalling this event brings him closer to the world of the Buddha once again—the narrator uses the word *hotoke sama* to describe the Buddhist statue with which Kenzō played. With the beginning of this recollection, Kenzō starts examining his childhood more or less objectively, as if he were embarking on a "path" to revive his memory.

Kenzō's memory of childhood often falls short. Not all his memories of Shimada are negative. He recalls that Shimada bought him Western clothes, a number of goldfish, a miniature suit of armor, a replica of a short sword, and drawings. Shimada held Kenzō's hand when taking him to various places. Kenzō vividly remembers those times but is unable to bring back the emotions he felt then.[32] Kenzō's incomplete memories suggest child abuse. Shimada and Otsune, known for being extremely stingy, pampered him as their only child, but that made them insecure about Kenzō because they were not his natural parents. Accordingly, the couple forced Kenzō to show his affection by asking him questions, such as "Who is your daddy?" and "Who is your mommy?" The more the couple tried to hold onto Kenzō, the more he disliked them. He grew selfish and especially loathed Otsune's hypocritical personality.

When the couple began fighting, the sounds of their beating, kicking, and screaming frightened Kenzō. They stopped arguing after hearing Kenzō cry, but later ignored him and continued abusing each other. Soon after, Otsune and Kenzō moved to another house. She kept telling him, "I have no one but you. You mustn't ever let me down—understand?" Otsune later abandoned him.[33]

Kenzō then found himself at his natural parents' home. His father neither welcomed his return nor felt sorry for him. Kenzō's father did not care about his youngest son because he had been responsible for so many children. He did not want to spend any money on Kenzō and considered Kenzō's return to be temporary. Shimada, on the other hand, assumed Kenzō's natural father would support Kenzō until he reached maturity. Kenzō was loved neither by his natural father nor by his foster father. When Shimada ordered Kenzō to become his servant, Kenzō left for good.

Recalling and examining his painful boyhood leads the narrator, who speaks for Kenzō, to develop an impartial view of the Shimada couple. Although Shimada is niggardly, Kenzō reevaluates him as being too honest to use money wisely and even perceives Shimada as being not so different from himself, wondering, "If god were to look at my own life, would he think I was much different from this greedy old man?" Kenzō sympathizes with the couple since they "must at one time have been happy together" and laments, "That shabby woman [Otsune] was once my foster mother. Had she been more decent, I would at least have tried to console her. And I would have been with her when she died."[34]

Kenzō further extends an unbiased perspective to Onatsu. He believes in the importance of education, but now realizes that intellect alone cannot control his complex feelings about himself. He considers Onatsu to be more sincere than he is. Kenzō then wonders if he might have been more like her had he not received a higher education. He is embarrassed by his arrogance and becomes humble.[35]

Kenzō also takes a hard look at himself vis-à-vis his wife. When arguing with Osumi, he always rationalizes his own behavior and argues her down. He never considers her suggestions might be correct. As an example, in Kenzō's opinion, a wife should always be subordinate to a husband. Osumi suggests that if he wishes her to be obedient, Kenzō should earn her respect. When she insists on her independence, he holds her in scorn: "You are only a woman." When she protests, he tells her off: "It's not because you're a woman that I consider you stupid—it's because you really are stupid. If you want respect from me, earn it." Kenzō thus finds himself repeating Osumi's words.[36] Although Kenzō shows his temper from time to time, he maintains a dialogue with Osumi. Both Kenzō and Osumi accept their karmic conditions, or causal relationship (*inga kankei*), as a shared experience—which does not make sense to others—and try to understand each other.

For Kenzō, the process of recovery is not straightforward. Judith Herman points to a spiral development of recovery from trauma, in which "earlier issues are continually revisited on a higher level of integration."[37] Despite his sympathy for Shimada and Otsune, Kenzō is often irritated by their visits and becomes angry with Shimada when giving him money. Kenzō justifies his contradictions and moral rigidity by saying, "only god could be just" and "even patience is beyond us mortals."[38] Kenzō also has a cavalier attitude towards Osumi. When his arguments with Osumi escalate, Kenzō hates her and even wishes her dead. Despite the recurrence of despair, Kenzō admires someone who is able to "overcome and control one's temper"[39] and feels ashamed of "his inability to treat ordinary harmless people."[40] Kenzō detaches himself from the memory of his boyhood days, investigates his past, and makes efforts to understand the intentions and situations of those who abused him. He becomes introspective and realizes that it is his words, behavior, and thoughts that have hurt his wife and children; accepts himself as a lonely, irrational, and less sympathetic person; and recognizes the working of karma that binds people's lives, including his own.

The narrative of *Grass on the Wayside*, in which Kenzō analyzes how his past led to his present and casts impartial views on the people around him, brings to mind the three-stage narrative structure of Buddhism consisting of "ground, path, and goal." In accordance with Richard Payne's study, the recurrence of Kenzō's frustrating activities (ground) leads him to investigate the qualities of his being (path)—his mental, verbal, and bodily behaviors, and their consequences. Kenzō is not liberated from the internal causes of his frustrating behaviors but idealizes the state where one can control one's temper (goal). Kenzō's spiritual development is slow, interruptive, and not unidirectional, as it progresses on a path; it is as if he takes three steps forward and two steps back. He seems to know that he can never attain the ideal spiritual state, but that what is important is staying on that path. For him, self-realization is an ongoing process as he continues to work on the causes and conditions of his problem.

Such a message appears at the end of *Grass on the Wayside* where Kenzō speaks of the instability in his life: "Hardly anything in this life is settled. Things that happen once will go on happening. But they come back in different guises, and that's what fools us."[41] At first glance, his remark sounds pessimistic—and his wife does not understand what he means, but Kenzō's words imply an understanding that life is full of problems and one cannot get away from them. This ending of *Grass on the Wayside* reminds us of how *The Gate* ends—despite Oyone's joy of the arrival of spring, Sōsuke says, "But it will soon be winter again."[42] As Sōsuke's transformation and positive attitude is evident on a subtextual level, which will be discussed in chapter 6, Kenzō's readiness to face the difficulties of life can be detected from the standpoint of path literature.

Sōseki's Method of Writing

According to Ueda Shizuteru, Kenzō's effort to see himself in others is a part of the plot that is enhanced by Sōseki's writing style. While writing *Grass on the Wayside*, Sōseki invented a method of writing by describing what Ueda calls "self and self" or "ego and ego." The hero not only sees every other character from his point of view while objectifying his perspectives but he also incorporates the images "seen by another who is not I, who comes into contact with I, and confronts the I." More precisely, Ueda observes that Sōseki attempted to depict a self—whether a protagonist, alter ego, or another character—from the point of its partner who questions and negates an absolute view held by the self. Ueda calls this method "writing without ego,"[43] and finds an example in the following exchange between Kenzō and Osumi:

> He [Kenzō] made up his mind to work harder and earn more money. Not long afterward he returned home with some extra money in his pocket. He pulled out the envelope containing the bills and threw it down in front of his wife. She picked it up and looked at the back to see where it had come from. Neither of them said a word.
>
> Her expression was blank. I could have shown pleasure, she thought, if only he had said something kind. Kenzō, on the other hand, resented her seeming indifference, and blamed her for his own silence. The money would help them satisfy their material needs. As a means of bringing warmth to their relationship, it was quite useless.[44]

Kenzō sees his reaction to Osumi from her perspective, while Osumi sees her response to Kenzō from his viewpoint. This interface, according to Ueda, makes *Grass on the Wayside* an "auto*hetero*biography" because Sōseki depicts Kenzō from the perspective of the other—Osumi is modeled after Kyōko, Sōseki's wife—while simultaneously reenacting his experience by using Kenzō as his surrogate.⁴⁵

In this development, Ueda argues that Sōseki's transformation begins on an ontological level and continues as a change in his writing style. Because Sōseki was dead for thirty minutes during his Shuzenji crisis, he must have grasped the "original reality (*Urfaktum*)" as being egoless. Ueda notes that "Sōseki's life as a drive toward reactualization of the nonego is lived in his personal existence and also in his way of writing as a novelist, on two different but not unconnected levels."⁴⁶

Based on Ueda's analysis, it can be said that writing was more than a profession for Sōseki. It was a way of life. While writing *Grass on the Wayside*, Sōseki adapted impartial views about each character and objectified his literary ego and the characters partially representing him. By writing *Grass on the Wayside*, Sōseki advanced his style of writing that also served as a means for him to objectify his own consciousness, cultivate his personality, improve his relationship with his wife, and gain spiritual strength.

While sitting in meditation and writing personal fiction were reciprocal for Sōseki later in life, Tayama Katai took it one step further. For the narrator of *Remaining Snow*, which was written at about the same time that Katai discussed "flat description," writing personal fiction was the means to reflect on and convey the Buddhist teachings. Unlike Sōseki, Katai explicitly discussed the connection between literary art and Buddhism.

Katai's Discussion of *Ari no mama*

Tayama Katai discussed the importance of describing things as they are. Refuting the criticism of *The Quilt*—that is, that the work was no more than a record of the author's repentance—he wrote, "I only wrote faithfully what I saw as it was, what I heard as it was, and what I thought I did."⁴⁷ Concerning the popular assumption in the reading of modern Japanese literature that the author, narrator, and hero are identical, Edward Fowler states that "Given the *bundan*'s [literary circle's] faith in the ability of the writer to apprehend and portray brute reality and to present himself without mediation, the distinctions between private person and narrating persona, between autobiography and fiction, lost their significance."⁴⁸ Fowler goes on to say,

> All these writers worked to camouflage the fictionality of their writing, a fictionality produced not by the nonreportive style's "lie"

of narrated consciousness but by the lie of authorial "presence" featured in the written reportive style. From this style has sprung the myth of "sincerity," in which the totally accessible author relates his experiences through the totally transparent text.[49]

The modern Japanese writers' claim that autobiographical fiction "truthfully presents" their experiences is partly based on the vagueness of narrative expression unique to the Japanese language. Fowler, at the same time, points out that literary imagination is a product of "representation"—no matter how closely author and hero resemble each other. To put it differently, Katai's belief in *ari no mama* depiction is a by-product of Western realism and traditional ideas, especially Buddhist sensibilities, that mediate his sensory experience.

Katai's theory of realistic depiction is known as "flat description" (*heimen byōsha*). According to Fowler, Katai was influenced by the Goncourt brothers and adopted a style of writing that permits the narrator to cope with events and characters with a degree of detachment.[50] In "My Attempt in Writing *Life*" (*Sei ni okeru kokoromi*, 1918), Katai wrote,

> By refraining from petty, subjective interpretation and from analyses of phenomena about which I had no direct understanding, and by presenting my material in unaltered [*ari no mama*] form.... I believed that my descriptions would actually come closer to the truth and would of themselves suggest the inner significance of things.[51]

The goal of plain depiction is to show things as they are. Shu Kuge considers it a "*fluid* writing that has no formal or manmade aspects,"[52] while Tomi Suzuki characterizes it as a method of depicting things "without a grain of subjectivity and without an abstract plot."[53]

Prior to the development of flat depiction, Katai wrote two short essays—"The Subjectivity of the Author: In Response to a Critique of *Wild Flower*" (*Sakusha no shukan: No no hana no hihyō ni tsuite*, 1901) and "On Subjectivity and Objectivity" (*Shukan kyakkan no ben*, 1901)—and discussed two kinds of subjectivity: "the subjectivity of great nature" (*daishizen no shukan*) and "narrow subjectivity" (*sakusha no shōshukan*). According to Tomi Suzuki,

> Katai further argued that a novelist should transcend his "narrow," "sporadic," "personal" subjectivity, which is full of "personal prejudices," and should attain, through "concrete and objective

description," "the subjectivity of great nature," which embraces and transcends various ideals and doctrines and which constitutes the innermost principle of human life. . . . Katai's primary concern appears to have been objective description of the subjective world of the protagonist, an objective description that assumes the transcendental perspective that he called the "subjectivity of great nature."[54]

The "subjectivity of great nature" reflects a writer's effort to assimilate himself into nature's perspective, and, as Matthew Fraleigh points out, aims at "transcending his individual authorial subjectivism and adopting the broad subjectivity of nature."[55] Although Katai did not mention Buddhism in these essays, his idea of a writer's subjectivity was inseparable from the writer's state of self-detachment.

The two kinds of subjectivities—the perspective of great nature and that of a writer himself—are intertwined. According to Katai, the subjectivity of great nature has developed through heaven and earth, and because of its presence, a writer is able to reflect on great nature and cultivate his subjectivity. As the writer's subjectivity matures, it corresponds to the subjectivity of great nature. Katai believed that only when a writer merges his perception into the perspective of great nature can a masterpiece be created.[56]

Katai's explanation of subjectivity resembles the unity of subject and object described by the Romantics in Western Europe. According to David L. McMahan, Friedrich W. J. Schelling considered the Newtonian perception of nature to be mechanical and nature to be an organic whole. For Schelling, McMahan states, "Objects are not independent of the subject, and the usual immersion of the ego in objects blinds the subject to its own positing of objects."[57] William Wordsworth deemed nature to be the "source of art and morality against the modern world's contrivances" and valued feeling and intuition more than intellect and reason.[58] Although Katai did not discuss the influence of Western Romanticism on his definition of a writer's subjectivity, he had read the works of the Romantics, including the poetry of Heinrich Heine and Wordsworth.[59]

In discussions of the impact of Western literature on Katai's realistic writing, traditional sources from which Katai developed his inclination toward realism are overlooked. As Katai himself acknowledged, when he was young he learned "realistic tendency" through a theoretical discussion of Japanese poetry. Katai studied *waka* with Matsuura Tatsuo, who had been affiliated with Kagawa Kagetsune's group. From Matsuura, Katai learned that "[p]oetry is not concerned with academically expounding, but with rhythmically expressing."[60] Rhythm in the original language is *shirabe*, and according to Judit Árokay, Kagawa Kageki (Kagetsune's teacher) reinvigorated Japanese poetry during the late Edo period by criticizing attempts by poets to rationalize their feelings and "emphasized the immediacy of poetic expression." Kageki recognized the importance of simplicity, spontaneity, and sincerity without incorporating argumentation into poetry. Árokay goes on to say that Kageki "equated emotion with the linguistic expression" and that he was "referring to language in its presentational function as opposed to its representational function." An example of this practice is equating the name of a *kami* in medieval Japan with a particular word that indicates its presence.[61] Although Katai did not discuss his study of poetry in detail, when the lineage of Kageki, Kagetsune, and Matsuura are considered as a background to his study of poetry, the intuitive nature of traditional poetry underlies his account of *ari no mama*. Further, in "A New Theory of Fiction" (*Shōsetsu shinron*, 1911), Katai juxtaposed the mental state of an artist who devotes himself to the discovery of the naturalness in a phenomenon with the spiritual state of a Buddhist monk who practices meditation.

Katai's idea of two kinds of subjectivity associated with nature is comparable to the two kinds of self as discussed in Sōseki's *Light and Darkness*. Sōseki and Katai never met and may even have disliked each other. Sōseki kept his distance from naturalism, which was promoted by Katai and Shimazaki Tōson, and described Katai's *The Quilt* as "drawings of an ugly house partitioned into small units in an alley."[62] Katai, on the other hand, viewed Sōseki's works as "incomprehensible" and stressed the difference between Sōseki's works, in which he saw the influence of English literature, and his own which were influenced by the naturalism of continental European literature.[63] Surprisingly, however, Katai and the narrator of *Light and Darkness* agree on the importance of realizing one's egotism as the first step to self-transformation.

In *Light and Darkness*, the narrator discusses "small self" (*shōga* 小我) and "great self" (*taiga* 大我) through an exchange between Tsuda and Onobu, a married couple. Onobu wishes to ensure her husband's love, but the more she suspects his love for another woman, the more Tsuda pulls back from her. The distance she creates between herself and her husband becomes the cause of her suffering, and she becomes more selfish in her conjugal relationship. Onobu thus represents a small self and "small nature" (*chiisai shizen*). From the narrator's perspective, however, Onobu could be part of "great nature" (*ōkina shizen*), if she understood her own personality or if she allowed herself to be absorbed into a great self—that is, if she started seeing the totality of her surroundings from a larger perspective. The small self and the great self are therefore inseparable and, furthermore, great nature may crush a small self if Onobu does not accept her egotism as the cause of her problems.[64] Although the narrator of *Light and Darkness* neither discusses great nature in terms of Buddhism nor extends his discussion of the two kinds of self to a writer's subjectivity, the Buddhist aspect of "great self" needs to be noted. In "A Fragment" (*Danpen*, 1915), Sōseki discussed in passing the great self in relation to no-self (*muga* 無我). He expressed his desire to attain the state of self-detachment and considered the state of no-self to be the same as the state of great self.

When Sōseki's equation of the three terms—the great self, great nature, and no-self—is taken into account, the narrator of *Light and Darkness* and Katai appear to share similar ideas. That is, when one realizes oneself in the totality of human activities and accepts the course of actions that develop naturally, one becomes relatively free from one's biases and is able to understand the views of others. In this respect, despite his insistence on being different from Sōseki, Katai is actually not so different.

Moreover, for Katai, great nature is inspirational and even mysterious. It moves a writer greatly, makes him contemplative (*meisō*), and brings him to an extraordinary state (*shinrai no kyō* 神来の境, or literally, the state in which *kami* arrive). It leads him to discover a wide range of dispositions, principles, and opinions beyond his narrow mind.[65] This discovery is, however, not made easily, and the writer has to train himself (*shūren*) in observing (*kansatsu*) phenomena and to develop his personality (*jinkaku*).[66] Katai wrote, "Writing is not so much about showing things to others, but about observing things for a writer himself; therefore, observing and writing are not two different activities."[67] To look at this idea more closely, *Remaining Snow* is examined next.

Remaining Snow: An Exploration of Dharma in Literature

Remaining Snow is another work of Katai's autobiographical fiction. Unlike *The Quilt*, it has not drawn the attention of scholars of literary studies, partly because of the narrator's intensive philosophical reflections. As Oscar Benl wrote about it, "The restraint of artistic creative power is undoubtedly lacking."[68] The phrase *Remaining Snow* is an oxymoron. While newly fallen snow symbolizes purity, remaining snow represents impurity. The title of this personal novel is therefore non-dual.

Remaining Snow is also a *bildungsroman* and a work of path literature. The hero seeks to overcome crises in his marriage and career (ground), models himself on the life of Durtal to solve his problems (path), and accepts Buddhist teachings (goal). Using Tetsuta as his alter ego, Katai confesses a triangular love affair, and as the narrator, he reflects Tetsuta's relationship on the Mahayana Buddhist teachings. Similar to *Grass on the Wayside*, *Remaining Snow* is written from the viewpoint of a person who understands Buddhism on a philosophical level and has come to realize the causes of his troubles, which he has not previously understood before, through the process of writing. Although the story ends with Tetsuta's Buddhist realization, the narrator's explorations of Tetsuta's relationships with his wife Eiko and with his lover, as well as events that take place before Tetsuta goes to a Buddhist temple and reads Buddhist scriptures, are already placed in Buddhist settings.

Tetsuta has a hard time keeping his life together. He has grown weary of his marriage and is frustrated by the stagnation of his career. As a result, Tetsuta has an affair with a young woman who is also dating another man because she knows she cannot marry Tetsuta. In order to redirect his career, Tetsuta goes to dilapidated quarters on a mountain, which is part of a renowned Buddhist temple, and secludes himself there for six months. Later he stays at a cottage on a plateau for another six months and lives like Durtal. He moves from one place to another while seeking a solution to his problems. Loneliness gradually leads Tetsuta to realize that the cause of his problems is attachment and that no one can possess anything forever. Tetsuta begins to understand why Christ carried the cross on his back on behalf of all mankind and why Siddhartha Gautama tolerated asceticism in order to liberate all sentient beings.[69] Later Tetsuta visits his old friend, O, a resident Buddhist priest in Hirano; peruses portions of the Buddhist *Tripiṭaka* (*Daizōkyo*) there; and realizes the subtlety of the correlation between self and others. Inspired by the notion of simultaneous affirmation and negation of all things—which echoes the Buddhist logic of *sokuhi*—and encouraged by O, Tetsuta decides to return to the city he once hated. Ultimately, Tetsuta's spiritual query revolves around his interaction with local people, sacred sites, Buddhist priests, and Buddhist texts.

Tetsuta projects romantic love onto the Buddhist teachings and reflects on it from a larger perspective, that is, from a less egocentric perspective. He recalls taking his lover on a strenuous trip to Mount Minobu, where Nichiren spent his later life, and considers that trip to be motivated by the "deep mystery of their love" (*karera no koini aru fukai shinpi*).[70] While there, they were inspired by Nichiren's legacy and recited the *daimoku*—the title of the *Lotus Sutra*, or *namu myōhō renge kyō* (literally, "I take refuge in the *Lotus Sutra*").[71] During the recitation, Tetsuta had the impression that his lover purified herself of her negative karma through the power of the *daimoku*. Reflecting on this experience, Tetsuta wonders if it is possible to realize the "truth of both sexes" (*ryōsei no makoto*) within egotistical love.[72]

For Tetsuta, the truth of love takes the form of reconciliation between the self and the other, and can be realized if he is able to share the sense of loneliness caused by his attachment with his partner. One day, Tetsuta's lover attempts to kill herself because the man she has fallen in love with—someone other than Tetsuta—is not serious about their relationship. She survives and talks to Tetsuta. Through his conversation with her, Tetsuta comes to learn that, like himself, she feels tormented by a sense of loneliness, albeit to different degrees, and that by relating her suffering to his own suffering from the standpoint of loneliness, they can be connected on a deeper level. This interrelation is the manifestation of the truth of love. Whereas the despair she had felt drove her to attempt suicide, the despair Tetsuta felt after this incident leads him to redirect his life more mindfully. Tetsuta travels aimlessly and accepts Buddhist teachings.

Based on his scriptural study of Buddhism, Tetsuta considers the great path to be both attached to and detached from all phenomena. He states, "liberation should not be liberation" and "the path to realization should not be a path to realization."[73] This expression points to the state of subtlety that is not fixed by a single perspective, but accommodates multiple perspectives, including its opposite position. However, this idea itself establishes a position and becomes a cause of conceptual attachment; therefore, in the end, it needs to be abandoned. Tetsuta's realization calls to mind the Buddhist notion of emptiness.

In *Remaining Snow*, the narrator extends his discussion of Buddhism to an analysis of art. In his view, religion and art are fundamentally different. Art can be a medium by which man is saved, but it conveys soteriological messages far less effectively than Buddhism does. Not only that, art may also delay man's spiritual development.[74] However, as the narrator feels the presence of Shakyamuni Buddha while reading Mahayana Buddhist scriptures, he believes that artists should cultivate and model their subjectivities on the Buddha's subjectivity:

> Unless an artist has the ability to introspect deeply, build a confidence that is indestructible and unshakable (*fudō fue na jishin*), and has the authority to express himself and confront society only after requested by the public to demonstrate his work, it is to be expected that his work ends up being sketchy and superficially depictive and

that he cannot do any more than dirty his fingers in creating an atmosphere which embraces only the exterior of human life. It is possible to reenact events in life, but real artists must go further and recreate *the Dharma body hidden there* (*sono soko ni kakureteiru hosshin o saigen shinakereba naranai*その底にかくれてゐる法身を再現しなければならない). Only then can great art be created. Once such a position is attained, an artist will no longer be concerned about whether people like his work or not.[75]

The narrator connects art and Buddhism through his discovery of great subjectivity, which transcends individualistic personalities, and through the value he places on the spiritual independence of the Buddha and artists. His expression of the Dharma body may be rhetorical, but it also suggests the artist's spiritual growth. The Dharma body is the "totality of the Buddha's qualities," "nirvanic essence of the Buddha," or "innate reality of Buddhahood."[76] The Dharma body implies a "Buddha nature" (S. *tathāgatagarbha*; J. *busshō* 仏性)—that is, the "innate *potential* for Buddhahood" found in man"[77] (emphasis added).

The narrator's implication concerning the relationship between nature and Buddha nature is made clear in Katai's essay *A Study of Long Fiction* (*Chōhen shōsetsu no kenkyū*, 1925). According to this essay, nature is to be found within a self. When the young writer, S, asks about the characteristics of nature, the narrator discusses the ubiquity of nature:

"What is nature after all? Is there an easy explanation?" S said somewhat superficially.

"It can't be explained. But nature is not something difficult. It's right there. It's here in this present moment. *It's inside of you*. It's neither a higher principle nor sacred scholarship. If you can sufficiently objectify yourself, then you'll find it. Objectifying the self is, however, not easy. You may think you have, but you haven't. There seems to be a set of stages or something like steps that you can't easily skip. So, although it is a bother, you need to do it step by step. This is not just about problems dealing with art; rather, they are related to every aspect of life. Ancient philosophers and religious thinkers alike have dealt with it. Kant's epistemology, Confucius's ancient way, and Shakyamuni's great nirvana, they all point to it. So we can't avoid it, whether we want to or not. It doesn't come off from our bodies regardless of how hard we shake. In fact, the harder we try to shake it off, the more difficult it is to get rid of."

[S said] "Perhaps that's true. But please continue, you were discussing the plot of the novel."[78]

The narrator identifies the common goal of all philosophies and religions to be a thorough objectification of the self and the discovery of nature within that self. When the account of the Dharma body by the narrator of *Remaining Snow* is considered in this light, nature and Buddha nature appear to be identical, since both are the immanent possibility for an individual to develop great subjectivity. For these narrators, a writer needs time and experience to discover the nature—and the Buddha nature—within himself, while literature serves as a vehicle for him to cultivate both his nature and Buddha nature, and to express his realization of it.

The equation of nature and Buddha nature needs to be understood in a Japanese historical context where "nature" emerges as a modern concept. According to Nanyan Guo, the word *shizen* (自然), which appeared in Japanese literature for the first time in 1518, came to suggest "all things in the universe" in the eighteenth century. In 1796, it became the translation of "nature" and, during the nineteenth century, *shizen* and nature became synonyms. Previously, medieval Japanese had pronounced the same characters as *jinen* based on Chinese classics, such as *Laozi* and *Huainanzi*, and Buddhist traditions.[79] Fabio Rambelli points out that *shizen* is a neologism in modern Japan that denotes the concept of nature in modern Western philosophy, the notion of *physis* in Greek—"the external, natural world in which human action takes place"—and the idea of *natura*, or "nature," in Latin. *Jinen* in Japanese, however, refers to "something that is unconditioned and absolute." *Jinen* came to imply the "ultimate nature of dharmas" only after the development of the original enlightenment theory associated with esoteric Buddhist rituals during the medieval period. Japanese nativists later incorporated *shizen* into their discourse and, since then, the Japanese admiration for *shizen* has become part of their national character. Rambelli states that the modern Japanese idea of "love for nature" is a "byproduct of cultural nationalism produced by a combination of erasure of the Buddhist intellectual tradition and absorption of Western notions."[80] Given this background, the expression of Dharma body in *Remaining Snow* can be seen as the narrator's attempt to bring back the Buddhist element of *jinen* to *shizen*.[81]

On that point, another similarity between Katai and Sōseki is found. Although the kanji compound word 自然 is read *shizen* in most of Sōseki's work, Sōseki occasionally gives the kana reading *jinen* to 自然. At the beginning of *The Gate*, Sōsuke "basked in the warm sunbeams that pierced through the weave of his newly-made kimono"[82]—*jinen to shimi konde kuru kousen no atatakami o* (自然と浸み込んで来る光線の暖味を).[83] In *Grass on the Wayside*, Onatsu is described as follows: "The poor woman was wasting away before his [Hida's] very eyes"[84]—*jinen to sugarete kuru kinodoku na nyōbō no sugatawa* (自然と末枯れて来る気の毒な女房の姿は).[85] In these contexts, *jinen* can be translated as "naturally," describing the way the warm sunbeams work and the way Onatsu ages; however, in the Buddhist reading of *jinen*, the sunbeam represents Buddha's light, the warmth of the light implies the Buddha's compassion, and Onatsu suggests being a Bodhisattva figure. It is fair to say that by using *jinen*, both Katai and Sōseki maintained the Buddhist aspect of 自然.

In *Remaining Snow*, the Buddhist notion of emptiness and the thorough objectification of the self and others enhance Katai's style of writing—flat description. Like Sōseki, who included the perspective of the hero's wife in *Grass on the Wayside*, Katai reflected Eiko's perspective in his description of Tetsuta. Like Tetsuta, who is agonized by his relationships with others and his inability to either withdraw from society or advance his career, Eiko is disturbed by the changes in her surroundings. When her mother dies, she loses her guardian, who shielded her from the negative aspects of life, and has to deal with Katai's infidelity all by herself. She also becomes aware of her sexuality:

> "You can enjoy yourself in every way you want, because you are a man. But what about me? What kind of pleasure can a woman have?" Eiko often asked Tetsuta. "Well, you have children," Tetsuta bluntly said. This was his usual response, but it always made her uncomfortable. Eiko realized for the first time that she had to deal with him as a woman, but not as the mother of their children.
>
> "I need to be beautiful. I have to attract attentions of other men. [At the same time,] I have to work hard to keep Tetsuta under control so that other women don't steal him away from me." With this line of thinking, Eiko started to look around the world, which she did not even care to look at before.[86]

Tetsuta looks at Eiko from her perspective, while Eiko perceives herself from his view of womanhood and feels miserable. This exchange makes *Remaining Snow* an "auto*hetero*biography," to apply Ueda's term.

The narrator's treatment of the female characters is, however, inconsistent. His description of the exchange between Tetsuta and his lover leaves the impression that the narrator is much closer to Tetsuta when depicting Tetsuta's relationship to her compared to when the narrator describes Tetsuta's relationship to Eiko. The narrator empathizes with Tetsuta's lover, especially when she attempts suicide. He analyzes her psychological development as Tetsuta's wishful thinking and constructs her agony from a Buddhist perspective of suffering. Still, Tetsuta is obliged to help liberate both his wife and his lover from their respective attachments and he becomes didactic, acting as though he is a spiritual leader. In *Remaining Snow*, Katai's flat description is not as successful as his intense Buddhist reflection.

Shiga Naoya's Spiritual Rhythm

Shiga Naoya often used the term *ari no mama* when he commented on his works. "At Kinosaki" (*Kinosaki nite*, 1917), "Incident on the Afternoon of November Third" (*Jūichigatsu mikka gogo no koto*, 1919), "The Flu" (*Ryūkō kanbō*, 1919), and "Yamagata" (1927) are based on real events, and he described those incidents just "as they are (*ari no mama*)."[87] Shiga's realistic approach also derives from both Japanese and Western sources. Nanyan Guo points out that Shiki's *shaseibun* and the haiku journal *Hototogisu* influenced Shiga's proclivity toward realistic writing, and that Shiga greatly admired the works of Ihara Saikaku and Lafcadio Hearn. From Saikaku's work, Shiga learned the importance of having a strong rhythm in writing and from Hearn's work, which he read in English, Shiga developed a style of writing that is "simple, natural, realistic, precise, and [had] no interpretation from the author."[88] Because of Hearn's work, Shiga came to reevaluate Japan's traditional literary expressions.

In "Rhythm" (*Rizumu*, 1931), Shiga wrote about the spiritual dimension of his writing. The rhythm of writing he felt when he read Saikaku's work is not about the pace of writing, but the writer's spiritual rhythm:

> Content and style have often been discussed in art, but that is not what moves a reader. In my opinion, the significance of rhythm goes beyond the importance of content and style . . . Suppose there is a novel which reads well. But it is boring if rhythm is weak. I can clearly feel it when I read a novel. What is important is the strength of a writer's spiritual rhythm (*seishin no rizumu*). That is all that matters.[89]

For Shiga, writing personal fiction was a spiritual activity. Although he did not discuss the writer's spiritual rhythm in religious terms, he pointed out the non-dual state of a writer: the spiritual rhythm of a good writer arises neither intentionally nor unconsciously and that rhythm makes a novel a good novel and, at the same time, helps tighten the reader's spirit.[90] For him, realistic writing is facilitated by the writer's spiritual rhythm that flows more or less naturally.

Further, for Shiga, writing personal fiction with a good spiritual rhythm was a means to achieving self-composure and a harmonious life. According to Makoto Ueda, later in life, after improving relations with his family, Shiga lost "the great urge to write."[91] The number of works he completed diminished significantly after 1928, but Shiga did not care about that. Shiga said, "The important thing for me to do is to spend this unrepeatable life of mine in the best way possible. The fact that I have written works of fiction is of only secondary importance."[92] On this point, Fowler makes the significant observation that

> literature is subordinate to life, that the goal is to be a content person, not a prolific writer. If we accept Shiga's motive for writing—to bring an emotional crisis to conscious light and liberate oneself from its burden—then we can see that this is precisely the goal that Shiga pursued. One might argue that this is the reason all writers write; but few writers have recognized, as Shiga did, its ramifications: if realized, it leads the writer to silence. For Shiga, literature was useful only insofar as it fulfilled a particular need in his life; once the need was met, he could discard his art as he would an outgrown pair of shoes. For Shiga, silence in the end signified a healthy reintegration into life.[93]

From Fowler's perspective, writing was a means to transform Shiga's sense of selfhood and to attain self-realization. Recently, however, Nanyan Guo has argued that Shiga had "a much higher creative mission"—that is, "how he positioned himself in nature, and how he viewed and represented it."[94] Although Fowler and Guo disagree on Shiga's attitude toward writing, both would recognize the spiritual fulfillment in his career. "At Kinosaki" is such a work that represents the Shiga hero's self-realization.

"At Kinosaki": Oneness of Life and Death

The short story "At Kinosaki" is based on Shiga's intense reflections on his survival after a train accident. The story recounts his experience in the hot springs town of Kinosaki where he convalesced after the mishap. Although Shiga said that the feelings he described in the story were direct and candid, he developed it from "Life" (*Inochi*, 1914?) which he wrote previously, in which the narrator admires man's tenacity of his life.[95] In "At Kinosaki," however, the narrator is less concerned about self-preservation, and instead the Shiga hero realizes the oneness of life and death. What appears to be an objective account of the author's experience in "At Kinosaki" actually represents the author's growing spiritual concern and is written from the standpoint of death that is in line with the Buddhist narrative pattern of ground, path, and goal.

The Shiga hero journeys to Kinosaki for hot spring therapy because there is a possibility that he would develop spinal tuberculosis from his injury. His survival and the possibility of death make him cognizant of death; hence, his goal is to come to terms with it. His trip to Kinosaki represents such a path. In the town, the Shiga hero sees a dead bee, a rat being tortured by children, and the killing of a water lizard by his own hand. His inquiry about death is answered by his observation of these three instances of death. Step by step, he develops an impartial view of life and death. "At Kinosaki" ends with the remark that the Shiga hero never developed spinal tuberculosis.

When the Shiga hero sees a dead bee, he feels lonely but finds the state of death to be calming and quiet. He is then deeply disturbed by seeing in a river a big rat that was skewered through its body by a group of children. The rat crawls up on a stone wall but continues to fall back into the river because of the skewer, while the children throw stones at it. The Shiga hero is disgusted by such cruelty, but reflecting on his own survival, he understands the rat's instinct for life: "I had the feeling that even if I had been told I was dying, I would have thought all the more of doing something to save myself. Doubtless I would not have been so different in that from the rat."[96] For the Shiga hero, being both able to and unable to accept one's death shows the reality of life, and he embraces both feelings.

The Shiga hero then considers death to be as incidental as life is random. During his evening walk, he finds a lizard sitting on a rock and throws a stone at it, expecting it to be startled and jump into a stream. The stone, however, hits and kills the lizard. The Shiga hero feels terrible, as he did not intend to kill it. When he faces the dead lizard, he feels "with equal force the gentle pathos of all living things."[97] He then recognizes that death by happenstance is inconceivable—"By chance I had not died. By chance the lizard had died"[98]— and is awakened to the unity of life and death: "Being alive and dying were not positive and negative poles. I had the feeling that there was not that much difference between them."[99] The Shiga hero's careful observation of the deaths of various small creatures and his reflection on his survival and their demise leads him to gain an objective perspective on life and death, and on himself and other living creatures. He realizes that from the standpoint of death, he is not so different from the bee, the rat, and the lizard.

The feelings of the inexplicability of what makes sentient beings live and die is enhanced by the narration that makes the Shiga hero's surroundings unclear. Nearby in the stream, a mulberry leaf flutters "rhythmically" without wind (*hirahira, hirahira, onaji rizumu de ugoiteiru*[100]). The Shiga hero wonders why, and even feels slightly scared, and goes down to look up into the big mulberry tree. The wind then starts to blow and the leaf stops moving. The narrator does not explain the cause of this phenomenon, only saying, "the cause was evident. I thought that somehow I could understand such things better now."[101] This self-serving narration, which is puzzling, makes the environment somewhat mysterious, one in which the Shiga hero has realized the oneness of life and death. For him, a mystical setting and nature's rhythm are supplemental to the development of a mode of detached observation.

Conclusion

This chapter has contributed to the discussion of Buddhist practice in modern Japan.[102] When the scope of lay Buddhism is expanded, Sōseki's sitting in meditation, Katai's wandering and reclusive life, and Shiga's viewing of Buddhist arts appear as forms of Buddhist practice that reinforced their attitudes toward detached observation. Further, when personal fiction is read as a written form of spiritual practice related to Buddhism—realistic prose writing as a medium of self-reflection that triggers self-transformation—the relationship between the author, narrator, and hero becomes interdependent. As the author transforms "the narrating *I*" into a "narrated *he*"—to borrow Fowler's words—to describe the author's attempt in autobiographical fiction to create an autonomous hero and to represent his own mental state at the same time,[103] the narrator advances his spiritual inquiry by using the hero as his surrogate. The hero, who has his own life and deals with his own problems, enables the narrator to develop multiple perspectives on the hero and people surrounding him, understand their circumstances, and become more sympathetic toward others.

Buddhist clergy also participated in this form of practice and were engaged in confessional writing. While the present chapter illustrates the connection between meditative Buddhist practice and realistic writing as literary practice, the next chapter explores the role of confessional writing in a Pure Land Buddhist tradition and analyzes the work of Akegarasu Haya, a modern Shin Buddhist priest. Zen monks did not confess a failure to attain Buddhist realization in the same way that Shin Buddhist priests did. Monastic practice was designed for Zen practitioners to achieve Buddhist realization by their own efforts (*jiriki*). Unlike Zen monks, young Shin Buddhist priests who took part in the *Seishin shugi* movement initiated by Kiyozawa Manshi confessed their problems and base passions, revealed their naked selves, and entrusted themselves to Amida Buddha's compassion. As the title of the Shin Buddhist book *A Record of Shōmatsu as He Is* (*Shōmatsu ari no mama no ki*, 1889) suggests, modern Shin Buddhists believed that Amida Buddha embraces them *just as they are*.[104]

CHAPTER FOUR

Shin Buddhist Confession and Literary Practice

Theory of Confession

According to Karatani Kōjin, "Modern Japanese literature may be said to have come into existence together with the confessional literary form" and "it is possible to define Christianity in an even more direct sense as a source of modern Japanese literature."[1] Western missionaries reintroduced Christianity to Japan after the Meiji government lifted the ban on it in 1873. Japanese intellectuals, who saw Christianity as part of Western European civilization, visited Christian churches, attended Christian groups, studied the Bible, and engaged in the practice of confession through which they formed a sense of selfhood.

Karatani argues that Protestant Christianity generated a change in the perception of Japanese writers—what he calls *tentō* or "inversion of consciousness." First, Protestant Christianity "inverted" the notion of sin, that is, it went from condemning immoral acts (physical behavior, such as adultery) to forbidding the thoughts and desires (interior motives, such as adulterous feelings) that led to them. Japanese intellectuals influenced by Protestant Christianity therefore placed their "interiority" under surveillance.[2] Second, Protestant Christianity helped former samurai, who could not survive after the Meiji Restoration, become spiritually independent. The fallen samurai—who, with the coming of the new era, became useless in Meiji society—changed their status from military masters (and being served by their retainers) to subservience to God, through which they became their own masters.[3]

Uchimura Kanzō was such an individual. He was born to a samurai family and later became spiritually independent through the inversion of consciousness. In *How I Became a Christian* (*Yo wa ikanishite kirisuto shinto to narishika*,

1895), he discusses how he had suffered from his traditional obligations to serve Japan's multiple *kami* and how he overcame that pressure by converting to Christianity, which led him to serve only one God. After that, Uchimura was able to perceive nature, which he had seen as a diverse world where multiple *kami* interacted and even collided, as "simply nature" that was created by God. Karatani observes that Uchimura developed his religious identity by repressing his polytheistic impulse and that Uchimura's perception of nature "exists only by virtue of the existence of the spirit or of an inner world."[4] For Uchimura and other Christian converts, confession was not about expressing remorse, but rather about taking charge of one's own life by accepting one's limitations and weaknesses.[5] Confession thus enabled the Christian converts to discover interiority.

Karatani, however, generalizes the Christian experiences of Japanese writers. He neither distinguishes the differences between the Protestant, Catholic, and the Orthodox Churches in modern Japan's experience of Christianity nor considers the tradition of hidden Christians in Japan prior to 1873 or the impact of Catholicism on modern Japanese thinkers.[6] Further, Karatani ignores the contributions made by thinkers of other religious traditions in the formation of modern Japanese literature.

Taking Karatani's theory of inversion as a point of departure, this chapter demonstrates that modern Japanese Buddhists also practiced confession. It helps expand the boundaries of modern Japanese literature by treating stories of religious conversion as personal novels and by comparing the concerns of Buddhist priests and the writers discussed in the previous chapter. Kiyozawa Manshi (1863–1903)—Japan's first modern religious philosopher and a minister of Higashi Honganji—wrote a testimony to his faith just before his death. One of his disciples, Chikazumi Jōkan (1870–1941), set an example for his followers to express their religious experiences in narrative form. Akegarasu Haya (1877–1954), another student of Kiyozawa's, not only revealed his spiritual growth in public but also commodified his sexuality. For them, confessional writing—sharing the stories of their religious experiences—was a form of religious practice. Generally, Shin Buddhists deny "practice" because they associate it with self-power Buddhism—the practice by which practitioners seek to attain birth in the Pure Land through their own efforts. In assuming that there is no "practice" in Shin Buddhism, however, various forms of spiritual cultivation, such as listening to Dharma talks, attending Shin Buddhist rituals, and writing introspectively, are overshadowed. This chapter explores Kiyozawa's "The Nature of My Faith" (*Waga shinnen*, 1903), and after a brief discussion of Chikazumi's work, investigates Akegarasu's *Before and after My Rebirth* (*Kōsei no zengo*, 1920). The present study does not discuss the confessional writings of Kiyozawa and Chikazumi to the same degree that it analyzes Akegarasu's work; rather, it illustrates the literary and fictive quality of Akegarasu's confessional writings.

While confessional writing helped modern Japanese intellectuals define their subjectivity, religion also provided them with a spiritual standpoint that added to the formation of a self as a modern concept. According to Björn Krondorfer, confession in Judeo-Christianity permits men to reveal their private affairs, immoral acts, and unethical thoughts as a way to console themselves and avoid divine punishment. Krondorfer writes,

> Believing in the possibility of a transcendental Other and harboring hopes for redemption, both of which widen the imaginary horizon, enable men to self-examine and to grant others a look into their hearts. In view of something grander than one's own mortal being, some men feel sufficiently secure to expose a vulnerable self.[7]

Religious confession requires the presence of a transcendent authority, to which a confessant can disclose his unwholesome state of being, and from which to seek forgiveness. Although God—as the absolute being—does not rule over the spiritual landscape of Japan in the same way as in the West, Amida Buddha is the "spiritual other" for followers of Pure Land Buddhism in Japan, including Kiyozawa, Chikazumi, and Akegarasu. It is thus useful to refer to Krondorfer's study of male confessions in examining the confessional writings of these Buddhist priests.

For Krondorfer, confessional writing is a gendered activity. In order to write about a self, one must first be educated and then have the social status to present oneself in public. Historically, men have been more privileged to write than women. Second, men need a space to reveal their personal feelings. Talking to family members and friends is not an effective way for them to organize their ideas, but writing about themselves helps them manage their own thoughts.[8] Third, for men, confessional writing is an act of adventure. According to Krondorfer,

> It is a titillating activity. It fills the writer with the invigorating sense of being suspended between risk and control. "Control," because the writer, in and through the process of creating a text, also creates a distancing from himself, others, and events in the past. He remains largely in command of the story he wants to

tell about himself. "Risk," because writing for an audience exposes men to public ridicule and censure. Male confessants relinquish the protection offered either by the privacy of direct conversations or by the secrecy of the religious confessional and therapeutic spaces.[9]

For male confessants, confessional writing—which includes religious elements—represents a paradox. It discusses their spiritual crises and recoveries, but may invite further crises to their lives. When men identify confessional writing as a work of adventure, the narrative becomes male-centered. It silences women's voices and neglects female spirituality. The confessional writings of Shin Buddhist leaders mirror the patriarchal society of modern Japan and reflect their masculinity and carnal desire. Print technology led them to circulate their thoughts throughout the country, and young Shin Buddhist followers who read their writings sympathized with them because the confessants' struggles resonated with their own. For Shin Buddhist leaders, particularly for Chikazumi and Akegarasu, confessional writing was an effective means of religious propagation. This characteristic of confessional writing in Buddhism is distinct from the nature of personal fiction. At the same time, for Akegarasu, confessional writing was a way to transform his experiences into a story, through which he debunked embarrassing aspects of his life, rebuilt his religious faith, examined his relationship with others, and expressed his self-realization. In that sense, Akegarasu represents a writer excluded from the disciplinary boundary formed around modern Japanese literature. Before a discussion of the Shin Buddhist clerics' confessional writings, a brief summary of Shin Buddhist teaching and its confessional practice is provided.

Shin Buddhist Tradition of Confession

Shinran, the posthumous founder of Shin Buddhism, asserts that "we are certain to attain Buddhahood only when we have Faith in the Original Vow and recall the Name."[10] According to the *Larger Sutra of Immeasurable Life* (S. *Sukhāvatīvyūha Sūtra*; J. *Daimuryōjukyō*; hereafter, the *Larger Sutra*), the most important sutra for Shin Buddhist followers, Bodhisattva Dharmākara made forty-eight vows and became Amida Buddha upon their fulfillment. The eighteenth vow of Dharmākara is the most crucial and is called the Original Vow (*hongan*): those who sincerely recite Amida's name—known as *nenbutsu* 念仏 or *namu amida butsu*—attain birth in the Pure Land and subsequently nirvana.

More than reciting the *nenbutsu*, however, Shinran realized that the devotee's mindset is important and concentrated on the arising of faith, or *shinjin* 信心, in Amida's Vow. For him, Amida Buddha directs both the *nenbutsu* and *shinjin* toward the practitioner; hence, they represent Amida's activity to awaken sentient beings and inspire them to seek birth in the Pure Land.[11] Shinran considered *shinjin* a matter of the present life, and by receiving it, one will "dwell in the stage of nonretrogression," which means "the attainment of the equal of perfect enlightenment" and attaining birth in the Pure Land.[12]

Gradually, Amida Buddha acquired the character of afterlife savior and became personified. Shinran's followers in turn structured his doctrine and practice and formed many organizations. Under the leadership of the eighth abbot, Rennyo (1415–1499), the Honganji became the most powerful Shin Buddhist order. Rennyo considered the benefit of receiving *shinjin* in the present life to be as important as that of attaining birth in the Pure Land in the next life.

Shin Buddhist followers developed a sense of intimacy with their spiritual authority by calling Amida Buddha *oyasama* (honorable parent), which is gender neutral, either male or female, or a combination of both. From the late Edo period to the Meiji era, the so-called *myōkōnin* (devout followers) wrote many Buddhist poems, addressing their ignorance and self-realization to *oyasama* while praising Amida Buddha's virtue. For Shin Buddhists, therefore, Amida Buddha represents two bodies: *dharmakāya* (*hosshō hosshin*)—Dharma body or Dharma itself—and *upāya dharmakāya* (*hōben hosshin*)—an avatar of compassion or the body that manifests the Dharma using skillful means.

Confession has been part of Shin Buddhist practice. First of all, traditionally, as institutions of discipline, Buddhist monasteries forced monks and nuns to keep an eye on themselves through the means of confession.[13] In ancient Japan, the term *sange* 懺悔 appeared in translated Buddhist sutras and monks performed repentance. It developed as a form of revelatory tale, which included elements of Buddhist conversion.[14]

Second, for Shinran, sexuality was one of the tenacious biological forces that prevented him from pursuing a monastic Buddhist path. He received a vision, which was later verbalized and popularized as the "Verse on Making Love to a Woman" (*Nyobonge*), when he was struggling with celibacy. He is believed to have joined Hōnen's group after this event. James Dobbins states that "the path to the Pure Land is discovered within sexual engagement, not in renunciation of it."[15] In *The Collection of Passages Expounding the True Teaching, Living, Faith, and Realizing of the Pure Land*, better known as the *Kyōgyōshinshō*, Shinran wrote,

> I now truly realize! How wretched I am! Ran [Shinran], the stupid bald-headed one, deeply submerged in the wide ocean of desires and cravings, confusingly lost among the huge mountains of worldly fame and interests, has no aspirations for being counted among the elite of the definitely assured group and feels no pleasure in approaching the really true experience. How deplorable! How heartrending![16]

Although Shinran was not explicit about his sexual desire in this context, it was part of "the wide ocean of desires and cravings." He lamented the difficulty of overcoming his desires, seen as a cause of worldly attachment, such as the desire for fame and power. Shinran's followers in medieval Japan expressed their burden of karma and repented, using the term *kaige* or *gaige* ("ga" as the voiced sound of "ka," as in *kaige*) 改悔. Rennyo particularly encouraged the practice of repentance in his followers when they gathered in observance of Shinran's passing (*Hōonkō*). One of the *Letters* (*Ofumi* or *Gobunshō*) he addressed to the regional followers reads as follows:

> In sum, during the seven days and nights of the thanksgiving services of this month, each person should deeply repent; and, leaving none of his own mistaken thoughts at the bottom of his mind, he should undergo a turning of that mind and confess before the revered image [of the founder] in this temple, telling of this every day and every night so that everyone will hear about it. This, in other words, is in accord with [a passage in Shan-tao's] commentary: "With a turning of the mind, [even] slanderers of the dharma and those who lack the seed of buddhahood will all be born [in the Pure Land]"; it also corresponds to the teaching of "realizing faith (*shin*) oneself and guiding others to faith."[17]

By Rennyo's time, repentance had become a popular religious practice among Shin Buddhists. *Hōonkō* services were held once a year at local temples. Such ritual practice became a matter of formality when Honganji leaders institutionalized their organization and Buddhist priests merely read aloud Rennyo's *Letters* to the congregation.[18]

Further, the revelatory tales gradually lost their Buddhist nuance. Christine Marran points out that at the beginning of the twentieth century a wide range of Japanese intellectuals and writers, including women, began using the term *zange* ("za" as the voiced sound of "sa," as in *sange*) when portraying their life stories and that records of *zange* eventually developed into the style of *kokuhaku*, or confession, literature, which did not necessary involve a sense of sorrow and regret.[19] The word *sange* is the traditional and Buddhist reading of 懺悔, whereas *zange* is the popular and Christian reading of the word.[20] In addition to the practices of *sange* and *kaige*, Kiyozawa's followers used the term *hyōbyaku* to express their faith in Amida Buddha and seemed to have differentiated it from *kokuhaku*, which meant disclosing base passions.[21] Confessional writing therefore represents both traditional and modern Shin practice. For Kiyozawa and his followers, it was a vibrant religious practice. By verbalizing their personal experiences as reportage of spiritual experiments, they redefined Shin Buddhist doctrine, their relationship to Amida Buddha, and their moral values, while educating their followers.

Kiyozawa Manshi (1863–1903): Modernizing Shin Buddhist Confession

In 1895, when Uchimura Kanzō published *How I Became a Christian*, Kiyozawa wrote *A Record of Repentance during My Sickness* (*Zaishō sangeroku*). Despite its title, *A Record of Repentance* is a doctrinal text and shows Kiyozawa's effort to redefine Shin Buddhism after his failure in pursuing ascetic practices. In 1903, just before his death, Kiyozawa wrote "The Nature of My Faith," which inspired many young Shin priests, who regarded it as a testimony of his spiritual achievement. Encouraged by Kiyozawa's rational approach to Buddhism and moved by his method of establishing a spiritual standpoint, they revitalized their religious tradition.

Kiyozawa was born into a low-ranking samurai family in Nagoya. His parents—his mother in particular—were pious Shin Buddhist followers. They could not afford to pay for his education so when they learned that he could study at Higashi Honganji's high school (*ikuei kyōkō*) by becoming a priest in its organization, they encouraged him to do so. Kiyozawa was ordained at the age of sixteen, and a scholarship from Higashi Honganji allowed him to attend Tokyo Imperial University, where he majored in philosophy. He could have remained in academia, but in 1888, upon the denomination's request, Kiyozawa became the principal of a junior high school in Kyoto. He resigned that position about two years later and began exploring the basis of his religious identity. He lived ascetically and pursued an experiment that he called "minimum possible"—his attempt to live with the minimum amount of material things, including food. He gave up this experiment when it led him to contract tuberculosis, and he came to understand Shinran's teaching on a deeper level.[22]

Natsume Sōseki is said to have modeled the character K in *Kokoro* in part after Kiyozawa. In the last segment of *Kokoro* titled "Sensei and His Testament," Sensei confesses his past, which involves K's suicide, to *watakushi* (literally, "I" as the narrator). While in Tokyo, Sensei takes room and board at a young widow's (Okusan's) house and falls in love with her daughter (Ojōsan). At the same time, he worries about his longtime friend K's well-being and brings him to Okusan's house. K was born to the resident family of a Shin Buddhist temple but was adopted by a physician, who sends him to Tokyo to study medicine. K, however, refuses to study medicine and pursues the study of religion and philosophy. K's adopted family grows angry with him and sends him back to his natural parents, who then disown him. Considering his difficult situation, Sensei suggests that K, who is ascetic and tends to "willfully proceed to his own destruction,"[23] move into Okusan's house and regain his strength. K gradually recovers his health, but at the same time, falls in love with Ojōsan.

The more K and Ojōsan interact, the more jealous Sensei becomes, but he is unable to reveal to K his feelings for Ojōsan. During a summer vacation, Sensei travels to the Bōsō Peninsula with K, hoping to confess to K his love for Ojōsan. They visit various places and stop at Kominato, where the medieval monk, Nichiren, was born, and go to a temple associated with his birth. The following night, K criticizes Sensei for not having responded to K's comment on Nichiren, saying "anyone who had no spiritual aspirations was an idiot."[24] Sensei replies that K is abnormal because of his past ascetic practice. Ultimately, Sensei is unable to tell K of his love for Ojōsan.

Several months later, K confesses to Sensei that he is in love with Ojōsan. K cannot decide whether or not he should propose to her, because having a relationship goes against his ascetic principle—"everything had to be sacrificed for the sake of 'the true way.'"[25] Sensei takes advantage of K's hesitation and throws K's words back to him—"anyone who has no spiritual aspirations is an idiot." He then suggests that K give up thinking about Ojōsan. At the same time, he asks Okusan for permission to marry her daughter, without telling K. Okusan agrees to Sensei's request and later shares this news with K, who remains calm. Before Sensei informs K about his betrothal, K cuts his own carotid artery. Later, Sensei marries Ojōsan but suffers from a deep sense of guilt. He eventually takes his own life when Emperor Meiji dies and after General Nogi and his wife follow the emperor to the grave.[26]

Unlike K, Kiyozawa did not destroy himself. However, like K, Kiyozawa initially abandoned the Buddhism of other-power he inherited from his natural parents and attempted to develop his spirituality pursuing the Buddhism of self-power. Only after failing in that practice, did Kiyozawa take refuge in Amida Buddha. Kiyozawa died at the age of forty-one from tuberculosis.[27]

Kiyozawa's exploration of Shinran's teaching is known as "cultivating spirituality" (*Seishin shugi*).²⁸ For him, *seishin* refers to a spiritual state in which one can "accept the Infinite" or the Great Compassion (*daihi*) of the Infinite (other-power).²⁹ Kiyozawa describes the gist of *Seishin shugi* as follows:

> It is important to establish our lives upon perfectly firm ground. Without a firm basis, all of our efforts will be in vain. It is like doing acrobatics atop a cloud—an impossible feat: The performers are sure to fall.
>
> How can one attain that perfectly firm ground? In my opinion, we arrive at it only through an encounter with the Infinite, or the Absolute. It is unnecessary to speculate whether the Infinite is within or without. Because the Infinite is where the seeker finds it, we cannot define the Infinite as internal or external. We cannot stand on firm ground except by encountering the Infinite. This is what we call spiritual awareness [*Seishin shugi*, spiritual cultivation]: The process of inner development through which we gain that perfectly firm ground.³⁰

Cultivating spirituality, which Kiyozawa also expressed as "activism" (*Jikkō shugi*), "subjectivism" (*Shukan shugi*), or "the way of introspection" (*Naikan shugi*),³¹ is pragmatic and "develops where the relative enters into the Absolute and the finite meets the Infinite."³² Kiyozawa thus defined the correlation of a self and all other things under the principle of unity of all things (*banbutsu ittai*). He employed such words as the "Infinite," "Absolute," and "Tathagata" in order to make Amida Buddha an inclusive religious symbol and related Shin Buddhism to other religions.³³

According to Kiyozawa, his exploration of the inner life is inseparable from his efforts to reform the organizational structure of Higashi Honganji. Although he failed in his reforms because of opposition from the denomination's conservative authority, he achieved several goals. In 1901, he established a university in Tokyo (which was later moved to Kyoto—present-day Otani University) and served as its first president. He also formed a private study group called the *Kōkōdō* ("capacious cave"³⁴) and began publishing a Buddhist journal, *Seishinkai* (literally, "spiritual world").³⁵

"The Nature of My Faith," published in *Seishinkai*, is the testimony to Kiyozawa's spiritual attainment. He wrote this essay just a week before his death. According to Yamamoto Nobuhiro, because the members of the *Kōkōdō* and the readers of *Seishinkai* often questioned the nature of their faith, Kiyozawa felt compelled to explain to them the characteristics of his own faith.³⁶ At the same time, Yamamoto points out that "The Nature of My Faith" does not always represent Kiyozawa's Buddhist realization word for word. It was edited by his immediate students, such as Akegarasu and Sasaki Gesshō (later the third president of Otani University), and even included ideas that were not Kiyozawa's.[37] In other words, although Kiyozawa must have deepened his self-realization while writing "The Nature of My Faith," the record of his experience was compromised by the editing that took place when the text was published.

In "The Nature of My Faith," Kiyozawa's spiritual trajectory develops in an order that is the reverse of "goal, path, and ground," and then follows the pattern of "ground, path, and goal." In order to attain Buddhist realization, he first took a path of self-power Buddhism. After he realized his attachment to ascetic practice was a problem, a new path—other-power Buddhism—opened for him, and that path allowed him to "course through this world calmly and without malice."[38]

Because Kiyozawa had studied Western philosophy, Christianity, Confucianism, and Theravada Buddhism, he was analytical and experimental in his approach to Shin Buddhism. Like Uchimura Kanzō, Kiyozawa questioned the traditional orthodoxy defined by religious authority, refused to blindly accept doctrine, and sought to verify the teachings through personal experience.[39] As Kiyozawa tested his spiritual strength to the limit, he inevitably exhausted his mental faculties.

Kiyozawa's spiritual development suggests what Karatani calls the inversion of consciousness. Although not typical within the Shin tradition, Kiyozawa first repressed his body through ascetic practice. By failing in his goal of owning the minimum possible, he gave up the self-power approach and took refuge in Amida Buddha. In his diary kept in 1902, he wrote, "*hobo jiriki no meijō o honten shietari* 略ぼ自力の迷情を翻転し得たり [I have almost been able to let go of my attachment to the Buddhism of self-power]."[40] It would seem that without seeing results, one might lose attachment to ascetic practice the longer it is performed, but Kiyozawa became even more attached to ascetic Buddhism during his experiment with living as minimally as possible until he ruined his health. In other words, only after inflicting damage on his body did he realize his ignorance and perceive his attachment to self-power Buddhism as the cause of his suffering. Ultimately, his spiritual failure transformed his way of living.

Because of his spiritual experiment, Kiyozawa insisted that "religion is a subjective fact."[41] He argued that belief in the Buddha or in *kami* is unrelated to the physical presence of such beings, but belief in them comes only after a spiritual crisis. In other words, one's spiritual quest necessitates transcendent authority, and Buddha and *kami* do not stand by themselves. Such a personal religious statement is clearly shown in "The Nature of My Faith":

> The third question queries the nature of my faith itself. The answer to this is that my faith believes in the tathāgata. The tathāgata is the embodiment of the sacred (*hontai*) that I am able to believe in and, moreover, cannot help but believe in. Faced with the truth of the powerlessness of my own efforts, I [know I] lack the ability to stand on my own, but this tathāgata in whom I am able to believe as the fundamental embodiment of the sacred has the power to make me what I am. Faced with a world filled with good and bad, truth and falsehood, happiness and unhappiness, and yet personally lacking the ability to know one from the other, I am unable to move, right or left, forward or backward [to accommodate these things]. This tathāgata in whom I am able to believe as the fundamental embodiment of the sacred is capable of enabling such a person as myself to course through this world calmly and without malice. Without believing in this tathāgata, I would neither know how to live nor how to die. I could not exist without believing in the tathāgata. This tathāgata is a tathāgata that I am incapable of not believing in.
>
> This, then, is a summary of my faith. In terms of my first problem [of anxiety], the tathāgata *for me* is infinite compassion. In terms of my second problem [of ignorance], the tathāgata *for me* is infinite wisdom. In terms of my third problem [of practice], the tathāgata *for me* is infinite power. As such, my own faith believes in the reality of infinite compassion, infinite wisdom, and infinite power.[42]

Kiyozawa used the first person pronoun "for *me*" (*watakushi ni taisuru*) to explain his relationship with Amida Buddha.[43] By doing so, he reinvented Shinran's tradition by bypassing the institutional authority of Higashi Honganji, which had fixed Shin Buddhist doctrine.

Kiyozawa's rhetoric of "for me" echoes Shinran's sayings. In the *Tannishō*, Shinran is quoted as saying, "When I reflect deeply on the Vow that Amida fulfilled after five *kalpas* of contemplation, I find that it was for me, Shinran, alone! How compassionate, therefore, is the Original Vow of Amida, who was moved to free me from so many karmic defilements!"[44] After twenty years on Mount Hiei, Shinran gave up monastic practice, became a disciple of Hōnen, and entrusted himself to Amida Buddha's compassion. By doing so, Shinran realized that Amida's salvific power works for each individual, irrespective of his or her condition. Both Shinran and Kiyozawa had to fail in ascetic practice and become spiritually lost before feeling sure that Amida was embracing them. Understanding the Buddhist concept of "no-self" on an intellectual level did not help Kiyozawa attain spiritual liberation. Rather, when he became self-centered and realized the burden of karma, he discovered an alternative path. The assertion of a self, therefore, transformed his sense of being and guided him to the Buddhism of other-power. While accepting the notion of self as a modern construct, Kiyozawa denied egotistic individualism and identified a self in relation to Amida Buddha, the spiritual other. Once his spiritual standpoint was established—and although he remained strongly disciplined—morality and ethics became less important to him.

Kiyozawa's spiritual experience and emphasis on Shinran's teaching was part of a larger effort to revive Japanese Buddhism undertaken by reformers of Buddhist denominations and lay intellectual Buddhist practitioners who interacted with them during this period. First, from approximately the third decade of the Meiji period, Buddhist leaders moved away from positivistic and scientific approaches to Buddhism, which had been derived from the West, and began stressing the importance of introspection and the growth of one's own spirituality. Within and beyond Buddhist communities, there was a tendency to view religious truth as being verified through one's own experience without resorting to science and philosophical speculations.[45] Second, as discussed in the previous chapter, lay Buddhist leaders, such as Nishida Kitarō and Suzuki Daisetsu, invented the idea of "inner experience" through one's own experiment. While they championed Kamakura and Muromachi Zen for its great achievement,[46] Kiyozawa confirmed Shinran's teaching as true and real based on his empirical experience.

Kiyozawa was not alone in recognizing the agency of a self as being indispensable to Buddhist liberation. For many young Shin Buddhists, confessional writing served as a means of discussing the nature of their faith.[47] In 1900, for instance, Chikazumi Jōkan published "The Lingering of My Faith" (*Shinkō no yoreki*), for which Kiyozawa wrote a preface,[48] in which he discussed his experience of the turning of the mind. Chikazumi had a tremendous Buddhist influence on the educated youth in Tokyo, including philosophers such as Miki Kiyoshi (1897–1945) and Takeuchi Yoshinori (1913–2002), and writers such as Mitsui Kōshi (1883–1953) and Kamura Isota (1897–1933).[49] A brief discussion of Chikazumi's work will help to bridge the confessional writings of Kiyozawa and Akegarasu.

Chikazumi Jōkan (1870–1941): Circulating Confessional Buddhist Writings

Chikazumi was born into the resident family of Saigenji, affiliated with Higashi Honganji, in Shiga Prefecture. In 1889, Kiyozawa's recommendation led Higashi Honganji to send Chikazumi to Tokyo to study at Kaisei Junior High School and First High School. Chikazumi then entered Tokyo Imperial University in 1895, where he majored in philosophy. In Tokyo, he joined Kiyozawa's reform movement, but the failure of the reform dispirited Chikazumi. At the same time, he had difficulty in making friends in Tokyo and illness further depleted his spirit. Still, on September 17, 1897, Chikazumi experienced a turning of his mind. According to *A Record of My Repentance* (*Sangeroku*, 1905), one day on his way home from the hospital, Chikazumi happened to look up and felt as if his chest had completely opened up to the blue sky and as if the sky had absorbed him, a figure "as small as a bean." At that moment, he realized that, unlike all his friends, the Buddha had accepted him unconditionally.[50]

After regaining his spiritual strength, Chikazumi grew active once again. Together with other Buddhist priests, he opposed the Diet passing the Religions Bill in 1899, by which Yamagata Aritomo's cabinet aimed to control religious organizations.[51] From 1900 to 1901, he traveled to Western Europe and the United States to observe religious institutions. Upon his return, Higashi Honganji helped him build a student dormitory (*kyūdō gakusha*) in Hongō in Tokyo. In 1915, he built a lecture hall (*kyūdō kaikan*) next to the dormitory and committed to sharing the Shin Buddhist teaching for the rest of his life.[52]

Like Kiyozawa, Chikazumi valued personalized religious experience. According to Ōmi Toshihiro, Chikazumi tried to internalize the spiritual liberation of fictional characters in Buddhist sutras and reflected on episodes for which Shakyamuni and Shinran are known. For instance, Chikazumi related the turning of his mind after recovering from an illness to an episode of the *Nirvana Sutra* in which Ajātaśatru, who succeeded to the throne of the Magadha Empire by killing his father but later suffered from a disease because of his guilt, took refuge in the Buddha's teachings and simultaneously recuperated from the sickness. Although the immediate causes of Ajātaśatru's and Chikazumi's agonies are different, Chikazumi considered the fundamental causes of human suffering to be the same and treated Ajātaśatru's problems in the same way he treated his own.⁵³

Chikazumi then organized religious gatherings (*shinkō danwakai*) every month and encouraged young people to share their agonies and the development of their religious faith. In the journal *Gudō*, which began publication in 1904, Chikazumi created a confession column (*kokuhaku-ran*), to which various people contributed essays. They included university students, Buddhist priests, housewives, schoolteachers, medical doctors, business owners, businessmen, mailmen, public service employees, factory workers, and even politicians and military officers. In their writing, these people expressed their afflictions, battles against illnesses, religious interests, and spiritual healings. This column not only helped them understand the nature of suffering and Buddhist salvation, but also created a series of dialogues between the writers and the readers.⁵⁴ Ōmi states that

> the words of "I" who spoke of personal agonies and, receiving of an entrusting mind in Amida, helped another "I" verbalize his/her religious experience. This pattern became structured as a linguistic practice, which generated further stories in a chain-reaction manner. This was the most outstanding characteristic of Chikazumi's activities during the early 1900s.⁵⁵

The column gave writers an opportunity to disclose their anguish, reflect on the Buddhist teaching, and describe their religious experiences. Those who read the essays sympathized with the writers, initiated religious experiments modeled on the stories in the columns, and reported developments in their spiritual growth. The readers, therefore, became embedded in the system of confessional writing as well.

Dennis A. Foster discusses the relationship between a confessant and a reader in terms of intersubjectivity. The reader does not merely understand or sympathize with a confessant's experience but recognizes it as a "shared discourse" that shapes his subjectivity.⁵⁶ Foster writes,

> In the activity of interpretation, a reader will almost inevitably find the text to be a confirmation of his own thoughts, both happy and fearful (or an almost personal attack on him, which amounts to the same thing). If the activity of the writer is motivated by a desire to confess his own sense of loss and desire, the reader will find himself engaged in the same motivations, though he may

not recognize that the history he strives to comprehend becomes increasingly his own, not the writer's. The writer's work, in short, becomes the field on which the reader attempts to realize himself.[57]

Confessional writings enable both writer and reader to form their sense of being, but writing is a discourse through which a confessant actually controls the readership and molds the reader's perceptions. To put it differently, those who are going to peruse confessional writings characterized by a narrator's conversion experience have already shown interest in religion and even might have sought salvation prior to reading religious journals. They are thus willing to question their ways of living based on the confessant's religious experiences. Given this nature of confessional religious writings, it is fair to say that Chikazumi employed confessional writing not only as a means for his followers to establish Shin Buddhist faith but also as a system by which he could further propagate Buddhism.

Confessional writing enabled both Kiyozawa and Chikazumi to recognize the self in relation to a spiritual other—in their case, Amida Buddha—but their expressions were quite different. Kiyozawa's writings are terse and even didactic. He discussed neither the moment of the turning of his mind nor the immediacy of a mystical encounter. "The Nature of My Faith" is a record of how Kiyozawa came to internalize the principle of unity of all things—a modern Buddhist concept he created. While Kiyozawa is rational in his confession of faith, Chikazumi is emotional. Although Kiyozawa did not live long enough to receive readers' responses, Chikazumi understood the importance of a readership and reinforced confessional writing as a way to promote Shin Buddhism. Modern Shin Buddhist confession took yet another turn when Akegarasu Haya revealed both his religious faith and his sexuality. He was clearly aware of the artistic effects of confessional writing.

Akegarasu Haya (1877–1954): Confessing Religious Wrongdoing in Literary Form

Akegarasu was born in 1877 into the resident family of Myōtatsuji, affiliated with Higashi Honganji, in Ishikawa Prefecture. He lost his father at the age of ten and was raised by his mother. After receiving a local education, Akegarasu went to the junior high school in Kyoto where Kiyozawa served as principal and became one of Kiyozawa's closest students. Later in life, Akegarasu became a charismatic leader of Higashi Honganji and in 1951 served as its chief administrator. Like Kiyozawa and Chikazumi, Akegarasu took a pragmatic approach to Buddhism and talked about his religious experience, but his confessional writing was different from theirs. Akegarasu expressed his confession in the form of fiction. He did not hesitate in disclosing his love affairs, which included sexual escapades. He was an eloquent writer, who considered Kiyozawa's writing style to be boring and too intellectual,[58] and a poet—Nishida Masayoshi, a literary critic, characterizes Akegarasu as a poet–Buddhist priest (*kasō* 歌僧, or *shisō* 詩僧).[59] It is worth mentioning that notable writers such as Shimada Seijirō, Nakano Shigeharu, and Saitō Mokichi were influenced by Akegarasu.[60] Miyazawa Seijirō, Miyazawa Kenji's father, was also an adherent of Akegarasu, and through his father, Kenji became familiar with Shin Buddhism (though Kenji later became a passionate believer of the *Lotus Sutra*).[61]

Akegarasu was fond of the *Tannishō* and spoke highly of the spiritual liberation of *akunin* (literally, "bad people," but this word has wider implications) in it, such as in the words "Even a virtuous man can attain birth in the Pure Land, how much more easily a wicked man [can]!"[62] Akegarasu denied morality and ethics while propagating the efficacy of the Buddha's "grace" (*onchō*), which he extended even to criminals and transgressors of a moral principle.[63] His essay "Even Evil Acts Are Embraced by Tathagata's Grace" (*Zaiaku mo nyorai no onchō nari*, 1909) expresses this attitude:

> My understanding [of Shin Buddhism] is that Tathagata's grace embraces both convenient and inconvenient matters, for which I remain grateful. I feel Amida's grace when I am encouraged and also when I am discouraged. I feel his grace when my wallet is full and also when my wallet is empty. I feel his grace when I meet a person I am fond of and also when I depart from him. I feel his grace not only because of teachers and friends who have guided me but also because of individuals who have led me to commit evil acts.[64]

For Akegarasu, entrusting in Amida Buddha's original vow implies accepting all phenomena without making any judgment based on binary values, such as good and bad, and convenient and inconvenient.

Akegarasu promoted the Buddha's grace to young people and converted them to Shin Buddhism. He questioned them about outward appearances, which caused them to realize their hypocritical nature and how spiritually ignorant they were. That realization caused them to joyfully sense Amida's compassion.[65] Conservative authorities in the Higashi Honganji organization considered Akegarasu a heretic, because he affirmed the evil aspect of human nature without expressing sorrow and because he considered the sacred scriptures of Shin Buddhism to be meaningless unless they were applied to one's religious experiment.[66]

Various events, however, forced Akegarasu to relinquish the Buddha's grace, and that resulted in a spiritual crisis for him, to which he responded by writing a series of confessions. In February 1913, he wrote an essay entitled "Is This How I Am Going to Ruin Myself?" (*Kakushite watakushi wa chōraku shite ikuka*). In July 1913, he published a small booklet titled *The Ruin* (*Chōraku*), which included "Is This How I Am Going to Ruin Myself?" and other short essays. In February 1914, he declared his spiritual recovery in "After Returning to the Womb of the Buddha" (*Tainai kuguri o idete*). Further, in 1920, he published *Before and after My Rebirth*, in which he reproduced some of his previous writings, including "After Returning to the Womb of the Buddha," and reiterated his previous discussions from *The Ruin*.

A pattern can be discerned in these writings. First, Akegarasu himself was the reader of his own writings. He then interpreted and reconstructed his experiences while expanding the narrative by adding fragmentary remarks and diary notes, as well as deeper self-analyses. The word "confessor" implies the dual activities of a person who makes a confession and a minister who listens to it.[67] In this framework, Akegarasu is a confessant who listened to his own voice.

Making confessions in piecemeal fashion, as seen in the series of essays mentioned above, created a mechanism for Akegarasu. Step by step, he disclosed his intimate private affairs, crises, and the process of healing. He thus placed himself in a situation where he was responsible for his own conduct, analyzed his past behavior, and forced himself to grow spiritually. By exposing his predicament to the public, he pressured himself to overcome his crises. Akegarasu's phased confessions must have been attractive and even titillating to his readers, who may even have felt they were reading a serialized novel.

Before and after My Rebirth is more than two hundred fifty pages long and consists of a short prelude and three sections. The prelude expresses Akegarasu's motive for writing the book:

> After raging flames of lust burned all my clothes and even my body—religion, morality, status, personality, determination, honor, everything—a tiny sprout of life budded, and a beautiful world began emerging from the ashes.
>
> This book represents four years of crying out after I died spiritually at the age of thirty-seven and exposes my painful footsteps during that time.

A sense of shame comes over me when I think of publishing these essays, but I feel I will suffer even more if I do not publically disclose my conduct. I know this book will cause problems for some, but through it I wish to receive guidance from those who are ahead of me and perhaps it will be of benefit to those who follow.

I am planning to publish my next work, *The Declaration of an Independent Man* (*Dokuritsusha no sengen*) as a continuation of my efforts towards spiritual emancipation.[68]

Before and after My Rebirth is a record of Akegarasu's battle with his sexual desire that, as a cause of attachment, is discouraged in Buddhism. He was aware of his readership and, employing literary techniques, deliberately constructed this work to be read like a work of literature—together with *A Man Moving Forward* (*Zenshin suru mono*, 1921), Akegarasu considered *Before and after My Rebirth* and *The Declaration of an Independent Man* (1921) a trilogy of his work, since producing three personal novels in sequence was a popular literary practice among modern Japanese writers, including Sōseki and Katai. Akegarasu was neither embarrassed about expressing his sexual frustration nor concerned about the damage that his confession might cause his family and those who were involved in his affairs. He resembles Tayama Katai, who ignored his family and protégée as he confessed. However, *Before and after My Rebirth* is significantly different from *The Quilt* and *Remaining Snow*.

The first section, "Preface: To Revered Teacher, Kiyozawa" (*Chogen, Kiyozawa sensei e*), is written in the form of a letter that Akegarasu addressed to Kiyozawa, who had passed away by then. This section, on which the present study focuses, shows Akegarasu's naked self. With regard to letters as a popular vehicle of confessional writing in modern Japan, J. Thomas Rimer states that "the epistolary form brought with it the possibility of producing a powerful confessionary thrust less easily managed in the more regular third-person narrative style," and recognizes Natsume Sōseki's *Kokoro* as "one of the greatest of the epistolary works of the period."[69] The last section of *Kokoro*, "Sensei's Testament," which describes Sensei's past, is the letter Sensei sent to a young man called "I." Akegarasu's style of writing thus mirrors a contemporary development in Japanese literature.

In *Before and after My Rebirth*, the narrator's shame disappears, section by section, while his exegesis on Buddhism increases. In the second section, "Worries after A Rebirth" (*Sosei no nayami*), he continues his confession, but shifts his emphasis from being in a state of hopelessness to his enjoyment of spiritual liberation and analyzes his personality and his past behavior from a new perspective. The third section, "The Joy of Birth" (*Tanjō no yorokobi*), is expository and written in the third person—using "he" (*kare*) when referring to Akegarasu himself. The narrator compares Shakyamuni and Jesus, and highlights his need to pursue a religion of self-realization but not by observing precepts and worshipping an idol. The last two sections are written introspectively and include dialogues between the narrator, his friends, and the people in his community.

Although Kiyozawa avoided modern literature, Akegarasu presented *Before and after My Rebirth* as a work of popular literature. The second and third sections contain a number of his poems. In addition, the narrator refers to modern Western literature, including the works of Tolstoy, Rousseau, Zola, Maupassant, Flaubert, Ibsen, and Oscar Wilde. Further, as will be discussed shortly, he sympathizes with Shimazaki Tōson regarding Tōson's incestuous relationship.

Akegarasu used the commemoration of the seventeenth year of Kiyozawa's passing as an opportunity to present his naked self to the public. *Before and after My Rebirth* begins with the narrator's greetings to Kiyozawa:

> To Revered Teacher, Kiyozawa
>
> I was twenty-seven years of age when you passed away on June 6, 1903. Seventeen years have passed since then and I am now forty-three. I thought I was doing well for about ten years following your death, but when I was thirty-five or thirty-six, I became gloomy, and then, after I lost my wife at thirty-seven, I became confused. My old self died by my immoral act. But then a new Akegarasu Haya was born. Please listen to my confession about the changes in my mind.[70]

Rather than honoring Kiyozawa, the narrator risks humiliating himself and embarrassing other followers of the deceased master. The narrator reports the problem of his sexuality, immoral affairs, second marriage, and how he has misrepresented Kiyozawa's teaching to a person who is no longer living. By declaring his intention to study the *Larger Sutra*, however—which, before his demise, Kiyozawa planned to peruse—Akegarasu reconnects with his teacher and claims himself as Kiyozawa's successor.

In this connection, the relationship between the "external other" and the "internal other" that Krondorfer differentiates in male confessional writings is useful. Krondorfer defines the external other as "*to whom* he speaks"—such as "the implied, anticipated, sympathetic reader"—and the internal other as "*about whom* he speaks," including his "wives, children, mother, and lovers." A male confessant unfolds his story through imaginary dialogues with both the external and internal others. The division between the two is not always clear. For Augustine, for instance, God can simultaneously be his external and internal other. Krondorfer, however, points out that "drawing a distinction between external and internal others in confessiographies heightens our awareness of the confessant's interdependence on flesh-and-blood people during his life."[71]

For Akegarasu, Kiyozawa is both his external and internal other. While imagining the presence of his teacher (and readers), Akegarasu writes about four women—his wife, the nurse with whom he had a relationship, his second wife, and his mother. At the same time, the late Kiyozawa is his internal other, because Kiyozawa continued to inspire him. Thus, Akegarasu fictionalized Kiyozawa as his guardian and transcending other, who forgives him and embraces his unwholesome karma.

Akegarasu's crisis begins when he is diagnosed with tuberculosis. Since a discussion of his initial frailty is not included in *Before and after My Rebirth*, it is first necessary to turn to *The Ruin*. After visiting a medical doctor, the narrator broods over his physical condition:

> "Was I a man like that?"
> "Is this how I am going to end my life?"
> When such thoughts rise within me, I become so sad that I cannot stop crying. It is useless trying to explain what kind of sadness it is, or even why I feel so sad. For some reason, when I think, "Is this how I am going to end my life?" I fear tears will begin pouring from my eyes. Perhaps this is what novelists (*bungakusha*) refer to as "going downhill."
> I first felt this frailty during May of 1908 when I was diagnosed as having tuberculosis. On May 31, a day that I can never forget, I went to the Sasaki Clinic in Surugadai. The doctor examined my lungs thoroughly and told me that I had the beginning stages of tuberculosis. I didn't think anything of it then, but after I left the clinic and went to a pharmacy, the thought "Is this how my life will end?" rose within me, and hot tears began rolling down my cheeks. What will happen to honorable mother? How distressed she will be. What will happen to my family, my wife? How miserable I felt when I considered that I might die without achieving anything. I want to go to a sanatorium but I can't afford it, nor

can I stop working. What am I going to do? I feel as if my body is being crushed into a thousand pieces. What saved me then was the *nenbutsu* which escaped so naturally from my lips.

Namu amida butsu. That's what brought me back to life. That was when I heard the voice of the Buddha saying, "Why are you worried? I will take care of everything—your mother, your wife, and yourself." I felt as relieved then as when dark and foreboding clouds clear up.[72]

The narrator reacts emotionally to the diagnosis and imagines the end of his life. His reaction to tuberculosis, however, is different from Kiyozawa's. Kiyozawa maintained his rational attitude because he knew that he could not control his death; that was why he entrusted himself to Amida.[73] Unlike Kiyozawa, Akegarasu never developed symptoms of the illness, but his wife was plagued by tuberculosis and that disrupted Akegarasu's career. In *The Ruin*, the narrator broods, "if her sickness continues, I feel my progress will stop. My friends are successful and being promoted, but I'm gradually being buried in this rural land. There is no hope for me."[74] Further, the narrator complains, "My father died long ago. My family is poor. I contracted tuberculosis. My wife now has the same illness. I'm in total darkness. How miserable my life is. But what can I do? Nothing! Ahh—!"[75] The narrator is frustrated not only because his wife's health has worsened but also because he has to care for her ceaselessly, thus interrupting his work. The narrator, who has a strong desire for fame, feels frustrated when his wife becomes a burden.

Two problems emerge for the narrator while caring for his wife. First, he begins losing faith in Amida Buddha and expresses anger: "Why does she have to suffer so much? She has worked hard throughout her life. Why doesn't the Buddha take her to the Pure Land immediately? That's why I hate the Buddha."[76] On a different occasion, the narrator says, "Seeing her agony, I wonder why the Buddha does not save her. I doubted the Buddha's power and therefore hated it. I lost all hope and became frightened. But in the end the *nenbutsu* saved me."[77] By personifying Amida Buddha, the narrator seeks a worldly benefit, but when his wish is not granted, he is displeased. Yet he continues seeking comfort in reciting the *nenbutsu*. His attitude toward Amida changes, depending on his wife's condition. It remains ambiguous as to whether the *nenbutsu* serves as a vehicle for Buddhist wisdom and makes him realize his selfishness, or whether it nullifies his senses and temporarily alleviates his pains.

Second, while crying over his wife's slow death, the narrator battles his sexual desires. In *The Ruin*, he vividly describes his wife's death in the section

"The Death of My Wife" (*tsuma no shi*) and his memories of her in the section "About Fusako" (*Fusako no koto*). However, *The Ruin* ends with a series of his poems titled "The Muddled Mind" (*Midare gokoro*), which reveal his rising sexual appetite:

> Scenes of awful sickness fill my eyes,
> But for some reason I am serene . . .
> I felt purged
> When Fusako died.
> Though I vowed to remain a pure priest,
> How shameful that I
> Long for a woman
> Only five days after her funeral.
> Hating myself,
> I cry over the ego that has ruined my life.[78]

In this poem, Akegarasu laments his sexuality but considers lamenting to be inappropriate because he is supposedly grieving over the loss of his wife. The poem also expresses mixed feelings toward his wife: He loved her very much, but he had already been distracted by another woman. In fact, shortly after his wife's death, Akegarasu did sleep with a woman. This incident caused him to question his ability to be a Buddhist priest.

While envisioning the presence of his teacher, the narrator confesses to Kiyozawa how hard he struggled against bodily desires. The narrator felt lust rise in him at about the age of twenty. During four years of university life, he worked hard to divert his sexual energy by writing haiku and reading novels, making friends with those who were less sexually active, and studying under strict teachers. The narrator tried to contain his lecherous impulses by actively participating in Kiyozawa's reform movement. A year before Kiyozawa's death, the narrator married Fusako. When she became terminally ill, his sexual desire grew unmanageable:

> My wife's illness dragged on and I nursed her as best I could. I was determined to have her recover her health. Two or three months later, however, my sexual desires became so intense that I started to fear young women. I could not accept the advice to hire a nurse because I felt I would not be able to resist the temptation to bed her.
>
> One day, a friend of mine told me that an acquaintance had slept with a nurse when his wife was sick. I was terrified, but my

friend told me, "But you aren't like him." He seemed impressed by my dedication to my wife, but I felt extremely lonely because he did not understand my true feelings. Because I was unable to interact with a young nurse, I asked my wife's mother to help me nurse her. What a frightening premonition that was! About a week before my wife's death, my friend finally sent a young nurse to our house and I could not refuse her. Was she an angel? Or was she a devil? Was she a daughter of Mātaṅgī, a tantric goddess? Or was she a reincarnation of Avalokiteśvara? Soon after my wife's passing, I was comforted by this sympathetic young woman. I was no longer a moral person, whom I had pretended to be, and in fact, I had never been. When the inevitable happened, I lost my faith, my character, my work, and my reputation. That was when I realized how truly ugly I was.[79]

The narrator's lust grows as his wife's illness worsens and his spiritual strength abates. He blames women for his spiritual weakness, but simultaneously praises them for his liberation. Fusako's tuberculosis prevents him from making love to her and the nurse entices him to do what goes against his moral judgment. With Fusako's passing, he is released from his conjugal obligation and his spiritual torment, and his physical needs are met by the nurse.

The narrator, who regrets his sexual affair, seeks comfort not in the *nenbutsu*, but in the behavior of those with similar experiences. Shimazaki Tōson's novel *New Life* (*Shinsei*, 1918–1919) is of particular interest in this regard. In that novel, Tōson, through the main character of Kishimoto, revealed his incestuous relationship with his niece who came to help his family after his wife died. The narrator feels a deep sympathy with Kishimoto, who represents Tōson:

I believe Kishimoto's agonies cannot be understood without having similar experiences, and I kept thinking that his anguish and my struggles were alike. Kishimoto went to France. I also thought about going abroad, but because I could not leave my mother alone, I could not. I also thought of taking my life, but again because of my mother, I could not. I could bear disgrace and pain for myself, but I could not make her suffer. I therefore gave up running away from life or committing suicide. There was no way other than for me to suffer. That was when I discovered a new world opening up for me—a vast sky and unending earth. My old self died and I found that three women—Fusako, the nurse, and my mother—

had guided me to this new life. For me, they are manifestations of Amida and Avalokiteśvara.

Tōson must have suffered by keeping his secret to himself, even after returning from France. Writing *New Life* made his brother angry and his relatives disowned him. Tōson's case demonstrates that there is a cause to suffering. The cause of his suffering was that he could no longer hide his secret. It did not matter how astonishing that secret was, how much his confession would trouble others, or how badly he would be humiliated by telling the truth. Tōson must have felt that he could not be saved unless he disclosed his past by writing *New Life*. I understand completely. In my case, I was somewhat relieved because a journalist had already written about my affair, though his article was not completely accurate. Still, I felt bad about it. I therefore must confess my affair to you, even though it will cause further trouble for the nurse.[80]

Tōson's *New Life* served as a point of reference for Akegarasu. The narrator of *Before and after My Rebirth* feels worse than Kishimoto, because he was unable to escape the incident by going abroad. (It is worth noting that the narrator of *New Life* calls Kishimoto a "man inspired to attain Buddhist truth" *[hosshin sha]*.[81]) For that, he blames his mother, but venerates all three women since they have formed a reverse karmic condition (*gyakuen*, or what seems to be a negative event in one's life becomes the opportunity for one to understand the Dharma) that allows him to understand who he is. Nevertheless, the narrator remains insensitive to the nurse who will become the subject of gossip.[82]

In addition to Kishimoto in *New Life*, the narrator sympathizes with Paphnutius in Anatole France's *Thais* and quotes Nietzsche's *Thus Spoke Zarathustra*. From his point of view, both Paphnutius and Zarathustra reject God and heaven as abstract entities, and instead embrace love and desire as proof of life. For the narrator, Paphnutius's words ("God, heaven—all that is nothing. There is nothing true but this worldly life, and the love of human beings."[83]) represent his own voice when he loses his wife. Zarathustra's sayings, such as "This old saint in the forest hath not yet heard of it, that *god is dead*!," "I love him," or "The Superman is the meaning of the earth," also resonate deeply within him.[84] Based on those words, the narrator constructs "the significance of the earth" in his own words:

> At my wife's vigil, I vowed to never marry again. But I had an affair, just three weeks after her death. Was I degenerate? Was I

sinful? But how can a degenerate and sinful person become more degenerate or become even more sinful? Is the true me the "I" that speaks about degeneration and who feels ashamed? Or is the true me the "I" who sleeps with another woman? Why are the flames of sexual desires that flare up in me called degenerate? After all, I was born because my parents had similar desires. Why is it considered sinful when such a fire burns my entire body and reveals the naked me? All right, call it degenerate, call it sinful, but that is who I am. Kiyozawa sensei, that is the significance of earth [that is what it means to be human].

That is why I decided to marry again. I took the woman I loved most as my second wife. That is Fusako [same pronunciation but different kanji characters from those of his first wife]. Remember? She may have sat on your lap when you came to Kyoto.[85]

The narrator is no longer brooding over his situation. His tone shifts to one of self-affirmation and he justifies his sexuality as part of human necessity. The death of his first wife leads to his spiritual death, whereas his second marriage brings him the joy of marital intercourse and a sense of rebirth. However, it is unclear how he reconciles with Amida Buddha, except for his renunciation of the idea of Amida's grace, which will be discussed momentarily. The narrator expresses a sense of guilt and *penthos*—which, in the Christian tradition, means "a subsequent process of intense grief and sorrow over the fallenness of humanity and over the felt distance to God and divine mercy"[86]—but not his reunification with Amida. In order to improve his understanding of Amida, the narrator decides to study the *Larger Sutra* and what Bodhisattva Dharmākara is.[87]

Kiyozawa's interest in the *Larger Sutra* makes the narrator realize how he has misunderstood Kiyozawa's life. The narrator apologizes to a person who now exists only in his memory. The narrator sees Kiyozawa as a leader who revolutionized the entire Buddhist world of Japan. He is proud of being his closest disciple. After Kiyozawa's death, despite opposition from conservative priests, the narrator and others promote his teaching, as if they are going to establish a new denomination named after Kiyozawa (*Kiyozawa-shū*). The narrator now recognizes that he did not understand the depth of Kiyozawa's self-introspective practice and that he had used Kiyozawa's teaching for personal gain. The presence of his teacher, as an imagined interlocutor, enables the narrator to reexamine his doctrinal understanding and decide on a new course of action—namely, studying the *Larger Sutra*. Now, like Kiyozawa, the narrator ceaselessly questions his selfhood through his engagement with sacred scriptures and declares that he is Kiyozawa's true successor.[88]

In *Before and after My Rebirth*, Akegarasu, at the same time, announced his independence from his teacher. First, he actively used modern literature as a means of explaining base passions and representing his mundane experience. For instance, the narrator quotes Tolstoy's "Father Sergius." If Kiyozawa had been alive, the discussion of modern literature would not have pleased him, but the narrator thinks that Father Sergius's experience resonates within him so he wishes for his teacher to hear the story of Father Sergius, who suffers from doubt about God and longs for the lust of flesh.[89]

Sergius renounces the world twice. The first renunciation does not involve the destruction of his inner self, but in the second renunciation, he becomes spiritually liberated and accepts death. According to the narrator, Sergius's act is similar to Siddhartha Gautama's renunciation. Siddhartha first went to the mountains in search of self-realization, while still believing in himself and deities, then descended the mountain after destroying his ego and abandoning his faith in the deities. Reflecting on Siddhartha's twice-born experience, the narrator states,

> I began worshipping the Buddha and propagating the efficacy of the Buddha's grace while you [Kiyozawa] were still alive. But whether I liked it or not, my Buddha had to disappear, together with my wife. Although it was a very convenient formula, because of the sinful person that I am, I can no longer believe in the idea of a sinful person being embraced by the Buddha's grace. If the Buddha does, in fact, have the power to do this, why did he not save my wife? I have come to understand that, unlike the God in Christianity, there is no transcendent Buddha who will manifest power in this world.[90]

For the narrator, the second renunciation means abandoning the idea of Amida's grace. He neither personifies Amida nor sees in Amida an absolute authority. By reflecting on his carnal desire and born-again experience through the episode about Father Sergius, the narrator sees himself in Sergius's struggle, but separates Sergius's experience from its Christian context and interprets it from a Buddhist perspective. While explaining his spiritual maturity, the narrator enunciates the difference between Buddhism and Christianity.

Intersections of the two religions seen through "Father Sergius" and *Before and after My Rebirth* can also be explained from the viewpoint of a narrative pattern. In both writings, the main characters are the clergy who come to question their understanding of God and Amida Buddha, respectively, but continue to search for an answer within their own religious traditions. Prince Stepan Kasatsky first leaves his imperial service after losing his fiancée to the emperor and becomes Father Sergius, and then relinquishes his monastic life because he realizes that he thought he had served people in the name of God but had only served himself, and he now wishes to serve God. In *Before and after My Rebirth*, Akegarasu's literary alter ego first propagated Amida Buddha's grace enthusiastically, and then breaks faith with his personified Buddha and becomes a "true" follower of Kiyozawa. In other words, in "Father Sergius," the narrative pattern of "fall" and "redemption" is repeated, whereas in *Before and after My Rebirth*, that of "ground, path, and goal" is replayed by the narrator, who thinks he has already discovered a path and attained a goal. In each respective cycle, Kasatsky and the Akegarasu hero significantly modify their spiritual perspectives with a deeper understanding of themselves and their religion. In each story, the narrative develops around the protagonist who suffers from the separation of his loved one(s) and whose sexual desires bring about higher self-realization.

The use of sexuality and references to popular literature in confessional writing set Akegarasu apart from Kiyozawa. Whereas Kiyozawa occasionally used Christian concepts to supplement the Shin Buddhist doctrine and showed no interest in the representation of Christianity in Western novels, Akegarasu incorporated literary expressions of Christianity into his confessional writings, but rejected Christian doctrine as a whole. For him, popular literature allowed base passions, such as sexual desire and longing for romantic love, and allowed the reality of human conditions in modern society to be portrayed. He read modern fiction not merely as a source of entertainment, but as didactic literature, which could be applied to his self-analysis. It was an innovative medium for him to discuss his problems, rebel against traditional religious authority, and yet express his need for spiritual comfort. Akegarasu also knew that he could attract a wider audience, who would read his confessional writings in the same way they read novels, and that popular literature could serve as a gateway to their religious experience, thus recruiting potential Shin Buddhist converts.

The second point where Akegarasu departed from Kiyozawa was in his employment of mystical expressions. In the second section of *Before and after My Rebirth*, Akegarasu replicated one of his earlier essays, "After Returning to the Womb of the Buddha." In order to announce his spiritual recovery, he had published this essay exactly one year after confessing his crisis in the previously mentioned article "Is This How I Am Going to Ruin Myself?" The essay "After Returning to the Womb of the Buddha" depicted his mystic encounter:

For about a year—from the autumn before last year to last autumn—I felt like I was returning to the Buddha's womb [like wandering around in the dark area beneath the inner altar of Zenkōji temple]. Surely my dead wife had dragged me there. Once in the womb, she briskly got out, leaving me behind. I heard that evil rascals who go there turn into cows, horses, dogs, or cats, but I became a beast that didn't look like any of those animals. My chest was human-like, but my head was like that of a Buddha. I was all tail below my waist and very hairy. I had imagined myself looking like a beast like this in the past, but that image never appeared as clearly as it did last year.

[Inside the temple hall,] I lost the vision of the Buddha and felt I was in total darkness. I called out to my wife but she didn't respond. Crying in that completely dark place of my mind, the *nenbutsu* suddenly came out of my mouth. I then felt a key in my hand. [Instantly] I knew that it was a key that would lead me to the lotus petal on which the Buddha was seated. I also sensed that this key could only be found by those in complete darkness.

As I moved aimlessly forward, I heard my uncle say, "I'll leave now." That was when I realized he was there too. I passed through the womb and found myself at the edge of a bright temple hall. Though I was no longer a beast, I couldn't help feeling that now that I was back to being a human, a beast would pursue me. Shaking with fear, I sat down in front of the statue of the Buddha and cried tears of remorse. In front of my tear-darkened eyes, I saw the Buddha looking at me compassionately, as if he were saying, "You must have suffered. You must have grieved. How terrible you must have felt!" Next to the Buddha, I saw my wife and uncle.

That was when I was saved. I was reborn! When I thought about it, I realized that I had passed through the dark womb that was right under the seat of the Buddha. How delighted I was![91]

It is unclear whether Akegarasu actually had such a vision or if he invented this scene to dramatize his twice-born experience. Either way, the narrator personifies Amida Buddha and mystifies the moment of his conversion. This mystic expression is puzzling, however, when compared with his previous statement in *Before and after My Rebirth*, where the narrator stops personifying Amida as a savior who can generate worldly benefits. *Before and after My Rebirth* was compiled about six years after he published "After Returning to the Womb of the Buddha." Akegarasu might, therefore, have avoided reproducing the story of his mystic encounter in *Before and after My Rebirth* if he had regarded it as not representing his renewed understanding of Amida Buddha. On the other hand, he may have purposely duplicated his supernatural experience with Amida and woven it into his confession because he was aware of the literary effect such a narrative would have to spiritually move readers.

Critics' assessments of Akegarasu's experience vary. According to Mizushima Ken'ichi, after giving up the principle of Amida's grace, Akegarasu began diligent study of the *Larger Sutra* and realized the need to internalize the scriptural passages as his own experience. He took the Buddha Sovereign Monarch of the World's words "you yourself will know,"[92] spoken to Bodhisattva Dharmākara, as a sign of questioning a self, and related it to Kiyozawa's statement: "Our true self is nothing but this: Committing our total existence to the wondrous working of the Infinite, then settling down just as we are in our present situation."[93] By studying the characteristics of Amida's original vow, in Mizushima's view, Akegarasu redefined Shin Buddhism as a religion of self-realization but not of self-consolation.[94]

On the other hand, Yamamoto Nobuhiro, who is skeptical about changes in Akegarasu's perspective, presents a different view. He believes Akegarasu continued to justify his base passions and avoided taking a critical Buddhist stance. That is why Akegarasu was easily carried away by the ideology of the day. Akegarasu passionately supported the Russo-Japanese War and took part in developing Higashi Honganji's so-called wartime theology. Yamamoto suggests that the series of Akegarasu's confessions demonstrates his "flip-flop" nature—easily changing his stance depending on external circumstances. Further, Yamamoto argues that despite his love for his teacher, Akegarasu did not comprehend Kiyozawa's religious point of view as deeply as he thought he had.[95] In fact, Akegarasu remained an amorous and provocative Shin Buddhist priest. Later he had what he called a "miracle-like love affair with two individuals"[96] and made no effort to hide his extramarital love affair.

Miyamoto Matahisa finds a middle ground in understanding Akegarasu. He argues that Akegarasu did not understand his love affairs in Buddhist terms, such as being embraced by Amida's grace, but held a so-what attitude toward his affairs. He then internalized the Shin Buddhist principle of *akunin shōki*—Amida Buddha embraces those who suffer unwholesome karma—and used it to illustrate his liberation from social conventions and obligations that had restrained his life. Because he was thrilled with the throbbing pulse of life, Akegarasu supported labor movements, socialism, democracy, and the Russian Revolution. On the other hand, he rejected institutions, sciences, and civilizations when they restricted the development of human life. In Miyamoto's opinion, Akegarasu was not rational but emotional.[97]

In addition to Yamamoto and Miyamoto, Soga Ryōjin—one of Akegarasu's contemporaries, who later became a prominent scholar of Shin Buddhist studies—had already questioned the nature of Akegarasu's confession. As early as 1910, when Akegarasu was propagating the principle of Amida Buddha's grace, Soga published the essay "Confession" (*kokuhaku*) in *Seishinkai*, in which he wrote the following:

> When confessing our faith, we say, "we believe in the evil nature of a self" and "we believe in the immeasurable power of the Tathagata's vow." But is our confession free from lies? When I think that confession has such a nature, I cannot stop shivering. . . . Are we really able to believe in our evil nature and entrust ourselves to the power of the Tathagata's original vow?[98]

For Soga, faith was not about expressing emotions and bursting into tears, but rather reflected Buddhist wisdom that enabled him to question all his assumptions, especially assumptions about himself.[99] Soga was thus skeptical about the notion of Buddha's grace and the practice of confession, although they were then becoming popular among young Shin Buddhists.

Conclusion

This chapter has demonstrated a literary aspect of Akegarasu's confessional writings and expanded the scope of personal fiction. *Before and after My Rebirth* can be read as an autobiographical novel and raises issues concerning the property of *kindai bungaku*, or modern Japanese literature, formed around the works created by literary writers. Disciplinary boundaries, such as Buddhist studies and literary studies, limit our perception of a work like *Before and after My Rebirth* and cause it to be read and interpreted only through the lens of an established framework with a disciplinary and denominational label on it.

The boundaries between Buddhist writers and literary authors are ambiguous in confessional writings. Buddhist thinkers, such as Kiyozawa, Chikazumi, and Akegarasu, assumed a specific readership when writing about their conversion experiences and published their confessions in Buddhist journals. For literary writers, such as Sōseki, Katai, and Shiga, the range of their intended audience was much broader. They wrote for literary circles and general readers. Sōseki, in particular, serialized his work, including *Grass on the Wayside*, in a national newspaper. Their personal fiction neither represented a particular Buddhist organization nor promoted a specific doctrine, although it included Buddhist ideas and was read without Buddhist knowledge. Sōseki, Katai, and Shiga did not confess their problems in order to start a new life; rather, writing personal fiction helped them understand themselves as well as that which had confused them in the past—to apply Karatani Kōjin's theory of inversion in his study of the system of confession in modern Japan. In the case of Akegarasu, writing *Before and after My Rebirth* was a way to regain and redefine his Buddhist faith. He placed confessional writing not only within a realm of religious activities conducive to self-transformation and inspiring to others, but also within popular culture. In the next chapter, a further effort is made to question and enlarge the scope of personal fiction by taking history into consideration and situating it at the intersection of literature, Buddhism, and history.

CHAPTER FIVE

A Shin Buddhist Historical Novel

Niwa Fumio's *The Buddha Tree* (*Bodaiju*, 1955–1956) is perhaps the best-known novel in the West depicting the life of a modern Japanese Buddhist priest. This chapter, however, concentrates on *Guardians of the Dharma Castle* (*Hōjō o mamoru hitobito*) written by Matsuoka Yuzuru. Because of their autobiographical elements, *The Buddha Tree* and *Guardians of the Dharma Castle* are similar. Niwa and Matsuoka were both born in Pure Land Buddhist temple families and were expected to become resident priests of their family temples, but became writers instead. They differ in that *Guardians* is documentary in nature. When read today, *Guardians* is an important work of historical fiction. It was also a bestseller that contributed to the so-called "Religious Boom," during Japan's Taishō period (1912–1926).[1] *Guardians* is one of the early works that portrayed the lives of Buddhist clergy in modern Japan, depicted characters associated with Buddhist temples, and included a discussion of Buddhist doctrine. Unfortunately, it is available only in Japanese.[2]

This chapter explores another aspect of Buddhism and literature in modern Japan. It situates *Guardians* at the intersection of the historical novel and the personal novel. Representations of a Shin Buddhist denomination and its two historical events, how Matsuoka placed his hero within the historical development of Shin Buddhism, and the ways in which the protagonist condemns an established Shin Buddhist organization based on his understanding of the historical development of Buddhism are analyzed.

Matsuoka was born the eldest son of a Shin Buddhist temple family. When he was grappling with his identity in his teens, the *Kōkōdō* continued to reform Higashi Honganji after Kiyozawa's death. In *Guardians*, Miyagi Entai, the main character and Matsuoka's alter ego, clashes with his father, who is a resident priest of a temple, and criticizes the Buddhist organization of which his father is a member. Miyagi questions the leaders of its reform movement because his vision of Buddhism as a living religion is radically different from theirs. To put it more broadly, Matsuoka documents the lives of his parents, lay members' attitudes, activities of Kiyozawa's followers, and a religious ceremony held at the Higashi Honganji head temple, while the narrator reflects the impact of the Shin Buddhist reform movement on Miyagi's life.

Although *Guardians* is a work of fiction, it can also be read as a religious testament. The text reveals Matsuoka's religious practice as he documented, interpreted, and fictionalized contemporary Shin Buddhist events. Additionally, the text drew public attention to the management of an established Shin Buddhist organization that Matsuoka criticized and to which he proposed a reform through his fiction. Despite Matsuoka's attempts to question Shin Buddhist authorities, however, his practice created an unintended consequence. Because *Guardians* depicted the lives of ordinary clergy and laity as well as local Shin Buddhist history, it made the story of Higashi Honganji a living history and contributed to the expansion of its institutional history.

Guardians is also a work of path literature. As Miyagi, like Matsuoka himself, is expected to succeed his father and become a priest, he identifies a Buddhist temple as the cause of his suffering (ground). Miyagi's goal is to change his father's perspective on priesthood—which is taken for granted as a hereditary profession in Miyagi's opinion—and to destroy the temple in which Miyagi was born and raised. In order to convince his father, Miyagi goes back and forth between Tokyo and his hometown in a quest for the knowledge of Buddhism (path). During these trips, Miyagi meets and engages in a series of dialogues with progressive Shin Buddhist priests; he visits Kyoto to observe a major Shin Buddhist event, which leads him to identify their problems and to justify his position against his father; and he befriends people who are sympathetic to his situation. Because his suffering is caused by the institutional Buddhist practice and because his goal is to change his father's perspectives—instead of transforming his own perspective, which might have allowed Miyagi to accept priesthood as his future occupation—*Guardians* differs from the works of path literature discussed in the previous chapters. Yet Miyagi experiences a series of self-realizations and gains knowledge of the Buddhist organization he criticizes.

To better understand the cause of Miyagi's suffering, an explanation of the concept of Temple Buddhism is useful. According to Stephen G. Covell, Temple Buddhism refers to "the Buddhism as lived by the members of those sects of Japanese Buddhism that were founded before the 1600s."[3] Temple Buddhism consists of Buddhist temples subsumed under a sect or denomination and maintained by the reciprocal relationship between clergy and laity. A priest officiates at funerals and memorial services for the temple members, who in return take care of the temple, the priest, and his family. Before analyzing Matsuoka's fictional treatment of Temple Buddhism, the conceptual frame of this chapter and the background of *Guardians* are discussed: characteristics of documentary fiction, which includes historical fiction; a biography of Matsuoka and the climate of religious literature in modern Japan—the rise of the so-called Taishō Religious Literature to which *Guardians* contributed; and a summary of the work.

History and Fiction

According to Barbara Foley, the scope of the documentary novel changed over time in the West, but this genre was in line with the literary trends of the day. For instance, during the seventeenth and eighteenth centuries, it was similar to what is today known as the "news/novel discourse." During the nineteenth century, it took the form of the historical novel, expanding from realism, and at the beginning of the twentieth century, it contributed to the discussion of modernism. The documentary novel further produced the fictional autobiography, in which an artist-hero "assumes the status of a real person inhabiting invented situations" and the metahistorical novel, in which a linear perception of the historical process is no longer assumed.[4]

Harry Shaw shares a similar view about the connection between the style of historical fiction and the mainstream literary form of the day. He states that "[i]n most respects, historical fiction depends upon the formal techniques and cultural assumptions of the main traditions of the novel."[5] It was therefore not surprising for Matsuoka to formulate *Guardians* as a work of personal fiction, because personal fiction was a dominant form of modern Japanese literature at that point.

When reading historical novels, Foley proposes a scheme similar to the one used in Gestalt psychology, in which a drawing simultaneously invites two kinds of perception—either a duck or a rabbit, but no other animal. It is a means of conveying two kinds of cognition—factual and pseudo-factual discourses—based on the "mimetic contract" between writer and reader.[6] Foley argues that in the case of documentary novels, the mimetic contract is that of an "analogous configuration"—that is, the writer explains historical events to the reader not simply by creating characters and events modeled after historical figures and incidents, but by totalizing "the mutual interaction of different textual features—characters, events, social conditions, philosophical debates."[7] The mimetic contract enables the writer to have the reader participate in his rendering of the past, and while the reader can disagree with the writer about the interpretation of that past, analogous configuration tends to "efface the reader's conscious awareness of the informing authorial perspective."[8] Historical fiction serves as a means to imagine and interpret historical events, but this process is also subjective and biased.

In *Guardians*, the representation of Temple Buddhism is critical. Miyagi takes temple life, a group of progressive young Buddhist priests, and a religious ceremony—all of which Matsuoka documented—as opportunities to propose a reform of Temple Buddhism. Miyagi's criticism of Temple Buddhism is driven by his belief in religious revolution; the narrator describes historical Shin Buddhist events ideologically with the emerging Buddhist movement of "returning to the founders of denominations." The narrator's views on Temple Buddhism are therefore judgmental from the beginning.

Matsuoka is not the first Japanese writer to integrate religious ideals into a historical novel. Mori Ōgai (1862–1922), who is often compared with Natsume Sōseki as an outstanding literary figure of his time, is the pioneer of Japanese historical fiction. According to J. Thomas Rimer, Ōgai examined Japan's past carefully in order to explore its future, and for him, historical novels served as a means of contemplation.[9] Further, Rimer states that "the best of Ōgai's work manifests both the moral power sanctioned in the Confucian tradition and a subtlety and finesse of style derived from the West, both fused into a harmonious whole."[10] David Dilworth shares a similar view, stating that for Ōgai, historical literature served as a vehicle to express exemplary human qualities linked to Confucian and Buddhist sensibilities, which he captured from historical chronicles of medieval Japan, such as *The Tale of the Heike* (*Heike monogatari*), *The Chronicle of Grand Peace* (*Taiheiki*), and *The Chronicle of Minamoto no Yoshitsune* (*Gikeiki*), as well as *The Treasury of Loyal Retainers* (*Chūshingura*) produced during the Tokugawa era.[11] Rather than recapturing the Buddhist sensibilities of medieval Japan, however, Matsuoka dealt primarily with the history of a Buddhist denomination with which his family temple was affiliated.

Matsuoka Yuzuru's (1891–1969) Life and the Rise of the Taishō Religious Literature

Matsuoka Yuzuru was born on September 28, 1891, the first son of Matsuoka Zen'en—the Shin Buddhist priest at Shōkōzan Honkakuji, located in present-day Nagaoka City in Niigata Prefecture—and Rue. He was given the name Zenjō 善讓, which he later changed to Yuzuru 讓 against his father's wishes, by removing the character 善 from his first name. This incident is recreated in *Guardians* when the hero changes his name from Miyagi Entai 宮城円泰 to Miyagi Yasushi 宮城泰. Matsuoka lived at his family temple until he attended First High School in Tokyo, so the observance of funerary rites was the norm in his juvenile life. As indicated by the fact that Matsuoka's literary alter ego reads aloud Shinran's magnum opus, *Kyōgyōshinshō*, Matsuoka was familiar with Shinran's writings.

Matsuoka graduated from First High School and entered Tokyo Imperial University, where he majored in philosophy. At First High School, he read a wide variety of literary works and became friends with Kikuchi Kan, Kume Masao, Naruse Seiichi, and Akutagawa Ryūnosuke. Through Kume and Akutagawa, Matsuoka joined Natsume Sōseki's Thursday Association (*mokuyō-kai*) in the fall of 1915 and was close to Sōseki for about a year until Sōseki's death. Matsuoka, Akutagawa, Kume, Naruse, and Kikuchi created the Fourth Edition of *Shinshichō*, a literary magazine, with Sōseki as their supervisor. Matsuoka then published his first novella, "A Blowfish Buddhist Priest" (*Fugu oshō*, 1916), in which the narrator criticizes Buddhist clergy in a comical yet serious way. The plot consists of a Buddhist priest raking in money by officiating at funerals and conducting memorial services.[12] From the beginning of his career, Matsuoka questioned the life of a resident priest, criticized Buddhist organizations, and searched for an alternative Buddhist way of life.

Matsuoka's career as a writer was not without problems. In 1918, he married Natsume Fudeko, Sōseki's eldest daughter, but this marriage became the subject of gossip among the literary writers, who referred to it as the "Wrecked Ship Incident" (*Hasen jiken*) named after *The Wrecked Ship* (*Hasen*) written by Kume Masao, who had also fallen in love with Fudeko.[13] Kume won public sympathy by presenting himself as the victim of a love triangle and confessing his agony, while Matsuoka appeared to have cheated his friend. According to Sekiguchi Yasuyoshi, who interviewed Fudeko, Sōseki's widow, Kyōko, initially suggested that Fudeko marry Kume because Matsuoka was supposed to take over his family temple. Kyōko's remark had given Kume the impression that he was entitled to marry Fudeko, although Fudeko herself preferred Matsuoka.[14] As a result of the scandal caused by Kume's work, Matsuoka ended his friendship with Kume, left the literary circle, and even thought about giving up his literary career.[15]

Matsuoka resumed his career by publishing *The Mona Lisa* in 1921. He wrote *Guardians* and short stories, as well as a variety of essays on the topic of religion.[16] He also wrote other historical Buddhist novels, such as *The Life of Shakyamuni* (*Shakuson no shōgai*, 1935) and *The Story of Dunhuang* (*Tonkō monogatari*, 1943).[17] Toward the end of the Pacific War, Matsuoka and his family evacuated to his hometown in Niigata. After the war, he resumed his friendship with Kume, and in 1947 they worked together to commemorate the thirtieth anniversary of Sōseki's death. Matsuoka remained in Nagaoka and continued to write until he died of natural causes on July 22, 1969. Perhaps because of his advanced age at the time of his death, Matsuoka had ceased to be critical of the priesthood as a hereditary profession and even asked his nephew, resident priest of Honkakuji, to officiate at his funeral when he died. Matsuoka's posthumous Shin Buddhist name is *Muryōjuin shaku zenjō*. As implied by the name *zenjō*, later in life he was able to accept the birth name his parents gave him.[18]

Today, Matsuoka is better known as a precursor of Sōseki studies than as a writer himself. After moving into Sōseki's house as a son-in-law, he kept Sōseki's study room intact until the bombing of Tokyo damaged it in 1945. Matsuoka published Sōseki's unpublished works,[19] and because of his dedication, the entirety of Sōseki's work came to be known. Matsuoka is also known as Sōseki's direct student who interpreted Sōseki's *sokuten kyoshi*—"leaving oneself by becoming one with heaven"—from a philosophical perspective. According to Matsuoka's *Religious Dialogue* (*Shūkyōteki mondō*), Sōseki is believed to have said,

> Recently, I have finally [attained] a state of mind which I wish to call "leaving oneself by becoming one with heaven," even though others might express it differently. This means to leave the small self, which is ordinarily called the "I," and entrust oneself to the commands of the great self in universal nature. Having said this, however, I feel that words are not enough to describe such a state. In its presence, arguments, ideals or principles, which are said to be very important, appear to me like trifling matters; yet, things that are usually seen as less important, appear to me as something that possesses some kind of meaning. In other words, from the viewpoint of the observer, this means that one is able to see everything equally, or that "difference is instantly non-distinction."[20]

In Matsuoka's words, *sokuten kyoshi* suggests a state of detachment and an impartial view that is less egocentric and more egalitarian. His explanation of *sokuten kyoshi* should not, however, be taken at face value, because his record appears to be the combination of his teacher's fragmentary words and his own interpretation of them from a religious perspective.²¹ Nevertheless, it shows one possible understanding of *sokuten kyoshi* that Sōseki never articulated clearly. As discussed in the previous chapters, because Sōseki was interested in Buddhism, it is not surprising that one of Sōseki's students chose Buddhism as his literary theme.

Guardians of the Dharma Castle became a best seller as part of an unprecedented upsurge in religious literature during the Taishō period. This literary movement began with the publication of Kurata Hyakuzō's (1891–1943) *The Priest and His Disciples*, based on the life of Shinran, which was also a best seller and sold well for a long time.²² According to Chiba Masaaki, who analyzes the Taishō Religious literature (*Taishō shūkyō shōsetsu*), the second decade of the twentieth century has been characterized as a period when literary authors reflected their attitudes of "seeking the way" in their works (*kyūdōteki sakuhin*). Further, movements such as the "Taisho elite intellectual cultivation" (*Taishō kyōyō shugi*) and humanism (*jindō shugi*) blossomed.²³ In addition, Tolstoy studies became popular among Japanese writers who reevaluated Christianity, intellectuals such as Watsuji Tetsurō and Yanagi Muneyoshi initiated a wide range of religious discussions, and Nishida Kitarō's *Inquiry into the Good* was widely read. All these factors paved the way for *The Priest and His Disciples* to become a bestseller.²⁴

Following the success of *The Priest and His Disciples*, the "Shinran boom" (*Shinran dairyūkō*) emerged during the 1920s. Honganji organizations also spread what was called the "Shinran illness" (*Shinran kaze*).²⁵ In 1921, *Letters of Nun Eshinni* (*Eshinni monjo*) was published, after the letters were discovered in a Nishi Honganji storehouse. These letters were proof of Shinran as a historical person. Several Japanese historians, using empirical methods of studying history that originated in the West, had asserted that Shinran never existed.²⁶ In 1923, ten denominations of Shin Buddhism jointly celebrated the seven hundredth anniversary of the founding of the Shin Buddhist sect (*rikkyō kaishū*). All these events added momentum to creating the so-called "Shinran Literature."²⁷ *Guardians* must have been seen as an extension of this literary development. Although this work does not deal with Shinran per se, it brings to light the internal affairs of a long-standing Buddhist denomination, Higashi Honganji, founded on his teaching and led by his descendants.

Despite its bestseller status, Japanese critics did not direct serious attention to *Guardians*. They seem to have lost interest in it because they perceived it to be a continuation of "Home to Protect the Dharma" (*Gohō no ie*, 1917), a short autobiographical work of Matsuoka's, on which they had already commented both positively and negatively. Literary critics considered *Guardians* to be narrowly focused and not artistic enough for serious evaluation, while Shin Buddhist leaders simply ignored *Guardians* because the suggestions made in the work were not useful for their organization. In other words, most of the critics and religious thinkers treated the work merely as one of personal fiction written by a person who was unhappy about his family's temple life, and overlooked its documentary importance.[28]

A Summary of *Guardians of the Dharma Castle*

Guardians consists of three sections: *Book of Life* (*Seikatsu-hen*, 1923), *Book of Faith* (*Shinkō-hen*, 1925), and *Book of Criticism* (*Hihan-hen*, 1926). The first section, which overlaps "Home to Protect the Dharma," is much more autobiographical than the second and third sections.[29] Throughout the series, Matsuoka portrays his hero's struggles over his personal obligation to become a temple priest and the clash between his literary ego and his father. Matsuoka then places the conflict in a larger historical event—the reform movement of the Higashi Honganji organization—and models his characters on historical figures, such as Tada Kanae (1875–1937) and Akegarasu Haya, leaders of the *Kōkōdō* movement after the passing of Kiyozawa Manshi.[30] In other words, Matsuoka directs his criticism to the entire Higashi Honganji organization and attempts to restore Shinran's spirit in his own way—using fiction as a form of protest.

The work begins with a heated exchange between father and son at Kōmyōji. Miyagi Entai considers the lifestyle of a resident priest to be the fundamental problem of Temple Buddhism and refuses to succeed his father, whereas the father insists that priests and temples are indispensable for the transmission of Dharma. The relationship between Miyagi and his father is complicated by a third person, Miyagi's mother. Whenever Miyagi attempts to move away from his family temple, the negative side of which is represented by his father, he returns because of the influence of his mother.

Miyagi takes the ordination examination at the age of eighteen for his mother's sake and in order to appease his father. Because the head temple in Kyoto is heavily indebted, administrative leaders come up with plans to have local priests and lay members make more donations. The ordination examination is a simple way to collect money, so they make the exam easy in order to increase the number of candidates. For the examination, Miyagi is taken to a regional temple by his father, but he detests what he sees there—a red-light district around the regional temple, his father's arrogant behavior, fellow ordination candidates who look unintelligent, and haughty proctor-priests.

Miyagi purposely misreads a sacred text and upsets the examiner. Despite his attitude, Miyagi passes. He then goes to Tokyo for higher education without continuing the ordination process.

Miyagi further rebels against his father by changing his name. He removes one character from his given name—which doubles as his Dharma name—in order to express his determination to not become a temple priest. He is now Miyagi Yasushi. He clashes with his father, who admits that he did not have an authentic religious experience when he took over the family temple at the age of twenty, because he was too busy officiating at services and caring for the congregation that supported him. The father is apologetic, but at the same time demands that Miyagi examine his own attitude toward Temple Buddhism because he has been fed by the temple members.[31]

Miyagi befriends Ōtsuki, who has a similar family background and studies at the denomination's university (*shūmon daigaku*). Ōtsuki does not deny the necessity of temples; he only proposes to reform their structure and financial conditions, as well as restore a spiritual life to the priests. In his mind, the system of hereditary abbots needs to be eliminated, because entrusting into Amida Buddha's original vow is more important than submitting to the abbot, who is considered a "living Buddha" (*iki botoke*), and because the Shin Buddhist order was founded on the spirit of "fellow followers." Ōtsuki also believes that the denomination's university must become an independent academic institution, free from interference by the head temple administrators who manipulate academic authorities.[32]

Many of Ōtsuki's positions actually embody Kiyozawa Manshi's visions. In his effort to reform Higashi Honganji, Kiyozawa advocated restoring doctrine as the foundation of the denomination. He then established Shinshū University in Tokyo in order to separate it from Higashi Honganji's traditional academic institutions in Kyoto.[33] He emphasized the importance of personal experience in spiritual understanding rather than fitting one's religious experience into the established pattern of Shin Buddhist life.

Miyagi, on the other hand, rejects both temples and priests because temple management has become the means by which the majority of priests make their living. He believes that temples are unnecessary and that each household should become a Dharma gathering place where each follower finds a spiritual standpoint. Miyagi argues that those who make religion their occupation should "have a regular job and dedicate themselves to others. They should neither covet nor talk about God, but give themselves to others and work with God because they are stray sheep. They should not sell their religion to others."[34] By using Christian terms such as "God" and "sin," Miyagi relates his discussion to other religions and points out that the religion promoted by Shin Buddhist priests lack those characteristics. He then directs his criticism to lay members. They are simply born into families registered with a temple with the obligation to make donations to their temple and the head temple in honor of the founder of the denomination. They merely observe funerals and memorial services according to tradition without understanding the teaching. Miyagi believes that a true religion cannot develop unless the head temple is destroyed, local temples are closed, and Buddhist priests are laicized.[35]

Ōtsuki suddenly dies of illness. For Miyagi, Ōtsuki was the hope for the denomination's future, because Miyagi could share his experience of temple life and religious ideas with him. Ōtsuki's last words linger in Miyagi's ears:

> First, return to the founder. Then go beyond him. "To return" means to honor his spirit and "to go beyond" means to transcend the conventions of old. It doesn't mean regressing to the society of seven hundred years ago; rather it means manifesting the founder's spirit in our lives today.[36]

Miyagi becomes depressed because of Ōtsuki's death and his health worsens. His parents bring him home to recuperate. He realizes his parents have not gotten along well after he left for Tokyo and feels bad about it.

In the second section, Miyagi is back in Tokyo and observes the reform movement of young Buddhist priests. One day he attends a Shin Buddhist gathering in Kudanzaka, Tokyo, in order to meet Tachibana Hōjin, whose talk has aroused his interest. After the meeting, he makes friends with Takamine, who is seeking a spiritual resolution to the survivor guilt he feels after a shipwreck. Miyagi and Takamine participate in another gathering in Kudanzaka organized by a group of young Shin Buddhists to honor the seventh anniversary of their teacher's passing. These students have carried on his spiritual movement, called *Seishin shugi*, in an attempt to reform their denomination. Miyagi and Takamine listen to various lectures, including Tachibana's, and continue conversing with him.

This section features characters modeled after historical figures. The gathering at Kudanzaka suggests Chikazumi Jōkan's activities in Tokyo. The bearers of the reform movement honor the passing of their teacher, Kiyozawa Manshi. Tachibana represents some parts of Kiyozawa's life and ideas, but also resembles Tada Kanae, one of Kiyozawa's leading followers. Miyagi and Takamine then meet Daidō Tesshin, a character who resembles Akegarasu Haya, known for his boldness and sensational remarks, as discussed in the previous chapter.[37]

Daidō is radical, but attracts the young. He strips away their hypocrisy as if peeling a fruit, leaving them spiritually naked. He leads them to realize how strong their base passions are and how strongly they are attached to themselves. Through this process, he guides them to understand the efficacy of Amida Buddha's compassion, by which they come to accept themselves as they are. Traditional Buddhist leaders consider him a heretic, but juvenile delinquents, tuberculosis patients, and prostitutes all come to take refuge in Shin Buddhism because of his charisma and what he says. While Daidō's followers become zealous, Miyagi remains skeptical about their religious experiences and questions Daidō's method of proselytizing.[38]

One day Miyagi returns to his hometown. He has not changed his attitude toward Temple Buddhism, but wishes to apologize to his parents for his past behavior. By chance, he finds his mother consulting Daidō at a gathering about losing her Buddhist faith after her son (Miyagi) abandoned the temple. When Daidō curses her and points out the incorrectness of her Buddhist understanding, Miyagi steps in. He protects his mother and criticizes Daidō's proselytizing method as brainwashing. She considers Miyagi's return to be the result of the Buddha's miraculous work and regains her faith. Miyagi angrily asks her, "Who is more important, the Buddha or me? If the Buddha is more important, then forget about me. If not, then forget about the Buddha. The Buddha you speak of is nothing but the reflection of your own desires by which you are deceived, and that prevents you from taking right actions." When Daidō becomes furious about this turn of events, Miyagi's mother grabs her son's hand and leaves the gathering. Not knowing what to do, Daidō tells his crowd, "Look at them, that's the manifestation of the Buddha's compassion!"[39]

Miyagi finds a common problem with the reform leaders, including Tachibana and Daidō. They tend to judge who is right and who is wrong under the name of the compassionate Buddha. No matter how seriously they talk about the importance of experiencing a turning of the mind, they are resident priests who are bound by institutional rules and can neither give up their own temples nor encourage their members to seek Buddhism in their own ways. That is their fundamental contradiction.[40]

The third section opens with a description of a ceremony which commemorates the passing of the denomination's founder, Shinran. This ceremony is held only once every fifty years. Although disgusted with Temple Buddhism, Miyagi goes to the head temple, still wishing to discover something sacred or a religious community that will assure him of the correctness of Temple Buddhism. He loses hope, however, when attending a series of services at the head temple. In Miyagi's eyes, power, hierarchy, and money overrule this once-in-a-lifetime event. Modeled after government amnesty, the head of the denomination reinstates priests who had previously been excommunicated from the order, celebrates the highest title bestowed on the late abbot by the government, honors the imperial royal family members, and displays their gifts. The seating arrangement in the main hall reflects the attendants' ranking. The most privileged people—represented by the abbot and his family—are placed highest, followed by high-ranking priests, regular priests and special guests, leaders of the confraternities and the Buddhist women's associations throughout the country, with ordinary lay members at the bottom. Only one-tenth of the regular followers are admitted to the hall. Miyagi finds a hidden message in this seating arrangement: "The Dharma can only be purchased with money. Do not enter here if you don't have any."[41]

A long procession passes by. It consists of thousands of priests wearing expensive and glittering robes. They are separated into ten ranks by the colors of their robes. Miyagi is somewhat consoled at seeing his father among these priests wearing worn-out robes. There are also thousands of affluent lay members whom the head temple recognizes as distinguished supporters of the denomination. The service reaches its finale when the abbot, the living Buddha, appears in front of the crowd. Suddenly, chanting of the *nenbutsu* echoes throughout the temple compound.[42] Miyagi and Takamine are disappointed at the extravagant Buddhist ceremony. For them, the city of Kyoto is where dead religions prevail. Later they meet Tachibana, but he only irritates them by defending the denomination against their criticism and discussing the righteousness of the head temple and the abbot's inviolable authority. Tachibana simply preaches to them about the importance of introspection.[43]

The reform movement loses its momentum after the founder's commemorative service. The *Seishin shugi* group is eventually dissolved. (It split into two factions led by Tachibana and Kasuga Daijō, who was a Zen priest until proselytized by Daidō—Kasuga is modeled after Fujiwara Tetsujō [1879–1975].) Those who tried to reorganize the denomination return to their own temples. Tachibana returns to his temple and begins life as an ordinary resident priest who submits to the head temple's demands and bows toward members of his temple.[44]

Miyagi finds himself more challenged than before by this spiritual decline and attempts to persuade his father one last time. However, his father is not easily persuaded:

"You talk about freedom and liberation as soon as you open your month, don't you?" the father said. "But Entai, do you really believe there is absolute freedom in this world? We are merely human beings shackled by the karma of the three worlds. Speaking for myself, I'm bound by this temple, the head temple, the founder, our ancestors and teachers, the members, and my family. I have only limited freedom. Freeing myself from these responsibilities means the end of my life. I have no other way of making a living that I consider sacred. That's why this is my duty. I'm obliged to perform this work and that's the life I enjoy. Entai, don't you realize that you are killing me by trying to save me?"[45]

There is no common ground between the two because the father remains affiliated with the denomination, while the son is not. The father renews his vow to maintain his temple and rejects the son's suggestion that he give up the priesthood.

Guardians ends with a series of twists. One night, a fire burns down Miyagi's family temple and kills his younger sister. The cause of the fire remains unknown but Miyagi suspects Takamine is the arsonist. Before the fire, Miyagi spoke to Takamine about his desire to destroy his home temple as a way of restoring the relationship between parent and child and Takamine agreed with him. Miyagi realizes that his lifelong desire has finally been fulfilled, but only with the loss of his sister, and that makes his parents frantic. Although he did not set the fire, Miyagi blames himself for being its cause.

The destruction of the temple surprises Miyagi in another way. Rather than considering becoming members of a neighboring temple, the congregation immediately decides to rebuild their temple. After the inauguration ceremony of the new temple hall, Miyagi's father dies of illness. On his deathbed, he apologizes to Miyagi for having imposed his values on him and thanks Miyagi for making him aware of his egotistical desires.[46] *Guardians* ends with the following words of the father: "Your life begins now."[47]

Marxism as an Interpretive Tool of Temple Buddhism

Hasegawa Nyozekan (1875–1969), a journalist and critic who helped publish *Guardians*, characterized *Guardians* as a novel of "religious anarchism."[48] Matsuoka had been inclined to socialism during his high school years and at the beginning of his college life.[49] Concerning his motivation for writing *Guardians*, Matsuoka identified hereditary priests and their families to be the primary cause of problems in Temple Buddhism:

Temple life, through which a priest propagates Buddhism and talks about doctrine and faith, is an abnormal form of economic life. Unless temple life becomes more religious, or unless it is examined more deeply on the principle of receiving offerings, there will be no salvation. That is the fundamental idea of this work.[50]

For Matsuoka, creating *Guardians* was a way to direct "revolutionary observation" of Temple Buddhism: the religiosity of Temple Buddhism is lost because its economic foundation is incorrect.[51]

Miyagi's observation of Temple Buddhism brings to mind Karl Marx's perception of religion. Marx is known for his famous remark that "[r]eligion is the opiate of the masses." At the same time, Marx wrote, "Religious suffering is at one and the same time the expression of real suffering and a protest against real suffering." For Marx, religion is the expression of both an ideology that enforces a social hierarchy and a "protest" against suffering caused by economic inequality.[52] Religion develops dialectically through piety and man's concerns for worldly living, which includes man's economic needs.

Whether or not Matsuoka was aware of the role of religion in social protest is unclear, but his attitude toward Temple Buddhism represented a Japanese consciousness of the day. In 1920, the Japan Socialist League was formed, and in 1925, the Japan Proletarian Literary Federation organized its first meeting and gradually adopted a Marxist vision of society.[53] That is, "the point of view of the exploited and the marginalized," to borrow John Raines's words.[54] During the twenties and thirties, Marxism influenced Japanese philosophers, men of letters, and all kinds of Japanese intellectuals. According to Yoshitomo Takeuchi, they learned to "utilize Marxism not only to apprehend social reality in such separate categories as economics, law, politics, and ethics, but also to provide a method of grasping reality in all its inner relationships. Moreover, this was a method which demanded social responsibility on the part of the intellectuals."[55] Proletarian writers, in particular, considered their role to be depicting and examining the social reality of the day.[56]

According to Barbara Foley, changing strategies of representation reflect the "changing terms of the fictional contract in different social formations."[57] The Marxist vision is an example of such a social development that connects writer and reader in a shared view of modern Japanese society. To put it differently, *Guardians* provides a Marxist mode of religious cognition vis-à-vis Temple Buddhism. For Miyagi, Temple Buddhism reveals inherent conflicts between a spiritual life and a materialistic way of living, as well as between Buddhist detachment and the attachment of ordinary people, including priests.

He criticizes the lives of resident priests, examines the expansion of man's egotism, and portrays the corruption of an established religious organization and the growth of a new spiritual movement within it.

At the beginning of *Guardians*, Miyagi questions the ways in which the Buddhist clergy make a living. While expressing anxiety for his future and embarrassment about being a son of a Buddhist priest—since he was expected to take over that position from his father—he uses the diary to fight his destiny:

> Why am I ashamed of having been born the son of a Buddhist priest? Two responses always come to mind. First, it can't be helped because it is my fate. Second, although I know it can't be helped, I also can't stop feeling ashamed. I try to accept my fate and live with it, but I always look for excuses. On the one hand, I try to resign myself to my destiny, but on the other hand, I resist it and seek a new life. These two different feelings arise simultaneously and are of no use in preventing the instinctual shame that arises. That's the beginning of my problem.
>
> Why do I feel ashamed? There are at least two reasons—the problem of bread and the problem of spirit. First, priests should refrain from forcing people to feed them; this is like an act of plundering. Second, it is wrong for priests to receive the offerings given with impure motives. Third, it is wrong for priests to receive bread without working for it. In other words, they neglect their responsibilities and yet demand their rights, which I find most disgraceful. Further, they live comfortably because of the misfortunes of others [in exchange for the funeral and memorial services they officiate at, they receive a lot of donations]. This is a betrayal of clerical life and should not be tolerated. These points lead without fail to the conclusion that Buddhist priests should be ashamed of themselves.
>
> Having said that, faith does seem to generate a power by which people can change their lives. Since I haven't experienced anything like that, perhaps I shouldn't say anything about it. But I wonder how many Buddhist priests who act wise and boast of their vocation truly do so from the point of view of "Becoming enlightened yourself and then leading others to that same enlightenment?" They give Dharma talks without spiritual experience and maintain their lives by selling the Buddha and by selling others and even themselves. There is no way other than feeling ashamed about this. . . .

> What is unfortunate is that first there is a temple, and then there are members. This is fundamentally wrong. A true and real teaching must come first and then places where that teaching can be taught come into existence. This must be the rule. But among the descendants of the founder who succeeded our denomination, some abbots went against the founder's will, made political connections, and built temples strategically. Despite their impressive outward appearances, the temples are hollow inside. Building Shin Buddhist temples had already been useless from the very beginning.[58]

For Miyagi, the history of Buddhism began with pure faith. After Shakyamuni Buddha died, a small group of his followers formed a religious organization based on their faith. Soon after, however, his disciples materialized his spirit: they worshipped his relics, made stone monuments, created Buddhist statues, and built Buddhist temples. In Miyagi's mind, Shinran regained Shakyamuni's spirit by rejecting superstition and explaining the importance of the entrusting mind. Shinran's followers, however, diverged from his teaching, longed for a better afterlife, and hierarchized their organizations.

Miyagi denounces a Shin Buddhist organization as an institution that exploits the poor. High-ranking priests and affluent lay members represent a privileged class. Differences between the clergy and the laity symbolize the division of labor and class struggle. In Miyagi's eyes, Shinran's teaching has become a religious ideology that makes his followers subservient, while the Honganji head temple has become a center of idol worship. The problems of Temple Buddhism originate in the head temple and penetrate the denomination as a whole. The reform of Temple Buddhism must therefore be revolutionary and Miyagi believes that a new religious life must be built on a firm foundation that reflects a new economic concept and responds to the needs of the present society.[59]

In Miyagi's critical accounts of Temple Buddhism, the extent of reductionism is significant. He romanticizes Shakyamuni Buddha and Shinran but does not take into consideration the fact that Shinran composed hymns about worldly benefits. Neither does Miyagi consider the long-standing local practice of ancestral veneration that is necessary for maintaining the unity of each household. Miyagi's criticism is also not constructive; he does not discuss the material basis of his ideal Buddhist organization and how the current economic structure of Temple Buddhism can be replaced with a new financial model. He believes only in the strength of faith and fantasizes about destroying Temple Buddhism. The accounts of the two historical events of Shin Buddhism described below are therefore biased.

Representations of the
Two Shin Buddhist Historical Events

Barbara Foley points out that historical fiction appears to be truthful because characters convey cognition of historical events through their engagement in them.[60] Miyagi appears to be real because of his involvement with the Higashi Honganji's reform movement carried out by Kiyozawa's followers and his observation of the service commemorating the six hundred fiftieth anniversary of Shinran's passing at the head temple in Kyoto. He considers both events to be instances of religious activities preventing Shin Buddhist followers from thinking rationally.

According to Fukushima Kazuto, for many of Kiyozawa's followers, including Tada Kanae and Akegarasu Haya, having a personal struggle and an awakening experience was more important than blindly accepting the doctrine established by institutional authority. They emphasized the importance of receiving Amida's grace, thereby single-mindedly praising Amida's virtue.[61] Tada, especially—and Akegarasu as discussed in the previous chapter—saw the grace of Amida Buddha as the basis of his existence. Tada wrote,

> When I think of myself as a living being, which is the most important matter for me, there is no such a thing as the power of a self (*jiko no chikara*). This body, this hair, and this skin are all here because of my parents. . . . My entire being reflects the grace [of Amida]. This selfhood is the crystallization of [Amida's] compassion. Isn't this the meaning of birth in the Pure Land?[62]

Tada considered all things to be given—conditioned by the Buddhist principle of dependent arising.

In *Guardians*, Tachibana Hōjin, who both inspires and disappoints Miyagi, is the avatar of Tada. Although some of Miyagi's revolutionary visions coincide with ideas held by members of the *Seishin shugi* movement—such as restoring the founder's spirit to the denomination and proclaiming Shinran as a true follower of Shakyamuni Buddha—Miyagi is critical of Tachibana's idea of receiving Amida Buddha's grace.

Miyagi questions Tachibana about the custom of Buddhist priests receiving offerings from their temple members. Tachibana replies that the clothes and food represent the grace of Amida and that he has never worried about the availability of daily necessities. Miyagi, however, says that resident Buddhist priests today do not deserve the offerings because their lives are corrupt and that the grace of Amida obscures the fundamental problem of priesthood since it justifies their situations as always given. Offended by Miyagi's criticism, Tachibana tells him angrily,

> "Everything I've said, Mr. Miyagi," Tachibana says, "is derived from my experiences and reflects my deepest feelings. But if forced to conclude our conversation, I'll concede that receiving offerings reflects the lifestyle that Shakyamuni Buddha taught."
> Miyagi attacks Tachibana without hesitation.
> "First of all, you're not a Buddha. Second, we live in a society that is 3,000 years later than his. A crab digs a hole that matches his size; it can never fit into a lion's lair. Let Hermes wear his own shoes. An ordinary man should wear straw sandals. Similarly, isn't walking the Path of the Sage detrimental to the spiritual growth of ordinary people, Master Tachibana?"
> Tachibana refuses to concede.
> "Don't misunderstand, Mr. Miyagi. I don't accept offerings in order to become a saint. I accept them because there is no other way for me to live."
> "Doesn't that mean you recognize what you do is the right form of living?"
> "That, I don't know. But as a lowly ordinary person, I'm always grateful for offerings. I believe this lifestyle is the only way to avoid plundering and containing greed in today's society."
> This reply annoys Miyagi because Tachibana always seems to justify himself by resorting to the grace of Tathagata—as if he were a politician using Imperial brocade to exercise power.[63]

From Miyagi's perspective, Tachibana is not really interested in fundamentally reforming Temple Buddhism because, after all, he is a resident priest who does not want to give up his position. The idea of Amida's grace only works inwardly for someone like Tachibana and prevents him from questioning the priesthood and leaving the denomination. It is like opium that paralyzes rational thinking.

While being able to receive Amida's grace is the goal of Tachibana's spiritual path, for Miyagi, the goal of his spiritual attainment is expanded outwardly through his personal struggles. Miyagi identifies the cause of his suffering as being socially constructed. He suffers because he is obliged to become a Buddhist priest, according to the Buddhist hereditary system. In order to remove the cause of his suffering, he cannot take the path of least resistance. He has to revolt against the system; seek a Buddhist organization that is built on pure faith; and urge his father to change his perspective on Temple Buddhism, abandon his priesthood, and leave his home temple.

The tension between Tachibana and Miyagi represents a debate regarding the degree to which Buddhists should be involved in social reform. The Association of Pure Buddhists (*Bukkyō seito dōshikai*), formed by Sakaino Kōyō and others in 1899, for example, promoted New Buddhism (*Shin bukkyō*) to allow free discussion of Buddhism and religion, reform the established religious system and ritual practice, and improve society through regaining healthy faith and knowledge. In contrast, Kiyozawa's group, the *Kōkōdō*, stressed the importance of introspection and avoided sociopolitical action.[64] In *Guardians*, Miyagi is determined to engage in socially reforming Temple Buddhism, while Tachibana rejects the notion of justice and concentrates on the importance of introspection. In Tachibana's mind, justice is nothing but blaming others without reflecting on one's own problems.[65] While relying on a life of receiving offerings, Tachibana remains conservative and evades Miyagi's criticism directed at the denomination. They depart without understanding each other and never meet again.

While Amida's grace is one of the features in the modern development of Shin Buddhism, Miyagi's exchange with Tachibana is ideological. Matsuoka, as the author of *Guardians*, may have intended to dialogue with Tada through a fictional exchange between Miyagi as Matsuoka's alter ego and Tachibana as Tada's surrogate. When Matsuoka published "Home to Protect the Dharma" prior to *Guardians*, he was severely criticized by Tada for it. In Tada's mind, Matsuoka—despite growing up in a Shin Buddhist temple—did not understand the significance of temple life. Although Tada recognized the degeneration of Temple Buddhism as Matsuoka did, he proposed to educate the priests, increase the dignity of the denomination, improve rituals, and reorganize the denomination's finances. Further, Tada considered Matsuoka to be "mentally ill," "too emotional," "lacking in intellect," and "not introspective enough."[66] It is likely that Matsuoka employed his artistic imagination to respond to Tada's attack by having Miyagi explain to Tachibana the corruption of Temple Buddhism and the limitations of Higashi Honganji's reform movement.

Another historical Shin Buddhist event described in *Guardians* is Higashi Honganji's commemorative service in Kyoto honoring the six hundred fiftieth anniversary of Shinran's passing. In the spring of 1911, the Jōdoshū, with

Chion-in as its head temple, honored the seven hundredth anniversary of Hōnen's passing, and Jōdo Shinshū (Higashi and Nishi Honganji and other smaller Shin Buddhist denominations) celebrated the six hundred fiftieth anniversary of Shinran's passing. Because of these commemorative events, the city of Kyoto became packed with Amidists. Records show that more than one million people visited the Nishi Honganji head temple between March and April. In the case of Higashi Honganji, the head temple conducted a series of commemorative services for ten days between April 18 and 28. According to records, more than ten thousand priests attended. On both April 26 and 27, fifty thousand people who could not enter the temple compound lined up outside the gates. The administrators opened the temple halls for night visitation, starting at ten o'clock, and more than four hundred thousand people paid their respects to the statue of the founder during nine nights. A temporary railway station had to be built next to the Kyoto station in order to accommodate the huge number of pilgrims.[67]

The Higashi Honganji head temple carefully planned the commemorative events and effectively carried them out. It organized a series of lectures and Dharma talks; sent priests to a variety of facilities in the city of Kyoto where pilgrims stayed; published many booklets; and involved students, who were going to be priests in the near future, in voluntary works. Prominent Buddhist scholars, such as Nanjō Bun'yū (who had studied Sanskrit in England under Max Müller and become the second president of Otani University) and Sasaki Gesshō, as well as popular Buddhist priests, including Tada and Akegarasu, spoke to the congregation. During the ten-day ceremony, the administrative office issued tickets that could be exchanged for various souvenirs, depending on the amount of the donation; served special lunch and dinner, and sold bento boxes; and organized recreational events, such as park visits and the viewing of Nō dramas performed in the temple compound.[68]

The institutional records of Higashi Honganji do not reflect the attendees' experiences, whereas *Guardians* replicates multiple voices of Shin followers. These experiences are "historical data"—collected, processed, and integrated into the narrative by Matsuoka. As a common representational strategy of historical fiction, Foley states, "empirical data enter the historical novel not to validate the author's honesty but to reinforce the text's claim to offer a persuasive interpretation of its referent."[69] In *Guardians*, the voices of the multitudes of Shin Buddhist followers become the "extratextual verification."[70]

The objective of historical fiction is, at the same time, not merely to duplicate social reality. Georg Lukács states, "What matters therefore in the historical novel is not the re-telling of great historical events, but the poetic awakening of the people who figured in those events. What matters is that we should re-experience the social and human motives which led men to think, feel, and act just as they did in historical reality."[71] *Guardians* conveys the behaviors of ordinary lay Shin Buddhist followers and the social circumstances of the day that drove them to act the way they did.

To give an example, during his stay in Kyoto, Miyagi hears both zealous and skeptical opinions about the commemorative services. He is particularly disturbed by the ignorance of pious lay members who are blinded by faith. An old woman, who happens to be a member of another temple in his hometown, waits a long time for the celebration. She single-mindedly saves money so she can hand it directly to the abbot. Miyagi also hears the story of an old man who orders a bowl of noodles but does not have enough small change to pay for it and ends up arrested by the police. The old man runs away from the noodle shop because he only has paper money, which he does not want to break into small change, in order to donate all of it to the head temple. At the same time, Miyagi hears that the abbot goes to a party with young geisha using the money the followers donated to the head temple. Miyagi feels sorry for them because they are competing with each other to buy what they think are tickets to the Pure Land without really understanding the abbot.[72]

Miyagi's negative perception of the abbot and his rejection of Shin Buddhist followers who worship the abbot single-mindedly illustrate his criticism of the feudal characteristics of Higashi Honganji, where the abbot is installed in the top echelon. Before Honganji was divided into Higashi (east) and Nishi (west) Honganji at the beginning of the Tokugawa era, it received the status of a *monzeki* temple in 1559—it was among the temples privileged by imperial and aristocratic families. During the Warring States period, Shin Buddhist followers fought regional warlords and the Honganji as a whole fought Oda Nobunaga in the Ishiyama War for about ten years.[73] The word "castle" in *Guardians of the Dharma Castle* thus brings to mind the political status of the abbot, which was equal to that of a *daimyō*, a feudal lord during the Warring States period.

In modern Japan, the power of the Honganji leaders remained strong because abbots of both Higashi and Nishi Honganji were related to Emperor Shōwa. Ōtani Kōshō, the twenty-third abbot of Nishi Honganji, was a cousin of the emperor and Ōtani Kōchō, the twenty-fourth abbot of Higashi Honganji, was the emperor's brother-in-law. Given this historical background, Miyagi's criticism of the abbot of a Shin Buddhist organization implies criticism of the imperial system of modern Japan.

Rewriting Shin Buddhist History

By means of fiction, *Guardians* replaced the accounts of two historical Shin Buddhist events created by ministerial authorities during Matsuoka's time. It is a history of lay Shin Buddhists and local Shin followers who were both part of and outside of the *Seishin shugi* movement. At the same time, because Miyagi interacts with ordinary priests and lay members, and with leaders of the reform movement, the narrator's account of Temple Buddhism ironically enriches its institutional history as a whole by adding layers of local Shin Buddhist events. First, while the clerical leaders who had driven the *Seishin shugi* movement created their own discourse and the critics evaluated *Seishin shugi*'s contribution to the modern development of Japanese Buddhism, in *Guardians* the narrator describes the *Seishin shugi* movement from the perspective of a layperson who disagrees with both conservative Shin Buddhist authorities and the members of the reform movement. Second, while the denominational authority celebrated Shinran's commemorative events from its viewpoint, in *Guardians*, the narrator describes a wide range of behaviors concerning the priests and lay members who gather in Kyoto. They have mixed reactions to the way the founder's memorial service is organized. The head temple becomes a place for social gatherings, exchanging information, a commercial market, and egotistic expressions, as well as for worship.

Matsuoka was able to create *Guardians*, in which the narrator challenges the master narrative of the history of Higashi Honganji, because he was born and raised in a Shin Buddhist temple family. He understood a priest's work, the Higashi Honganji organization's hierarchy and bureaucracy, Shin Buddhist doctrine and rituals, and the activities of the *Kōkōdō* members. The two historical Shin Buddhist events discussed above demonstrate not only Matsuoka's ability to create a documentary work but also his personal experience with Temple Buddhism. As a documentary writer, he was privileged to make use of his observations, and as an artist, he amplified the effects of his discoveries with his imagination.

Guardians does not, however, provide a complete picture of the *Seishin shugi* movement. According to Sekiguchi Yasuyoshi, Matsuoka finished the first section of *Guardians* in 1923 and immediately began planning the remaining sections.[74] By that time, the leading followers of Kiyozawa had already changed their perspectives. For instance, Tada had given up his ideas regarding Amida's grace. In 1919, he even went so far as to rebel against Kiyozawa's teaching. Akegarasu had also stopped promoting Amida's grace by 1915 and even indicated interest in Marxism in 1919.[75] None of these developments are reflected in the descriptions of Tachibana and Daidō in *Guardians*. It is important to remember that Matsuoka's fictional treatment of the history of the Shin Buddhist reform movement is not impartial.

Further, because *Guardians* is concerned not only with the history of Higashi Honganji but also with Matsuoka's own past, the ending of the novel seems to have mirrored Matsuoka's wishful thinking. A less well-known fact is that Honkakuji, Matsuoka's home temple, was burned down for unknown reasons and his sister died, but his father survived that incident and lived a long life.[76] Although in *Guardians* the destruction of Miyagi's home temple leads his father to accept his attachment to the temple, it is unclear if that was the case for Matsuoka's father. Miyagi's father's insistence on the temple's hereditary system causes a feud in his family and suffering for his son. The father's self-realization results in his son's apology for not being filial, leading the two to finally reconcile. Although Miyagi softens his attitudes toward his father only after his sister dies, he maintains his critical stance on Temple Buddhism. It is only his father who changes his attitude significantly. In this aspect, *Guardians* differs from the personal fiction discussed in the preceding chapters and betrays its pattern in which transformation of the hero, and narrator, is a theme.

One final note: in large part, criticism of Temple Buddhism began entering popular consciousness because of *Guardians*. It was only after the Pacific War and further organizational reforms that Higashi Honganji stopped worshipping the abbot as a living Buddha, banned the temple ranking system, and became a democratic religious organization. In that sense, *Guardians* predicted a new era of Temple Buddhism.

The next section shifts gears and analyzes the personal novels written by Natsume Sōseki, Tayama Katai, and Shiga Naoya as Buddhist allegories. In these works, Buddhism is part of the main characters' spiritual dynamics by which they grow introspective, realize the nature of suffering, gain self-awareness, undergo a self-transformation, and become positively engaged in their relationships with others—at least in their thinking. While treating these personal novels as works of path literature, Part 2 examines both implicit and explicit aspects of the protagonists' Buddhist experiences through their associations with words and symbols that are suggestive of Buddhist ideas (chapter 6), the mystical experiences of the main characters at the height of their spiritual inquiries (chapter 7), and the impact of Buddhist funerals on the fictional characters (chapter 8). Although allegorical readings of the texts are dissociated from discussions of the authors' Buddhist experiences, their Buddhist engagement appears on subtextual levels.

PART 2

The Buddhist Reading of Personal Fiction

CHAPTER SIX

Buddhist Words and Buddhist Symbols in Personal Novels

This chapter focuses on the words and symbols suggestive of Buddhist ideas that appear in Natsume Sōseki's *The Three-Cornered World* and *The Gate* and in Tayama Katai's *The Quilt*. These personal novels do not seem to be Buddhist except for scenes in which the main characters in *The Three-Cornered World* and *The Gate* interact with Buddhist clergy; however, allegorical analyses, or allegoresis, of certain words, such as *ōjō* 往生 and *mondō* 問答, and objects, such as a futon and Daruma doll, as well as exploration of Buddhist themes, demonstrate otherwise. Concerning allegoresis, Susan Klein states, "the interpretation of a symbolic text appears to require only naturalized discursive conventions that we accept unconsciously, but an allegorical text demands the use of political and/or religious discourse, and this dependence on 'extrinsic' discourse forces the process of interpretation into consciousness."[1] The allegoreses of the three works listed above, when interpreted through the narrative pattern of Buddhism, lead to the conclusion that for a main character who struggles to come to terms with himself, accepting his problem is the beginning of a path and self-transformation is a goal that is an ongoing process. To better understand the Buddhist implications of the main characters' actions, Buddhist symbolism is first introduced.

The Role of Language and Symbols in Buddhism

Nāgārjuna, the founder of the Madhyamaka school of Buddhism, elaborates the idea of dependent arising through the notion of emptiness (*śūnyatā*). He argues that all things lack inherent existence, because they "arise and pass away due to certain conditions."[2] Emptiness is not the same as nonexistence because existence is already assumed in a discussion of nonexistence. The goal of the Buddha's teachings is for us to develop an insight into the nature of the conventional world and see things as they are—that is, nothing exists by itself, as something comes into being only in relation to all other things.

According to Nāgārjuna, suffering, or failure to understand the nature of impermanence, is caused by attachment: conceptualization causes us to fix our relationships to objects and others by assigning words to objects and names to others. At the same time, language can serve as a means of overcoming the kind of ordinary, materially bound thinking whereby we separate ourselves from others. According to Paul Williams, Nāgārjuna elaborates the Buddha's teachings in terms of conventional and ultimate truths—the so-called two truths. Ultimate truth, or emptiness, is inexplicable; however, without using language as a means of communication, neither Buddhist practice nor spiritual liberation can be explained. For Nāgārjuna, "when the everyday conventional world is thus seen correctly it is apparent that emptiness (the ultimate truth) and the world are not opposed to each other but rather mutually imply each other."[3] Ultimately, the notion of emptiness itself needs to be negated.

In the Yogācāra school of Buddhism, "mind-talk" or "mental verbalization" (S. *manojalpa*; J. *igon* or *shinchū ni kataru*[4]) facilitates the realization of ultimate truth and plays a crucial role in Mahayana Buddhist practice. In his study of *manojalpa* in the *Mahāyāna-sūtrālaṃkāra* (J. *Daijō shōgonkyōron*), Taiki Motomura describes mental verbalization as part of a threefold training of Buddhism consisting of hearing, reflection, and practice:

> One takes outer-object in the mind converting it to a name or word in the stage of hearing (*śruta*). This name or word in mind is called mental verbalization (*manojalpa*). In the next stage, reflection (*cintā*), the *Yogin* manifests the image from this mental verbalization and he considers that that object appears solely from mental verbalization, and realizes that there is nothing other than mental verbalization. After going through these stages, in the stage of practice (*bhāvanā*), the *Yogin* fixes his mind upon the name, that is, mental verbalization, and perceives true reality (*tathatā*) extinguishing the duality of object.[5]

While listening to and reflecting on Mahayana Buddhist teachings, a practitioner first identifies an external object using a word and then reverses the process of the identification by creating an image of the object referring to that word. Through meditation, the practitioner comes to realize that the object is the product of mental recognition—conceptualization—and that the object neither exists apart from the mind nor does the mind exist by itself. The practitioner thus closes the dichotomy between subject and object. In Buddhism, conceptualization becomes the cause of attachment but can serve as a means of liberation if language is properly applied.[6]

Medieval Japanese Buddhists considered language to be a double-edged sword, representing both material attachment and spiritual detachment. As early as 806, Kūkai said, "Dharma has no language, but it is not apparent except through language."[7] As Susan Klein points out, the soteriological power of sacred words, which transform our relationships to the mundane world, are shown by the use of *dharani* in Shingon esoteric Buddhism, recitation of the *nenbutsu* in Pure Land Buddhism, the use of kōan or Zen riddle, and so on. Medieval Japanese Buddhists believed that with proper training, the unity of language and reality were attained.[8]

In the same way that language works on two levels, from a Buddhist perspective, symbols are two-tiered but also non-dual. According to William LaFleur, who analyzes the role of the Buddhist system of symbols in medieval Japan, images from nature were often used to represent Buddhist teachings. For example, the lotus flower, which grows out of mud, was seen as a symbol of a pure life amidst the muck and mire of this material world and the scattering of cherry blossoms was associated with an understanding of impermanence.[9] At the same time, the scattering of cherry blossoms can indicate the residue of attachment, such as the mourning of a broken heart or the desire implied by pining for someone. A Buddhist symbol brings together dualistic visions, such as attachment and detachment, thereby demonstrating non-dualism. In Japan, meditation on the aesthetic dimension of natural scenery enabled poets and prose writers to realize both worldly desires and a longing for detachment from this attachment.

According to LaFleur, Buddhist symbolization derives from the notion of original enlightenment (*hongaku*)—that is, Buddhist realization is not a matter of the future but of the present. Enlightenment can be attained with an ignorant mind. It does not affirm ignorance per se but closes the gap between the deluded mind and the enlightened mind through which dualistic thinking—that itself is the cause of delusion—collapses.[10]

As an example of the system of Buddhist symbols appearing in medieval Japanese literature, LaFleur considers the phrase "traveler's inn" (*kari no yado*) in a poem by the twelfth-century poet Saigyō (1118–1190) to be a case of signification. It is a metaphor for impermanence as suggested by "a temporary inn" (based on the reading of *kari* 仮り as transitory) and as a signifier of sexuality which is suggested by "a rented inn" or brothel (based on the alternate reading of *kari* 借り as rented). The interplay between the sense of impermanence, which motivates the poet to leave the mundane world, and lust, which brings him back to the world of desires, adds a didactic element to Saigyō's poems. In Buddhism, the implications of a symbol can be paradoxical, changeable, and yet interconnected.[11] LaFleur concludes, "Many poets, essayists, and people articulating a theory of literature appear to have been simultaneously involved in constructing and demolishing the system of Buddhist symbols; and this was the case *because* they pursued the implications of their understanding of Buddhism and tried to express it in literary form."[12]

The symbolic interpretation of Buddhism continued in early modern Japanese literature. In *Narrow Road to the Far North* (*Oku no hosomichi*), Matsuo Bashō considers chestnuts (*kuri*) to be sacred trees that grow in the profane world. He bases this idea on his reading of the two radicals that form the kanji character for 栗 (*kuri*), which is made up of 西 (west) and 木 (a tree), and the association of "west" where Amida Buddha's Pure Land is said to exist. He then relates walking sticks (*tsue*) and pillars (*hashira*) made from chestnut trees, which imply "reliance" as in "to rely on" the sticks and "to be supported" by the pillars, to the goal of Pure Land Buddhism—that is, to rely on Amida Buddha's compassion in order to be born in the Pure Land.[13]

Scholars have also noted the non-dual nature of Buddhist images and symbols appearing in Chikamatsu Monzaemon's plays on the theme of double suicide. According to Steven Heine, for instance, the blade that "causes physical death simultaneously and paradoxically creates spiritual rebirth in paradise [Amida's Pure Land]" and the net (*ami*) is transformed "from a symbol of karmic judgment to the Buddha's promise to catch and save all humankind."[14] The system of Buddhist symbols remained strong in Japan during the late seventeenth and early eighteenth centuries.

In modern Japan, Buddhism was neither given hegemonic status in the intellectual establishment nor treated particularly well by political authorities. Japanese writers were neither didactic nor eager to explicitly articulate Buddhist worldviews in their works. This does not mean that Buddhist imagery disappeared from modern Japanese literature. As examples, Buddhist symbolism in Natsume Sōseki's *The Three-Cornered World* and *The Gate* and Tayama Katai's *The Quilt* are discussed next.

The Three-Cornered World: Buddhist Detachment and Artistic Fulfillment

Natsume Sōseki considers *Kusamakura*—translated as *The Three-Cornered World*, but literally "grass pillow"[15]—a "haiku novel." He wrote it all at once within a week. Steve Odin calls it a "plotless novel with a discontinuous story line and no development of events," which "aims only to disclose the beauty of events in nature so as to produce an aesthetic effect in the mind of the reader," and "a precursor of the *nouveau roman* or 'new novel' of postmodernist literature." Odin defines the philosophical theme of the novel as a "role of psychic distance in the aesthetic experience of beauty in art and nature" and discusses both traditional aesthetic principles connected to Zen Buddhism (such as the notion of *yūgen*) and contemporary aesthetic practice, including Masaoka Shiki's style of composition known as "sketching."[16] Odin also points out that Sōseki's aesthetic visions anticipate the Western theories of psychic distance developed by Edward Bullough and José Ortega y Gasset.[17] Odin focuses on the philosophical aspect of *The Three-Cornered World* but not on the soteriological aspect of the novel.

The Three-Cornered World is characterized by the aesthetic inspiration and Buddhist interest of a painter/poet whose name is not given. He admires the beauty of nature, contemplates artists' attitudes toward the world, and finds a Zen master's personality liberating. Although he is inclined toward Zen Buddhism, ambivalent images of the Pure Land emerge through his aesthetic vision. When the word *ōjō* (birth in the Pure Land) is examined at the intersection of his aesthetic and religious quest—which is facilitated by female characters—the Pure Land known as a glorious manifestation of Buddhist enlightenment becomes a more complex realm.

The protagonist's spiritual growth can be explained in terms of the narrative pattern of "ground, path, and goal." For him, living in the world itself is a problem (ground)—"It is not a very agreeable place to live, this world of ours"[18]; and yet, as he admits, if he were able to accept the fact that there is no perfect place to live, then he would be able to write a poem and draw a painting without being disturbed. He escapes the bustle of everyday life; journeys to and stays in a town known for its hot springs, where he entrusts himself to the healing power of nature and interacts with spiritually inspiring people (path); and fulfills his spiritual-artistic needs before returning to the city (goal).

A remote hot-springs town called Nakoi is where the main character seeks spiritual liberation and artistic fulfillment. The beauty of nature, which inspires him poetically, and Buddhist detachment lead him to feel there is a better realm in this world. The story develops through his interaction with Nami, the daughter of the innkeeper at Shihoda. She is associated with the legendary Nagara maiden, the daughter of a wealthy man, who took her own life by throwing herself into a river when she suffered from being courted by two different men. In a like manner, two men proposed marriage to Nami at the same time. Although she wanted to marry the one in Kyoto, her parents arranged for her to wed the other man, the son of the richest man in a nearby town. After her husband's business went bankrupt, Nami was divorced and returned to Nakoi. Villagers considered her strange and even insane; however, the protagonist enjoys conversing with her. He finds her mysterious, charming, witty, and suicidal.

One day Nami asks the protagonist to draw her portrait. He does not feel like doing so because in his mind she lacks a sense of pathos (*aware*).[19] He finally sees a moment of pathos when she goes to see off a cousin—who is going to join the Japanese Imperial Army to fight the Russians in northern China—at the train station, where she finds her ex-husband getting on a train to leave Japan.

The state of artistic detachment the protagonist seeks is called *hininjō* or "detachment from human feelings."[20] The narrator, who calls himself *yo* (literally, I),[21] explains it as being "free from personal interests," standing "three feet away from the canvas [so] you can look at it calmly," and "taking a pace back to give yourself the room to move that a bystander would have, [in order to] examine your feelings calmly and with complete honesty."[22] Awareness of *hininjō* suggests his capacity to separate himself from his attachments, including his feelings and emotions, and to experience spiritual freedom.

The main character of *The Three-Cornered World* experiences spiritual aloofness on three levels: view of nature, association with poetry, and interaction with those who have attained a state of detachment. His life becomes enjoyable when he is surrounded by nature. It helps him forget the bustle of everyday life and even his material being. By blending into natural surroundings, he is able to objectify himself, as if looking at a person in a drawing. What he sees and hears from a "purely objective standpoint"[23] allows him to enter a poetic world where he is able to renounce ordinary thoughts, enjoy being in a realm of transcendence, and write a poem. Artists do not live in a world regulated by rules—a "four-cornered world"—but in a "three-cornered world" where the angle called common sense is removed.[24]

The protagonist enjoys both classical and modern poetry. He is versed in classical Chinese prose and poetry, Bashō's haikai and Shiki's haiku, and modern English poetry by Shelley, Swinburne, and Wordsworth. The protagonist's familiarity with classical Chinese reflects the narrator's profound knowledge of the classics of Chinese literature, such as the *Analects*, *Book of Odes*, *Zhuangzi*, and *Chu Ci*. The narrator is also acquainted with Chan/Zen literature, such as *The Blue Cliff Record*, and uses specific idiomatic expressions that are found in the *Records of Master Mi'an Xianjie*, the *Collection of Hakuin's Dharma Talks*, and the *Writings of Zen Master Dahui*.[25] For the narrator, poetic realization is similar to Buddhist attainment: "to become a poet is one way to achieve supreme enlightenment."[26]

At the inn, the protagonist happens to see calligraphy brushed by Daitetsu, the Zen master of a local temple called Kankaiji, and is impressed with it. He finds Daitetsu's calligraphic touch to be similar to that of Kōsen, whom the protagonist admires as a superb Zen calligrapher. As the protagonist interacts with Daitetsu, he finds the Zen master to be a person who has attained a state of complete detachment. He thus reflects on the similarity between religious figures and artists:

> I believe it was Oscar Wilde who remarked that Christ's approach to life was supremely artistic. I don't know about Christ, but I certainly believe this statement could justly be applied to the abbot of Kankaiji. . . . His heart is a bottomless well. Everything passes straight through it without hindrance. He moves freely through all places, creates at will, and moves on, and there's not the least hint of any sullying particle of experience remaining lodged within him. If just a touch of discernment and taste could be added to his brain, he would become the perfect artist, at one with whatever situation he found himself in, maintaining the artist's essential state of mind even in the most trivial everyday moments of life.[27]

The protagonist is impressed that Daitetsu is spiritually free while immersed in the mundane world, whereas he himself finds peace of mind only when he is surrounded by nature.

The protagonist's sense of tranquility, however, is disturbed by two events. First, during his first night in Nakoi, he dreams of the Nagara maiden transformed into Ophelia, who runs down a river while singing beautifully, and he follows her from the riverbank in order to save her. This dream reminds the protagonist of the story of Dahui, a prominent Buddhist monk in Song dynasty China, who was said to have attained enlightenment but was troubled by ordinary thoughts recurring in his dreams.[28]

Second, the protagonist meets Nami, the eccentric young woman. According to a local barber, when Taian, a young Buddhist trainee at Kankaiji, sent her a love letter, Nami came to the temple, put her arms around his neck when he was chanting a sutra with the master, and said to him, "If you really love me so much, let's make love here before Buddha."[29] Taian was astonished and fled the temple. Nami comes naked to take a bath when the protagonist is present. Later she tells him that she purposefully showed him her body because he is a painter and that someday she will drown herself in Kagami Pond, and asks him to make a painting of her body floating peacefully there.

Kagami Pond is where the forces of life and death, as well as religious and artistic sensibilities, join. It represents the collective karma of the young women who took their lives by drowning in it. In addition to the Nagara maiden who threw herself into a nearby river, many years ago a beautiful young woman in the Shihoda family fell in love with a Buddhist monk who stayed at the inn. Her father opposed their marriage, so she followed the monk to the pond where she committed suicide. These stories help the protagonist conjure up the image of Ophelia from Millais' painting, and that is how he relates Ophelia to Nami.

One day the protagonist visits Kagami Pond. We are told that he finds at the bottom "long slender tendrils of weed which looked as though they had given up the ghost. This is the only phrase I can think of which describes their appearance." The narrator continues:

> Lying submerged in water which was obviously not going to move in a hundred years, it had preened itself and struck a pose waiting for the time when it too could play the coquette. It had waited in vain through an endless succession of days and nights, its long unsatiated desire to love expressed in the tip of every stem, until now it led a paralysed existence, unable to die.[30]

The protagonist then picks two small stones and throws them in the pond. The stalks of waterweed slowly begin to move, conjuring up an image of women's hair, and he says, "May your soul rest in peace." Concerning this scene, Kin'ya Tsuruta observes that the pond "has become a grave for the still restless souls of women" and that its bottom implies a utopia.[31]

Tsuruta's assessment of the pond is much to the point, but both Tsuruta and the translator(s) are quick to dismiss the sense of ambiguity felt through the word *ōjō*, which is used to describe the stalks of waterweed.[32] First, the long slender tendrils of weed remind us of the women who died in the pond. At the same time, they give an impression that those women are still alive. In the source language, what is translated as "on the bottom I could see long slender tendrils of weed which looked as though they had given up the ghost" is *sokoniwa hosonagai mizukusaga ōjō shite shizundeiru* 底には細長い水草が、往生して沈んでいる. The word *ōjō* is "the only word" that the narrator can think of to describe the stalks of waterweed.

Ōjō has several meanings. It derives from the Amidist notion of birth in the Pure Land, but also means "death," "to give up" after exhausting oneself, and "being troubled." On the one hand, the women who died in the pond after giving up their love rest in peace as suggested by their attainment of birth in the Pure Land, but on the other hand, they are still attached to romantic love and are being exhausted, or being troubled, by their own desires. In other words, the bottom of the pond only serves as a temporary utopia, and therefore the protagonist wishes them to attain eternal peace by saying *namu amida butsu* or *nenbutsu*—which is translated as "may your soul rest in peace"—and throws small stones into the pond as a way to direct his merit (*kudoku* 功徳). The word *ōjō* thus implies both women's spiritual impasse and liberation, and the protagonist's act of saving their souls.

Such ambivalence of the word *ōjō* associated with birth in the Pure Land is noted at the beginning of the novel. Before the protagonist meets Nami, he senses the mysterious presence of a young woman at the inn—which appears to be Nami. The narrator relates his desire to draw her out from the world of shadows to the sensation that people feel when they see a dying person. They are eager to bring that person back from the world of eternity, instead of saying the *nenbutsu* and wishing that she will attain birth in the Pure Land. Those who are about to lose a loved one cannot easily accept that death as birth in the Pure Land.

The atmosphere of Kagami Pond does not bring an image of the Pure Land to the protagonist either. He finds camellias blooming around the pond and associates them with an enchantress and the blood spilled by her victims. At the same time, he envisions Nami as an incarnation of Ophelia. This is when he happens to discover Nami on top of the steep rock standing by the pond where she thinks about committing suicide. According to Tsuruta, while the notion of *hininjō*, or "detachment from human feelings," prevents the protagonist from expressing his feelings about Nami, he is able to articulate his attitude toward her through his response to the flowering of camellias because he is not obliged to restrict his feelings arising just from viewing the camellias. And yet the protagonist juxtaposes the image of death with the camellias in order not to be overcome by Nami's vitality and charm.[33]

The protagonist's creative association of Kagami Pond and the camellias is far from the conventional representations of the Pure Land, the land of Amida Buddha. According to the *Shorter Sukhāvatīvyūha Sutra* (*Amidakyō*), the Pure Land is decorated with many things of beauty. Ponds are made of gems and mandara flowers fill the air.[34] The Pure Land, however, is a provisionary place. It is the realm of nirvana, which cannot be conceptualized or verbalized. The glorious image of the Pure Land only serves as a skillful means (*hōben*) to lead sentient beings to realize the emptiness of all things.

Nami represents a figure of skillful means. She is not an enchantress but a spiritual guide for men. Daitetsu of Kankaiji praises her highly, even though Nami thinks the Zen master talks nonsense. Because of her outrageous behavior, Taian left Kankaiji but later became a prominent Zen master at Daibaiji in Rikuzen. The protagonist sees in her face qualities of both ignorance and wisdom. Her appearance even reminds him of the bodhisattva Kannon. The sense of pathos he finally detects in her face is "unknown to the gods, and yet it is the very emotion that can elevate man to near-deity."[35] While being enticed by Nami, the protagonist progresses in his study of art—"Thanks to her, my study of art had been considerably advanced"[36]—and when he sees her express pathos, he is able to put the final touch on her. He concludes that Nami's behavior and her mode of life is "more beautiful than those of any woman" he has met because she is not "consciously trying to give a beautiful performance."[37] He is impressed with Nami because she is not pretending to be someone she is not, but because she is just as she is.

Nami's advanced spiritual quality resonates with the sacred powers of women depicted in revelatory tales of medieval Japan, where they play the role of bodhisattvas and guide men to spiritual attainment.[38] Her eccentricity and spiritual liberty represent what Michele Marra would call the "aesthetics of madness," a discourse of Buddhist aesthetics. This is a new literary paradigm that emerged in the collections of "explanatory stories" (*setsuwa*) during the late twelfth century by which antisocial and unethical behaviors of reclusive unorthodox characters were embraced paradoxically as indications of spiritual attainment, in contrast to the aesthetic sensibility (known as *miyabi* or refinement) shared by the Heian aristocrats and the hero of *The Tale of Genji*.[39] Although Nami still interacts with people in Nakoi, she is mentally reclusive. For the protagonist in *The Three-Cornered World*, her madness is central to his learning process.

In addition to the word *ōjō*, other words closely associated with Buddhism appear in secular contexts and describe the protagonist's religious sensibilities. When the narrator arrives at Kagami Pond, he lights a cigarette. The smoke from the matchstick takes the shape of a lizard-like dragon and then "immediately disappears"—*sugu jakumetsu shita* すぐ寂滅した. This phrase implies a sense of impermanence and resonates with the bubbles that form and burst on the surface of the pond when the narrator throws small stones into the pond. The word *jakumetsu* also means nirvana, which can be associated with a sense of eternity. When the protagonist reflects on an image of the enchantress on the camellias, he comes to believe that no one who catches a glimpse of her will ever be able to escape her spell—*konrinzai nogaruru koto wa dekinai* 金輪際、免るゝ事は出来ない. In Buddhism, *konrinzai* is a realm that borders the deepest part of the earth, indicating the depth of ignorance of which man is unaware; by contrast, in secular use it suggests a conscious articulation of denial expressed as "never" or "absolutely not."

This reading of *The Three-Cornered World* sheds light on the soteriological aspects of the novel seen through the protagonist's travel experience. Travel is an indicator of the path that includes a destination within its concept and religious elements. In ancient Japan, when travelers entered a new terrain, they made a small offering, recited a poem as a form of offering to a deity, and prayed for a safe trip.[40] Pilgrimages to shrines and temples were another popular form of travel that required travelers to engage in religious actions by which they revived their energy. Travel enables one to move away from one's ordinary life, adventure into an unknown place where one receives spiritual nourishment, and then to return home.

While away from home, the protagonist meets Nami, who guides male characters to self-realization, and attempts to rescue the souls of women who took their lives in Kagami Pond. For the protagonist, Nami is a symbol of his attachment to human life and longing for aesthetic detachment. The word *ōjō* that the narrator uses to rhetorically describe the souls of the women suggests a non-dual Buddhist perspective of life and death, which develops from his observation of Kagami Pond involving the stalks of waterweed and camellias as manifestations of charm, fear, beauty, and death. It is unclear, however, whether the protagonist is able to apply the mental state he thinks he has attained in Nakoi to his city life. By contrast, Sōsuke, the literary character examined next, continues to engage with his path after he returns to his everyday life.

The Gate: Zen Kōans as Ongoing Zen Dialogues

In 1894, at the age of twenty-nine, Natsume Sōseki stayed in the Engakuji compound in Kamakura and practiced sitting in meditation for about two weeks. In *The Gate*, he reflected and refracted his Zen experience. Like Daitetsu in *The Three-Cornered World*, Zen priests appear as extraordinary characters in *The Gate* and impress the main character, Sōsuke. In conventional readings of *The Gate*, the protagonist Sōsuke is perceived as a man who is unable to find his "deepest self" and fails to take a leap of faith. Critics consider the impact of Buddhism on Sōsuke to be of little significance because of his inability to solve a kōan. In the reading of *The Gate* through a Buddhist lens, however, Sōsuke's engagement with Zen continues.

Sōsuke lives quietly with his wife, Oyone. He fell in love with her when she was dating his friend, Yasui (Oyone and Yasui might have been married—their exact relationship is unclear). Sōsuke stole her away from Yasui and married her despite opposition from his own family, relatives, and friends. As a result, the couple was ostracized. Although Sōsuke and Oyone make a good couple and hardly fight, they do not share real concerns. She suffers a sense of guilt when she has a third miscarriage and goes to see a fortune-teller who tells her that her infertility is caused by the bad karma she created (as she hurt Yasui). Oyone is disturbed by what appears to be her karmic punishment but keeps it to herself until the opportunity arises for her to share her agony with Sōsuke. On the other hand, when the possibility for Sōsuke to meet Yasui arises by chance, Sōsuke conceals this from Oyone. Rather, he goes to a Zen temple to seek "direction to his deepest self" and "find a way to exercise a firmer command over his life."[41]

In Kamakura, Sōsuke meets Gidō, a young Zen priest and caretaker of Issō-an, a boarding house for Zen trainees in the temple compound. He finds Gidō pleasant, but with a tinge of pathos. Gidō looks after Sōsuke and teaches him the basics of Zen, particularly the mindset required for novice trainees. Gidō reminds Sōsuke that *zazen* is a serious undertaking and that even those who practice Zen for two or three decades suffer from their attachments from time to time. Sōsuke gradually realizes that *zazen* is much harder than he initially thought and how imprudent he was to expect to attain spiritual enlightenment in such a short time. He is especially taken aback when Gidō tells him that Gidō has not slept in a bed for two years and how long it has taken to get to his present stage.

Gidō introduces Sōsuke to a Zen master, whose gaze reminds him of a "sudden flash of a cold sword blade in the dark."[42] The master gives Sōsuke a kōan: "What was your original state before your parents were born?" The next day, Sōsuke lines up in front of the wall with advanced trainees and awaits his turn to present his solution. The master evaluates his answer and says, "It is no good unless you bring something glaring."[43] The master continues, "Anyone with even a little education could say as much as you said."[44] Shortly after, Sōsuke leaves the temple. He never meets Yasui.

Sōsuke fails to solve the kōan for three reasons. First, he looks for a quick solution and tries to find an answer in Zen literature, such as *The Blue Cliff Record*. Second, Sōsuke has trouble concentrating and is disturbed by mundane thoughts from his everyday life; he feels obligated to write to his wife and wonders about Yasui's whereabouts. Third, his time for Zen practice is too short; the more he hurries, the further he moves away from his goal. After all, the narrator says,

> He [Sōsuke] had come here to have the gate opened to him, but its warden had remained obstinately within, and had not so much as shown his face, however long he knocked. The only greeting he had received was, "It's no use knocking. Open the gate yourself and enter." . . .
> It seemed to him that he had been fated from birth to stand forever outside the gate, unable to pass through. There was nothing he could do about it.[45]

Sōsuke could not resolve the kōan because he is a man who can never enter the "gate," no matter how hard he tries.

The critic Damian Flanagan associates Sōseki's "gate" with "the Gate of Eternal Return" in Nietzsche's *Thus Spoke Zarathustra*. This connection is based on an anecdote that suggests Natsume Sōseki allowed two of his students to decide the title of this novel, and during that discussion the students happened to refer to the gate in *Zarathustra*. Flanagan discovers significant marginalia included in an English translation of *Zarathustra* found in Sōseki's personal library and concludes that Sōseki must have been familiar with the notion of "eternal return."[46]

In his reading of *The Gate*, Flanagan considers "adventurer" a key word. Sakai, Sōsuke's landlord, uses this word when he describes Sakai's younger brother who has gone to Manchuria and Yasui. Flanagan observes that Sōsuke also embarks on an adventure by going to a Zen temple, but his failure to answer the kōan leads him back to the beginning, and thus Sōsuke never changes. The way *The Gate* ends seems to reinforce Flanagan's idea of repetition: Oyone tells Sōsuke, "It's a good thing, isn't it. Spring is finally here," to which Sōsuke responds, "But it will soon be winter again."[47] Flanagan's reading of *The Gate* represents the popular perception of the novel—that is, Sōsuke is a "will-less person" and Zen has no impact on his life, although he is surrounded by various religious images.[48] However, clear signs of change in Sōsuke's attitude toward himself and his marriage can be detected through the analysis of the religious symbols that permeate the novel from beginning to end.

A careful reader will notice how *The Gate* begins: "Sōsuke had brought a cushion on to the veranda and plopped himself on it, cross-legged, and was now basking in the midafternoon sun. After a time he tossed aside the magazine he held in his hands and stretched himself out full length on his side."⁴⁹ In the source language, what was translated as a "cushion" is *zabuton* 坐蒲團, which indicates a cushion used for Buddhist sitting in meditation.

Zabuton is related to futon, which in Japan refers to both a mattress and a quilt to cover one's body—"buton" as "zabuton" is a voiced "futon."⁵⁰ Today, *zabuton* is commonly known as a square cushion used for sitting on a tatami floor, but it was also called futon. A number of references to futons are found in Buddhist commentaries written in medieval China and Japan. For instance, in *Treasury of the True Dharma Eye* (*Shōbōgenzō*), Dōgen introduces the story of Master Huileng who "wore out twenty sitting mats" during his twenty-nine years of training.⁵¹ In a section titled "Rules for Zazen," Dōgen discusses how to position one's body for sitting meditation:

> When sitting zazen, wear the kashaya [*kesa*, patched robe] and use a round cushion. The cushion should not be placed all the way under the legs, but only under the buttocks. In this way the crossed legs rest on the [soft] mat and the backbone is supported with the round cushion. This is the method used by all buddha ancestors for zazen.⁵²

Translations of futon vary and include words such as "mat" and "round cushion," but there is only one usage in the source language: Buddhist monks employed futons in their religious training.

The implication of the cushion that Sōsuke sits on is not just that it is a seat—if it were, the kanji character 座 might have been used—but is associated with 坐, as in *zazen* 坐禅. "Cross-legged" also suggests a bodily posture required for sitting meditation. The very first line of *The Gate*, therefore, indicates Sōsuke's effort to sit in meditation before giving up on it by changing his posture and lying down on the veranda.

In addition to the cushion, a Daruma doll suggests Sōsuke's involvement in Zen. One day he finds a balloon that takes the shape of Daruma when inflated. He brings this children's toy back home and shows it to his wife and his brother Koroku. They play with the Daruma doll and Koroku blows over it. The doll tips over but bounces back because of its resilience. Furthermore, the critic Kumakura Chiyuki points out that the words Sōsuke later hears from the Zen master—"it is no good unless you bring something glaring" (*motto girori toshita tokoro o motte konakereba dameda* もっと、ぎろりとした所を持って来なければ駄目だ)—brings to mind an image of the Daruma doll, as the homophone *girori* alludes to Bodhidharma's rolling eyeballs.⁵³

Kumakura argues that Sōsuke changes his attitude after returning from the temple. He carefully examines the implications of Sōseki's choice of unusual kanji characters and how they might be symbolic of Sōsuke's psychological transformation. At the end of *The Gate*, Sōsuke goes to a public bath and hears a conversation between a young merchant and a middle-aged Buddhist priest about the arrival of spring. The merchant tells the priest that he had just heard a bush warbler sing for the first time that year. The priest also says he heard the song of a bush warbler a few days earlier. The merchant continues, "It's still the beginning of the season, so he wasn't in very good voice." The priest says, "Yes, his tongue is still thick." When Sōsuke returns home, he repeats the conversation he overheard at the bathhouse to Oyone many times. In this scene, Kumakura points out that non-standard kanji characters 洗湯 are used for public bath, which is usually written 銭湯, indicating Sōsuke's decision to wash away his old self (洗 means "to wash or clean").[54]

Kumakura further predicts Sōsuke's growth in his reading of a passage in which Sōsuke clips his nails: "Sōsuke stepped onto the veranda and began to clip his finger nails, which had grown to quite a length. 'But it will soon be winter again,' he said, as with downcast eyes he continued to cut his nails (*sōsuke wa enni dete nagaku nobita tsume o kirinagara 'un shikashi mata jiki fuyu ni naruyo' to kotaete shita o muitamama hasami o ugokashiteita* 宗助は縁に出て長く延びた爪を剪りながら「うん、然し又じき冬になるよ」と答えて、下を向いたまま鋏を動かしていた)."[55] Kumakura points out that the kanji character 鋏 is used for the nail clipper, a character that usually refers to scissors, and the character 剪る is employed for "to clip," instead of the character 切る. The character 剪る means "to shave off unnecessary parts to encourage new growth." Based on the ways in which the kanji characters 鋏 and 剪 appear in this passage, Kumakura concludes that the phrase "he continued to cut his nails" indicates Sōsuke's determination to transform his sense of being by removing unnecessary impediments.[56]

Sōsuke's desire to change himself also suggests his ongoing engagement with Zen. A closer look at the conversation between the merchant and Buddhist priest shows that the word *mondō* (dialogue or exchange) is used: "When Sōsuke got home, he recounted to Oyone the conversation (*mondō*) he had overheard at the bath (*Sōsuke wa uchini kaette oyone ni kono uguisu no mondō o kurikaeshite kikaseta* 宗助は家に帰って御米に此鶯の問答を繰り返して聞かせた)."[57] Here the word *mondō* is not the same as the usual word for conversation, *kaiwa* 会話, but instead evokes the image of Zen. First, there is the phrase *Zen mondō* 禅問答, referring to Zen dialogue between a master and a disciple, which is part of Buddhist training. It includes the exchange over a kōan. Second, as the verb "to repeat" (*kurikaeshite*)—instead of "to recount"—suggests, Zen dialogue is something that needs to be reiterated for the purpose of the training. Third, in Japan, the singing of a bush warbler is characterized as *hō-hokekyō*, a word that reminds the Japanese of the title of the *Lotus Sutra* known as *Hokkekyō*. As Jacques Derrida would say, "the movement of signification is possible only if each so-called 'present' element, each element appearing on the scene of presence, is related to something other than itself, thereby keeping within itself the mark of the past element"[58]; here the implication of Sōsuke's interest in Zen becomes clear through the associative chain of the middle-aged Buddhist priest, the word *mondō*, the meaning "to repeat," a bush warbler, and the *Lotus Sutra*. It is fair to say that, textually at least, Sōsuke begins to perceive ordinary matters from a Buddhist perspective.

Although Sōsuke does not attain Buddhist enlightenment, his Buddhist development calls to mind the three-stage narrative structure of Buddhism, which consists of "ground, path, and goal." Concerning nirvana as the goal of one's spiritual path, Buswell and Gimello state, "To 'achieve' nirvāṇa, then, is not to 'arrive at,' much less to 'settle,' anywhere. Rather (if we may hazard some descriptions that are themselves only metaphors, but perhaps less misleading than the metaphor of 'destination'), to 'achieve' nirvāṇa, is to be released from confinement, to embark on a continuing transformation, to participate in unfettered change and in unbounded interrelation with all things and beings."[59] The path itself becomes a goal when one accepts one's problems and realizes that life is in a state of flux. Spiritual cultivation is therefore constantly needed. In this sense, Sōsuke's trip to the Zen temple was never meaningless. Self-transformation becomes a lifelong challenge for him, and he will continue to work on his spiritual strength.

This reading of *The Gate* raises an interesting question, which can easily be overlooked, concerning the author's strategy of writing and the reader's interpretation of the subtextual Buddhist message embedded in the narrative. In fact, the English translator misses *ateji*, kanji characters substituting for other characters with the same sound—however, it is extremely difficult for such a subtextual meaning to be translated into English. The question, therefore, is whether it represents Sōsuke's consciousness or is Sōseki's strategy to get the reader into a Buddhist mood with a novel that does not appear at all Buddhist.

It must be noted, however, that the word *mondō*, discussed above, appears in *The Gate* more than once. At the beginning of the novel, Sōsuke and Oyone repeatedly debate (*mondō suru*) whether or not he should see his uncle in Tokyo, who has been avoiding talking to him. As it turns out, the uncle mishandled Sōsuke's inheritance, which had been entrusted to him after Sōsuke's parents died. In addition, when Sōsuke visits his landlord, he overhears laughter during the conversation (*mondō*) between his family members and a peddler trying to sell merchandise to them. In these secular contexts, the word *mondō* is used.

The ordinary exchange between Sōsuke and Oyone, concerning the arrival of spring and the recurrence of winter, can also be read via a Buddhist context. Here, Dōgen's notion of "Being-Time" (*uji*), or "being that is inseparable from time," serves as a reference. According to Norman Waddell and Masao Abe, spring passes not because spring moves forward, but because of man's perception of spring at different stages, even though spring manifests itself only moment by moment.[60] To put it differently, time does not pass by in and of itself but is instead inseparable from one's realization of the present moment. Given this Buddhist notion of time, what appears to be Sōsuke's ironic response to Oyone's joy about the coming of spring at the end of *The Gate*—"But it will soon be winter again"—may instead be his Buddhist awareness of time in the present. In this line of thinking, Sōsuke's "downcast eyes" while cutting his nails can further be interpreted in terms of Zen practice: downcast eyes as a practitioner's half-closed eyes during his sitting meditative posture and Sōsuke's cutting his nails as an act of repetition suggesting Zen *mondō* as a repetitive practice.

In conventional readings of *The Gate*, Sōsuke remains unchanged because of his negative Zen experience; however, the present study has demonstrated that sitting in meditation and kōan practice had a great impact on him and that Sōsuke is going to change. At the same time, Sōsuke remains uncertain about what to do with Yasui if Yasui happens to visit Sakai again. Most likely, in the near future, Sōsuke will share his anxiety over Yasui's visit with Oyone, who confessed her guilt to Sōsuke, which was caused by her third miscarriage and subsequent visit to a fortune-teller. He made a mistake by treating Yasui's visit as his own problem, not telling Oyone about it, and by escaping to a Zen Buddhist temple. If Sōsuke had been able to open up himself to Oyone, she would have played a therapeutic role in his struggle against Yasui and helped him find a solution.

Next, Tayama Katai's *The Quilt* is discussed. The protagonist's struggle, with the Buddhist notion of suffering, is considered and the futon, sleeping mat and quilt, is treated as a Buddhist symbol.

The Quilt: *Futon* and Buddhist Imagery

The Quilt (*Futon*, 1907) is perhaps Katai's most popular autobiographical novel and has been frequently studied by Western scholars. Irmela Hijiya-Kirschnereit evaluates the work as "not a drama about marriage and love, as is *Einsame Menschen* [Gerhart Hauptmann's drama], but is confined to present the inner life of a man with only very limited insight into his own spiritual problems who delights in indulging himself in unrealistic, adolescent daydreams."[61] Tomi Suzuki introduces the view of many Japanese critics who consider *The Quilt* to be the "first modern Japanese novel to depict faithfully the 'facts' of the author's life."[62] Edward Fowler, however, suggests that modern autobiographical fiction "would have emerged with or without the appearance of *Futon*."[63]

The Quilt is written in the third person, but through a mode of reading whereby the singular identity of author, narrator, and hero is assumed, it also gives the sense of first-person narration.[64] The interchangeability of the narrator and hero, as well as the author's "sincere" attempt to depict his "true" experiences are, however, questionable. Fowler, for instance, points out that "Despite his [Katai's] theoretical insistence on the privileged status of lived experience, then, Katai's allusions to other literary texts [such as Gerhart Hauptmann's *Lonely Lives*] can only be described as a conscious attempt to mediate that experience."[65] *The Quilt* is a work of fiction, which represents the author's own experience, and is mediated by form and the narrative style.

A Summary of *The Quilt*

The novel depicts the anguish of a middle-aged fiction writer, Takenaka Tokio, who struggles simultaneously to help his beloved student, Yoshiko, and to contain his carnal desires. Tokio is married and has three children. His tedious marriage and the boredom of his work as an editor of geography books have gradually exhausted his spirit. That is when he meets Yoshiko, a beautiful young college student attending a Christian college in Kōbe. She is a fan of his work and wishes to become a writer herself. Tokio accepts her as a protégée. Tokio becomes captivated by her beauty and her passion for literature, but he manages to combat temptation and keep his distance as a teacher.

Yoshiko soon starts dating a young man named Tanaka, who studies religion at a Christian university in Kyoto. After visiting her hometown, Yoshiko spends two days in Kyoto with Tanaka on her way back to Tokyo. Tokio is enraged by her conduct and becomes jealous of Tanaka. Yoshiko swears to Tokio that her relationship with Tanaka is platonic and asks him to conceal her love from her parents. Tokio maintains his role as her mentor and even becomes a "kind-hearted guardian" of Yoshiko's love.[66] Tanaka moves to Tokyo soon after. He gives up his religious studies and leaves the university against the advice of his benefactor, a member of a Christian church in Kōbe, who had supported his education. Tokio meets and tries to persuade Tanaka to return to Kyoto and at least complete his education. Tanaka, however, refuses, and Yoshiko asks Tokio for permission to live with Tanaka. Tokio defers to Yoshiko's father to settle the matter.

Yoshiko's father comes to Tokyo and meets Yoshiko and Tanaka. He dislikes Tanaka who is rather rebellious, but is reluctant to take Yoshiko home because, as a local politician, he is concerned about his family's reputation in the community. He suggests that Yoshiko and Tanaka stay apart for three years and study individually to see how their relationship develops. Tanaka, however, presses him to promise to give them permission to marry. Tokio then discovers that the couple's relationship has not been platonic from the start. He hates Tanaka and despises Yoshiko, whom Tokio now sees as a liar, and he regrets treating her gently when he assumed she was a virgin. Tokio is haunted by remorse for being her "kind-hearted guardian" and for not having slept with her when he had a chance.

Yoshiko's father eventually takes her home. Tokio finds joy in separating Yoshiko and Tanaka, although laments his decision to send her home. After her departure, Tokio's life again becomes monotonous. Five days later, he receives a letter from Yoshiko, apologizing for having caused him so much trouble. The novel ends with Tokio's psychological impasse:

> He went upstairs to Yoshiko's room, which was still as she had left it the day of her departure. Overcome with nostalgia and longing, he wanted to recall something of her from those of her things that were left behind.... Presently he stood up and opened the sliding partition. Three large wicker traveling-cases, tied with cord, were waiting to be sent off, and beyond them in a pile lay the bedding that Yoshiko normally used—a mattress of light green arabesque design, and a quilt of the same pattern, with thick cotton padding. Tokio drew them out. The familiar smell of a woman's oil and sweat excited him beyond words. The velvet edging of the quilt was noticeably dirty, and Tokio pressed his face to it, immersing himself in that familiar female smell.
>
> All at once he was stricken with desire, with sadness, with despair. He spread out the mattress, lay the quilt out on it, and wept as he buried his face against the cold, stained, velvet edging.
>
> The room was gloomy, and outside the wind was raging.[67]

Tokio's depression coincides with the weather outside, which is cold and miserable. He is once again a lonely man who has no incentive in life.

Katai expresses his own frustration and erotic desire by using Tokio as his hero. As an author, Katai appears to reveal his struggle, carnal desire, and spiritual gridlock through his protagonist. According to Karatani Kōjin, however, Katai must have realized his sexuality through literary confession, which helped him construct his inner life.[68] While critics have generally considered *The Quilt* to be a work focused on love and sexuality, it can be read as a work of path literature informed by impermanent sensibilities, which depicts various types of suffering.

Representation of Religions and a Buddhist Perspective on Impermanence and Suffering in *The Quilt*

A careful reader will notice the significance of the names with which the novel begins: "As he started down the gentle slope of that road in Koishikawa that leads from Kirishitanzaka to Gokurakusui, he thought things over"[69] (*koishikawa no kirishitanzaka kara gokurakusui ni deru michino daradarazaka o oriyōtoshite karewa kangaeta* 小石川の切支丹坂から極楽水に出る道のだらだら坂を下りようとして渠は考えた). Tokio is moving from "Christian Hill" (*kirishitanzaka*) to "the fountain of the Pure Land" (*gokurakusui*). These are historic places—the former derives from the Tokugawa-period prison where "Hidden Christians" were locked before interrogations, whereas the latter indicates the place where Denzū-in, a family temple of the Tokugawa shogunate, was built.[70] The first line of *The Quilt* thus indicates Tokio's dissociation from Christianity and his descent toward the Buddhist themes of loneliness and impermanence.

Yoshiko's devout parents had her educated at a Christian school, which was open-minded about modern literature, even though the Ministry of Education discouraged students from reading contemporary novels. At the school church, Yoshiko learned the importance of prayer, enjoyed Christmas nights, cultivated ideals, celebrated the beauty of mankind, and turned a blind eye to man's base passions. She enjoyed the freedom of living in a boarding house, which means that she grew up differently from most Japanese girls. In Tokio's eyes, Yoshiko exhibits both the positive and negative aspects of modern young Japanese women, but because she is both socially active and spiritually conservative, she is an enigma to him.

Tokio, for instance, cannot understand why Yoshiko dates Tanaka. He finds Tanaka "annoyingly smug and too mature for his years," and with the "distasteful, unpleasant attitude of one raised in the Christian faith."[71] Tanaka abandons his religious faith and ignores Yoshiko's father's compromise—that is, if the relationship between Yoshiko and Tanaka "accords with the Will of God," they will be married in three years.[72] Tanaka's carnal desires override the piety he once had when studying at Dōshisha University. Tokio ends his relationship with Tanaka (the former Christian) and Yoshiko's father (the devout Christian) when Yoshiko returns home.

Throughout the novel, Tokio is depicted as a lonely person who is sympathetic to Johannes Vockerat in Hauptmann's drama *Lonely People*.[73] His wife is not interested in the novels that Tokio laboriously writes, because all she cares about is their children. Tokio feels like "screaming his loneliness out loud."[74] With or without Yoshiko, he is unhappy with "a life that a man in his mid-thirties should expect rather to enjoy," and is disturbed by "unhealthy thoughts about his job" and "his sexual frustration."[75] Tokio has tasted "the bitterness of lonely torment," because he stands apart from his family, society, and the literary establishment.[76] For Tokio, loneliness is a form of suffering.

The nature of Tokio's suffering can be understood within a Buddhist framework. Shakyamuni Buddha considered birth, illness, aging, and death to be the fundamental causes of suffering. Birth activates interaction with the so-called "five *skandhas*" or five aggregates—one's biological needs, sensations, cognitive functions, volitions, and discernments—that forms one's personality and behavior. The five aggregates intensify Tokio's base passions and become the cause of his suffering (*goun jōku*). He suffers even more because of his unattainable desires (*gufu tokku*), the loss of and separation from loved ones (*aibetsu riku*), and contact with those he detests (*onzō eku*).

In *The Quilt*, illness, aging, and death have a psychological impact on Tokio. He drinks to overcome his loneliness and to relieve frustrations about Yoshiko. At the same time, Yoshiko, who frets over her relationship with Tanaka, suffers from neurasthenia (*shinkei suijaku*) and constantly takes medicine. Tokio compares himself unfavorably to Tanaka: "Young birds flock only with other young birds—the wings of old birds like me aren't beautiful enough to attract the young ones any more."[77] As an old bird, Tokio broods over his life as a married man who "has his wife taken from him by his children and his children taken from him by his wife."[78] Tokio's despair increases when he reads Guy de Maupassant's *As Strong as Death*, which deals with the second love of an old painter. All these anxieties lead Tokio to a spiritual stalemate.

Tokio also suffers because of his pride. He neither divorces his wife nor commits infidelity because he is too conscientious to degrade himself. Society expects him to be a "correct and trustworthy man," while morality forces him to taste "the bitterness of standing on the outside of destiny." Tokio regrets "being controlled by this strength."[79]

Such moral judgment generates ironic effects for Tokio. He detests Tanaka but becomes the "kind-hearted guardian" of Yoshiko's love. Tokio lies to himself and never confesses his love for Yoshiko. He then creates a situation in which he has to communicate with the person he dislikes most—Tanaka—and fools himself even more. Tokio's conscience creates a chain reaction that puts him in a position where he does not wish to be.

Tokio's frustration is accentuated by the images of a futon. When he discovers Yoshiko's romance, he regrets losing his beloved student to Tanaka. He takes it out on his wife, scares his children, gets dead drunk, and recites a childish poem:

> Halfway through the verse he suddenly stood up, still wearing the quilt [futon] with which his wife had covered him, and, looking just like a little mountain, moved towards the parlor. His wife, very worried, followed and asked where he was going. He paid no attention and tried to enter the toilet, still clad in the quilt. His wife was flustered:
>
> "What are you doing? You shouldn't get drunk like this! It's horrible! That's the toilet!"
>
> Suddenly she pulled at the quilt [futon] from behind, and was left holding it there in the entrance to the toilet. Tokio was relieving himself in a dangerously erratic manner, and on finishing he promptly flopped straight down on his side, still in the toilet. His disgusted wife tried her best to move him, but he would neither move nor stand. Yet neither did he fall asleep, but rather, with wide piercing eyes in a face like red clay, he just stared at the rain pouring down outside.[80]

Unlike Yoshiko's futon, the futon with which Tokio's wife covers him does not excite him. However, Tokio expresses his loneliness through the futon his wife brings to him as well as Yoshiko's futon. The futon is therefore a symbol of Tokio's falling out of love with his wife and his fantasy for Yoshiko.

According to Michael Wheeler, who examines the representations of death during the Victorian era, Western beds are symbols of "sexual irony." Concerning a painting of the deathbed by W. I. Walton titled *The Last Moments of HRH The Prince Consort*, in which doctors, politicians, and royal family members assemble in the state bedchamber, Wheeler states,

Walton's picture, however, not only suppresses emotion, but also conceals a potential for sexual irony, with the children of a fruitful marriage gathered near the bed. The overt analysis of the relationship between *eros* and *thanatos*, however, was largely the preserve of the Gothic in the nineteenth century, where the "normal" (and safe) compartmentalizing of birth, marriage, and death was disrupted. The marriage-bed is shown to be a deathbed, for example, in *Wuthering Heights*, and in Sheridan Le Fanu's terrifying story, "Schalken the Painter."[81]

Accordingly, when a futon is viewed in relationship to a bed as a natural environment for copulation, it can also suggest an erotic paradox. There is, however, a fundamental difference between beds and futons, and this adds another layer of irony. Whereas beds are fixed, futons are transportable, as the futon with which Tokio's wife covers Tokio becomes an extremely long overcoat (futons are folded, unfolded, placed in a closet, or carried to other places). The mobility of the futon, its association with sadness (as is the case for Tokio), and the futon's Buddhist implication (as discussed in the reading of *The Gate*) highlight a sense of impermanence that undercuts it as a focus of erotic obsession.

Furthermore, Tokio's loneliness invokes an aesthetic sensibility connected to nature, and again, evokes a sense of impermanence. We are told he is sad not because of his inability to express his love for Yoshiko, but because there is "a more profound and greater sadness, a sadness inherent in the innermost reaches of human life." That sadness is the "irresistible force" of nature in which water flows and flowers wilt, and there is nothing that anyone can do about it because man is also ephemeral and powerless when it comes to the phenomena of nature. With these ideas running through his head, Tokio ascends the *Nakane* slope and goes to the grove at Hachiman—a Shinto shrine in Ichigaya—passes the lanterns in the precincts, and stands on the high slope of the shrine where he used to listen to the faint sounds of a *shamisen* that his wife played when she was still single. He wonders how he lost his passion for the woman he had married eight years earlier and realizes the "frightening power of time." Tokio then looks up and sees a "large and lusterless copper-colored moon" whose dreary appearance fills his heart with "unbearable sadness."[82]

Tokio neither gains a sense of relief nor seeks salvation; he only cries out in sadness. According to Motoori Norinaga (1730–1801), a scholar of classical Japanese literature and national learning, misfortunes are caused by a vengeful *kami*—*Magatsuhi no kami*—and there is nothing that people can do about it. They simply cry their eyes out and endure disasters without seeking an answer through the teachings of organized religion.[83] Steven Odin points out that Norinaga valued "human feelings that move the heart-mind (*kokoro*) to spontaneous overflow of deep emotions" and that Norinaga's aesthetic sensibility was very different from aesthetic contemplation related to Zen Buddhism and the aesthetic taste sought by the protagonist of *The Three-Cornered World*.[84] Whether or not the narrator of *The Quilt* is aware of Norinaga's religio-aesthetic sensibility, we are left with the feeling that Tokio only relates his sense of pathos with depressing scenery and that deities of nature, or *kami*, are actively out to get him.

This reading of *The Quilt* illustrates the degree to which religious objects, moral values, and Christianity are plot devices that dramatize Tokio's loneliness, discontent with his life, friction with other characters, conflict with his own interests, and his spiritual impasse. By leaving Yoshiko, her father, and Tanaka, Tokio rids himself of Christian influences and returns to his previous state where life was weary and unproductive. At first glance, *The Quilt* does not appear to follow the Buddhist narrative pattern. Tokio's descending Christian Hill only corresponds to his spiritual descent and the story ends without his gaining a sense of direction in life. Tokio, however, has a serious existential problem and his interaction with Yoshiko only worsens his pessimistic view on life. In order to overcome these conditions, he takes a traditional path: he embraces Buddhist sensibilities after associating with and dissociating from Christianity, a symbol of Western power. He ascends the hill, visits a Shinto shrine, and reflects on his past. When Yoshiko leaves for good, he releases his emotions for the first time by bursting into tears, showing a sign of change.

By reading *The Three-Cornered World*, *The Gate*, and *The Quilt* through the lens of Buddhism, we get a clearer picture of the struggles that modern Japanese intellectuals had with regard to religious faith and spirituality, struggles that both literary critics and Buddhist scholars have ignored. This way of reading, which pays careful attention to how imagery can be read in a multivalent way to reveal subtextual meanings connected to spiritual deadlock, also problematizes the assumption often made with regard to realist or naturalist fiction: that the author's goal was to create a smoothly realist experience for the reader.

CHAPTER SEVEN

Buddhist Attainment and Mystical Experience

A narrative that features a protagonist's spiritual growth based on his awareness of causality and interpersonal relationships can be found in personal fiction written on the theme of self-transformation. Unlike the artist-protagonist in *The Three-Cornered World*, Sōsuke in *The Gate*, and Tokio in *The Quilt*, the characters examined in this chapter experience Buddhist, or quasi-Buddhist, awakenings. Tayama Katai's *The Miracle of a Buddhist Monk* and Shiga Naoya's *A Dark Night's Passing* are analyzed in light of the main characters' turning of the mind. Whereas Jikai in *The Miracle of a Buddhist Monk* becomes a devout Buddhist priest after his mystical experience, Kensaku in *A Dark Night's Passing* attains spiritual liberation through an inexplicable unity with nature. Jikai was a Buddhist trainee in his youth, so it appears natural for him to return to the temple and become a priest after the exhaustion of personal struggle and social unrest. Kensaku, however, is critical of Buddhist clergy and organized religion that promotes worldly benefit. Instead, natural settings affect his spiritual state, which develops dialectically between his rational thinking and irrational behavior. The main characters' mystical encounters and self-examinations in both novels are part of a Buddhist narrative pattern known as the "ground, path, and goal." Before discussing the transformative power of the path Jikai and Kensaku followed, defining Buddhist mysticism is necessary.

Mysticism and Mystical Experience

Definitions of mystical experiences vary, depending on scholars' approaches and religious traditions. William James recognizes a broad range of mystical experiences and characterizes four psychological aspects of mystical experience: "ineffability," "noetic quality" or intellectual quality, "transiency," and "passivity." For mystics, the mystical experience is too sacred to be conceptualized, but at the same time, they express their experiences in a paradoxical way: they simultaneously reveal and obscure parts of their experiences. In other words, mystical experiences are both intelligible and unintelligible. Mystical experiences occur during a short period of time and mystics often receive revelations "not as active seekers, but as passive recipients."[1]

William Harmless characterizes mysticism as a "domain" of religion and points out its "life-altering aftereffects," regarding a "profound revelation of who we are, what the world is, and especially (for the religions of the West) who God is."[2] Mysticism is a feature of monotheistic religions, such as Christianity, Judaism, and Islam, but Harmless also finds elements of mysticism in Buddhism:

> "[M]ysticism" might be circumspectly applied to Buddhism, which advocates contemplative disciplines and experiential breakthroughs and a liberating knowledge of the deeper truths and about the self and others and world, but which does so in nontheistic terms and which denies anything like a substantial self (and thus any "experiencer").[3]

Mysticism is a concept useful in explaining the sudden awakening of Buddhist practitioners, for whom the self is not a fixed entity, but rather one that comes into being in relation to others and all other things.

Ernst Tugendhat separates "mysticism" and "religion," defining the former as "putting the weight of one's wishes into perspective, or even denying them." This process triggers a *transformation of one's self-conception.*[4] Whether a mystic feels the presence of God (or an ultimate reality) or develops awareness of being one with reality through meditative practice,[5] when the mystic becomes aware of the numinous (i.e., the universe, Being, Dao, or even God), he "steps back—be it absolutely or only minimally—from his wishes and seeks to reach peace of mind."[6] In the case of Buddhism, Siddhartha Gautama stepped back from his determination to solve his problem when he collapsed after a long period of ascetic practice. He was rescued and fed by a young girl. After he gained strength, he meditated under the bodhi tree and became the Buddha.

Meditation and the ritual practices associated with contemplation can be considered a form of "rational mysticism." According to Alexi Procyshyn and Mario Wenning, who interpreted Tugendhat's study, this type of mysticism illustrates "a problematic desire to flee from this world by abandoning all desires in a paradoxical act of wanting not to want, or an egocentric escape from egocentricity."[7] Seeking and experiencing Buddhist enlightenment can be a self-centered act, as practitioners think of only their spiritual well-being. When Siddhartha Gautama attained the Buddhahood, however, he returned to the world and shared his realization with others. In the case of Mahayana Buddhism, mystical experiences enhance practitioners' "compassion," one of the two qualities of bodhisattvas, known as wisdom and compassion.[8] Initially, both Jikai in *The Miracle of a Buddhist Monk* and Kensaku in *A Dark Night's Passing* only care about themselves, but after their awakening experiences, which took the form of rational mysticism, Jikai returns to his community and Kensaku returns to his wife, and they seek to reconnect themselves to others. The narrators, who have a Buddhist worldview, tell us these stories.

The Miracle of a Buddhist Monk: Mystical Self-Realization at a Buddhist Temple

In *The Miracle of a Buddhist Monk*, Katai models the protagonist Jikai, a middle-aged Buddhist priest, partly on his friend Ōta Gyokumei (1871–1927). Ōta was the resident priest of Kenfukuji, affiliated with Sōtō Zen sect, in present-day Hanyū City in Saitama Prefecture. He was also known as a poet. Katai married his younger sister, Risa.[9]

Jikai returns to Chōshō-in, a Buddhist temple, where he spent his youth as the youngest student of the old resident priest, and recalls bygone times. He fell in love with the priest's daughter, but the priest had already decided to have her marry a senior disciple, Jiun, who was expected to take over his position. Jikai gives up his training and moves to Tokyo, where he joins a group of self-indulgent people, and then sets out on an aimless journey to Taiwan and Manchuria. On his return to Japan, Jikai hears of the arrest and execution of those in the "dreadful group" (*osoroshii mure*) in Tokyo who had been his friends. When he is tormented by this incident, a caretaker of Chōshō-in asks Jikai to return to the temple and become the resident priest. Jikai accepts the offer because that temple is the only place he can stay and because none of his activities have made much sense to him since leaving it. Back at Chōshō-in, Jikai discovers that after the master's death Jiun became the resident priest but did not marry the master's daughter. Jiun womanized, exhausted temple funds, sold off its properties, and disappeared. The temple, with its distinguished history, was thus left in ruins for years without a resident priest. Jikai is overwhelmed by his lack of readiness to resume his career as a

Buddhist priest. He becomes introverted and spends most of his time passively in his room, not even interacting with the caretakers.

One day a storm causes more damage to the temple. Although the roof of the worship hall leaks badly and the floor is covered with water, the statue of the Buddha remains unaffected. Jikai feels as if the statue has absorbed and removed his negative karma. He is now reborn. After this event, Jikai goes to the worship hall and eagerly chants sutras, not to gain the merit in chanting them, but to praise the Buddha's virtues. He is filled with energy after discovering a diamond-like mind in the statue of the Buddha, and no longer feels bothered by his past.

Jikai goes to seek for alms and observes the people's base passions. At a troubled household, he chants a sutra for a long time. His sincerity and devotion move many people, including a criminal, a woman who survived a double suicide, an obnoxious blacksmith, and a young girl who has suffered from an incestuous relationship. These people begin worshiping Jikai as a living buddha. Jikai neither recruits temple members nor repairs the temple by himself—all he does is chant sutras as resident priest. The power of his chanting, however, inspires the community. Temple membership increases and the parishioners restore Chōshō-in, which seems only natural to Jikai.

The Miracle of a Buddhist Monk is a narrative of religious conversion and a work of path literature. The kanji compound of "kiseki" 奇蹟, as in *Aru sō no kiseki*, translated as *The Miracle of a Buddhist Monk* in the present study, also suggests "unusual marks," "unusual footprints," or "an unusual trace (奇跡)." When Jikai's spiritual development is taken into account, the title of this work can be translated as *The Unusual Path That a Buddhist Monk Takes*. The story fits the narrative pattern of Buddhist praxis consisting of "ground, path, and goal," which Richard Payne describes as "frustrating repetitive behaviors (ground), attention to the nature of one's existence and the consequence of one's mental, verbal, and bodily actions (path), and freedom from the delusions that drive the round of frustrating repetitive actions (goal)."[10] Jikai, who grew up at a Buddhist temple as a minor priest trainee and who failed to come to terms with his past, is transformed into a genuine Buddhist priest. As a result, Chōshō-in is rebuilt, although Jikai is not initially concerned with its rebuilding.

The fall and rise of Chōshō-in reflects Jikai's spiritual impasse and regeneration. Out of despair, Jikai leaves the temple at the age of nineteen, becomes unethical, and even purposefully violates the Buddhist precepts. Everything he does turns out to be a failure. When a caretaker of Chōshō-in approaches him, it provides him an opportunity to examine the ideas of freedom and free will with which he was occupied. He gradually recognizes his egocentric nature and that he has been attached to himself and to the ideas of love and freedom. His contemplation of change over time, recollection of the past, and self-examination lead him to discover his karmic connections to the temple. It is the only place that connects his past, present, and future. Chōshō-in thus becomes a symbol of unity for Jikai—his being and the existence of the temple become one.

Buddhist awakening takes place as Jikai internalizes his inevitable relationship with the temple. Although he does not actively seek mystical guidance, when the time is right and he is at the peak of his spiritual inquiry, he awakens to a state of unity. According to Tugendhat, mystical experience can be interpreted in two paradoxical ways: a mystic only thinks of himself and wishes to "become one with the One" and "instead of seeing everything from the egocentric perspective, he [the mystic] sees himself from the perspective of the world."[11] In the case of Buddhism, a mystic's desire for unity naturally causes him to change his perspective,[12] as is the case for Jikai. He is no longer attached to his past, which was the cause of his suffering, and is free from ordinary problems that concern most people. Further, Jikai loses his sense of survivor guilt over the deaths of those in the dreadful group. Yet his awareness of the dark side of humanity allows him to be more sympathetic with those who need spiritual guidance. His life as resident priest of Chōshō-in really begins as he starts seeing the world from the Buddhist standpoint.

Jikai's sudden awakening can further be explained in terms of Zen practitioners' awakening experiences. Zen meditation is both mystical and not mystical. It is mystical because meditation helps a practitioner direct his spiritual energy toward the moment of a sudden awakening. Zen meditation is not mystical because the inherent existence of the self, the perpetuity of what one may call the "mind" or "soul," is denied in Buddhism. According to William Harmless, realizing the lack of the inherent existence of the self is liberating because it is a "life-altering, world-shattering breakthrough. It offers an utterly new way of seeing, thinking, feeling, acting, being. That experience is said to open a radical, nondual way of seeing that shatters both illusory distinctions between and false conflations of self and others and world."[13] The moment of awakening itself is less important compared to the change of perspective that takes place as a result of the mystical experience. While living his everyday life, a practitioner starts looking at his life and the world from a new perspective. In order to do this, Zen practitioners must continue to meditate. As Dōgen would say, sitting in meditation is "at once practice-in-realization and realization-in-practice."[14] After his mystical experience, Jikai continues to sit in front of the Buddhist statue and recite the sutras in the temple hall, but he does not do this because he seeks a mystical unity again. For him, sitting, chanting, and praising the Buddha's virtue is a form of practice.

Jikai's mystical experience and self-realization do not take place out of the blue. Rather, he is guided through a series of events. Initially, he pursues his own gain and then thinks about reforming society by joining the dreadful group, finally turning to introspection. This process illustrates the shifting of his attitude toward life—from the extrovert to the introvert. The narrator states,

> Civilization generated hypocrisy, decadence, rights of winners, and the notion of individuality. In fact, he [Jikai] insisted on those rights. In order to obtain everything he had wanted, he fought his way out with knowledge he had gained. He pursued wealth, glory, and power. For him, mountains and hills had to be as flat as plains. However, equality does not mean equal material distribution. Equality does not appear on the surface of human life and through personality. Equality does not fall into the hands of victors who rack their brains and use every means to get it. When he reflects on these things, memories of the dreadful group begin to haunt him. Suddenly, the thread he has grabbed was cut off.[15]

As Jikai questions the utopia of an egalitarian society and the limitation of social justice, a reformer of society becomes a reformer of a self. He perceives individualism and free will as egotistic expression and locates the roots of social problems within individuals.

Considering the historical time frame and the magnitude of the incident, the dreadful group can be identified as the group of socialists whom the Meiji government arrested and punished in 1910, in what is known as the High Treason Incident. Today, this incident is understood to have been a government conspiracy to eliminate socialism from Japan. The government rounded up socialists and anarchists and indicted twenty-six of them for planning to assassinate Emperor Meiji. In December of that year, twenty-four of them were sentenced to death, and within a week, twelve of them were executed, including Kōtoku Shūsui, the alleged leader of the group. Among those indicted, three Buddhist priests were prosecuted: Uchiyma Gudō of the Sōtō sect, Takagi Kenmyō of the Higashi Honganji denomination of Shin Buddhism, and Mineo Setsudō of the Rinzai sect. Uchiyama was put to death by hanging, Takagi killed himself in prison, and Mineo died in prison.[16]

Although Jikai did not join the dreadful group as a Buddhist priest, he continued to think about the fate of his former comrades when he became the resident priest of Chōshō-in. According to the narrator, their actions, based on the notion of free will, caused them to be censored and death was the price they paid for practicing that freedom. Yet Jikai's sympathy for them indicates that the narrator's criticism is directed at the political authority of the day. For Jikai, who is unable to either rationalize the consequences of the incident or free himself from the guilt of surviving, redemption comes only through divine intervention. Through his mystical encounter with the Buddhist statue, which cleanses his negative karma, Jikai realizes that his guilt was caused by his mental attachment.

The empirical interpretation of Buddhism prevailed in Japan after the turn of the twentieth century, but mystical experiences remained strong among individuals. The revelation by the Buddha, which plays a decisive role in Jikai's mental transformation, illustrates the continuation of a tradition, in which an individual makes a personal connection to a local deity and receives a divine oracle, and the reconstruction of Buddhist values against Western concepts, such as freedom and free will, which do not help Jikai solve his problems. While an institutional Buddhist setting is necessary for Jikai to be liberated from his attachments, for Kensaku, the protagonist of *A Dark Night's Passing*, examined next, spiritual liberation takes the form of total immersion in natural surroundings. Kensaku's self-realization, which is similar to Buddhist awakening from the narrator's perspective, occurs through the seemingly dissimilar processes of denying superstition and accepting supernatural forces.

A Dark Night's Passing: Mystical Union with Nature

Shiga Naoya spent some twenty-five years writing *A Dark Night's Passing*. He began writing drafts in the year 1912, at the age of twenty-nine. The early drafts consisted of fragmentary pieces, including "Tokitō Nobuyuki." Shiga seems to have intended to publish these fragments as a serialized novel titled *Tokitō Kensaku*, in the *Tokyo Asahi Shinbun*. In 1921, Shiga renamed this work *An'ya kōro* 暗夜行路, *A Dark Night's Passing*, and published the first half (parts 1 and 2) in the journal *Kaizō*. There is an almost sixteen-year gap before he finished the second half (parts 3 and 4). He was forced to complete *A Dark Night's Passing* in 1937, because the Kaizō Press planned to publish his collected works.[17] For a work of personal fiction, especially one produced over a long period of time, the writing span is crucial. Time helps a writer rethink and reorganize his ideas. This process affected the writing of *A Dark Night's Passing* and it is no surprise that many episodes—particularly the plotlines between the first and second halves of the novel—appear to be inconsistent.[18] Many critics, however, both in Japan and overseas, consider *A Dark Night's Passing* to be a great work, namely, Shiga's "longest and his finest novel," according to Sibley, and his "magnum opus," as lauded by Roy Starrs, who treats and analyzes *A Dark Night's Passing* as a representative work of modern Japanese fiction that describes the "ineffable wisdom of Zen."[19]

Although *A Dark Night's Passing* is a widely used English translation for *An'ya kōro*, the implications of the original title need to be examined carefully. *An'ya* means "a dark night" and *kōro* suggests a "passage" or "passageway"; therefore, the combination of those words hints at two actions: a dark night that is about to pass or a pathway in the dark that someone must take. If *An'ya kōro* as a title is read more figuratively, it suggests Kensaku's pursuing a way through a dark night and in this context *An'ya kōro* is more clearly a work of path literature. With this caveat, the translation of *A Dark Night's Passing* by Edwin McClellan is used in this study.

Tokitō Kensaku is the author's alter ego, or what William Sibley calls the Shiga hero. The ambiguity of the author's subjectivity appears as a contradiction in the narrative style, corresponding to differences in first- and third-person narratives. In the case of personal fiction, such a problem is insignificant. Referring to the structure of the Japanese language, in which distinctions between "represented speech/thought" and "direct utterance/reflection" are unclear, Edward Fowler writes,

> Faced with the contradictory desires of creating an autonomous hero and representing his own mental state, Shiga arrived at a compromise commonly elected by *shishōsetsu* writers. As in the "Yamashina" cycle, he simply transformed the narrating "I" (*watakushi*) into a narrated "he" (*kare*), thus "objectifying" his hero without, however, granting him the true autonomy found in a conventional third-person narrative."[20]

Given this mode of writing style, the reader is likely to relate the author to the main character by ignoring the first- and third-person narratives. Although the issues of self-referentiality are important to the study of autobiographical fiction, the following analysis of *A Dark Night's Passing* focuses on Kensaku's spiritual journey, which develops dialectically between his reading of Buddhist stories and his interactions with Buddhist priests, while mediated by the power of Mother Nature. Kensaku's attitude toward mysticism and superstition are also explored. A synopsis of *A Dark Night's Passing* is provided first.

A Summary of *A Dark Night's Passing*

A Dark Night's Passing begins with a short preface titled "The Hero's Reminiscences," a first-person narrative. It is Kensaku's recollection of five episodes related to his childhood and family—those associated with his mother, father, and paternal grandfather. Kensaku loved his mother, but did not receive much affection from his father and did not understand why. His mother died when he was six, and he met his grandfather for the first time. His grandfather brought Kensaku to his home, where he lived with a young mistress, Oei. Kensaku did not like his grandfather because of his vulgarity.[21]

The main text of *A Dark Night's Passing* is a third-person narrative and consists of four parts. Part 1 portrays the degeneration of Kensaku—who is living with Oei after the demise of his grandfather and trying to establish himself as a writer—depicted through "a life of idleness, irregularity, dissipation, and finally debauchery." Kensaku is much closer to his brother, Nobuyuki, whom he trusts and from whom he often seeks advice. Kensaku toys with several geisha but is unable to advance to a serious relationship. He feels betrayed when his family and relatives reject without explanation his marriage proposal to the daughter of the woman whom Kensaku's mother's parents had adopted and who knew Kensaku's mother very well. In the meantime, Kensaku develops strong sexual desires, goes to a brothel, and even fantasizes about Oei. The first part ends with Kensaku's determination to straighten out his life and move to Onomichi (in Hiroshima Prefecture), where he hopes to live simply and to write.[22]

In part 2, despite a good start in Onomichi and a strong determination to produce an autobiographical work, the "old malaise returns" to Kensaku. He cannot deal with a simple and isolated life, and his health declines. In order to overcome his loneliness, he thinks of marrying Oei and contacts her through Nobuyuki. A "double blow," however, strikes Kensaku. Nobuyuki not only delivers Oei's refusal but also reveals the truth about Kensaku's birth. Kensaku was born as a result of the incestuous relationship between his mother and his grandfather on his father's side (though this was not true for Shiga Naoya). Kensaku now understands why the person he had understood to be his father was so cold and indifferent to him and why his previous marriage proposal was turned down. He is driven into darkness. The deterioration of his health eventually forces him to return to Tokyo, where he abandons his attempts to marry Oei and once again engages in a life of debauchery. Womanizing is the only thing that fills the "vacuum of his existence."[23]

In part 3, Kensaku is in Kyoto. He consoles himself by visiting Buddhist temples and looking at traditional art. He soon falls in love with a young woman, Naoko, whom he is urged to marry. Naoko helps Kensaku see the bright side of life. Kensaku is happy and is determined to avoid backsliding. Naoko is soon pregnant and has a baby, but the baby dies of a bacterial infection. Naoko finds it difficult to get over this loss, whereas Kensaku accepts the baby's death as another incident of fate, which has cursed his entire life.[24]

In part 4, Kensaku finally liberates himself from what he had perceived as an ill-fated life. Oei, who has gone to Manchuria to work with her cousin, once again enters his life. When Kensaku discovers that Oei is in trouble there, he, with Naoko's agreement, brings her back to Japan and allows her to live with them. In his absence, Naoko is seduced by her cousin. Kensaku outwardly forgives Naoko but inwardly blames her for being seduced. Relations between Kensaku and Naoko become awkward, though Naoko and Oei get along well.

One day Kensaku bursts out in frustration. On a family trip to Takarazuka, Kensaku and Naoko try to board a train that is about to depart. He pushes Naoko off onto the platform and Naoko is seriously injured. This incident makes Kensaku realize that he is the one with a problem, and he decides to cure himself. For spiritual solace, he goes to the area around Mount Daisen, a place sacred to the Tendai Buddhist sect, climbs the mountain, and experiences a spiritual awakening. After that, he becomes seriously ill. *A Dark Night's Passing* ends with Naoko's visiting the half-dead Kensaku and renewing her resolution to continue living with him.[25]

Buddhist Texts, Buddhist Clergy, and Nature

Given Kensaku's spiritual liberation as a denouement of the story, *A Dark Night's Passing* follows the narrative pattern of ground, path, and goal. Because of the family discord and the secret of his birth, he becomes a debaucher. Despite his efforts to redirect his life, he is caught by the idea that his life has been cursed and that he cannot change his lifestyle. Only after hurting his wife does he accept his problem and seek a spiritual cure. A trip to Mount Daisen then becomes a path that leads him to experience spiritual liberation. Buddhist clergy do not help Kensaku recover, but Kensaku learns from books that he can attain an ideal spiritual state. He reaches his goal by realizing how trivial his egotistic concerns are—compared with the vastness of Mother Nature—and by feeling his mind and body slowly assimilate into the surroundings of Mount Daisen. Kensaku's turning of the mind is therefore driven by Buddhist ideas, although it does not represent a perspective specific to any Buddhist sect.

In *A Dark Night's Passing*, a series of Buddhist experiences develop dialectically, creating a tension between Kensaku's dislike of Buddhism as an organized religion and his inclination toward "book Buddhism"—Buddhism that he understands through books, which leads to his spiritual attainment on Mount Daisen. The first instance of his engagement in Buddhism comes in part 2, where Nobuyuki—"Nobuyuki" as a kanji compound of *shin* 信 (faith) and *gyō* 行 (practice)—tells Kensaku that he has decided to quit his current job and study Zen at Engakuji under a distinguished master. Kensaku responds negatively and cautions him against "awfully fashionable" Zen. On the other hand, Kensaku is delighted to listen to Zen stories Nobuyuki has read, which are artistically written, and is deeply moved by them. Despite Nobuyuki's recommendation, Kensaku avoids attending Zen temples, because he hates to imagine himself "sitting humbly at the feet of some smug Zen priest."[26]

While staying at an inn at the foot of Mount Daisen, Kensaku is actually frustrated by Buddhist priests. For advice on renting rooms, he visits Renjō-in but is disappointed at hearing from a rickshaw man about the vulgarity of its resident priest. Still, Renjō-in offers to rent him three rooms, so Kensaku decides to lodge there. He finds the priest's wife and daughter kind and caring. Kensaku's dissatisfaction with the Buddhist priests turns to anger when the resident priest of Manshōji later visits and flatters him because the priest wants to use Kensaku's Renjō-in rooms for kōan practice during a ten-day Zen seminar he plans to organize:

> Kensaku lost his temper completely. He might not have been quite so angry if he had not been gulled into taking the priest's invitation to the lectures so seriously. "If you had asked me that in the first place," he said hotly, "I would have given some thought to your request. But you tried to flatter me first. You tried to manipulate me, didn't you?" He continued to berate the priest thus for some time.[27]

For Kensaku, who dislikes hypocrites, the personality of Buddhist clerics matters. He also learns from Nobuyuki that the quality of a Zen master makes a difference in a practitioner's meditative training and kōan practice.

Despite these unpleasant experiences with Buddhist priests, Kensaku is pleased with the environment of Mount Daisen. He visits the Amida Hall and finds all life beautiful. A sense of reverence comes over Kensaku and he reflects on his past:

> Three or four years ago, when he was so absorbed in his own work, he had praised man's tenacity of purpose, man's conquest of the sky and of the sea. But since then, his attitude had changed completely. Now he wondered if nature had ever intended that man should fly like birds or go down into the sea like fish. Would not such limitless ambition lead man to some kind of misfortune? Would he not in time be severely punished for his overweening confidence in his own intelligence? . . .
>
> He felt very differently now. True, he was still tied to his work; it still was capable of upsetting him. But his present state of mind was such that if he were told that man would be destroyed together with his planet, he would gladly have accepted that fate. Though he knew nothing about Buddhism, such realms believed in by Buddhists as "nirvana" and "the realm of bliss" seemed irresistibly attractive to him.[28]

Kensaku leafs through the *Sayings of Lin ji* that Nobuyuki gave him. He sheds tears while reading the story of Genshin and Kūya in *Lives of Eminent Priests*. Interaction with genuine local people also helps him get rid of his stubbornness and makes him humble. Several days later, Kensaku climbs the mountain with a group of company employees from Osaka. Affected by minor food poisoning, he becomes easily exhausted and falls behind. While resting alone, he passively experiences an extraordinary sense of detachment:

> He [Kensaku] felt his exhaustion turn into a strange state of rapture. He could feel his mind and his body both gradually merging into this great nature that surrounded him. It was not nature that was visible to the eyes; rather, it was like a limitless body of air that wrapped itself around him, this tiny creature no larger than a poppy seed. To be gently drawn into it, and there be restored, was a pleasure beyond the power of words to describe. The sensation was a little like that of the moment when, tired and without a single worry, one was about to fall into a deep sleep. Indeed, a part of him already was in a state hardly distinguishable from sleep. He had experienced this feeling of being absorbed by nature before; but this was the first time that it was accompanied by such rapture. In

previous instances, the feeling perhaps had been more that of being sucked in by nature than that of merging into it; and though there had been some pleasure attached to it, he had at the same time always tried instinctively to resist it, and on finding such resistance difficult, he had felt a distinct uneasiness. But this time, he had not the slightest will to resist; and contentedly, without a trace of the old uneasiness, he accepted nature's embrace.

It was so still a night, even the night birds were silent. If there were lights in the villages below, they were quite hidden by the mist that lay over the rooftops. And all that he could see above him were the stars and the outline of the mountains, curved like the back of some huge beast. He felt as if he had just taken a step on the road to eternity. Death held no threat for him. If this means dying, he thought, I can die without regret. But to him then, this journey to eternity did not seem the same as death.[29]

Kensaku is liberated from all his concerns—the fear of death and delusions of man's progress, all things that Shiga Naoya struggled with in the past—in a dreamlike, mysterious trance.[30] He then falls asleep and wakes at dawn, further perceiving the splendid scenery of nature. For Kensaku, a "dark night" passes both literally and figuratively. The climax of his journey to Mount Daisen takes place a little before daybreak, and union with nature ends his spiritual struggle.

Kensaku's acceptance of anxiety over death can be explained by the Freudian notion of the "uncanny." Sigmund Freud examines this word through a linguistic inquiry. The word *heimlich* is not necessarily antonymous to its opposite, *unheimlich*. *Heimlich* not only means "homely" but also "secret" and "hidden," while *unheimlich* suggests "uncanny" or what is uncomfortable and frightening. It therefore appears that the hidden nature of a thing or unfamiliarity with it triggers an uncanny feeling.[31]

According to Freud, excessive self-love generates a process of "doubling," by which a child tends to share his knowledge, sentiments, and experiences with others, or to associate himself with a hero (or fictional character) in order to define his own self. Doubling is the process that divides and reciprocates a self and simultaneously protects the ego. When a child grows up, doubling produces the opposite effect. While it helps prevent a child from destroying his ego, for an adult it becomes "the uncanny harbinger of death."[32] That is, an adult is open to a new world and directs self-criticism to the early stage of his narcissism based on new knowledge. Doubling further produces a retroactive effect by which an earlier mental stage is reintroduced to him. The uncanny thus implies not only unfamiliarity with something, which may generate a sense of fear, but also a recurrence of what used to be familiar. Frightening incidents experienced earlier are repressed and hidden, but then re-emerge. Such ambiguity is inherent in the concept of the uncanny.

On Mount Daisen, the frightening thought of death that Kensaku has repressed recurs. He has been afraid of death since the loss of his mother in childhood and continues to suffer after the loss of his own child. At the same time, the familiarity with death caused by the loss of a loved one helps Kensaku sublimate death to a state of eternity when he rids himself of his attachment and blends into the spectacular scenery of Mount Daisen. As a result, Kensaku experiences what seems to be "nirvana" or "the realm of bliss" that he had longed for. Roy Starrs perceives that experience to be "a genuine Zen *satori*" attained "naturally" without seated meditation or Zen kōan practice.[33]

The equation of Kensaku's spiritual attainment to the sudden awakening of Zen, however, needs to be examined more carefully. On Mount Daisen, Kensaku is simply completing his previous encounters with nature. Prior to reading Zen texts, he found himself engrossed by nature several times, as he "had experienced this feeling of being absorbed in nature before." For instance, in part 2, after Kensaku learned that he is a "child of sin,"

> [h]e made himself think of the vastness of the world around him. There was the earth, there were the stars (unfortunately it was cloudy that evening and he could not see them), there was the universe; and in the midst of this vastness there was this minute particle that was himself, busily weaving a web of misery in the little world of his mind. Such was his *customary way of* combating his own fits of depression; and this time it seems to have some effect.[34] (emphasis added)

Further back, at the beginning of part 2, when Kensaku takes a ship to Kōbe on his way to Onomichi, he views the dark seascape from the deck and feels as if he were "about to be swallowed up by the great darkness around him."[35] In addition, he has an aesthetic experience of nature and recalls the magnificent landscape he had seen before.[36] Apparently, the Buddhist knowledge of detachment and tranquility he gains by reading books helps him relativize his consciousness. It is, however, uncertain whether or not Kensaku's experience of attaining unity with nature should be understood only in Buddhist terms, because there is no discussion of Buddhist philosophy. Rather, it is an indication of other traditional religious elements and contemporary literary influences, such as the expression of impermanence through the perception of the transient beauty of nature, Zhuangzi's philosophy, the long-standing *shugendō* practices on Mount Daisen, and the naturalist writers' influence in both Japan and the West, although the narrator does not speak of them.[37]

Mysticism and the Change in Narrative Style

The state of detachment that Kensaku experiences is related to the development of the narration. In Shiga's unusual style of writing, the hero's perspective is neutralized. Edward Fowler's narrative analysis, which deals with the narrator's relationship to the hero, is helpful here, even though Fowler shows no interest in the representation of Buddhism in Shiga's works. Fowler points out that in the aforementioned description of Kensaku's awakening on Mount Daisen, the author deprives Kensaku of his identity and makes him "person-less" in both an "ontological *and* grammatical sense," while substituting "Kensaku" with the third pronoun, "*kare*" (he). Fowler goes on to say, "The hero, at the threshold of death, yields his monopolistic point of view to a suddenly omniscient narrator intent on transforming his *shōsetsu* into a novel."[38] "Kensaku" does not return until "he," who happens to fall asleep, wakes up, and fully sees the shadow of Mount Daisen projected onto the landscape before him. The scene on Mount Daisen, therefore, gives the narrator spatial and temporal release.

However, Kensaku is unable to internalize his spiritual attainment for good and Shiga Naoya cannot continue keeping his distance from the Shiga hero. After returning from the mountain, Kensaku becomes critically ill at Renjō-in. The priest's wife sends for a doctor and contacts Naoko, but prevents Naoko from seeing Kensaku immediately since she feels that if Kensaku is relieved by seeing Naoko, that relief might trigger a decline in his unstable condition. Nevertheless, when Oyoshi, the priest's daughter, goes to Kensaku's room to check his condition, she comes back and tells her mother, Naoko, and the doctor "he knows, he knows madame's here," referring to Naoko.[39] Kensaku has detected her presence, perhaps, through the sacred power of Oyoshi, whom Kensaku earlier dreams of as being a divine medium (Kensaku's interaction with Oyoshi is discussed shortly). The supernatural power brings Kensaku back to his mundane life and evokes a desire to see his wife.

The recovery of Kensaku's consciousness coincides with a change in the narrative style. Fowler's study becomes relevant here once again. He observes that Shiga's narrative experiment is inconsistent, because omniscient narration disappears at the very ending of *A Dark Night's Passing*. It reads,

Kensaku seemed too tired to say anymore. His hand still in hers, he closed his eyes. She [Naoko] had never seen him look so tranquil. Perhaps, she thought, he is not going to live through this. But the thought somehow did not sadden her very much. As she sat there looking at him, she felt herself becoming an inseparable part of him; and she kept on thinking, "Whether he lives or not, I shall never leave him, I shall go wherever he goes."[40]

A Dark Night's Passing ends with Naoko's determination to live with Kensaku, but as Fowler points out, the last sentence sounds as if "the narrator of his hero" speaks of his will to live or as if "Kensaku's soul has taken flight and migrated to the body of Naoko."[41] Depending on Kensaku's spiritual state, therefore, the distance between the hero and the narrator changes. When Kensaku is on Mount Daisen and stands aloof from the mundane world, the distance between the hero and the narrator widens, whereas when Kensaku longs for his wife at Renjō-in, his attachment closes the gap. In both settings, Mount Daisen and Renjō-in, mystical and supernatural elements become part of a literary device, though working in opposite directions: they lead Kensaku to become spiritually awake, accept death, and unite with nature on the one hand, and encourage him to live and meet his wife, on the other.

As the narrative style changes, representations of the rational Buddhist mysticism are inconsistent. It is unclear how Kensaku changes his attitude toward himself and others, including his wife, and how he incorporates the vision of nonattachment into daily life. As the story ends with the worsening of his illness, Kensaku's spiritual aftereffect is unknown, just as we do not know whether he lives or dies. On one hand, Kensaku's desire to see his wife implies his effort to show her his new self after his experience of ego eradication. He overcomes his fear of death and maintains that spiritual state when Naoko comes to see him at Renjō-in. Although Kensaku does not return to Naoko with a halo around his head and although he is in critical condition, Naoko "had never seen him look so tranquil."[42] Kensaku thus fulfills his promise to her of self-transformation, at least temporarily. On the other hand, Kensaku's desire to see his wife may be wishful thinking and represent the recurrence of his egocentric behavior. Kensaku's mental state slips back from the height of his spiritual attainment to show the difficulty of integrating a state of self-detachment into ordinary settings.

Kensaku's Attitude toward Tenrikyō and Superstition

Kensaku's contradiction found between the ordinary setting and the extraordinary environment is also observed in his attitude toward Tenrikyō. In part 2 (chapter

12), Kensaku, with Nobuyuki's help, looks for a new place to lodge. They return home after not finding anything suitable. While telling Kensaku about Buddhist stories from *The Blue Cliff Records*, Nobuyuki suggests looking at planted shrubs, and they come in contact with Kamekichi, the gardener. Kensaku remembers having met him in the past. At that time, he was suspicious of Kamekichi because the gardener was "a little too good to be true."[43] Kensaku's observation of Kamekichi turns out to be correct; Kamekichi was double-dipping.

This negative image of Tenrikyō, as represented by Kamekichi, is somewhat corrected when Kensaku goes to Mount Daisen and lodges at Renjō-in. He meets Oyoshi, who lives with her husband in Tottori Prefecture but has temporarily returned to the temple with her baby, and Také, a roofer replacing shingles at Daisen Shrine. Kensaku has a strange dream the night after Oyoshi serves him dinner and makes a seemingly suggestive remark. In that dream, Oyoshi emerges from a crowd as a young "divine medium" and founder of Tenrikyō. Kensaku appears to be her follower and is sexually aroused by her. Kensaku tells Oyoshi about his dream and then learns more about Také:

> "Také's father was a Tenri believer you know," she said finally. "He was ruined because of that."
>
> "I see. Is Také the only one in his family that comes here to worship, then?"
>
> "His family were always members of the congregation here until his father's time. And when his father went bankrupt, I suppose Také got fed up with the new religion. . . ."
>
> "Mind you," Kensaku said, "he has a touch of the Tenri zealot, doing all that work on the roof for nothing."
>
> "But he's a really admirable person, don't you think?"[44]

Oyoshi goes on to tell Kensaku about Také's present hardships. Také was married to a loose woman who was always having relationships with other men. Také knew about her sexual proclivities before marrying her but never attempted to leave her. After learning about Také, Kensaku becomes convinced that Také is either "very saintly or a pervert of some kind." Kensaku later comes to respect him as a person who manages to "rise above his misfortune" because after all Kensaku came to Mount Daisen "hoping to rid himself of that hardness in him, of his incapacity to be truly gentle."[45]

How is it possible for Kensaku to accept Také, who has "a touch of the Tenri zealot," as a spiritually inspiring person? One possible answer is that in order for Kensaku to "become a Buddha" and return to Naoko with a halo around his head,[46] he must free himself of bias toward others. Kensaku's experience with Také enables him to sublimate the negative feeling about the new religion that he developed from his acquaintance with Kamekichi. To some degree, therefore, Tenrikyō becomes a reverse karmic condition that helps Kensaku find a person on whom he would like to model himself.

Parallel to Kensaku's ambivalent associations with Tenrikyō, other episodes illustrate both Kensaku's rejection and acceptance of superstition. When Kensaku's baby is plagued by erysipelas, Naoko's mother engages in a feng shui ritual (in part 3). Kensaku considers divination to be irrational and rejects her urging to accept this practice. On the other hand, when he listens to Schubert's "Erlkönig"—"a song about the child who was taken by the demon of death on a stormy night"[47]—on the day his baby is born, he regrets having gone to the concert with his friends because that song makes him uneasy. Kensaku, who has denied magical beliefs until then, accepts the coincidence of the two events—his child's birth and the music he hears that day—as an omen:

> They were in Teramachi, on their way home, when Mizutani said with emotion, "What a marvelous piece 'Erlkönig' is!"
> "Yes, it is," said Suematsu. He could not play any music, but he was fond of it and knew a great deal about it. To Kensaku who was silent he said, "I think that it's the best thing Schubert wrote."
> Kensaku gave no reply. He didn't know enough about music to want to express openly unqualified opinions about it. Surreptitiously he pulled out the crumpled program from the pocket of his Inverness cape, and let it drop to the ground—rather in the manner of someone trying to *shake off a curse*.[48] (emphasis added)

His superstitious behavior does not prevent his child from dying and as mentioned earlier, Kensaku continues to link the baby's death to some "evil force bent on hurting him."[49] Kensaku's attitude toward superstition is therefore ambiguous. Despite his rejection of petitionary prayer and seeking worldly benefit, he is swayed by supernatural powers and irrational beliefs.

Kensaku's resort to supernaturalism can be considered a plot device. Freud's discussion of the uncanny becomes relevant here once again. Freud highlights the difference between the uncanny in actuality and its representation. He points out that readers of fairy tales will be unlikely to sense the uncanny in reference to strange events described in stories which include the return of the dead, lifeless objects gaining life, and a character's desire to harm others. Similarly, fiction writers can transform an event, which could have been dreadful if it had actually happened in real life, into an imagined incident. They dramatize the incident and agitate readers, make it appear natural in a plot development, or change it into a harmless event.[50] Referring to the relationship between a writer and his readers regarding the uncanny in literature, Freud states,

> We adapt our judgment to the imaginary reality imposed on us by the writer, and regard souls, spirits and ghosts as though their existence had the same validity as our own has in material reality. In this case too we avoid all trace of the uncanny.
>
> The situation is altered as soon as the writer pretends to move in the world of common reality. In this case he accepts as well all the conditions operating to produce uncanny feelings in real life; and everything that would have an uncanny effect in reality has it in his story. But in this case he can even increase his effect and multiply it far beyond what could happen in fact. In doing this he is in a sense betraying us to the superstitiousness which we have ostensibly surmounted; he deceives us by promising to give us the sober truth, and then after all overstepping it. We react to his inventions as we would have reacted to real experiences; by the time we have seen through his trick it is already too late and the author has achieved his object.[51]

In the course of developing a narrative, successful writers incorporate superstitions and naturalize supernatural events. They achieve such literary effects by embracing irrationality and "deceiving" readers, and avoid a provocation of the uncanny. *A Dark Night's Passing* includes the "world of common reality" where people worship the supernatural with awe, embrace superstitious behavior, and express uncanny feelings. Michael D. Foster refers to the Japanese expression *hanshin hangi* ("half belief, half doubt") in his study of *yōkai*, or monsters, in modern Japan, and states that "seemingly irreconcilable beliefs [belief and doubt] do not cancel each other out but actually prove to be, if not quite harmonious, a least productively resonant with each other."[52] In *A Dark Night's Passing*, Kensaku's rational attitude is paradoxically enhanced by his acceptance of irrational beliefs.

Kensaku's mystical experience, read as the pinnacle of his spiritual development, is similar to Jikai's mystical experience. However, while Kensaku experiences spiritual freedom in natural settings, Jikai experiences spiritual liberation at a traditional Buddhist temple facilitated by a statue of the Buddha, a man-made object. For Kensaku, his inclination toward "book Buddhism," his admiration of a Tenrikyō follower, the magnificent natural landscape, and even his rejection and acceptance of superstitious belief come together to direct him toward an experience of eternity. Kensaku, as well as the narrator, considers his unity with nature to be Buddhist-like, although Kensaku's experience includes other religious elements and Kensaku is not committed to any kind of disciplinary practice. Neither does Jikai understand Buddhism in terms of the doctrine of a specific Buddhist sect, but basic Buddhist practice is central to his life. Despite these differences, both gain peace of mind and fulfill their spiritual inquiries. The paradoxical nature of mystical experience—that is, both rational and irrational—is supplementary to the non-dual aspect of Buddhism in modern Japanese literature.

Although Kensaku and Jikai have different personal problems, death is one human condition that leads them to take spiritual journeys. In the next chapter, literary responses to death seen through descriptions of funerary Buddhism are investigated.

CHAPTER EIGHT

Literary Representations of Buddhist Funerals

Readers of modern Japanese literature often find many vividly depicted instances of death. Sōseki and Katai, in particular, dealt with the inevitability of death,[1] and portrayed rites of passage, including Buddhist funerals and liminal persona, in their works. On one hand, funerals can be sources of great agitation and opportunities for characters to consider matters of life and death. On the other hand, as Alan W. Friedman points out, both narrative and funeral facilitate engagement with and working through issues related to separation and displacement, and help stabilize the difficult transition period by embracing loss.[2] Either way, funerals provoke the fictional characters to reflect on their being and, as a result, they start to change their attitudes toward themselves and others.

In this chapter, fictional accounts of Buddhist funerals are analyzed in conjunction with the Buddhist narrative pattern of the path, and the impact of Buddhist funerals on the fictional characters and authors are examined. Sanshirō, in Sōseki's *Sanshirō* (1908), comes across a funerary procession for a child and idealizes the tranquility of death. *Jibun* (literally, "I"), in Sōseki's *The Miner* (*Kōfu*, 1908), watches a funerary procession for a miner, intensifies his anxiety, and advances his contemplation on life and death. In Katai's *The Diary of the Second Army Corps at War* (*Dainigun jūsei nikki*, 1905), the narrator witnesses the Buddhist funeral of a Japanese Imperial Army officer in northern China. His perception of loneliness and impermanence heightens in response, and he relates instances of unnatural death to the uncertainty of human life. Unlike those three works, Katai's *Life* (*Sei*, 1908) and Sōseki's *To the Spring Equinox and Beyond* (*Higan sugimade*, 1912) are personal fiction accounts in which the funerary services for a loved one provide members of a surviving family with a place to gather that helps them recover from the sorrow of the loss.

When Buddhist rituals are treated as literary texts, liminality serves as an analytical tool for exploring the spiritual growth of the characters. Although the ambivalence of liminality is not the same as the oneness of duality in Buddhism, the concept of liminality is helpful in understanding a funeral's function in literature and the non-dualistic nature of rites of passage.

Narrative and Rites of Passage

Victor Turner, who builds on Arnold van Gennep's study of rites of passage, considers isolated social interactions that involve psychological discomfort "social drama." It consists of events that are structured in four stages: "*breach* of regular, norm-governed social relations"; "*crisis*" of an individual or a group that violates the rule; "*redressive or remedial procedures*" to resolve conflicts; and "*reintegration*" of the disrupted person or group, meaning the restoration of peace and order. Among these phases, the third redressive stage is crucial for those facing a crisis to process anxiety and grief, during which time they develop liminal characteristics.[3]

Turner defines liminality as a "betwixt-and-between condition of involving seclusion from the everyday scene," which is situated between the two phases of "separation from antecedent mundane life" and "re-aggregation to the quotidian world."[4] Liminality suggests a period of transition for an individual or a group that is neither separated from nor fully integrated into everyday life where binary forces of order and chaos converge and realms of life and death merge. It involves self-reflection on an incident that has led to the life of an individual being disrupted and a group being disintegrated. In this stage, those who are affected construct stories, in order to make sense of the events that have led them to experience spiritual breakdown, and share these stories with others.[5] Turner states that social drama "may provide materials for many stories, depending upon the social-structural, political, psychological, philosophical, and, sometimes, theological perspectives of the narrators."[6] Social drama also takes the form of "text."

According to Susan Ackerman, while rites of passage help transform a person or a group from one phase of life to another, they also serve as a means of communication and convey "information about religion."[7] The analysis of religious stories, including myths, is similar to the examination of ritual and its mediation of liminality. Ackerman goes on to say,

Turner concluded that in the same way that rituals, and thus ritual expressions of liminality, most typically manifest themselves during the third or redressive phases of social dramas, it was during the redressive phases of narratives structured according to the social drama pattern that liminal characteristics and liminal symbolism most commonly occurred.[8]

Just as narratives that follow the patterns of rites of passage are characterized by the ambiguity of liminality, fictional treatments of Buddhist funerals include liminal personalities.

Liminal imagery, which emerges from such a reading of personal novels, corresponds to the non-dualistic nature of Buddhism. The ambivalence of liminality, however, is not the same as the unity of the binary explained in Buddhism. As Bjørn Thomassen points out, liminality refers to the transition of time and is "a world of contingency where events and ideas, and 'reality' itself, can be carried in different directions."[9] While liminality is marked by a sense of uncertainty, Buddhist non-duality is liberating. Despite these differences, because—according to Thomassen—"liminal moments are characterized by very real spiritual experiences that profoundly shake the personality,"[10] analyses of liminal characters and their responses to Buddhist funerals in the works of Sōseki and Katai help us understand the phases of those characters' spiritual growth through their reactions to death.

Sanshirō: A Child's Funeral

Sanshirō can be considered a work of path literature, given that Sanshirō stands at a crossroads in his life. He graduates from a high school in Kumamoto and moves to Tokyo to study at a university. Moving to a city and becoming a college student represents a transition in his life. Sanshirō embodies both the temporal and spatial dimensions of liminality, and his persona is defined by the ambiguity of his numerical name. "Sanshi 三四" literally means "three four." It is therefore neither three nor four, but both three and four, or between three and four. Sanshirō's personal irresolution is reflected in the indecisiveness between the two numbers.

Sanshirō begins with Sanshirō's becoming acquainted with a woman who loses contact with her husband after the Russo-Japanese War. They happen to meet in Nagoya when Sanshirō is on his way to Tokyo and end up spending a night in the same room at a cheap inn. Sanshirō is immature and unable to sense the woman's mood. He finds the situation awkward and hesitates to interact with her. The next day, she smiles and says to him before they separate, "You're quite a coward, aren't you?"[11] Sanshirō is bewildered as she points out his indecisiveness.

After arriving in Tokyo, Sanshirō meets several people but remains indecisive in his interactions with them. He befriends Nonomiya, a scientist at the university, as his mother in Kumamoto suggests. One day, Nonomiya asks Sanshirō to bring a change of clothes to Nonomiya's sister, Yoshiko, who has been admitted to a hospital. At the hospital, Sanshirō hesitates and pushes the "door open *halfway*," looking inside while holding the doorknob. He then finds "a union of languid melancholy and unconcealed vivacity" in Yoshiko, who is "a most precious fragment of human life and a great discovery" for him.[12] Sanshirō, however, does not enter the room until Yoshiko calls him in and makes his decision for him.

Further, when his friend Yojirō introduces him to Hirota, Yojirō's high school teacher, Sanshirō greets him awkwardly. His awkwardness belies his earlier acquaintance with Hirota; Sanshirō actually conversed with Hirota as they ate peaches together on the train to Tokyo. However, Sanshirō is unable to talk to him. He only removes his hat and bows, an action "too polite for Yojirō, but rather too curt for Hirota—a middle path that was appropriate to neither."[13]

Sanshirō's indecisive personality makes him hesitant when he meets Mineko. She is a new breed of woman—intelligent and independent—but ironically, her strong personality makes her unfit for a modern society that has not yet overcome traditional constraints for women. Mineko calls Sanshirō a "stray sheep" and considers herself to be the same. Sanshirō falls in love with her, but is unsure whether she likes him or makes a fool of him.

Yojirō, a playful friend, sets the stage for Sanshirō to meet and declare his love to Mineko. He borrows money from Sanshirō, but because Yojirō is unable to pay Sanshirō back, he arranges for Mineko to lend money to Sanshirō. After receiving money from his mother in Kumamoto, Sanshirō pays Mineko back. On his way to the art studio where Mineko is posing as a model, Sanshirō reads Thomas Browne's *Hydriotaphia* and is struck by a passage that deals with death. He neither comprehends the passage nor is mature enough to fully conceptualize death, but it nevertheless inspires him.[14] He then comes across a funeral procession:

> A child's funeral procession came toward him. Two men in formal coats were the only mourners. The little coffin was wrapped in a spotless, white cloth, a pretty pinwheel attached to its side. The

wheel kept turning. Each of its five blades was painted a different color. They blurred into one as the wheel turned. The white coffin moved past him, the pinwheel spinning constantly. He thought it a lovely procession.

Sanshirō had viewed another's writing and another's funeral from a distance. If someone were to come along and suggest that, while he was about it, he should look at Mineko from a distance, he would have been shocked, for his eyes were no longer capable of doing that. First of all, he was not conscious of a distinction between the distant and the not-distant. He knew only that, while he sensed a tranquil beauty in the death of another, there was a kind of anguish beneath the beautiful pleasure he felt from the living Mineko. He would move straight ahead, trying to sweep away this anguish. If he went forward, it seemed, the anguish would leave him. He never dreamed of stepping aside to shed it. Incapable of such a thought, Sanshirō viewed the rites of extinction [a gathering of nirvana—"*jakumetsu no e* 寂滅の会"] from afar, as a word on a page, and he felt the pathos of early death from a place apart. What should have brought him sadness he viewed with pleasure and a sense of beauty.[15]

As an onlooker, Sanshirō perceives the child's funeral procession as someone else's tragedy, yet finds the innocence of death in it. He reflects on the sorrow caused by the loss of the infant—which he sublimates into the tranquility of death in its connection to nirvana—and believes that the removal of agony, which has underlined Mineko's existence, would make her more beautiful. He then realizes that he can make that happen for her. The observation of the child's funerary procession becomes a turning point in Sanshirō's attitude toward Mineko.

The beginning of Sanshirō's change is reflected in the narrative pattern of "ground, path, and goal." Being indecisive is Sanshirō's problem, but he does not intend to overcome this weakness; rather, by setting a goal to help Mineko, he becomes strong-willed and, as a result, starts to overcome his problem. In other words, love makes Sanshirō take a path to adulthood. In the text, the funerary procession signifies forward movement that does not allow turning back, so Sanshirō finally confesses his love to Mineko, who, however, sighs and ignores his feelings. Although Sanshirō's love is never realized, he has taken a decisive step forward by expressing his love to Mineko, showing one sign of growth.

Sanshirō's sublimation of the child's death is very different from his reaction to the death of a young woman who took her own life. Previously, he had looked after Hirota's house, which is built near a railway. One night, he happens to hear the hopeless mutterings of a woman outside. Soon after, Sanshirō hears that someone just committed suicide by jumping in front of a train. It turns out that the woman Sanshirō heard is the woman who has killed herself. The scene of her death terrifies him. For the first time, he feels "the roots of life, which appear to us so sturdy, work loose before we know it and float off into the darkness"[16] and realizes the impermanence of life through this cruel incident. Sanshirō, however, avoids thinking further about the irrationality of human life, exemplified by the suicide of an adult woman, yet later he idealizes a child's death. His refusal to engage with the complexities of society that cause people to commit suicide reinforces Sanshirō's unwillingness to cope with the irrationality of human life.

Unlike Sanshirō, who is not quite initiated into adulthood and remains in a state of in-betweenness, Mineko is initiated into womanhood through marriage. She searches her place in society and looks for a man equal to her, but is unable to find what she seeks. Mineko then quickly chooses to marry her brother's friend. Just before her marriage, Sanshirō goes to a church where she is attending a service and waits for her in order to return her money, which he failed to do at the art studio. The church door opens and people begin "returning from Paradise to the fleeting world of men."[17] Knowing that Sanshirō is aware of her engagement, Mineko sighs slightly and then mumbles, "I acknowledge my transgression, and my sin is ever before me."[18] After attending the Christian service, Mineko accepts her mistakes and the conditions that have led to her engagement, yet she still marries. As Norma Field points out, Mineko personifies "the dying of youth."[19] The Christian service represents her initiation into adulthood and by beginning a new life with her husband, she completes her rite of passage.

The Miner: The *Jumbō*

The Miner is a first-person narrative that is based on a story Sōseki heard from a young man. Jibun (literally, "I") is an educated young man and the son of a wealthy family in Tokyo. He runs away from home at the age of nineteen because of trouble with two women and the problems he caused his family. He first identifies the cause of his suffering to be his desire to change others but considers his other self—that is, what is "incubating inside of" him (*senpukusha*)[20]—to be the problem, because *senpukusha* is unpredictable and uncontrollable when it emerges at the surface of the self. Jibun leaves home and wanders aimlessly. He is accidentally recruited by a trickster to join a group of mine laborers and taken to the Ashio copper mine in Tochigi Prefecture. *The Miner* is the story of how Jibun experiences various kinds of hardship at the mine, overcomes those challenges, and becomes an adult. It is structured to fit the narrative pattern of "ground, path, and goal," although there is no reference to Buddhism.

The miners' world is beyond Jibun's comprehension. They live at the lowest stratum of society, yet a hierarchy exists among them. They are rough, vulgar, uneducated, and unsympathetic. They harass Jibun and with one voice tell him to go home because he is fresh off the boat and does not look like a manual laborer. When Jibun eats cheap Chinese rice (*nankinmai*) for the first time and frowns, the miners heckle and laugh at him for having grown up as a wealthy child unfamiliar with cheap rice. Jibun feels as if they are attacking him because they see him as a member of a society that mistreated them. Jibun finds himself in a "perfect fix, wedged between ordinary society and the society for the miners."[21]

While the miners abuse Jibun, a *jumbō* ジャンボー—funerary procession—approaches the boardinghouse and they all go to the window to watch it:

> The jangle [*jumbō*] continued indifferently to appear around the corner of the stone wall. Was it never going to end, I [Jibun] wondered, stretching to look down at the road, which brought me another rush of horror. Between the bearers of the wash basins, dangling in space as it made its way down the mountain road, was a square coffin. The top had been covered in a white sheet, a bare cedar pole passed through the wooden loops at either end, and there was a man shouldering each end of the pole with all the matter-of-factness he might have evidenced if entrusted with a load of water. From here it looked as if they, too, were cheerfully singing the chant. It was then that I realized the meaning of "jangle." The moment of understanding came with a piercing clarity I shall never forget for the rest of my life, whatever else is left in store for me. A "jangle" was a funeral, a kind of funeral that can only be performed—indeed, *must* be performed—for miners of the four classes—miner, digger, setter, and shopper. It was a funeral in which phrases from the sutras are sung in the emotional Naniwa-bushi style, the music of shattering wash basins is played, the

coffin is carried past the barracks, dangling like a barrel of water on a pole, and, finally, a half-dead miner is dragged from his bed and, despite his protests, forced to look on. It was the height of innocence, the height of cruelty.²²

The *jumbō*—translated as "jangle" in English²³—does not give Jibun a sense of a proper funeral. Because of the noisy banging of washbasins and the absence of a Buddhist priest, it does not evoke solemn feelings in Jibun. In such funeral processions, however, it was not uncommon for a dead body to be scrunched to fit into a tight wooden bucket (*oke*)—rather than a rectangular-shaped coffin—and carried like a large bucket of water. Such a practice is depicted in *Shank's Mare* (*Tōkaidōchū hizakurige*, 1802–1809), a popular comic travel novel written by Jippensha Ikku during the late Edo period. Jibun's bewilderment during the *jumbō* suggests his recognition that he, a man who grew up in a wealthy family, has joined men of the lowest rank in society who use a wooden bucket as a coffin and whose families do not attend their funerals.

The ambiance in the boardinghouse changes completely after the funeral procession passes. When the miners return to the hearth, Jibun, who was sitting away from them, is "admitted to the ranks of the savages" and "able to approach the fire" without being jeered at.²⁴ Jibun feels somewhat relaxed and listens to their conversation. The miners suddenly become nervous about their future:

"I wonder where it came from?"
  "What's the difference? A jangle's a jangle."
  "Maybe from Kuroichi's. Somewhere up there."
  "I wonder where you go after a jangle."
  "To the temple, stupid. Everybody knows that."
  "Who you callin' stupid? I'm talkin' about after the temple."
  "He's right. It sure as hell doesn't end at the temple. You gotta go somewhere."
  "That's what I mean. The last place. I wonder what it's like there. Think it's the same as here?"
  "Sure, human souls go there. It must be pretty much the same."
  "I think so, too. If you go somewhere, it's gotta be there."
  "They talk about 'heaven' and 'hell,' but ya hafta eat there, too, I guess."
  "I wonder if they've got women."
  "Of course they've got women. There's no place in the world without women."²⁵

The miners seemingly joke and talk nonsense, but Jibun realizes that they are serious about the afterlife. He is surprised that in being so concerned with their afterlife, these "savages" have expressed piety. For the first time in his life, Jibun observes a "germ of all true religious feeling and, in the presence of these half-animal—half-humans, felt a genuine sense of awe."[26]

Initiated by the *jumbō*, a liminal group experience takes place at the boardinghouse. According to Turner, liminal persons have "no status, property, insignia, secular clothing indicating rank, role, or position in a kinship system."[27] When they gather, a group of liminal people becomes egalitarian because they do not possess anything. They dissolve hierarchies and boundaries, which previously defined their places in society and experience "intense social togetherness" or "union with one's fellow human beings."[28] Viewing the *jumbō* causes the relationship between Jibun and the miners to change. In other words, the partitions of educational and cultural disparities between them have been removed and the hierarchy within the miners' world has broken down. Both Jibun and the miners are confounded by death. All are deficient in knowledge concerning the meaning of life, the afterlife, salvation, and religion. Further, their poverty and lack of a religious perspective equalizes the relationship between Jibun and the miners.

Jibun's reflections on life and death continue when, the next day, he is guided into a mine to see the miners' work. In the pitch-dark tunnel, the meandering passages become narrower and wet. As the underground trip intensifies, Jibun physically and mentally hovers between the realms of life and death. When he loses his way out, he meets Yasu, an unusual miner who is digging into a rock wall. Yasu is educated and detects Jibun's nobility as he struggles in the mine. He treats Jibun well and briefly tells him about how he himself ended up working in the mine—Yasu committed a crime and as a result gave up everything he had and fled his home. Yasu advises Jibun to return home and not to make the same mistake he did. While reflecting on Yasu's experience of "a living death in the depths of degeneracy,"[29] Jibun determines to face his own weaknesses and to confront his problems.

Jibun's experiences at the mine lead him to change his perspective on life. He accepts the twists of fate that have brought him to the mine and caused him to be humiliated by the miners, that threw him into a world of pitch-darkness, and yet that have also kept him alive. When he watched the *jumbō* procession, he became concerned about his own funeral. In the aftermath, however, Jibun stops worrying about what will happen after his death because he is not even sure what will happen while he is alive. Jibun decides to entrust himself to his fate and "let things run their natural course."[30] When this thought arises in him, he no longer considers the miners to be filthy, but rather sees them *as they are*—"They were not ugly, not frightening, not hateful. They were just faces, as the face of the most beautiful woman in Japan is just a face,"³¹—and decides to stay at the mine. He becomes a bookkeeper and keeps the ledger, recording the miners' purchases of daily necessities and sundry items. He interacts with them positively, earns their respect, and finally returns to Tokyo. For Jibun, the state of going to and returning from the mine corresponds to the beginning and end of a rite of passage.

In Jibun's transformation, religion hardly plays a role, but his awareness of fate suggests that he is able to develop a metaphysical perspective on the human condition. For him, fate is not predestination and his liminal experience does not bring him into contact with God or another transcendent being. Instead, fate is powerful and intangible. Further, because his understanding of fate enables him to accept his present condition, it also indicates his encounter of the law of causality. In that sense, *The Miner* is a work of path literature that is built on the notion of karma, a concept that has been incorporated into Buddhism. Although Jibun does not have a preconceived goal, the path he takes by accident—going to a mine and down its pitch-dark tunnel—and his encounter with Yasu, whom he meets by chance, helps Jibun stand on his own two feet. The despair Jibun feels during the *jumbō* echoes the sense of displacement that the narrator of *The Diary of the Second Army Corps at War* feels, which will be discussed next.

The Diary of the Second Army Corps at War: A Battlefield Buddhist Funeral

Between March 1904 and September 1905, Tayama Katai observed the Russo-Japanese War as a member of a photography team. In *The Diary of the Second Army Corps at War*, he reproduced letters that he had written while in service and the descriptions he had recorded in a pocket notebook. In *The Diary*, Katai wrote about the Second Army Corps that advanced through the Battles of Nanshan, Delisi, and Dashiqiao. He was unable to report on the Battle of Liaoyang, which had been the goal of his role in his corps, because of illness. In *The Diary*, Katai described the various battles, the Japanese army's formations against enemy troops, scenes of atrocities, the geography of China, the food he ate, appearances of local houses and towns, and the lives of the Chinese, simultaneously weaving poems and observation of the landscape into his narrative.³² He also wrote about his interactions and conversations with military officers and with Mori Ōgai, a prominent literati figure of the day and a physician who served as an army surgeon. Despite its title, *The Diary* not only records what Katai observed and felt at the moment but also is a collection of his later reflections on the Russo-Japanese War. In that sense, *The Diary* can be considered fictional.[33]

Katai dedicated *The Diary* to his father, who fought on the side of the Meiji government during the Seinan War of 1877 and was killed. For Katai, dying in battle was irrational because the surviving family suffered as a consequence of the soldier's unnatural death. He wrote, "After a while, I came to think that death on the battlefield is a grave problem that we must seriously consider,"[34] and treated death as a major theme. In essence, the narrator's inquiry of unnatural death constitutes the ground portion of the narrative structure of *The Diary*. His travel to China signifies a path—his effort to analyze the causes and conditions of unnatural death. Coming to terms with unnatural death is the narrator's goal; however, he himself is caught by the plight of the war and is unable to achieve his mission. During this trip, the narrator feels marginalized and embraces the Buddhist sensibility of impermanence.

The narrator develops a liminal persona on two occasions. First, before advancing to the battlefield, he witnesses the Buddhist funeral of Lieutenant Katsura from the Second Army Corps. The service is held during a quiet and relatively peaceful time in Manchuria and the narrator enjoys the sight of a magnificent night sky and countless stars. On the afternoon of May 13, he attends the ceremony:

> Referring to the pages of my pocket diary, I noticed that my visit to Shukakō [Zhoujiagou, a place near Fengtian] also records the unforgettable rite for Lieutenant Katsura. Since the commander and various officers were going to attend, we had left our station after lunch. Shukakō is about one *li* [four kilometers] north of the Daiyōka [Yaojiatun] station. On the highland to the right of Shukakō, three companies of soldiers stood in a row. Beyond them was an altar nicely made up of willow branches and corn shells. Food, including a pig, hen, and pots of sake, were offered in memory of Lieutenant Katsura. When I arrived, the commander and the division commander had already been seated, and the chanting of a sutra was about to begin. The first loss of the corps caused all to feel sorrow. I especially recognized the great sadness of those who were going to fire blank shots. Three unshaved Buddhist priests were in attendance. It was strange, however, to see them wearing

Western shoes with their robes. I even found it comical to hear their chanting, loud and often interrupted. This, however, made me much sadder. I vividly imagined how the lieutenant had died, covered with blood and in agony, in a deserted place far from home.

The sky with a wisp of gray cloud appeared to be sending condolences. When the service concluded and condolences were expressed, the commander and the division commander returned to the station on horseback, as did the infantrymen. *The altar and burial marker are now abandoned. The wind and rain will decay it in a few years. Ahh . . .*[35] (emphasis added)

The narrator finds an avenue by which the pent-up energy of the servicemen can be released—through the strange appearance of Buddhist priests—but he also finds disturbing a Buddhist funeral performed in a foreign land without proper arrangements, such as a pig and hen being offered on the makeshift altar.

Like Jibun, in *The Miner*, who was initially regarded as an outsider by the miners, the narrator of *The Diary*, as a member of the photography crew, is also an outsider. Military personnel treat him differently because of his civilian status. Whereas the miners accept Jibun after they watch the *jumbō* together and find themselves equally disturbed, the narrator of *The Diary* seeks redressive action by himself. He overcomes the sense of displacement he felt after the unconventional funeral of Lieutenant Katsura by embracing traditional sensibilities of loneliness and impermanence. This incident creates a situation where "the external custom is always a material support for the subject's unconscious," as Slavoj Žižek states.[36]

According to Žižek, although religious belief seems to be the embodiment of interiority, it is actually external to an individual in the same way that the unconscious is. Žižek writes,

> When we subject ourselves to the machines of a religious ritual, we already believe without knowing it; our belief is already materialized in the external ritual; in other words, we already believe *unconsciously*, because it is from this external character of the symbolic machine that we can explain the status of the unconscious as radically external.[37]

This is what Žižek calls the "paradoxical status of a *belief before belief*."[38] That is, "we find reasons attesting our belief because we already believe; we do not believe because we have found sufficient good reasons to believe."[39] An individual rationalizes a belief only because he already believes it and conversion, or a turning of the mind, is only the affirmation of that belief and "merely a formal act by means" of what he knew before.[40] In the case of *The Diary*, the external characteristics of belief embedded in the Buddhist ritual suggest that the narrator develops feelings of impermanence and loneliness in response to Lieutenant Katsura's death because he has already accepted that life is fleeting—feelings he developed after attending Buddhist funerals many times in Japan.[41]

According to Naoko Shimazu, Japanese conscripts during the Russo-Japanese War consider death in battle to be "tragic" and "heart-wrenching."[42] This circumstance propels the conscripts to embrace a traditional religious perspective:

> In war death, one became a victim of the ultimate state of loneliness by dying in a foreign land away from one's home. Moreover, as mentioned previously, physical death did not mean a complete break from the world of the living, as the soul of the dead continued to "live" on, and only after a while did it leave "this world" to go to the "other world." Around the time of the Russo-Japanese War, it is safe to assume that most conscripts subscribed to the notional cosmic framework of "this world" and the "other world," deriving from a mixture of beliefs from ancestor worship (with shamanistic practices) and Buddhism, which as a late comer had had to accommodate the existing indigenous belief system.[43]

A set of Buddhist funeral and memorial services, through which a surviving family and fellow soldiers honored the loved one who fell in battle, was the indispensable means for both soldiers who were going to die and the people who were left behind to relate this world of the living to the world of the dead. It was the source of spiritual comfort that allowed them to accept a lonely, tragic death in a foreign land.

The second time the narrator develops a liminal persona is when he reflects on unnatural death and his own near-death experience. Three days after Lieutenant Katsura's funeral service, *The Diary*'s narrator hears the sound of cannon fire for the first time and begins witnessing the tragedy and horror of war. He witnesses the agony of dying soldiers, a pile of dead bodies deformed and torn apart, blood spilled on the roadside as well as blood stains on bandages and handkerchiefs, and the enemy formation full of trenches with overhead cover, loopholes, pitfalls, and barbed wire spread all around.[44] When the narrator discovers a bag belonging to a dead officer, he cannot stop imagining how it will be delivered to the officer's wife. He is thus led to question unnatural death: "For some people, death is life itself and it is the proof of living. Man obviously must accept death. However, [those soldiers] died without any spiritual shock or struggle. They were shot and stabbed and died instantly. Isn't it worth crying over their unnatural deaths?!"[45] For the narrator, war not only causes people to die inhumanly but also makes death mechanical.

The death of Major Tachibana—a brave man who took good care of Katai's photography team—further disturbs the narrator. Tachibana died in the Battle of Liaoyang, one of the fiercest battles about which the narrator hears. Although Tachibana succeeded in taking a hill previously held by the Russians, he was shot several times during the Russian counterattack. The narrator looks at the hill where Tachibana lost his life and imagines Tachibana's last moment:

> While lying and bleeding in a field of cannon smoke, the sorrow he must have felt—not looking back at the happiness he gave up for the sake of the nation, what kind of life is this? Is it still a kind of sorrow we experience in this world? I cannot explain . . .[46]

The narrator is perplexed about the death of an officer with whom he became acquainted, but unlike the heroic account of Tachibana's death, about which he hears repeatedly, the narrator avoids glorifying the major. Instead, he attempts to understand Tachibana's inner feelings, which are concealed by patriotism and the fellow soldiers' deification of his spirit.

The narrator's concern with unnatural death is intensified by reflections on his own potential death. He once entered a combat zone where bombshells were flying everywhere and later contracted typhoid. Dying of disease would have been the most miserable way to end his service and his life, but because of Mori Ōgai's help, the narrator received decent treatment at a hospital for officers. He might otherwise have been treated in a regular soldiers' ward, where poor sanitary conditions might have made his survival unlikely.

The Diary is a record of impaired mourning for the dead. The narrator is traumatized by the atrocity of war and challenged by the irrationality of unnatural death. While he considers the conflict between man and society to be unavoidable, he is unable to explain the causes of his society's collective action, which supersede individual choices, and unable to accept the unnatural deaths of so many soldiers. Although the narrator maintains the detachment of an objective reporter in the midst of a battle and depicts the cruelty of mankind as impartially as possible, his narration becomes more sympathetic with regard to the circumstances of individual deceased servicemen.

Sanshirō, *The Miner*, and *The Diary of the Second Army Corps at War* illustrate instances of impersonal Buddhist funerals. The funerary processions that Sanshirō and Jibun encounter and the funeral service that the narrator of *The Diary* attends are not for their loved ones. Their liminal experiences are characterized by the lack of a personal connection with the deceased whose funeral services they witness. In the next section, personal accounts of funerals are examined. In the portions of *Life* and *To the Spring Equinox and Beyond* considered, the main characters, their family members, and narrators mourn the loss of loved ones. As we shall see, for the narrators and main characters of these two works, funerary rites and the period of mourning serve as both the beginning and end of their liminal experiences.[47] Especially for Sōseki, writing *To the Spring Equinox and Beyond* was itself a way to recover from the loss of a loved one.

Life: A Buddhist-Shinto Funeral

Katai wrote *Life* (*Sei*, 1908) about nine years after his mother's passing and immediately after the sensational debut of *The Quilt*. In this personal novel, while reenacting his mother's death and her funeral, he fictionalized his brother's family feud and conflicts between a parent and sons. By writing *Life*, Katai aimed not only to come to terms with the loss of his mother but to also firmly establish himself as a naturalist writer. Confessing his family's problems and critically examining each of his family members was part of that process.[48]

Life centers on the family of Ryō, the elder brother of Tetsunosuke—Katai's alter ego—and his dying mother. His mother grew up in an era during which patriarchal authority was the norm. After the premature death of her husband, Ryō's mother raised four children all by herself. She was frustrated, however, because her children did not succeed in society and because Okei, Ryō's third wife, did not live up to her expectations. As a result, she constantly collided with Okei and her children, whose perspective on life was different from her own. The narrator is critical of the mother's traditional ways of thinking but sympathetic to her idiosyncratic struggle. For him, and Tetsunosuke, her death indicates the transition of time and change in the family system.

Life can be read as a work of path literature in which Tetsunosuke finds a way to come to terms with his complex feelings toward his mother. His mother's death becomes the impetus (ground) for Tetsunosuke to think about relationships between Ryō's family members and his mother, the nature of individual ego, and his own place in the entire family. The funeral service provides the opportunity for the surviving family members to interact and understand each other, and it becomes the way (path) for Ryō's family members and Tetsunosuke to sublimate their negative emotions toward their mother. The procession to, and burial at, the cemetery not only marks the end of the funeral service but also characterizes Tetsunosuke's relief (goal) at the idea that his mother and her late husband are now reunified in the land of their ancestors.

The mother's funeral service is not conducted in the traditional Buddhist style, but in the contemporary Shinto fashion. At the beginning of the Meiji era, the government initiated changes in funeral arrangements. According to Nam-lin Hur,

> In a show of trying to divest imperial rites and ceremonies of any Buddhist character, Emperor Meiji conducted Shinto-style memorial services for his father, Emperor Kōmei (r. 1847–66), who had previously been buried with a Buddhist service. After this, the imperial house no longer conducted Buddhist funerary rites for its members. In the fourth intercalary month, the Meiji government moved to order all Shinto priests to conduct Shinto funerals for their family members, effectively freeing them from the bondage of the *danka* ["the enduring relationship between a Buddhist temple and its funerary patron household, cemented from generation to generation through recurring rites and services related to death and ancestral veneration"] system. At the same time, it encouraged the populace to leave their *danna* temples [temples with which "the funerary patron household or individual" is affiliated] voluntarily and to switch to Shinto funerals.[49]

The introduction of Shinto funerary liturgy was part of the Meiji government's effort to reduce Buddhist influence in society and promote Imperial Shinto. However, the Shinto funeral was not without its problems. It lacked a standard ritual procedure, and Shinto specialists did not solve the problem of defilement in death; therefore, Shinto funerary services were unpopular. Buddhist funerals and memorial services continued to prevail.[50]

Life depicts both the crisis and revival of funerary Buddhism. Because Ryō's father is enshrined at Yasukuni Shrine, a Shinto priest officiates at his mother's funeral, but Buddhist customs persist throughout the service. The Buddhist sensibility is enhanced by the narrator's choice of Buddhist words describing the funeral rituals, such as *hotoke* referring to the deceased and *kaimyō* referring to her posthumous name. At the same time, the hybrid funerary service becomes a gendered practice: while male characters are introduced to a set of new Shinto practices, female characters hold onto traditional Buddhist customs. As a result, when Ryō's family members participate in his mother's funeral, their liminal experience as a group involves the inversion of a male-female hierarchy. Yet sorrow over the loss of the mother keeps them unified and the funeral service itself helps them complete the first step of mourning.

During the mother's last moments, her niece, Okoma, recites *namu amida butsu* and moistens her lips with a brush. The mother takes her last breath after jerking up her chin:

> The head of the family [Ryō], who is checking her pulse, also knows that this is the end of her life.
>
> The last moment! Death! Sorrow fills everyone's hearts. Death makes people forget everything and purifies all unhealthy thoughts [about that person]. There is nobody who is not touched by the sadness and sympathy of the occasion.
>
> Okoma continues to recite *namu amida butsu* and says to Tetsunosuke and Hideo [Tetsunosuke's younger brother], "Why don't you moisten her lips with the last water. This is the end of the karmic relationship to your mother.[51]

Tetsunosuke cries, as does everyone else, and their attitude toward their mother changes drastically. The curiosity of death is now superseded by sadness, which is mixed with a sense of solemnity. Although now released from filial duty, they have ambiguous feelings of relief and loneliness.

With the arrival of relatives, the family contacts a high-ranking Shinto priest from Hibiya Great Shrine (*Hibiya daijingū*). Before the priest's arrival, however, the family makes a Buddhist arrangement based on the female members' suggestion that the mother is a buddha until a Shinto priest conducts the ceremony.[52] During the all-night vigil, the Shinto priest delivers words of blessings and bestows on the deceased a posthumous Shinto name, which ends with *mikoto*—the narrator, however, following the Buddhist custom, calls it *kaimyō*. The family offers three kinds of mountain vegetables and seafood at the altar. After the service, people express their thoughts about the deceased, speak of their own interests, and chat pleasantly with each other. A good-looking modern coffin then arrives. It is spacious enough to accommodate the entire body without breaking her legs or crooking her neck. Before encoffinment, and while reciting *namu amida butsu*, the people wash her body with hot water.

Tetsunosuke finds it difficult to bear but decides to wash his mother's feet, and only realizes how cold a dead body is. When dressing the body, the women place a Buddhist bag on her chest and put coins into it. The women do not care that the Shinto procedure does not allow it and continue by placing a cane and a pair of sandals in the coffin.[53]

The next day, Ryō and Tetsunosuke attend the funeral wearing Shinto robes. They appear out of place in the outfits and those in attendance can hardly keep from laughing. Before the procession to the cemetery, the Shinto priest delivers a long prayer. The attendees then gather around the coffin and burn incense. After the last viewing, undertakers nail the coffin lid down and take it out of the house. The attendees form a line and move to Aoyama Cemetery, where many of Tetsunosuke's family members and relatives are buried. At the Aoyama funeral hall, the Shinto priest offers another prayer and reads aloud the mother's biography, which moves the attendees deeply. After the service, undertakers carry the coffin to the graveyard and place it in a hole dug in the ground. The attendants fill the hole with sand, set up a burial marker, and offer water. The funeral is now over. The family members feel a sense of completion that allows them to return to their everyday lives.[54]

During the series of funerary rites, Tetsunosuke presents a liminal persona that both witnesses and experiences the reversal of a Japanese man's dominant role in a household. Sara Cobb points out that the liminal is more than the state between separation and reconnection, but is "a phase, a place of transformation for those that engage in and witness the (playful) dramatic inversion of hierarchy and return to a different relation within that hierarchy."[55] While Tetsunosuke and his brothers are ignorant regarding the treatment of dead bodies, Okoma and Oyone, Tetsunosuke's sister, prepare for the vigil and funeral by placing the mother's body with her head to the north, removing her clothing and washing her body, and dressing her in a white kimono. In other words, the women who have been subservient are empowered at the time of the funeral: they are in charge of its preparation. While accepting their suggestions, the male characters work behind the scenes, doing things such as inviting guests, ordering a coffin, and discussing payment for the funeral. This atmosphere, in which the inversion of gendered authority in the household occurs, provides Tetsunosuke another opportunity to reflect on the deceased and the relationship with his wife, brothers, sisters, and relatives. He learns complex karmic relationships inside his family and understands the shifting values in Japan's family system.

Tetsunosuke's liminal phase can be situated in a larger context, that is, a Shinto funeral as an immature religious practice. Although a kind of State Shinto had emerged as the political apparatus of modern Japan by then, according to Naoko Shimazu, the enshrinement of loyalist spirits at Yasukuni Shrine and the notion of an honorable death for the country had not yet appealed to the general public.[56] Despite the government's efforts to promote State Shinto, most Japanese, as represented by Tetsunosuke's family, maintained their own traditional Buddhist customs, while Shinto priests attempted to develop their liturgy on extant Buddhist rituals. Because of the surviving family's confusion caused by Shinto practice being introduced to the traditional Buddhist funeral, the funeral's cathartic effect on them is not as strong as on Chiyoko, a character in *To the Spring Equinox and Beyond*, which is examined next.

To the Spring Equinox and Beyond: Yoiko's Buddhist Funeral

To the Spring Equinox and Beyond is Sōseki's first major novel after recovering from his Shuzenji crisis. Sōseki claims to have chosen this title without much consideration; he intended to finish the work by the time the spring equinox had occurred.[57] The title of this personal novel, however, suggests Sōseki's acceptance of Japanese Buddhist customs. First, the Japanese honor their ancestors and hold Buddhist services at the times of the spring and autumn equinoxes. Traditionally, these time periods were (and still are) called *higan* or *ohigan*, which literally means "the other shore," implying that the world of enlightenment lies across a gulf, compared to the shore where we live, or the world of samsara. The Buddhist service held during the times of equinox is called *higan-e*. Second, "A Rainy Day," part of *To the Spring Equinox and Beyond*, which the present study analyzes, was Sōseki's tribute to one of his daughters who died suddenly about one month before he started writing. Her funeral service was held in the Buddhist style, and her 100th-day Buddhist memorial service was held several weeks before the equinox. These Buddhist episodes should be kept in mind as Yoiko's Buddhist funeral is analyzed.

To the Spring Equinox and Beyond is a novel consisting of six sections with a preface and a conclusion. The plot develops from section to section, as the narrator describes the experiences of Keitarō, the main character. Some sections are third-person narratives but describe what Keitarō experienced, while other sections are first-person narratives in which the characters associated with him confess or discuss their experiences.

After graduating from a university in Tokyo, Keitarō looks for a job, and is introduced to Taguchi by Sunaga, Keitarō's friend. Taguchi is Sunaga's uncle-in-law and a successful businessman. Through Taguchi's detective assignment,

Keitarō meets Matsumoto who has two elder sisters—one is Sunaga's mother and the other is married to Taguchi. Keitarō finds out that Taguchi has two daughters, Chiyoko and Momoyoko.

The section "A Rainy Day" contains an account of a Buddhist funeral narrated from Chiyoko's perspective. Matsumoto and his wife, Osen, have five children. The eldest daughter, Sakiko, is thirteen, and the youngest, Yoiko, is two. Matsumoto's niece, Chiyoko, often visits them and takes good care of Yoiko. One rainy evening in November, when someone is visiting Matsumoto, Yoiko suddenly collapses while Chiyoko spoon-feeds her. A doctor is called but he cannot help Yoiko. The cause of Yoiko's death is unclear.

A vigil is immediately held at the Matsumotos' home. A branch of anise tree, an incense burner, and rice dumplings are placed on a white table. Seeing the dim lights of the candles, the Matsumoto couple and Chiyoko are "struck for the first time with the lonely feeling that a great distance now separated them from Yoiko, who would never awaken."[58] The next day all the women present help make a white *kimono* and dress Yoiko. Chiyoko then asks each of the mourners to write *namu amida butsu* as many times as possible on a piece of paper:

> Everyone sat formally writing the prayer for Buddha's mercy. "Don't look at me while I'm writing," said Sakiko, screening her paper with her kimono sleeve as she composed her crooked strokes. The ten-year-old son said that he would write his prayer in *kana*. He copied several lines, all in syllabary letters as in a telegram.
>
> In the afternoon just before Yoiko's body was to be placed into the coffin, Matsumoto told Chiyoko to dress it in the newly sewn kimono. Chiyoko, so choked with tears that she was unable to reply, took off Yoiko's clothes and raised the cold naked body in her arms. All over the child's back were purple spots. When it had been changed into its hemp kimono, Osen passed a small string of beads around its folded hands. A small braided hat and an equally small pair of straw sandals were placed into the coffin, as were the pair of red woolen socks that Yoiko had worn until the evening before. At once there drifted before Chiyoko's eyes the image of the dangling tassels attached to the strings of those socks. All the toys that had been given to the child were crowded into the space at the child's head and feet. And last of all, over the body were strewn like piles of snow the strips of paper containing the prayer to Buddha. Then the lid of the coffin was put into place, and a cloth of white figured satin was placed gently over it.[59]

They dress Yoiko properly, according to Buddhist protocol, place her and her belongings in the coffin, and wish that she will attain birth in the Pure Land. That night a Buddhist priest comes to their home and chants sutras on behalf of Yoiko, after which Matsumoto talks to the priest about the Three Sutras of the Pure Land, Shinran's hymn, and a piece of writing by Rennyo.

The family delays Yoiko's funeral service for a day because Osen accepts a popular belief that scheduling funerals on a day of *tomobiki* is inauspicious—a day on which one's death is believed to cause a person related to him or her to die. Yoiko's funeral is held at a Buddhist temple on the following day and she is cremated. When the entire family gathers for a meal, Matsumoto says, "I don't think I made so much of the child while she was living, but now that she's gone . . . it seems I've lost the most precious thing. So much so that I almost wish one of these here could take her place."[60] After that, Matsumoto never receives a visitor on rainy days.

Yoiko's funeral illustrates the combination of traditional Shin Buddhist practice and the popular sentiments of the mourners. First, instead of reciting the *nenbutsu* for the deceased child, those gathered around Yoiko's coffin try to multiply the efficacy of Amida Buddha's compassion by writing *namu amida butsu*. Second, although Shin Buddhists do not accept superstitious beliefs, the Matsumoto family delays the funeral service because of Osen's belief in *tomobiki*. These practices lead to the conclusion that the mourners do not really understand the Shin Buddhist doctrine but arrange the funeral in a Shin Buddhist style for Yoiko simply because members of the Matsumoto family are affiliated with a Shin Buddhist temple.[61]

Matsumoto's conversation with the Shin priest is not fully described, but it indicates a discussion of Rennyo's "Letter on White Ashes" (*Hakkotsu no gobunshō*, or *Hakkotsu no ofumi*). Traditionally, a Shin Buddhist priest reads it aloud during a funerary service to remind mourners of the reality of human life. It reads in part, "Hence we may have radiant faces in the morning but in the evening be no more than white bones [white ashes]. With the coming of the wind of impermanence, both eyes are instantly closed, and when a single breath is forever stilled, the radiant face is drained of life and its vibrant glow is lost."[62] Although neither the narrator nor Chiyoko speaks about "Letter on White Ashes," the Shin Buddhist funerary service, which includes a reading of the passage, helps Matsumoto conceive of Yoiko's sudden death as an instance of impermanence.

The series of Buddhist rituals brings relief to the Matsumoto family and brings them closer together. Despite the gloomy atmosphere, the house is lively because of the funerary arrangement. The second son, Kakichi, plays a drum and is scolded because he is noisy; Sakiko and Shigeko bother their mother because they also want to go to the crematorium; Matsumoto and his wife discuss their outfits for the funeral service; and out of curiosity Chiyoko and Momoyoko wish to peek into the coffin. During the funeral service, neither of the parents looks extremely sad nor does Chiyoko cry. She even bursts into laughter when Matsumoto's second daughter, Shigeko, pinches ash from the incense burner and throws it into an incense container, instead of putting the incense from the container into the burner. On her return from the temple in a rickshaw, Chiyoko even misses the sense of anguish, which she also felt as pure and beautiful, from before the funeral.

The account of a Buddhist funeral in "A Rainy Day" can be explained in terms of the narrative pattern of "ground, path, and goal." The death of Yoiko is the cause of suffering for Chiyoko and the Matsumoto family. Participating in funerary Buddhism in the form of vigil, funerary rites, and crematory services is a way for them to console themselves over the loss of Yoiko. The bereaved family gathers together, shares sadness, and renews a sense of intimacy. To put it differently, funerary Buddhism, which requires the presence of a Buddhist priest and a set of liturgies, helps the mourners accept the loss of loved ones, overcome the feelings associated with death, evoke awareness of the brevity of human life, and embrace the preciousness of the present moment. It assures the Matsumoto family and Chiyoko that Yoiko does not remain in a realm of limbo but is embraced by the world of *kami*, Buddha, and ancestors. Although there is no "goal" in coping with the loss of a loved one, for Chiyoko, the completion of the series of Buddhist funerary services marks the end of her immediate mourning period.

The Buddhist funeral is not only cathartic to Matsumoto and Yoiko but also to the writer, Natsume Sōseki, himself. He wrote "A Rainy Day" in part to express his love for his fifth daughter, Hinako, who had died suddenly on November 29, 1911. In "A Rainy Day," he fictionalized her death and the funerary services, dedicating that section to her.

Some of the descriptions of Yoiko's funeral in "A Rainy Day" derive from a diary that Sōseki kept during the time of Hinako's death, vigil service, and funeral. For instance, he wrote, "While she [Hinako] was alive, I didn't think she was more important than other children. But now, when she is dead, I think she was the most adorable child"[63] and "My stomach has cracked. My mind, too, it seems, for I feel an incurable sorrow each time I recall [the loss of my child, Hinako])."[64] Sōseki also copied part of the passages from "Letter on White Ashes," and expressed a sense of relief and achievement when he completed that portion of "A Rainy Day." In his letter to his friend, Sōseki wrote, "I began writing 'A Rainy Day' on Hinako's birthday [March 2] and finished it on her hundredth-memorial day [March 7]. I'm glad I did it, because it has become a tribute to her."[65] In a fragmentary note he writes, referring to his conjugal relationship, "the death of a child, the reconciliation of a couple."[66] The writing of "A Rainy Day," therefore, illustrates Sōseki's healing and the creation of a narrative memory from a trauma. This was the means by which he reaffirmed his love for Hinako and felt that the life of a two-year-old child was just as precious as the lives of his other children (Sōseki had seven children).

Although the author must be critically distanced from the narrator and Matsumoto's losing Yoiko is not identical to Sōseki's losing Hinako, Chiyoko and Matsumoto do speak on behalf of Sōseki. While using the character of Matsumoto as his literary alter ego and narrating Yoiko's death and her funeral from Chiyoko's perspective, Sōseki opened up his emotions and let out his sorrow over losing Hinako. He recalled and mourned the loss of his fifth daughter by revisiting his diary entries three months after her passing and responded to his loss in the form of fiction. In other words, "A Rainy Day" demonstrates the author's path to healing. Sōseki found Hinako's death to be the cause of his suffering (ground), overcame the sense of loss by transforming a traumatic memory into a narrative memory (path), and accepted her death and paid tribute to her (goal). Just as the recitation of "Letter on White Ashes" by the Shin Buddhist priest during Hinako's funeral reminded Sōseki of the impermanence of life, Buddhist funerals and writing "A Rainy Day" allowed him to overcome the bereavement caused by her sudden death. While the characters are products of individual creativity, the funerary Buddhism represented in personal fiction mirrors the religious experiences of the people of the day, including those of the writers. The main characters' religious expressions and the narrators' Buddhist perspectives demonstrate the authors' knowledge of Buddhism on either an intellectual or practical level.

Conclusion

Since the "death of the author," literary studies scholars have moved away from biographical criticism—that is, to explore the connection between an author's life and work—and have analyzed literary texts without considering the interests of the authors. Especially in studies of modern Japanese autobiographical fiction, the author and a main character are not always considered to be identical and views of narrators are not necessarily reflective of the author's view. As Fowler points out, however, whether we read autobiographical fiction as nonfiction or fiction, "it does not deny ipso facto the possibility of the other."[1] As demonstrated in this book, it is also difficult not to find reflections of the authors' Buddhist experiences in personal fiction when the texts are read from the standpoint of the path.

The Buddhist formula of spiritual development known as the path is helpful for analyzing narrative structures of personal novels. For some characters, path is associated with their efforts to identify the causes of their problems and their desire to redirect their lives. The beginning of a path is acceptance of the irrational aspects of the human condition. The end of a path, however, varies. Self-transformation can be a goal for a main character, but it can also be an ongoing process for others. For some of the main characters examined in this book, the paths develop as rites of passage—that is, reflecting on the issues of life and death while observing Buddhist funerals, whether or not they actually experience illumination with regard to death. The characters' paths also intersect with the authors' paths and are framed by a particular Buddhist doctrine and ideology.

Buddhism is artistically represented in the works of path literature examined in this book. A sense of loneliness and displacement, as well as the nature of suffering, is transformed into an art of impermanence. Stories of spiritual liberation are presented as arts of awakening and dramatized by mysticism. Buddhist funerals of loved ones are portrayed as memorial art. These aspects of personal fiction make prose literature different from Buddhist scriptures and Buddhist writings. At the same time, the writings of a modern Shin Buddhist priest can be read as a work of art. Akegarasu was familiar with modern Japanese and Western literature, and incorporated literary techniques of the day into his work. He included an anecdote of a mystical encounter in order to make his story of conversion dynamic, which in turn undermined his new realization that Amida Buddha is not a savior who can generate worldly benefits. He did so because, just as Sōseki, Katai, and Shiga, he was aware of his readers. While the social standing of literary writers and Buddhist priests created boundaries in their work, these writers shared the same problems and expressed their concerns by writing personal fiction. In this regard, their written experiences of Buddhism are similar.

First, in the personal novels produced by both Buddhist and literary authors, the main characters "refigure" their lives. For example, Buddhism plays a key role in Jikai's conversion in *The Miracle of a Buddhist Monk*, Tetsuta's self-realization in *Remaining Snow*, Kensaku's awakening in *A Dark Night's Passing*, and Sōsuke's search for spiritual strength in *The Gate*. In these works, the spiritual development of the main characters is traced following the narrative pattern of "ground, path, and goal" and in a way similar to the development of Buddhist faith, as demonstrated by the narrators of "The Nature of My Faith" and *Before and after My Rebirth*. For these characters and narrators, the trajectory of ground, path, and goal is not straightforward, but can be characterized as diverging, spiral, and even regressive. Especially for Kensaku and the narrator of *Before and after My Rebirth*, attaining the goal does not suggest that they will stay within the ideal spiritual state forever. Rather, they can relapse to a former mental state and suffer again, redirect their lives as they accept new challenges, or continue to stay on the path. The goal may simply be a milestone on the path, similar to the way that enlightenment "unfolds endlessly, an endless beginning, an ever-fresh start into long-familiar territory," to use Harmless's words.[2]

Second, writing personal fiction, especially episodes dealing with the death of loved ones, enables the narrators and authors to reflect on the deceased and learn about their present being, whether they are Buddhist priests or not. For Sōseki, who wrote "A Rainy Day" in *To the Spring Equinox and Beyond*; for Katai, who wrote *Life*; and for Akegarasu, who wrote *Before and after My Rebirth*, writing itself represents a phase of spiritual recovery from the loss of a loved one. As David Stahl points out, constructing a narrative helps those who are traumatized to reconstitute, communicate, work through, and come to terms with agonizing experiences.³

Narrators embody themselves differently within the narrative structure of a path. According to F. K. Stanzel, in the personalized first-person narration, the hero's experiences are part of the narrative process. Narration is existential and almost always relevant to the first-person narrator. In the authorial third-person narration, in which the third-person narrator may refer to himself as "I," the narrator selects what is narrated based on his literary-aesthetic concern but not on his existential cause, and the narrating self is more detached from the experiencing self than the narrating self in the first-person narration.⁴ Although Stanzel's narrative study does not directly apply to the readings of modern Japanese personal fiction, which include both first- and third-person narrations, authorial presence in *Before and after My Rebirth* is as strong as in *The Diary of the Second Army Corps at War* and in "At Kinosaki," and much stronger than in *The Quilt*, *A Dark Night's Passing*, and *Grass on the Wayside*. In *Before and after My Rebirth*, the narrator is less concerned with aesthetic sensibilities connected to the transient beauty of nature than the narrators of *The Three-Cornered World* and *A Dark Night's Passing*.

The Buddhist notion of path is useful for the future consideration of Buddhism and gender in personal fiction and even for the study of contemporary Japanese literature. Here Higuchi Ichiyō's (1872–1896) "Child's Play" (*Takekurabe*, 1895–1896), Aoki Shinmon 青木新門's *Coffinman: The Journal of a Buddhist Mortician* (*Nōkanfu Nikki* 納棺夫日記, 1993), and Murakami Haruki 村上春樹's *Kafka on the Shore* (*Umibe no kafuka* 海辺のカフカ, 2002) serve as cases in point.

A discussion of Ichiyō's work is beyond the scope of this book, but it is worth mentioning unrecognized elements of Buddhism in one of her short stories. According to Robert L. Danly, she is, "with no serious contenders, Japan's first woman writer of stature in modern days."⁵ Ichiyō has been consecrated in the Japanese literary establishment, partly because of her premature death, which prevented her extraordinary talent from blossoming further. During the short period of the twenty-four years of her life, she wrote twenty-one short stories, many essays, and almost four thousand *waka* poems, while keeping a diary throughout her life, which can be read as a splendid autobiographical novel.⁶

Ichiyō was very interested in Buddhism. Because her family was affiliated with a Shin Buddhist temple, she attended Shin Buddhist funeral and memorial services and, as a result, seems to have been able to distinguish scriptures in the Shin Buddhist tradition. According to Sugisaki Toshio, her familiarity with Shin Buddhism does not, however, suggest that Ichiyō was an active Shin Buddhist member, but rather, she was interested in a broad range of Buddhist ideas and Buddhist philosophy. Poverty and unfulfilled love led her to reflect on the conditions of her suffering, nature of impermanence, and her attachment, as well as to seek spiritual liberation through Buddhist teachings. Ichiyō was especially attracted to the Buddhist teachings highlighted in the *Avataṃsaka Sutra*, according to which the object is the product of mental recognition and it does not exist apart from the mind, nor does the mind exist by itself. The correlation of object and mind suggests that the existence of an object depends on its relationships to all other things—in other words, all things are essentially void. According to Sugisaki, although Ichiyō understood the Buddhist concepts of emptiness and co-arising, she was unable to feel spiritually liberated because her attachment to love was too strong.[7]

"Child's Play" is one of Ichiyō's representative short stories that can be read as a work of path literature.[8] The story is about friendships, competition, and instances of bittersweet love among a group of young teenagers who live in the neighborhood of the red-light district called Yoshiwara. The heroine is Midori, a teen whose sister works as a courtesan. Midori is in love with Shinnyo, the son of the Buddhist priest at Ryūgeji, who also has feelings for Midori but cannot express them to her. It is about their growth and entry into adulthood, as shown by the title of the work, which literally means "comparing [their] heights,"[9] indicating their physical growth.

In "Child's Play," Buddhism is represented in several ways. First, Buddhist temples and Shinto shrines appear as part of the landscape where characters interact. A greedy Buddhist priest, Shinnyo's father, is depicted from the viewpoint of Shinnyo, who hates him and wishes neither to become a Buddhist priest nor to succeed his father. In the end, however, Shinnyo enters a school of the Buddhist denomination with which his temple is affiliated and wears a Buddhist robe. At the same time, Midori has her first period and, "she hated, hated, hated, this growing up!"[10] "Child's Play" depicts the rites of passage through which Shinnyo and Midori enter adulthood.

The first line of "Child's Play" indicates the path that Midori takes—path, as exemplified by the rites of passage. The short story begins with "It's *a long way* round to the front of the quarter, where the trailing branches of the willow tree bid farewell to the nighttime revellers and the bawdyhouse lights flicker in the moat, dark as the dye that blackens the smiles of the Yoshiwara beauties"[11] (emphasis added). Although this is a description of the red-light district, "a long way" implies how long it would take for Midori to become a courtesan. Her liminal phase corresponds to the interstitial space, where she is located—between the profane as represented by Yoshiwara and the sacred as marked by a Buddhist temple and a Shinto shrine.[12] Her liminal character is enhanced by a would-be Buddhist priest, Shinnyo, who represents both her love and her effort to detach herself from her love for him. Although Midori's goal to become a courtesan does not suggest spiritual liberation, it is parallel to, or reflects, the Buddhist path taken by Shinnyo, who also finds problematic aspects (ground) of growing up.

According to Edward Fowler, by the mid-1920s, Japanese writers had lost interest in writing about themselves using their own voices and that "more aesthetically inclined neo-perceptionist and more socially conscious proletarian literature" became popular.[13] This shift in the literary establishment does not, however, suggest that literary characters and Japanese writers stopped exploring the self. Japanese writers continued to cultivate a sense of selfhood through different forms of writing. The influence of personal fiction and path literature remained strong in the making of modern and contemporary Japanese fiction, and Buddhism continues to influence contemporary Japanese writers.

Nōkanfu Nikki became widely known in Japan largely because it was made into the film *Departures* (*Okuribito* おくりびと, 2008), the winner of Best Foreign Language Film at the 2009 Academy Awards. It was translated into English in 2002.[14] Since I have already discussed the relationship between *Coffinman* and *Departures* elsewhere,[15] here I will only mention *Coffinman* as the author's exploration of Buddhism.

Coffinman is more than a diary. It derives from the diary Aoki kept when he worked as a mortician. It does not, however, belong to a category of diary, autobiography, or novel. As Aoki himself acknowledges, this work is not a religious exegesis.[16] It is a combination of his diary and essays that include his later reflections on life and death and on the passages of various Buddhist scriptures—especially Shinran's writings—and Japanese poetry, including poems written by Miyazawa Kenji and Kaneko Misuzu.

Aoki recalls painful childhood experiences that eventually influenced him to work as a mortician. He survived in Manchuria until the end of the Pacific War, when he was eight. He was forced to return to Japan, leaving the bodies of his little brother and sister in a makeshift cremation site.[17] The sorrow Aoki felt when placing the dead body of his little brother on the coals, and the beauty of the sky he witnessed at that moment, made a deep impression on him; as a result, death became his lifetime theme. Because of this influence and the fact that he needed money, Aoki became a mortician, against his uncle's advice. Gradually, however, he changed his attitude toward his occupation, which is often looked down upon by many, when he realized the impermanence of life and the power of death that reconnects a dead person and people around him or her. He began associating death with a light that was both indescribable and marvelous. He read various religious literature and found Shinran's definition of light compelling—that is, "The Buddha is what we thus come to experience as that mysterious Light; the Tathagata Buddha [issuing from Reality-as-Such] that we thus come to experience is that Light."[18]

Coffinman follows the pattern of narrative based on "ground, path, and, goal" and can be read as the story of the author's spiritual journey in his own voice. The work of morticians, which the author initially disliked, reminded him of the problem of death that he first experienced at the age of eight, forcing him to consider human predicaments and helping him come to terms with his problems. He finally developed a perspective to see all things from the point of death and accepted the Buddhist soteriology that embraces all sentient beings. In other words, the occupation of mortician formed a reverse karmic condition for the author to experience Buddhism.

Writing *Coffinman* played a crucial role in forming Aoki's identity. According to Aoki's own words, he revisited the diary he kept during this period and began writing, not because he wished to become a novelist but because he felt it necessary to understand his life and the problem of death.[19] (Aoki, however, acknowledges that when he was young, he wanted to become a writer and wrote short stories while interacting with a literary circle of the day.) Writing, while weaving back and forth between his diary and Buddhist literature, enabled Aoki to organize his thoughts, connect Buddhist "theory" and his "practice" as a mortician, and transform his perception of death.

Kafka on the Shore is not personal fiction. The *New Yorker* reviewed it as "an insistently metaphysical mind-bender."[20] There are two different stories, narrated alternately in odd- and even-numbered chapters, and they join at the end. The protagonist is Tamura Kafka, a fifteen-year-old boy referred to as *boku*—a first-person male pronoun in Japanese—and the story in the odd-numbered chapters develops in the first-person narrative. A further introduction to this best-selling novel is perhaps unnecessary—*Kafka on the Shore* has been translated into multiple languages and the *New York Times* listed it as one of the ten best books of 2005.[21] Analyzing *Kafka on the Shore*, whose plot and themes are very complicated, is beyond the scope of this study. Nevertheless, it is worth discussing Murakami's relationship to Buddhism—which has not drawn adequate attention in the West—and aspects of path literature in the novel, although critics have already pointed out religious and spiritual components in the work. Philip Gabriel, in particular, discusses forgiveness as a Christian theme of *Kafka on the Shore*, together with violence and evil.[22]

Murakami grew up in a Buddhist environment. According to an interview by the *Prague Post* in November 2006, Murakami's father was a teacher and a Buddhist priest, which greatly affected his childhood.[23] Murakami recalled his father as follows:

> My father died last year at the age of 90. He was a retired teacher and a part-time Buddhist priest. When he was in graduate school, he was drafted into the army and sent to fight in China. As a child born after the war, I used to see him every morning before breakfast offering up long, deeply-felt prayers at the Buddhist altar in our house. One time I asked him why he did this, and he told me he was praying for the people who had died in the war. He was praying for all the people who died, he said, both ally and enemy alike. Staring at his back as he knelt at the altar, I seemed to feel the shadow of death hovering around him. My father died, and with him he took his memories, memories that I can never know. But the presence of death that lurked about him remains in my own memory. It is one of the few things I carry on from him, and one of the most important.[24]

Through the ritual practice of a Buddhist priest, who happened to be his father, Murakami learned about the tragedy of war, impermanence of life, and the impact of despondency caused by the loss of human life.

Although it is unclear how much Murakami knew about Buddhism when he wrote *Kafka on the Shore*, worldviews that the novel presents are similar but not limited to Buddhist perspectives. To name just a few, Tamura Kafka, who suffers from amnesia but attempts to seek his identity, considers his encounter with Sakura to be the result of actions he had committed in the past; Hagita, a truck driver who gives Nakata a ride, tells him that this world is in constant flux, changing day by day—therefore, nothing is permanent; and Oshima, while referring to *The Tale of Genji*, explains to Kafka that what Kafka sees is Saeki's doppelganger (*ikiryō*). A young man named Hoshino also wonders about his personal identity when he travels with Nakata. One day, Hoshino recalls a story that his grandfather told him when he was a child. Myōga (S. Cūḍpanthaka) is a mentally challenged disciple of the Buddha and polishes the shoes of other disciples. Myōga does this for many years and then one day suddenly attains enlightenment. Recalling this story, Hoshino realizes that it was not that "polishing shoes for decades" is the "crappiest kind of life" but that "life is crappy, no matter how you cut it."[25] Hoshino therefore decides to keep supporting Nakata's aimless trip and helps him rediscover his old self. Further, Hoshino's remark about Nakata's ultimate self-transformation—"death was the only road back to being the 'normal Nakata' "[26]—resonates with Natsume Sōseki's view on death: "I will return to my original self when I die." (Note that both Kafka and Murakami favor Sōseki's works.) The identity crisis (ground) that Hoshino, Nakata, and Kafka each undergo leads them to seek who they are (path/goal).

Although their self-discoveries do not seem to represent the author's own experience, exploration of the self was part of Murakami's literary theme. In *A Guide to Short Stories for Young Readers* (*Wakai dokusha no tameno tanpen an'nai*, 2004), Murakami discusses why he did not find modern Japanese autobiographical fiction interesting and instead chose to read Western novels:

> When I read novels [produced in English], I tried to understand how those writers dealt with the relationship between the ego and the self. That was a big problem for me. Actually, I feel that the issue of ego-expression (*jiga hyōgen*) might have been the reason I looked away from Japanese literature for a long time.[27]

Murakami avoided reading *shishōsetsu* (I-novels) because he did not like them, but he also knew that he could not continue turning away from the literary tradition of his own country. Instead of reading Japanese I-novels, he began exploring the relationship between a writer and his or her work through Western novels. Based on Murakami's statement above, Suzuki Takami believes that, for Murakami, writing contributes to the formation of selfhood.[28]

A dialogue between Nakata and Saeki in *Kafka on the Shore* represents such a position. Saeki, who senses she will die soon, asks Nakata to burn three notebooks she has kept after she dies. She had written in detail all her activities in the past so that she could understand who she was and what kind of life she had lived. It was very difficult, but she has just completed that task when they speak:

> "Writing things was important, wasn't it?" Nakata asked.
> "Yes, it was. The process of writing *was* important. Even though the finished product is completely meaningless."[29]

For Saeki—and possibly to some extent Murakami—writing served as a method of self-analysis through which she came to terms with herself.

Although the characters in *Kafka on the Shore* do not show knowledge of a specific Buddhist doctrine, general Buddhist principles underlie their spiritual journeys. Realization of the working of one's karma and the nature of impermanence help the characters better understand their conditions and relationships. If one is able to accept oneself, one can become lenient with others. Forgiveness will then take its own course. While changing its form and containing varying degrees of Buddhist presence, path literature still attracts many readers of contemporary Japan and the rest of the world.

APPENDIX 1

Before and after My Rebirth

AKEGARASU HAYA

Preface

To Revered Teacher, Kiyozawa

[1]
    I was twenty-seven years of age when you passed away on June 6, 1903. Seventeen years have passed since then and I am now forty-three. I thought I was doing well for about ten years following your death, but when I was thirty-five or thirty-six, I became gloomy, and then, after I lost my wife at thirty-seven, I became confused. My old self died by my immoral act. But then a new Akegarasu Haya was born. Please listen to my confession about the changes in my mind.

[2]
    I first sensed shame when sexual desires emerged as a child's natural growth. During my adolescence, I tried to keep it a secret, but felt guilty about it. From about the age of twenty, I fought my continuing sexual desires and cried because I was always defeated. That was when I entered Shinshū University. During the four years of college, until graduation at the age of twenty-four, I was more concerned about containing my sexual desires than studying. While I longed for a burning love, moral lessons taught me that lusting for love was a sin and evil. Therefore, I tried to subdue my sexual desires and struggled

tremendously to maintain my puritan ideals. To alleviate my agony, I composed haiku, read novels, and debated with friends. I associated with colleagues who appeared sexually inactive and followed professors who appeared to live puritan lives. It was during that time that I visited you.

When I asked, "What should I do about my raging sexual desires?" you said, "I used to have a similar problem so I consulted an old Buddhist master. He told me to avoid situations where I would be aroused. This problem of sexual desire is indeed troublesome."

During the times I was tempted by the opposite sex, I was consoled by a passage in the *Tannishō*: "Even a virtuous man can attain Rebirth in the Pure Land, how much more easily a wicked man!"[1] That passage made me feel as if I was in the embrace of the Buddha. But lust emerged gradually and strongly even in my joy and continued. I apologized to the Buddha and repented the arousing of desires only in a way to justify my desires. I recited the *nenbutsu*, read scriptures, and meditated. I then cried with joy at being a true guest of Amida Buddha, who had extended compassion to even such a hopeless man as I. I thought I had real faith, bragged about it, considered others to not be pious, and therefore tried to force them to believe in Amida.

When I graduated in 1900 at the age of twenty-four, I wanted to contribute to world peace. Because of my polluted body, I felt I was not qualified to be a Buddhist priest or a religious leader. I thought I should abandon the robe and become a diplomat. I talked to Reverend Ishikawa Shuntai of Higashi Honganji and then he arranged a scholarship for me so I could pursue study along those lines. Because of the advice of the late Konoe Atsumaro, to whom I was referred by the late Okumura Ioko, I decided to study Russian and so entered a foreign language school.

Being a diplomat requires a strong mind. Hoping to receive spiritual inspiration from you, I asked if you would allow me to live with you in your house in Hongō, Tokyo. How delighted I was when you welcomed me. I lived there with Tada Kanae and Sasaki Gesshō—my classmates whom Higashi Honganji had sent to Tokyo. Tada studied Buddhist sutras and Sasaki read commentaries on the *Tripitaka*, while I studied Russian and also economics and law. You opposed my decision to become a diplomat and even consulted with Higashi Honganji's administrative leaders regarding my career. I told you, "I drink and chase after women. That will make it difficult to be active in religious circles, so I should work in a secular environment." Your reply to me was, "You can rejoice in the tathāgata's compassion the way you and like-minded people want. Lust alone should not be the reason for you to give up your robe." You repeatedly advised me to maintain my priesthood, but I did not change my mind. Twenty years have passed since then, and I still want to be neither a bureaucrat nor a religious man. I remain a student who continues to inquire about the meaning of life.

In January 1901, the three of us decided to publish the journal *Seishinkai* under your supervision. I became the editor in chief and devoted all my energy to it. In the fall of 1902, you resigned as dean of Shinshū University in Sugamo and returned to your hometown. You told me to quit the journal then, but we insisted on continuing it. You passed away about half a year later—after moving back to Saihōji in Ōhama [present-day Aichi Prefecture]. I was deeply discouraged by your death, because I had relied on you so much. How gloomy I felt and how much I cried. Somehow, however, strength welled up in my heart and I was determined to stand on my own feet.

[3]

After your death, I, together with friends, worked hard to introduce your name, virtue, and teaching to others. I spoke passionately about the renovation of Japanese spirituality and publically urged Buddhist reform. Within five or six years, our efforts resulted in a new movement with the name Kiyozawa school. The gatherings of December Fan (*Rōsenk-kai*, annual gatherings to commemorate Kiyozawa) were organized throughout Japan and "The Nature of My Faith," the last essay you wrote, was read everywhere. Conservative Shin Buddhists became concerned about our new movement and called us heretics. Because I challenged them the most, they considered me the leader of heretics, but I took pride in being a reformer. In retrospect, I was filled with emotion. Like Paul, who founded Christianity because he respected Jesus, and Kakunyo, who built the Honganji because he admired Shinran Shōnin, I was trying to establish the Kiyozawa school. Not knowingly, I had become a leader of "religious merchants."

Tada, Sasaki, and I began visiting you back in 1896 when you were living in Shirakawa village. Although you were a great scholar and we respected you, we often discussed how to guide you to taste the dynamic of Shin Buddhism. While living together in Tokyo, the three of us discussed Shin Buddhism with you. Ten years after your demise, however, rather than sharing your spirit with others, we ended up explaining and interpreting your vibrant teaching according to standard doctrine, which had been corrupted since the Tokugawa era, and reinvigorated the same old beliefs under the fashionable name of "Kiyozawa." We were not aware of our mistake, however, and earnestly pushed it forward. I soon lost all humility and accepted the praise of others as a matter of course. I felt as if I dominated religious circles and grew arrogant as a result.

Still, I continued to be troubled by my sexual desires. I married Fusako on December 8, 1902, which was before your death. When I saw you in March of the following year, you said, "You've made a karmic connection, haven't you?" Fusako assisted me greatly in my efforts to promote your teaching. She even helped me compile the first volume of the *Collected Works of Kiyozawa*. We loved each other and for a while things went well.

[4]

Knowing that Ānanda was succumbing to the carnal influence of the spell, the Thus-Come One ended his meal immediately and returned to the monastic grounds. The king, his senior ministers, the elders, and the other laity, desiring to hear the essentials of the Dharma, followed after the Buddha. Then from the crown of his head the World-Honored One poured forth invincible light which was as dazzling as a hundred gems. The Buddha Śākyamuni made appear within that light a Buddha who, seated in full-lotus posture on a thousand-petaled sacred lotus, proclaimed a spiritually powerful mantra.[2]

The Buddha instructed Mañjuśrī to go to Ānanda and protect him with the spiritually powerful mantra and, once the evil spell had been defeated, to give support to Ānanda and also to the young Mātaṅgī woman, and to encourage both to return with him to where the Buddha was.[3]

When Ānanda saw the Buddha, he bowed and wept in sorrow. He regretted that, since time without beginning, he had devoted himself to erudition but had not fully developed his practice on the Path. Respectfully and repeatedly he asked the Buddha to explain for him the elementary steps that lead to attainment in the wondrous practices of calming the mind, contemplative insight, and meditation in stillness—practices through which the Thus-Come Ones from all ten directions had become fully awakened.

Meanwhile, as many Bodhisattvas as there are sand-grains of the River Ganges, along with the great Arhats, Solitary Sages, and others from the ten directions, all eagerly wished to listen. They sat down and waited silently to hear instruction from the Sage.[4]

The Buddha said to Ānanda, "You and I are members of the same family, and we share the affection that is natural among relatives. At the time you first made the resolution to become enlightened, what excellent attributes did you see in my Dharma that immediately led you to reject the deep familial affection and conjugal love found in the world?"[5]

We used to call our house, in Morikawa-chō in Tokyo, "capacious cave." While reading books on economics and law, I also carefully read the *Śūraṅgama Sutra* (*Shuryōgonkyō*) in order to calm my raging sexual desires. In this sutra, Shakamuni Buddha explains the Dharma to Ānanda when Ānanda was about to succumb to his carnal passions. Unfortunately, the sutra did not help me extinguish the flames burning within me. To divert my excessive sexual energies, I read the novels of Ihara Saikaku and Tamenaga Shunsui, and the work of Chikamatsu Monzaemon, but their descriptions of human emotions only fed the fires of my sexual passions.

> Further, in this samādhi, once this good person has seen the aggregate of form disintegrate, he will see the aggregate of sense-perception appear. He may then have a vision of his own superiority, for which he feels an overwhelming gratitude. Immediately, a boundless courage and intensity may arise within him so that he comes to believe that his resolve is equal to the resolve of all Buddhas. He will announce that he can accomplish in a single moment of thought what others need three quadrillions of eons to accomplish. This state is called 'an excessive and improper haste in trying to excel in one's spiritual practice.' If he understands this state, he will not suppose that he has become a sage, and he will not become confused. Eventually the state will disappear of its own accord. But if he thinks that he has become a sage, a demonic insanity will enter into the depths of his mind. He will boast about himself to everyone he meets. In his boundless arrogance he will acknowledge neither Buddhas nor ordinary people. Having lost his ability to enter the correct samādhi, he is certain to fall.[6]

Based on these words, I became introspective:

"People who undertake a spiritual practice but who fail to realize the ultimate enlightenment—people such as the Hearers of the Teaching and the Solitary Sages, as well as celestial beings and others, such as demon-kings and members of the demon's retinues, who follow wrong paths—all fail because they do not understand two fundamentals and are mistaken and confused in their practice. They are like someone who cooks sand, hoping to prepare a delicious meal. Even if the sand were cooked for eons numberless as motes of dust, no meal would result from it.[7]

"Ānanda, what are the two fundamentals? The first is the mind that is the basis of death and rebirth and that has continued since time without beginning. This mind is dependent on perceived objects, and it is this mind that you and all beings make use of and that each of you consider to be your own nature.

"The second fundamental is full awakening, which also has no beginning; it is the original and pure essence of nirvana. It is the original understanding, the real nature of consciousness. All conditioned phenomena arise from it, and yet it is among those phenomena that beings lose track of it. They have lost track of this fundamental understanding though it is active in them all day long, and because they remain unaware of it, they make the mistake of entering the various destinies.[8]

"The Thus-Come Ones in all ten directions chose one of the eighteen constituent elements of perception for their practice that led to their gaining the perfect, supreme, complete awakening. For them, none of the eighteen constituents was superior or inferior. But because you are at a lower level and have not yet fully developed that wisdom which is independent of conditions, I have explained all this to you in detail so that you will be able to choose one faculty as a gateway to deep practice. If you take that path until you have left behind all distortion within that one faculty, then all the other faculties will be purified as well."[9]

You can imagine how I was thrilled by these words of Shakyamuni Buddha.[10] I seem to have contained my exploding sexual desires after I married, but because we lived separately—she lived in her hometown and I lived in Tokyo—my body was almost entirely burned by the flame of love. While appreciating the tathāgata's grace and compassion, I was tormented by, and afraid of, the instinct that would betray my conscience. I agonized and wailed. I was somehow able to briefly overcome my desires by repenting, reciting the *nenbutsu*, purifying my thoughts, and practicing other means, but clouds of doubt sometimes overcame me. As a Buddhist reformer, I cared about fame and merit so much that I hid my excessive sexual desires and pretended to have pure faith in the tathāgata. My followers increased in numbers and the reform movement gained momentum, parrying the old guard's suppression. I furthered the reform while hoping to forget my carnal desires. I mixed up the objective of the reform with the need for controlling my lust. As a result, even though I started out as a seeker of religious truth, I really became a splendid religious propagandist. Disaster was, however, quickly approaching and I was about to fall.

[5]
    In 1910, the Higashi Honganji denomination held a commemorative service to mark the six hundred fiftieth anniversary of Shinran Shōnin's passing, and his name resonated throughout Japan. Because of this once-in-a-lifetime event, our reform movement grew rapidly. Sales of the *Seishinkai* journal increased and we were busy propagating the service throughout the entire country. The more I felt deceived by my sexuality, the more I strove for reform.

    During that time, I felt that in order to spread the teaching of other-power, I had to point out that a life of evil could be lived only through the grace of Amida Buddha. I felt I should emphasize that those who are sure to fall into Hell could yet live a life of ease and comfort only because of a marvelously mysterious power. That power is Amida Buddha, the being who saves us, which I sensed to be a power that could not be doubted. That is the power I wanted others to also feel. Again and again, I cried over my guilt and Amida Buddha's power. I cried over my evilness and also the grace that forgave me for that wickedness, and my explanations of the other-power seemed to be accepted by many. Because of my comparisons with the materialistic world, the previously unseen power of Amida could now seem to be tasted right before their eyes. It is no coincidence that the number of my followers increased so dramatically. I did not think I was trying to coerce others into believing what I had believed. Among the things I wrote then are essays about the pure blood and sweat that so overflowed and took over my entire being.

    I had a formula then that seemed to work. That formula was to accept myself as sinful and then repent—I cried when I felt guilty but then appreciated my present materialistic life, sensed Amida Buddha's grace, and thanked Amida. While I did not completely believe in this formula, I decided to accept it based on my reading of the *Tannishō*. The *Collection of Words by Zen Master Xuefeng Huikong* (*Ekū goroku*) and the *Sayings of Shūzon* (*Shūzon goroku*), a Shin Buddhist priest, compiled by Sasaki added fuel to the fire of my faith, which was about to extinguish. My formula seemed romantic and worked beautifully.

This dreamlike illusion became strong when naturalism—which had dominated the intellectual world of Japan—lost its momentum and before the passion of sex burned everything in my life.

[6]   Emperor Meiji died on July 30, 1912 and the world suddenly became pitch-black. Fusako became ill at the end of the fifty-day mourning period, September 19. I nursed her as well as I could, but she died on February 21 of the following year. I expressed my agony and bewilderment in *The Ruin*. I suppose you heard about it. As I wrote in *The Ruin*, I sank to the bottom of complete darkness. I reflected on the legend of Pierre Abélard, an ascetic who fell in love with Eloise in a monastery and suffered because of that. I also reflected on the story of an immortal who lost his supernatural power after being aroused by a young woman's sensual limbs. I was troubled just like those men.

My wife's illness dragged on and I nursed her as best I could. I was determined to have her recover her health. Two or three months later, however, my sexual desires became so intense that I started to fear young women. I could not accept the advice to hire a nurse because I felt I would not be able to resist the temptation to bed her.

One day, a friend of mine told me that an acquaintance had slept with a nurse when his wife was sick. I was terrified, but my friend told me, "But you aren't like him." He seemed impressed by my dedication to my wife, but I felt extremely lonely because he did not understand my true feelings. Because I was unable to interact with a young nurse, I asked my wife's mother to help me nurse her. What a frightening premonition that was! About a week before my wife's death, my friend finally sent a young nurse to our house and I could not refuse her. Was she an angel? Or was she a devil? Was she a daughter of Mātaṅgī, a tantric goddess? Or was she a reincarnation of Avalokiteśvara? Soon after my wife's passing, I was comforted by this sympathetic young woman. I was no longer a moral person, whom I had pretended to be, and in fact, I had never been. When the inevitable happened, I lost my faith, my character, my work, and my reputation. That was when I realized how truly ugly I was.

I neither felt love for that young woman nor even had an ulterior motive. I was just unable to control my carnal desire. That lust could only be satisfied by a woman. I would like to say that lust was in the mind of another, but that was not the case. That lust was in a self that even I was unaware of, and caused my mind and body—like in a dream—to commit such evils.

I described my confusion in *The Ruin*. I grieved over the loss of someone I loved, but then became a slave of a lust that destroyed my reputation. I thought about hiding, giving up my robe, going overseas, and even killing myself.

My relationship with that woman was very brief. We were unable to marry—I was not passionate enough to renounce all my duties just to marry her. She seemed to suffer afterwards, but I suffered even more.

I was right about why Shimazaki Tōson left for France. I wondered why he left Japan without taking his two children after his wife died. In his personal fiction, *New Life*, the protagonist, Kishimoto, seems to be the author. After Kishimoto's wife died, his niece, Setsuko, came to care for his two children. Kishimoto agonized over the fact that Setsuko became pregnant not long after.

> Unexpectedly sad thoughts suddenly came over Kishimoto. He thought about paying for what he did by taking his own life and thought about asking Setsuko's parents to take care of her. Incestuous marriage violated the law and his conduct infringed that rule, so he wanted to be punished. He sympathized with many sinners who quietly accepted the punishment, instead of being laughed at in a merciless society. . . .
>
> Until imagining a phantom marker of his own grave, Kishimoto wondered how to hide from his friends and relatives. Escape to a remote island was one option. Running to a desolate temple was another. But he was too exhausted, too burdened to do either. How ashamed he was of his conduct. Other than a path that led to a grave, there was nothing he could do.[11]

I believe Kishimoto's agonies cannot be understood without having similar experiences, and I kept thinking that his anguish and my struggles were alike. Kishimoto went to France. I also thought about going abroad, but because I could not leave my mother alone, I could not. I also thought of taking my life, but again because of my mother, I could not. I could bear disgrace and pain for myself, but I could not make her suffer. I therefore gave up running away from life or committing suicide. There was no way other than for me to suffer. That was when I discovered a new world opening up for me—a vast sky and unending earth. My old self died and I found that three women—Fusako, the nurse, and my mother—had guided me to this new life. For me, they are manifestations of Amida and Avalokiteśvara.

Tōson must have suffered by keeping his secret to himself, even after returning from France. Writing *New Life* made his brother angry and his relatives disowned him. Tōson's case demonstrates that there is a cause to suffering. The cause of his suffering was that he could no longer hide his secret. It did not matter how astonishing that secret was, how much his confession would trouble others, or how badly he would be humiliated by telling the truth.

Tōson must have felt that he could not be saved unless he disclosed his past by writing *New Life*. I understand completely. In my case, I was somewhat relieved because a journalist had already written about my affair, though his article was not completely accurate. Still, I felt bad about it. I therefore must confess my affair to you, even though it will cause further trouble for the nurse.

[7]

I read Anatole France's *Thais* at the height of my confusion. The story resonated deeply within me. Paphnutius had a group of twenty-four disciples and lived in a hut where he "observed the most rigorous fasts, and often went for three entire days without taking food," "wore a very rough hair shirt," and "flogged himself night and morning, and lay for hours with his face to the earth." One day, he went to a city to save Thais, a famous actress. After meeting Paphnutius, Thais, who had seen the degeneration of philosophers, wished to live in a convent. Paphnutius returned to the desert, but Thais's beautiful image kept bothering him, so much so that he climbed to the top of a pillar in a dilapidated temple and performed ascetic practice while exposed to the wind and rain. He then wandered into a cemetery and prayed for eighteen hours in front of a tomb, after which he heard a voice and looked up. He saw a beautiful man and woman depicted on a wall, talking to each other. Paphnutius even heard the sound of their kissing. One night, he heard a woman's voice, saying a man was lying on her. Upon awaking, Paphnutius saw himself lying on the top of a woman. She moved away, so he grabbed her, saying "Stay, stay, my heavenly one!"[12]

Because of his desires, Paphnutius lost his senses and fell to the floor. After regaining consciousness, he saw a number of priests in black robes pouring water into his mouth. Since Saint Anthony was returning to heaven, Paphnutius joined their procession. He then learned that Thais was about to die, and so immediately visited her deathbed.

Where could Paphnutius possibly find heaven other than on the lips of Thais? He cried, "I love thee! Do not die! Listen, my Thais. I have deceived thee! I was but a wretched fool. God, heaven—all that is nothing. There is nothing true but this worldly life, and the love of human beings. I love thee! Do not die!" But Thais could not hear him and died.

Paphnutius's shout—"God, heaven—all that is nothing. There is nothing true but this worldly life, and the love of human beings"—was also my shout when separated from my wife. In *Thus Spoke Zarathustra*, Nietzsche wrote, "This old saint in the forest hath not yet heard of it, that *god is dead*!" Isn't that the same as Paphnutius's cry? Zarathustra also says, "I love him," and

"The Superman is the meaning of the earth." I cannot stop being inspired by these words of Zarathustra.[13]

[8]

At my wife's vigil, I vowed to never marry again. But I had an affair, just three weeks after her death. Was I degenerate? Was I sinful? But how can a degenerate and sinful person become more degenerate or become even more sinful? Is the true me the "I" that speaks about degeneration and who feels ashamed? Or is the true me the "I" who sleeps with another woman? Why are the flames of sexual desires that flare up in me called degenerate? After all, I was born because my parents had similar desires. Why is it considered sinful when such a fire burns my entire body and reveals the naked me? All right, call it degenerate, call it sinful, but that is who I am. Kiyozawa sensei, that is the significance of earth [that is what it means to be human].

That is why I decided to marry again. I took the woman I loved most as my second wife. That is Fusako [same pronunciation but different kanji characters from those of his first wife]. Remember? She may have sat on your lap when you came to Kyoto.

After remarrying, I was asked by a newspaper reporter why I decided to marry so quickly after wailing over my wife's death. I told him that I remarried because I am lecherous. I should have told him that I remarried because of my mother and because family life was important to me. But the truth is, it was to satisfy my lust. Marriage was nonsense to me otherwise. I have a much stronger desire to live than to mourn my wife's death. I could not tolerate the impermanence, the pacing back and forth with past memories. I had to begin a new life.

[9]

You said Tolstoy's religion is ethical. Once, you summarized his *War and Peace*, which you read in just one week while in bed. There is also Tolstoy's short story titled "Father Sergius," which resonates within me.

> In the 1840s there took place in St Petersburg an event which caused general surprise: a handsome prince, commander of the sovereign's squadron of a regiment of cuirassiers, whom everyone expected to become an *aide-de-camp* and have a brilliant career at the court of Nicholas I, a month before his marriage to a beautiful lady-in-waiting who enjoyed the special favour of the empress, suddenly resigned his commission, broke with his fiancée, made over

his modest estate to his sister, and retired to a monastery with the intention of becoming a monk. To those who knew nothing of the circumstances, the whole thing was odd and unaccountable, but for Prince Stepan Kasatsky himself, it was all so natural that he could not conceive of any other possible course of action.[14]

When Kasatsky was twelve, his father—a retired guards colonel—died. Kasatsky was brilliant and had pride. Had he not been short-tempered, he would have been an exemplary student. He neither drank nor womanized and hated lying. At the age of eighteen, he joined an aristocratic guards division, where the Emperor Nicholas paid him special attention. Kasatsky had respected the emperor since he was a child and had ambitions of serving as the imperial *aide-de-camp*.

Kasatsky worked hard since his childhood. He appeared to be talented in many ways, but he actually always tried his best. He performed his duties perfectly because he wanted to receive everyone's admiration. His life seemed devoted to surpassing others—Kasatsky was ambitious. He fell in love with the daughter of the Countess Korotkova, proposed marriage, and was accepted. He was extremely happy but felt something was wrong with his fiancée and her mother. Because he was blinded by love, Kasatsky was unaware of her secret that almost everyone in the city knew—that she had been the emperor's mistress.

His fiancée revealed her secret to Kasatsky two weeks before the marriage. He was astonished and then angry with her and her mother. Pretending illness, he quit his work, refused to meet with anybody, and returned to his estate. He took care of his family business during that summer and, instead of returning to St. Petersburg, went to a monastery and became a monk. He had actually come to despise all those things that had formerly been important to him and others, and wanted to demonstrate his supremacy over those who had looked down on him. But he was also pure enough to seek religion after being betrayed by his love, Mary.

In the monastery, Kasatsky devoted himself to religious practice singlemindedly. He prayed and accumulated virtue. Lust and desire for fame gradually diminished. Prayer and obedience comforted him, and he made great strides along the religious path. When thinking of Mary, however, he regretted the choice he had made. So he tried praying even more, sometimes for two days at a time, but he could not concentrate. He felt he was ruled by something indescribable that was neither his own efforts nor God's power. Not knowing what else to do, he could only submit to the orders of the monastery elders.

Seven years had passed since Kasatsky entered the monastery. By the end of his third year, he had adopted Sergius as his monastic name. He was initially excited by the Communion service but then became used to it. He learned everything within the first seven years, so he became bored and indifferent to both the world and monastic life. He was neither affected by his mother's death nor ruffled by Mary's marriage when he learned of them.

When transferred to a monastery in town, Sergius found himself being approached by women. An indecent woman asked him to visit her at home. Although rejecting her invitation, he was terrified that he had wanted to accept it. He not only confessed his desire to the elder but also asked young disciples to watch him and prevent him from leaving his room except for making prayers and repenting. At the elder's suggestion, Sergius donated all his belongings to the monastery and moved to another monastery in Tambino, where Hilarion, a mendicant, had spent eighteen years of his ascetic life in wilderness, and confined himself to a cell.

One day, an unusual woman came to the Tambino monastery. She pretended illness and tempted Sergius. He hacked a finger off with an axe and showed her his dripping blood to demonstrate his determination not to be tempted. She repented and later took religious vows.

Six years had passed since Father Sergius moved to his chamber in the Tambino monastery. He was then forty-nine. Fasting and praying did not cause him any problems. What did was containing his doubts about God and his lust. This was unexpected. Doubt and lust came over him as if they were one enemy, but he fought them as if they were two separate evils.

"Oh, God, why dost thou not give me faith?" he thought. "Lust is one thing. St Antony struggled against it, and others, too. But they had faith, and there are times—minutes, hours, days—when I have none. What is the point of the whole world and its delights, if it is sinful and has to be renounced? Why didst thou create temptations to sin? Sin? But is it not sinful fancy for me to leave the pleasures of the world and prepare for myself a reward in a place where there may after all be nothing?" At his words he was seized with horror and self-loathing, and castigated himself: "Vile creature—you, who would be a saint!" And he knelt to pray. But no sooner had he begun than he pictured himself vividly as he had been in the monastery and how grand he had looked in his monk's cap and robe. And he shook his head. "No, this is no good. It is a deception. But it is others I deceive, not myself or God. There is nothing grand about me. I am just pitiful and absurd." He drew back the sides of his cassock, looked at his pathetic legs clad in underdrawers, and smiled.[15]

Father Sergius then put the cassock back into place and began praying, crossing, and bowing. He prayed, "And shall this bed be unto me a coffin?" He then heard a devil's voice, "A solitary bed is a coffin, anyway. It's all a lie." He then saw an image of the shoulders of the widow with whom he had previously lived. He continued to pray and read the Gospels. He saw a familiar passage that he had memorized and often recited: "Lord, I believe: help thou mine unbelief." He now removed all his doubts. He regained his faith and repeated a prayer he used to say when he was a child—"Lord, take me, take me." How relieved and joyful he felt. He then fell asleep. That was when that amorous woman came to visit him. He shed blood but won the battle of temptation.[16]

Father Sergius continued living in seclusion for seven more years. He initially accepted offerings, such as tea, sugar, white bread, milk, clothes, and firewood, but later declined such things except for brown bread once a week. Or he received them but gave them away to the poor, maintaining his ascetic way of living. He was always in his chamber, either praying or talking to visitors. Because Father Sergius had not been seduced, he gained a reputation as a hermit and a number of visitors came to see him every day—some of them from afar.

It was during his eighth year in Tambino that Father Sergius cured a sick person for the first time. He initially considered healing the sick to be arrogant. When requested to do so by the mother of a fourteen-year-old boy, Father Sergius had doubts about supernatural powers but prayed mechanically while placing his hand on the boy's head. Surprisingly, the child was cured. After that, the sick rushed to visit him.

After thirteen years, Father Sergius's hair turned gray. He began to realize that the monastery was taking advantage of his reputation and that he was being used as a tool to attract visitors and donations. He felt as if his spirit was being destroyed by such external demands, and as if he was not serving God but rather himself and others. He wanted to leave his chamber and hide. To prepare for that, he kept in his cell farmer's clothing: a vest, jacket, and a hat. But once ready to get out, he hesitated.

The more visitors came to see Father Sergius, the less time he had for himself and prayer. He often compared his situation with a dried-up well. "There was a weak spring of living water which poured from me and through me. That was the true life when 'she' had tempted him (he always remembered with rapture that night and 'she,' who was now the Reverend Mother Agniya). She has tasted of that pure water, but since then, before ever any water can gather people come to drink it, jostling and pushing each other. And the spring has been trampled in and nothing is left but mud."[17] He felt pleasure in the compassion, even though it left him weary. He was always tired.

One spring, Father Sergius received a number of visitors seeking his blessing. A merchant in the crowd pushed forward and stood before him. He said to Father Sergius, "Holy father, have mercy on my ailing child. Deliver her from the pain of her infirmity. I make bold to supplicate at thy holy feet."[18] His daughter was twenty-two and single, and had become ill after her mother passed away two years before. The merchant had brought his daughter a thousand miles for Father Sergius's miraculous treatment, and she was then waiting at a guesthouse for the appointment with Father Sergius. She could not go out during the day because of her fear of sunlight, but was willing to visit him at night. Father Sergius accepted the merchant's request and told him to bring her that night for prayer.

Father Sergius often wondered how a person like his old self, Stepan Kasatsky, had become a miraculous healer. Although amazed at the efficacy of the prayer, he had no doubt about possessing a supernatural power. After curing the boy and recently opening the eyes of an old woman, all the miraculous events he had participated in were real.

Father Sergius was interested in seeing the merchant's daughter because, although he was going to see her for the first time, she already had faith in him. Father Sergius wished to further test his supernatural powers and become even more famous. If it works, he thought, people will gladly travel a thousand miles just to see him. National newspapers will write about him. The emperor and even people in Europe, where they had lost faith, will know about him. Father Sergius then felt ashamed of his own vanity, and so prayed: "Lord, heavenly king, comforter, the spirit of truth, come unto us and dwell in us, and cleanse us from all impurity, and save, good Lord, our souls. Cleanse me from the corruption of worldly fame by which I am afflicted."[19] He then realized that although he had repeated this prayer many times, it had no effect on him. Although he had often prayed on behalf of others, his prayers for himself had not allowed him to renounce his desire for fame.

Father Sergius remembered when he prayed for the first time, seeking purity, humbleness, and love. He thought God would recognize his prayer. Recalling he had been pure enough to chop off his finger rather than be seduced, he kissed the scar that remained. He thought of how humble and compassionate he had been then, but now he was not pure, humble, or even loveable. It was necessary for him to be loved, even if he did not love others.

When Father Sergius heard about the merchant's daughter, he was excited about her age. He wanted to know whether or not she was beautiful and attractive. He then thought, "Have I sunk so low?" and began praying, "Lord, help me and raise me up, oh Lord, my God." He heard the warbling of nightingales and felt a beetle fly onto his head and crawl around. He brushed it off and wondered, "But does He exist? I might be knocking at a house locked on the outside. . . . The lock is on the door and I might see it. The lock is the nightingales, the beetles, nature." Father Sergius began praying aloud until that thought disappeared. He relaxed and felt his faith arising again, so called a lay brother to bring the merchant and his daughter immediately.[20]

The merchant departed soon after leaving his daughter at Father Sergius's cell. She was fair-haired and extremely pale, plump, and short, though her body was well developed. Her face had a childish look and she seemed afraid of something. Father Sergius sat on a bench at the entrance. She walked straight to him and stopped, so he blessed her. He was afraid he might be gazing at her body. When she passed him, he felt something about her—that she was amorous and not stupid. He got up from the seat and walked into the chamber. She was sitting on the stool, waiting for him.

> When he came in she stood up.
> "I want to go to Daddy," she said.
> "Don't be afraid," he said. "Where is the pain?"
> "It's all over," she said, and a smile suddenly lit her face.
> "You will get well," he said. "Pray."
> "What's the point of praying? I have prayed and it doesn't do any good." She was still smiling. "But you say a prayer and lay your hands on me. I've dreamt about you."
> "What was your dream?"
> "I dreamt that you put your hand on my heart like this." She took his hand and pressed it to her breast. "Just here."
> He gave her his right hand.
> "What is your name?" he asked, trembling all over and feeling that he was vanquished, incapable now of controlling his lust.
> "Mary. Why?"
> She took his hand and kissed it, then she put her arm around his waist and hugged him.
> "What are you doing?" he said. "Mary. You are a devil."

"Well, what does it matter?"

And holding him in her arms she sat down with him on his bed.[21]

At dawn, Father Sergius went outside. "Did all this really happen? Her father will come. She will tell him. She is a devil. And what shall I do?" He picked up the axe with which he had chopped off his finger and walked towards his chamber. The lay brother saw him and said, "Do you want me to chop some wood? Let me have the axe, then." He gave it to him and went into the chamber. She was still sleeping. Father Sergius glanced at her in horror and went further back. He put on peasant's clothes and cut off his hair. He then went out on a path along the river, which he had not seen for the last four years, and walked for a while. In the afternoon, he came across a rye field and lay down. In the evening, he passed a village by the river but without stopping went on to the precipitous riverbank.[22]

Sergius got up very early the next morning. His surroundings were gray and gloomy. Cold winds blew in from the west before sunrise. "Yes, I must make an end of it. God does not exist. How shall I do it? Throw myself into the river? I can swim, so I would not drown. Hang myself? Yes, there is my girdle, just put it over a branch."[23] It was easy to commit suicide, and so he was disappointed. He felt like praying as he used to do, but there was no point in it, because there was no God. He lay down and rested a cheek on a hand. While thinking, he fell asleep.

Sergius suddenly remembered Pashenka, his cousin, and that her family was poor. Because of his interest in the life of ordinary people, he visited her and witnessed her miserable life. Pashenka had fallen in love and married a man of whom her father disapproved. She gave birth to a girl, but her husband kept drinking, used up all their money, and died. Her daughter married a feeble man and had a child. Pashenka supported her family by teaching music and went to a church to socialize. After hearing about her life, Sergius left.

Sergius now knew that he should have lived like Pashenka. He served people in the name of God, whereas Pashenka lived for both others and God. Giving someone a cup of water without seeking a favor was more precious than the miraculous deed he was considered to have performed. "But surely in some part I genuinely wished to serve God?" Sergius thought. "Yes, but that was defiled and choked by human glory. And God does not exist for one such as I, who lived for human glory. I will seek Him now."[24]

Sergius wandered from village to village, as he did when he visited Pashenka. He walked together with pilgrims, or by himself, and begged for food and lodging. A mean mistress would sometimes insult him and a drunken peasant would make fun of him, but because he accepted their rude behavior without reacting, they gave him bread, tea, and even travel expenses. Some people were inspired by his looks, while others were delighted to see a gentleman begging. His warm heart always seemed to have won the minds and hearts of others.

Sergius found the Gospels while begging alms. He read them aloud and always inspired those who heard him. Even though they had heard the passages before, they felt as if they heard them for the first time. Sergius made himself available for consultation, wrote letters on behalf of illiterates, and intervened in quarrels. He left before being thanked for these acts. God began emerging in his mind while he spent his days like this.

Kasatsky [Sergius] continued his travel for about eight months, after which, while staying in a refuge with other pilgrims, he was arrested for not carrying a travel permit. When interrogated about his identity, Kasatsky said he was a servant of God. The police arrested him for vagrancy and the court sent him to Siberia.

In Siberia, he settled down on a wealthy peasant's estate. He still lives there, cultivating a farm, teaching reading and writing to children, and taking care of the sick.

[10]

Kiyozawa sensei, I've ended up summarizing Tolstoy's story written in 1899 based on Yamauchi Kazusuke's Japanese translation. You must have frowned at part of this summary, but I believe this story represents a part of my inner life and that is why I wanted you to listen to it.

Sergius renounced the world twice. In the first renunciation, he gave up external materials, but kept his inner thoughts unchanged. In the second abandonment, or in the self-destroyed renunciation, Sergius was an independent man standing on the verge of life and death. Like Sergius, Siddhartha Gautama also renounced the world twice: he ascended into and descended the mountains. In his first attempt, he continued to believe in himself and deities. The second time, he destroyed his ego and deities.

I began worshipping the Buddha and propagating the efficacy of the Buddha's grace while you [Kiyozawa] were still alive. But whether I liked it or not, my Buddha had to disappear, together with my wife. Although it was a very convenient formula, because of the sinful person that I am, I can no longer believe in the idea of a sinful person being embraced by the Buddha's grace. If the Buddha does, in fact, have the power to do this, why did he not save my wife? I have come to understand that, unlike the God in Christianity, there is no transcendent Buddha who will manifest power in this world. Because of my sexual affair, I began to realize that I had just observed myself subjectively. I understood that there was no Buddha who had a power to stop my immoral acts as a guardian. If you speak of evil, then you must say that it exists and that there is no salvation without it. For me, therefore, whether subjectively or objectively, there is no Buddha. I understood then that all I had done until then was to accept the words of the ancients and my own thoughts and feelings.

I was arrogant to believe that I could revive Buddhism. After my ego was destroyed, however, my Buddhism was destroyed as well, and the lights of the world disappeared. Everything was ruined. I did not know to whom I should pray and on whom I should depend. Many friends sympathized and cried for me. I am grateful to them, but I have realized that their tears cannot relieve my pain. No one in the three thousand worlds can do anything about my suffering.

I now know that I was wrong about believing in Amida Buddha as a miraculous godlike figure. When I came to this awareness, I saw a king who had abandoned his kingdom and called himself Bodhisattva Dharmākara after receiving the teaching from the Buddha Sovereign Monarch of the World (Buddha Lokeśhvararāja). He lived the life of a mendicant and eventually became the Buddha referred to as Amida Buddha. I clearly saw that I was completely wrong in trying to "have faith" in a godlike magician who would save me—that, rather than a request to be saved, the *nenbutsu* is the shout of those who are already saved.

At present, I am free from ideas of sin and punishment because neither Buddha nor *kami* exist as a savior for me. This is the vast world in which I am living right now—the Land of Immeasurable Light and the Buddha of Immeasurable Light. I am neither a man of religion, nor a politician, nor a scholar. I am simply a man. I am not bound to norms but free to create a living. Thanks to my wife's death, my love affairs, and my mother's love, I was able to leave a life of hypocrisy in which people are disguised as saints. This book that I am dedicating to you succinctly describes my agony, pains, and burning during that time.

I admire Shinran Shōnin who felt close to Kyōshin, a Buddhist novice. Kyōshin had been a scholar-monk at Kōfukuji, but left the monastery and labored on a ferryboat that crossed the Kako River, while following the life of a lay Buddhist with his wife and children.

I joyfully reflected on scriptural passages, such as "Greed, anger, and ignorance are Nirvana. Within the three base passions, innumerable Dharmas exist. Apart from them, one is far away from the Buddha, like the distance between heaven and earth" from the *Sarvadharmāpravṛttinirdeśa Sutra* (*Shohō mugyōkyō*), and "Lust is instantly the path. Anger and ignorance are also the same. Paths of an infinite number of Buddhas are there" from the *Mahāprajñāpāramitā-śāstra* (*Daichidoron*).

[11]
 Kiyozawa sensei, in your last letter to me, you asked me to bring an English translation of the Three Pure Land Sutras because you were studying the *Larger Sutra of Immeasurable Life*. You were forty-one then. After I turned forty-two, the *Larger Sutra* also touched my heart. Bodhisattva Dharmākara said,

> "Imagine buddhas by the hundreds, by the thousands, by the millions, by the tens of thousands, innumerable Great Saints, as many as there are sands in the Ganges, and think of someone honoring all these buddhas with offerings, all of them, as many as they are. This would still not be equal to seeking the Way, steadfastly, rightly directed, without retreating."[25]

And the Buddha Sovereign Monarch of the World responded,

> "It is as if one man were to bail out the great ocean with a ladle during many cosmic ages. He should be able to reach the bottom, and obtain the wonderful treasures in the bottom of the sea. In the same way, if a person single-mindedly exerts himself in seeking the Way without faltering, he will surely attain the goal. What desire would not be attained by this person?"[26]

I read these passages with tears in my eyes. Since I no longer create a Buddha or a *kami* for my convenience, the Buddha and *kami* have touched my heart for the first time. I am happy to report that I am now able to understand the state of "a buddha minding other buddhas" and the indication of "the perception of wisdom only shared by buddhas."
 Kiyozawa sensei, I am engulfed in flames of lust. But I neither feel sinful nor am bothered by it. All young women look beautiful to me. In the spring, all things between heaven and earth grow lively. Can't we appreciate Bodhisattva Dharmākara's vow?—"Even if my body falls into all kinds of bitter torments, I will continue to exert myself, patiently accepting all to the end, without regrets."[27]

I dedicate this book to the seventeenth-year commemorative Dharma gathering in your honor. Please continue watching over me.

Dated May 3, 1919

APPENDIX 2

Guardians of the Dharma Castle

MATSUOKA YUZURU

Preface

"So, are you saying you won't become a Buddhist priest and succeed me—no matter what?!" The father spoke harshly while carelessly hanging up his light-blue robe. He has just concluded a morning service in the main worship hall of the family temple, assisted by his son, whom he was now addressing. The father was desperate. His eyes were red with anger, completely devoid of any affection that a father would have toward a son. His words were not those of a father chastising a son with affection behind his words, but were full of anger. The father was about to crush the son.

Like father like son, the son erected a stonelike wall to shut out those words. All emotions other than anger and hatred disappeared from his face. A resentment as cold as ice that felt as if it would explode took over his entire body. The son managed to maintain a little composure, but there was recklessness in his attitude.

"That's right!" the son said. "I don't want to follow in your footsteps. Chanting sutras in the *naniwabushi* style of reciting ancient tales, preaching in a *chongare* style about things you don't believe, guarding the dead, worshipping a lifeless idol, living off of donations—I hate it!¹ You bow to temple members you hold in contempt and beg them to donate money because you are pressed to do so by the head temple. I don't want to spend the rest of my life doing things like that! And most of all, I don't want live in this large structure that

I'm not even sure is ours. My conscience will be paralyzed if I'm forced to do things I don't believe in. I don't want to sell myself by wearing baggy robes even if they are gilded, chanting sutras, talking about spiritual peace, and even selling the Buddha while ignoring how diligently others work. You should be ashamed of doing so! I will never become a Buddhist priest!"

"All right then!" the father shouted in reply. "But don't forget what you've just said. Don't forget that you were nurtured by this temple. Everything you have has been given to you by the Buddha and by our ancestors, but you don't appreciate any of it! I can't put up with such an attitude any longer! I regret having fed you rice that I first offered to the Buddha. I disown you! From now on, do whatever you want. Let's see what you make of yourself all by yourself! I don't want to see you until then!"

The father's voice shook as he spoke. But that made no impression on his son, who looked blank and heard his father's words only as noise. The son remained silent, his face pale. He didn't even blink. The father stood up but almost lost his balance because of his anger. He went to a chest, took an envelope out of a drawer, from which he removed several ten-yen notes.

"Here, take this," the father said as he handed the money to his son. "I disown you, but we were originally father and son. You won't be able to support yourself immediately, so use this. It's my parting gift." The father's words were polite enough, but there was no tone sporting emotion in them. He seemed to be explaining as reasonably as he could why he was giving his son this money while actually suppressing the rage and indignation that kept rising up within him.

The son could not understand why the money was placed in front of him. He looked blankly, first at his father's face and then at the money. The father appeared to be unconcerned, but indignation that he had tried so hard to suppress again found expression.

"Take the money and leave!" the father shouted. "You talk big but you're really just a coward! If you can't leave this house now, then be a man and apologize! Which are you going to do?!"

With these words, the son suddenly came to himself. Without reflecting on his father's words, he bowed, stood, and began walking out of the room. His steps felt so light, but he didn't even feel his feet pressing down on the tatami floor matting.

"What are you going to do with this money?!" the father roared from behind him."

"I don't need it," the son said, not even turning around . . . but the words didn't come out right. Then, as if in a great hurry, he was about to cross the threshold to the room when he heard sobs and felt a weight so heavy it made him stagger. His mother had thrown herself on him from the temple veranda and was pressing her face into his chest.

"Why did you lose your temper?" his mother said between sobs. "Why do you defy your father like that? What will happen if you leave home? How can we be happy if you do? How can you destroy yourself and everyone else's happiness just because of a temper tantrum? Let me apologize to your father for you. Then apologize to him. Please! This is the most important thing in my life . . . !"

"I don't care what happens to me!" the son shouted. He tried to push his mother away but she held tight. Since there was nothing else he could do, the son just remained there with his mother clinging to him. The fragrance of her hair oil entered his nostrils. Gazing vacantly at his mother's coiffure, he noticed the decorative piece of light-blue cloth that tied his mother's hair at the nape of her neck. For some reason, the slight grime on that bit of cloth bothered him.

Between sobs, his mother continued pleading until, finally, the son relented—at least slightly. He had expected more provocative words from his father, but his father had just stood there with his head down, neither moving nor saying a word. He seemed to be praying.

When his mother saw that he had calmed down, she gathered the scattered bills. She then took her son's hand, led him in front of his father, gently got him to kneel and took a similar position. "Your son was wrong," she pleaded to the father. "Please forgive him," she said and urged her son to say the same. The son bowed deeply but did not say anything. The father nodded silently.

The father went to bed and stayed there for the rest of the day. The son could hardly pass anything down his throat. The mother cared for both, going back and forth between father and son.

Three days later, the son finally acquiesced to his father's request that he take the ordination examination at the regional temple of the head temple. "I guess I can do at least that for mother," the son muttered, resignedly trying to console himself.

The head temple, of which the father's temple was subordinate, had an enormous debt then—several million yen—and the central administrators took various measures to raise the money to repay it. They sold properties and cultural treasures that had been preserved for generations. The ordination exam, which generated votive offerings, was another way to collect money. They also demanded three or five yen from each subordinate temple member, depending on the number of members in the temple. When a temple raised the money assigned them, the status of that temple was raised. The local priests thus worked hard to gather donations from their members.

Not all members were affluent, of course, and most complained about the extra donations demanded by the regional temple. When it came to helping the head temple, however, they became excited by slogans such as, "For the abbot's sake," "For the head temple's sake," and even, "For the sake of my temple," and donated generously. That was how the administrators of the head temple and priests of local temples were able to take advantage of temple members.

More money was raised by offering pictorial scrolls of Amida Buddha with the abbot's signature on the back. The larger the donation, the larger the scroll. There were scrolls for two hundred yen, three hundred yen, and even five hundred yen. When a representative from the head temple in Kyoto came to deliver a scroll, the excitement felt by the resident priest and temple members was beyond words.

The head temple also sent missionary priests to preach and representatives to make the rounds of local temple members to gather even more donations. Those who collected those donations claimed rebates to the head temple administration. Even directors of dioceses were part of this commission system. All the campaign staff made strenuous efforts to raise funds not only for the benefit of the head temple but also for personal gain.

The ordination of priests was an easy way to increase revenue. Although those in the administration talked about the importance of "peace of mind" gained through the Buddhist teaching, what they were primarily interested in was the votive offerings made by the priests they ordained. They highlighted three features of the current ordination examination that made it very attractive to resident priests who needed their sons to succeed them. First was that attendance at the head temple was not required, thus saving on travel costs to Kyoto. Second, the central administration discounted the ordination fee, pointing out that the fees would be higher in the future. Third, they implied that the examination would not be difficult. Resident priests jumped at this rare opportunity and rushed to bring their sons to the regional temple where the examination would be held.

The son had felt insulted when his father first approached him with this news and had rejected taking the examination. He had never wanted to succeed his father. Besides, he had long felt that even if he did decide to become a Buddhist priest, ordination was just a formality—that all it took to be a priest was a mind that was pure and behavior that was virtuous. The son was even more turned off when he heard that the ordination fee would be reduced and that the examination would be made easy. The father, however, was very attracted by news of the easy ordination and ignored his son's wish to not take it. That was what had led to the conflict following that morning's service, at which the son had assisted.

The son had reluctantly learned to read the preface to the *Kyōgyōshinshō* (*The Collection of Passages Expounding the True Teaching, Living, Faith, and Realizing of the Pure Land*—Shinran's magnum opus, written in Chinese and the sacred text in Shin Buddhism) from his father. That text was said to be the entire subject of the examination. But the son purposely upset his father by misreading the kanji Chinese characters derived from the Chinese Han dynasty by using the Wu dynasty reading and ignoring traditional pronunciations. Still, in just two days, he had progressed to where he was able to recite the preface perfectly without even looking at the text. Because it was so easy, the son suspected there was going to be something more to the examination. His father, however, was overjoyed at how quickly the son had picked up the reading and explained its meaning in simple Japanese terms. The son was not interested in or grateful for his father's efforts; he just mechanically swallowed whole what he was told.

The day before the examination, the son was brought by his father to the city where the regional temple was located. On the train there, the son acted as if he were alone because of embarrassment about the Buddhist robe his father was wearing. When the roof of the regional temple—which people in this area referred to as the honorable priest's residence—appeared like a small mountain towering above the roofs of private homes, the passengers on the train suddenly began reciting the *nenbutsu*—"*namu amida butsu, namu amida butsu . . .*"

When the train stopped, the majority of the passengers got off. Hundreds of old men and old women wearing straw sandals, holding a *juzu*, a string of beads, in their hands, and with their belongings wrapped in a *furoshiki*, or wrapping cloth, tied to their sash, descended onto the train platform. The custom in that area was for farmers to make a pilgrimage to the regional temple after a long winter, just before the start of the agricultural season. The train station was especially crowded that day because a family member of the abbot, who would be in residence as the ordination-examination supervisor for the next three days, was scheduled to arrive. Hiding his hands in the square bag sleeves of his new kimono, the son made his way through the crowd. He felt rather shy but also quite excited.

The inns surrounding the regional temple bustled with activity. The music of *shamisen* and the flirting voices of women from the inner rooms mixed with the sounds of merrymaking from groups on the second floor. The father seemed to be in a good mood as he ate dinner. A mature woman served him sake and they gossiped about people whose names the son had never heard. They seem to have known each other from the time the father had been a student and lived in this area.

The skin of the woman's face was coarse and freckled. She had covered it with a white powder that looked like wheat flour. Her hair was put up in a rounded style that—no matter how you looked at it—seemed to be a wig. She must have been close to forty. The powder, which covered even her neck, made the worn-out collar of her old kimono look even dirtier. Her cheekbones were chaffed and looked red where they swelled out. Despite her age, the woman acted like a young girl, coquettishly serving the father. She spoke with a lisp, making her seem like an obnoxious monster.

"This is your young brother, isn't he?" the woman said coyly, pointing at the son. "You look so much alike."

"You've got to be kidding!" the father replied. "This is my son. But doesn't he look great?"

"Really? You two do resemble each other, though you seem a little taller . . . Are you sure you're his father?"

"Of course I am!"

"How old is he?"

"Eighteen."

"Hmmm, then you must have married a beauty and been blessed with her favors much earlier than I thought. What a naughty boy you are!"

"Oh, well, please forgive me for not informing you, honorable lady, about my entering into a matrimonial relationship when I did. I offer a thousand apologies and beg your forgiveness!"

"Oh, you're still so young," the woman said to the father, her hands flopping around like the flippers of a seal. She fell over laughing. The father also laughed, his voice resonant.

"What a strange woman!" the son said in disgust when she stepped out of the room.

"Well, yeah! She's something. When I was young and kinda wild, attending the Buddhist seminary here, she was also young. She used to wear a hand towel to cover her bald head but she soon replaced that with what she's wearing now. Look closely when she returns—it's a wig.

"Anyway, after we students drank and were feeling good, we tore that wig off her head, stripped her, and dressed her in a Buddhist robe. We then played scissors-paper-rock with the loser having to wear the wig, dance, be her bridal partner, and be made the butt of jokes. In time, she became pregnant.

We learned she slept with more than just one or two of the guys . . . in fact with quite a few. I guess everybody wanted to get in on it while the getting was good. That demon was about eighteen then. I guess there's a time in their prime when even monsters are attractive . . .

"The resident priest of Raigō temple, who looks so cool now even with his swollen face, was one of those who had a piece of her. I won't say she slept with everybody, but anyone who expressed the slightest interest in her could expect to have some fun. Ha-ha-ha . . ."

The father rubbed his alcohol-induced red face and laughed, showing teeth full of tobacco stains. The son suddenly felt embarrassed at seeing and hearing his father like this.

After dinner, the father took his son to the entertainment part of town. On one street, a Buddhist priest was chanting the story of Iwami Jūtarō, a legendary samurai warrior, in the traditional narrative style. Festive music could be heard from a tent on another street. A man at the entrance was giving a spiel in a loud voice, trying to attract customers. Two small girls who seemed to have what looked like bowls over their faces were eating something while mounted on a horse. Many other freak-show tents could be seen. The father suggested they go inside one of the tents but his son refused and continued walking on.

On their way back to the inn, the father and son entered the regional temple compound from the rear gate. When they arrived at the main gate in front, they saw white-robed priests slowly closing the huge door to the main worship hall. The light from a huge suspended lamp flickered in front of the entrance. Although not clearly determinable in the dark, the entire structure seemed strangely gloomy and even depressing. Despite its size, there didn't seem to be much space, giving rise to a cramped feeling. The roof that weighed so heavily on the temple structure may have contributed to such a feeling, but that didn't seem to be the only reason.

When the son asked about this, the father explained that after the temple was rebuilt, strong winds damaged some of the pillars. Supporting pillars were then installed to compensate for the damaged ones, and that is what made the hall look cramped, the father said.

"I'm very impressed that you noticed that about the temple!" the father said after his explanation. But those words didn't seem very sincere to the son. Fully grown blossoms were falling gently from a plum tree located next to a hand basin that was shaped like a large lotus flower. When the son looked up at them, he realized how natural it was to be engulfed in such a pleasant aroma. It brought to mind a fragment of a poem about the fragrance of flowers at night.

After leaving the barrack-like precincts of the regional temple, the father and son walked south. The street was lined with rows of houses with beautiful lanterns in front. Voluptuous women, their faces covered with powder, stood at the entrance of each house, calling to the men passing by, trying to seduce them into entering. Groups of young men and women, their backs turned to and oblivious of the people passing by, were engaged in conversation.

Embarrassed and making himself as inconspicuous as possible, the son walked through this scene without once glancing around. But the color and the nature of what was going on burned clearly and deeply in his mind. A drunken man staggered directly in front of the son, who stepped aside without thinking. And when he did, a woman who had passed his father without a glance, whispered in the son's ear, "Young master, young master! Be sure to come back later for some fun!"

The son shivered. He felt as if he had heard the words of a witch and regretted hearing them. But those words that he should not have heard awakened something like sweet regret because they had a certain charm that seemed to mature him. A mysterious world seemed to be opening up for him—a world that was like a beautiful dream and yet with unknown fears. The son was becoming an adult.

"She asked you in for some fun, didn't she?" the father said after they returned to their room at the inn. He smiled broadly and looked fondly at his son.

"Do you remember that place?" the father asked when they were lying in bed. "That's where they cater to the sexual needs of both priests and laypersons who attend the regional temple. The system is, the regional temple during the day and that place during the night. It's funny, but over a long period of time a tradition has developed in which customers from the same diocese end up going to the same house—both priests and laypersons. What's ironic, however, is that the houses rake in more money than the donations made to the regional temple."

Compared with the dreary regional temple, the houses lining the street near it were quite warm. The son understood completely his father's words.

"However," the father continued, "the property on which those houses are located belongs to the regional temple. While complaining that what goes on in those houses is against their teaching, administrators of the regional temple gouge the owners of those houses. I hear their take in rentals is twice what they receive in donations. It's a lot like raising chickens—which is both time consuming and requires a lot of work, but in the end is worthwhile because of the eggs that the chickens produce. If only the regional temple administrators were better at keeping track of that money . . ."

The son found it difficult to sleep that night. He was haunted by the words whispered to him by that woman on the street: "Young master, young master! Be sure to come back later for some fun!" Those seductive words had a strange way of reappearing in his mind, regardless of how he tried to drive them out.

Large placards with the words "Donations" and "Diocese Offices" were hung in front of the regional temple's office area, to which there were several entrances. The father and son entered the main entrance, passed through several dimly lit rooms, and arrived at a gaunt room with dirty tatami mats and a sign: "Test Takers Waiting Room." Inside, they found four or five young men and two priests with shaved heads and robes, huddled around a square wooden brazier. The young men seemed depressed and anxious. One or two seemed older than the son, but most were younger. Their faces were pale but they looked suspiciously at the newcomers entering the examination room.

The father bowed slightly and while removing a cigarette from his sleeve, said, "Too bad. I thought we would be first in line, but I guess we're a little late."

"Would you like to go first?" one of the priests asked.

Both father and son nodded.

"You would?" the other priest said. "More than ten young men arrived before those who are here, but none of them wanted to go first. They're waiting in the main worship hall. You can be first if you want."

The father happily accepted the ticket labeled Number One. He then told his son to unwrap the *furoshiki* containing the son's working robe and to put it on.

The son threw the robe carelessly over his shoulders and made a trial pass at chanting the preface to the *Kyōgyōshinshō*. It went so well that the son relaxed. When he looked around, however, he felt the other examinees were looking at him white-faced and shivering in fright. "What sense is there in becoming a priest with these guys?" the son thought. "I'm going to take the exam today because I don't have a choice, but I'll never be the same as they . . ." While denouncing other examinees in his mind like this, the son was called in to be tested. Looked on by the others, he stamped on the floorboards with an attitude of "Take your best shot. I can handle whatever you send me!"

After making several turns in the corridor, the son was brought to a room facing a small garden. "Quiet, now" his escort said, and led the son into the room while in a stooped position. A priest wearing a brown, ring-shaped surplice indicated that the son should sit in front of a table on which sacred texts were placed. The son looked around for the first time. On his left, he saw an old priest sitting on a platform wearing a surplice with five strips of a light chestnut color with a pattern that included golden peonies and eight wisteria blossoms. The man looked just like the wrinkle-faced character Kōno Moronao who appears in the opening act of *Chūshingura* (a classical play about the forty-seven masterless samurai). He seemed to be someone who would be difficult to get along with, probably an eminent scholar with the rank of high academic honor in the denomination.

While considering such things and awaiting further instructions, the son looked more closely at the old priest. The priest kept his eyes closed and twitched his white eyebrows while softly reciting the *nenbutsu*.

Some time passed with no one saying anything. Then the shadows of three men, the sounds of footsteps, and the rustling of robes could be seen and heard through the translucent paper sliding door behind the old priest. The old priest suddenly popped his eyes open and glared at the son. "Prostrate!" he commanded, tapping the tatami floor with his ceremonial fan. The son was annoyed, but bent forward until his forehead touched the table and held it there until he sensed the old priest move. He then raised his body to its former erect position and saw a regal-looking man sitting on the upper platform. The man's face was oval-shaped and pale, with magnificent gold-rimmed eyeglasses. He looked rather thin and was wearing a gold-patterned surplice with a red background over his black working robe.

A strangely beautiful light flashed from a ring on the man's left finger. The son guessed he must be the *renshi*, the abbot's family member. The son then noticed two men sitting on either side of him, though separated by some distance. They were dressed in formal traditional clothing and must be his attendants.

All officials now seemed in place. The old priest suddenly threw his fan in front of his knees, turned his body slightly towards the *renshi*, placed both of his hands on the fan, bowed in full prostration, and announced that the ordination examination under the patronage of the abbot's representative would now begin. The *renshi* nodded slightly.

A man who seemed to be the head priest of the regional temple was waiting at the lower right-hand side. He read the son's name aloud: "Miyagi Entai, member of Kōmyō Temple." The son was not sure what he should do, so he just sat there, looking blank. The old priest tapped the tatami with his fan, and whispered, "Bow, bow . . ." His voice was soft but scathing. The son bowed once again. That ended his introduction.

The old priest then commanded in a hoarse voice, "Open the sacred text and read aloud the preface to the *Kyōgyōshinshō*!" Two service books were laid out on the table. The son was fairly sure that he should pick up the volume bound in red, but intentionally selected the one bound in black and opened it. That volume contained Rennyo's *Letters*. He closed that volume, quickly picked up the volume bound in red, and opened it.

In a whisper, the old man said the sacred literature should not be handled recklessly, that it should be venerated by bringing it to one's forehead before being read reverently. "Hmph!" the son thought, but because he planned to surprise everyone, kept this thought to himself. He closed the volume and then brought it to his forehead with exaggerated movements. In the shadow of the volume where he could not be seen, however, he stuck out his tongue. Then, without even looking at the text, he began reciting the words as quickly as he could.

The old priest was caught off guard. "Wait! Wait!" he said, striking the tatami flooring with his fan. The son acted as if he had not heard the old priest. He completed reciting the text, brought the volume to his forehead in the same exaggerated way as before, and then closed the volume. The son glanced at the *renshi*. He thought he saw a slight smile on that person's pale face.

"No! No! No!" the old priest said. "That's no way to read the sacred text! Now read it again, this time much slower!" Now that the son was sure he had irritated the old priest, he relaxed completely. This time he took the opposite approach. He took a deep breath and began reciting very slowly. The old priest nodded in approval at each word and each phrase, as if biting them off.

When the son read, "Therefore, let it be known . . ." the old priest stopped him. "Start again from 'let it be,'" the old priest ordered. The son suddenly remembered how angry his father had become when he read that kanji character combination. His father had insisted on reading it so it meant "Let it be it known, therefore . . ."

When the old priest ordered the son to read it again, he again read it, "Therefore, let it be known." When the old priest ordered him to read that phrase a third time, he read it the same way that he did before, in an even louder voice: "Therefore, let it be known."

The old priest faced the son directly. "Were you taught to read that character combination so it means 'Therefore, let it be known . . . ?'" he asked.

"No," the son replied calmly. "I was taught to read it so it means 'Let it be it known, therefore . . .'"

"Then why don't you read it that way?"

"Because I didn't think it needs to be read in a way that makes it sound more complicated than it is."

"But that's the way our predecessor scholars have always read it," the old priest said. "There's no need for you to arbitrarily change how to read it now. It's true that character combination can be read as you just did, but not in this context. From now on, read it in the way that I just taught you!" The old priest glared at the son in a menacing way, indicating that his words were more an order than a suggestion.

The son had already decided to make fun of the examination so when he was reprimanded in this way, he decided to fight back. "I'm not satisfied with your explanation," he began. "Why is the usual way of reading that character combination wrong?"

"Today you are being examined on your competence in reading the sacred text," the elderly priest said. "This is not the time for a lecture on the meaning of what you're reading. A time will come when I give you a lecture on that subject."

"I doubt that I will ever learn anything from you," the son countered. "But be that as it may," he continued, "is reading the text, even if there is no understanding of it, the entire ordination examination? Don't we have to understand what we are reading? Are you saying that I will be qualified to be a Buddhist priest if I pass an examination as simple as this?"

"That's right," the elderly priest said. "This test is to ascertain that you can read the text correctly. If you pass, the abbot will have your head shaved and ordain you at the Founder's Hall at the head temple in Kyoto. You will then receive a certificate that you are an ordained Buddhist priest."

After saying this, the elder priest turned toward the *renshi* and bowed. But the son was not through yet. "That's stupid!" he said. "It's time consuming for the *renshi* to travel all the way here to oversee this examination and meaningless for us to be tested at such a simple level. Why don't you just eliminate the formality of an examination and just give us the certificate in exchange for a donation?"

"What are you saying?!" the old priest shouted. "The abbot kindly takes care of all matters in our denomination, which ordinary people can't understand. Greenhorns like you should just respect what has been decided and keep your mouth shut!"

The son decided to use this occasion to make the old priest even angrier and to embarrass his father by failing the examination. He looked directly at the elderly priest. "Even if I wanted to become a Buddhist priest," he said, "taking such a childish test to become one is insulting. If the head temple needs money, why doesn't it just come out and say so? Why talk about the abbot's generosity in ordaining me? My coming here to be examined is not only stupid, it's just insulting!"

"What?!" the old priest shouted, "You have the nerve to say things like that in front of the *renshi*? Out! Get out!"

The old priest theatrically and recklessly waved his fan in an attempt to drive the son out of the room. Unable to just look on, the head priest of the regional temple also tried to coax the son to leave. The son finally bowed slightly to the *renshi* and walked out. When he looked back through the sliding screen, he saw the old priest in a rage and breathing hard, looking like a small version of enraged spider.

When the son returned to the waiting room, he found three times the number of worried-looking test takers than when he had left. He threw off his working robe.

"What happened?" the father asked. "You were in there for a rather long time."

The son tried not to show the excitement he had felt, but was unable to do so. "Oh, I just had an argument with the old priest," he replied, trying to sound as casual as he could. "It was such an easy examination that I felt they were making a fool of me so I gave it to them."

"Well, well," the father said, very pleased.

A resident priest who had brought his son to be examined, stuck out his lower lip. "Was there an oral examination?" he asked.

"Yes, there was," the son replied.

There was a stir in the group of test takers. Clearly, fear rippled through their breasts. Some began leafing through the pages of the sacred texts. The son got the feeling that some looked up to him as a sort of small hero, but he considered them nothing but sissies and hurried his father out of the room and away from them. He wanted to see the main worship hall.

The hall had just been rebuilt and the altar was still incomplete, making the place look like a huge empty warehouse. All four sides of the spaces above the paper sliding doors decorated with wooden carvings, called *ranma*, were hung with wooden tags containing the names of those who had contributed to rebuilding the main worship hall through the perpetual sutra-chanting services at this regional temple. Special painted tags were nailed on round columns where the names of those who made large donations and the amount—five hundred or a thousand yen—were shown in gold letters.

The father entered, stood in front of the still incomplete altar, and bowed reverently before the image of the founder of the denomination. Offertory coins were scattered here and there, and several strings of beads were hung from a round column—probably lost articles.

"I'll show you an interesting place," the father told his son and led him further behind a corridor in back of the main worship hall. The area was called a *tsumesho* (the place where priests could stay inexpensively while visiting the regional temple). Dirty rooms grouped by diocese, with a shabby robe hook in front of each entrance, could be seen. Robes stained with candle wax and surplices that could barely be called that were hanging on the hooks. Hidden by a clothes rack, a man dressed in a dirty white robe could be seen sitting on a kettle-boiler stand, smoking a cigarette. He seemed to have spent decades waiting for something.

"This is where priests from other dioceses can stay cheaply while visiting the regional temple," the father explained. When the son heard this, he could not resist asking, "Do these priests come here from their family temples on some business . . . ?"

"Them? They're the lice of the *tsumesho*. They're priests without a home temple or even a place to live so they make their way here looking for a job. They arrange flowers and conduct services—sometimes they are even invited to conduct services at a parishioner's home. Many have been here for decades, but they're just parasites."

"But there are a lot of them, aren't there?"

"Well, yes. . . . There was a time when there were twenty or thirty, but with that many priests, it was difficult to compete, so there seems to have been a thinning out. I think there's a bit fewer of them now. Despite their appearances, each priest has his own clients."

This said, the father looked into one of the rooms and exchanged greetings with a white-robed elderly priest with a beard that contained quite a few white hairs. This priest had moved in several decades ago and had established himself as the doyen of the *tsumesho*.

The son found it difficult to believe that this old priest was even human. Outwardly, the priest did seem simple and refined, but there was something sordid about him. The son could not see him as anything other than an animal with four legs that mischievously assumed the form of a priest who had suddenly grown old. There was nothing like human emotion or even rationality that showed on the old priest's face.

The son looked in amazement at the strange lives in that strange world, but could not understand it. Oddly, the word "parasite" that his father had used remained in his mind. Could it be that the priests in the *tsumesho* were not the only parasites? Could all Buddhist priests, all local temples, all the different regional temples, and even the head temple be described with that word?

When this thought occurred to the son, he could not help feeling that the *renshi*, the old priest, the head priest of the regional temple, and even his father were also parasites. They were all like lice, crawling around and making a fuss about little things. And when he considered that he might have become a louse just like them, he could not help laughing. Hiding his face in the sleeve of his splash-patterned kimono, and suppressing his voice as much as he could, the son continued laughing.

After returning home, the son waited to be notified that he had failed the ordination examination. He was slightly disappointed at not receiving such notification, and finally forgot about it. Regardless of how much time passed, a notice never arrived.

This was in early spring, when the son was eighteen.

Notes

Introduction

1. Yukawa Hideki, *Yukawa Hideki Jisenshū* (Tokyo: Asahi Shinbunsha, 1971), 5:451 (hereafter cited as *YHJ*).

2. At the age of thirty-four, Yukawa wrote: "As it extends further, the path that science is taking today, similar to other paths, is getting steeper and narrower. It is an endless path that leads to a vast and unknown world. That is the direction in which the study of physics is moving today. It may lead to a lonely world that goes beyond language. But because we find it difficult to deal with that loneliness, we call out to our friends. That calling voice [may be how we console ourselves and is the path to the world beyond language]." *YHJ*, 1:146; author's translation.

3. Jonathan Culler states, "To study something as literature . . . is to look above all at the organization of its language, not to read it as the expression of its author's psyche or as the reflection of the society that produced it." *Literary Theory: A Very Short Introduction* (New York: Oxford University Press, 2000), 30. He also states that "the authors' statements about a work" may be essential in "analysing the thought of an author or discussing the ways in which a work might have complicated or subverted an announced view or intention," whereas the meaning of a work is "context-bound, but context is boundless" (66–67).

4. Robert H. Sharf, "Buddhist Modernism and the Rhetoric of Meditative Experience," *Numen* 42 (1995): 249.

5. Edward Fowler, *The Rhetoric of Confession: Shishōsetsu in Early Twentieth-Century Japanese Fiction* (Berkeley: University of California Press, 1988), 41.

6. Karatani Kōjin, *Origins of Modern Japanese Literature*, trans. Brett de Bary (Durham, NC: Duke University Press, 1993), 83.

7. There are many more modern Japanese literary works in which images of Buddhist priests, Buddhist symbols, and Buddhist messages appear. The works of Shimazaki Tōson, Kasai Zenzō, Kamura Isota, and Kurata Hyakuzō, can be studied within the framework of path literature. (Masako Nakagawa Graham discusses Kasai

Zenzō's relationship to Zen Buddhism in *The Autobiographical Narrative in Modern Japan: A Study of Kasai Zenzō, a Shi-shōsetsu Writer* [New York: Edwin Mellen, 2007].) The study of Buddhism in modern Japanese literature can also be fruitfully applied to short stories, poetry, travelogues, and essays. Akutagawa Ryūnosuke's work is of particular interest in this regard.

8. *YHJ*, 1:166.

9. See Takeda Taijun, "Watashi ni totte shūkyō towa nanika: Shūkyōsha to bungakusha wa dōshi de aru," in *Bukkyō no meizuihitsu*, ed. Kokusho Kankōkai Henshūbu (Tokyo: Kokusho Kankōkai, 2006), 2:215–28; Okamoto Kanoko, "Bukkyō no shinkenkyū," in *Bukkyō no meizuihitsu*, 1:207–61.

10. "Dasheng qixin lun," in *The Princeton Dictionary of Buddhism*, ed. Robert E. Buswell Jr. and Donald S. Lopez Jr. (Princeton, NJ: Princeton University Press, 2014), 221.

11. This book also speaks to the surge of interest in the study of Buddhist literature in the United States, indicated by John Whalen-Bridge and Gary Storhoff, eds., *The Emergence of Buddhist American Literature* (Albany: State University of New York Press, 2009), and

John Whalen-Bridge, Gary Storhoff, and Jan Willis, eds., *Writing as Enlightenment: Buddhist American Literature into the Twenty-First Century* (Albany: State University of New York Press, 2011).

Chapter 1

1. Masunaga Reihō, trans., *A Primer of Sōtō Zen: A Translation of Dōgen's Shōbōgenzō Zuimonki* (Honolulu: University of Hawai'i Press, 1975), 33–34.

2. William R. LaFleur, *The Karma of Words: Buddhism and the Literary Arts in Medieval Japan* (Berkeley: University of California Press, 1986), 7. In the West, organized religion was at odds with literature as well. According to Ernest Rubinstein, in Judaism and Christianity, religious authorities initially emphasized the "univocity" of faith and practice; hence, they rejected literature empowered by creative imagination. See *Religion and The Muse: The Vexed Relation between Religion and Western Literature* (Albany: State University of New York, 2007), 2. For a discussion of the impact of the Bible on Western literature through language, myth, and metaphor, see Northrop Frye, *The Great Code: The Bible and Literature* (New York: Harcourt Brace Jovanovich, 1982). In modern Japan, Christian novelists, such as Endō Shūsaku, aimed to reconcile Christianity and literature. See Mark Williams, "From Out of the Depths: The Japanese Literary Response to Christianity," in *Japan and Christianity: Impacts and Responses*, ed. John Breen and Mark Williams (New York: Palgrave Macmillan, 1996), 156–74.

3. For a discussion of Dōgen's poetry, see, for instance, Steven Heine, *The Zen Poetry of Dōgen: Verses from the Mountain of Eternal Peace* (Boston: Tuttle, 1997).

4. LaFleur, *Karma of Words*, 7–8.

5. Esperanza Ramirez-Christensen, *Emptiness and Temporality: Buddhism and Medieval Japanese Poetics* (Stanford, CA: Stanford University Press, 2008), 88–89, 108–109. Concerning Fujiwara Shunzei's Buddhist poetry practice, Michael Marra holds a different view. Rhetorical *topos* of poetry became "a kind of exorcism, a magic formula that all poets had to follow in order to dispel the possible evil consequences that might come from an improper use of words, that is, a use removed from religious practice, which was directly linked to the praise of the Buddha. The poets' actual concern was mainly *poetic* in the sense that they aimed at creating the language of poetry, and making poetic language work differently from other types of language." *Essays on Japan: Between Aesthetics and Literature* (Leiden: Brill, 2010), 352.

6. See, for instance, R. Keller Kimbrough, *Preachers, Poets, Women, and the Way: Izumi Shikibu and the Buddhist Literature of Japan* (Ann Arbor, MI: University of Michigan Press, 2008).

7. Haruo Shirane, ed., *Early Modern Japanese Literature: An Anthology 1600–1900* (New York: Columbia University Press, 2002), 17.

8. Laurence R. Kominz, *The Stars Who Created Kabuki: Their Lives, Loves and Legacy* (New York: Kōdansha USA, 1997), 37–41, 79–81.

9. See Steven Heine, "Tragedy and Salvation in the Floating World: Chikamatsu's Double Suicide Drama as Millenarian Discourse," *Journal of Asian Studies* 50, no. 2 (1994): 367–93.

10. Heinz Morioka and Miyoko Sasaki, *Rakugo: The Popular Narrative Art of Japan* (Cambridge, MA: Harvard University Press, 1990), 1.

11. Morioka and Sasaki, *Rakugo*, 211–17.

12. Paul Varley, *Japanese Culture*, 4th ed. (Honolulu: University of Hawai'i Press, 2000), 183.

13. Shirane, *Early Modern Japanese Literature*, 885–86. For a discussion of Buddhism and literature in early modern Japan in Japanese, see Aoyama Tadakazu, *Kinsei bukkyō bungaku no kenkyū* (Tokyo: Ōfū, 1999).

14. For example, *Bukkyō bungaku* (Buddhism and Literature), an academic journal in Japan, tends to focus on the medieval and early modern periods.

15. James Edward Ketelaar, *Of Heretics and Martyrs in Meiji Japan: Buddhism and Its Persecution* (Princeton, NJ: Princeton University Press, 1990), 9, 45.

16. The separation of Buddhist studies and literary studies as subjects of academic inquiry can also be situated in a broader milieu. According to Wlad Godzich, disciplinary boundaries represent social abstraction in academia: "The disciplinary outlook, in other words, permits each discipline to function as if the problem of fragmentation did not arise since the concepts that it mobilizes and the operations it performs are adequate, if not isomorphic, to its object—an elegant variant of the Parmenidean principle of the identity of thought and being. This may well account for the blindness of the disciplinary perspective to the problem of fragmentation: it is constitutive of that perspective." Foreword to *Heterologies: Discourse on the Other*, by Michel de Certeau, trans. Brian Massumi (Minneapolis: University of Minnesota Press, 2010), 4. Categories of

discipline create interstitial space where subjects of inquiry pushed out by the disciplines slip through the cracks of intellectual fragmentations. Disciplinary divisions help us distinguish one field from another; however, the specialization of knowledge prevents us from perceiving a culture from a larger perspective. On this topic, recent efforts to connect Buddhist studies and art history are worth mentioning. In her recent study of Buddhist art in medieval Japan, Pamela Winfield connects two disciplines related to religion and art. She argues that the division of labor between religious studies scholars who focus on canonical texts and art historians who specialize in the analysis of religious images began after the late nineteenth century when Nishida Kitarō, Suzuki Daisetsu, and Nishitani Keiji (1900–1990) defined Zen as a religion of unmediated experience and ignored the importance of Buddhist icons. Together with other scholars, Winfield calls for a collaboration of scholars of religious studies and art historians with the aim of breaking down the "artificial and wholly modern disciplinary boundaries that have kept these interrelated fields from joining forces." *Icons and Iconoclasm in Japanese Buddhism: Kūkai and Dōgen on the Art of Enlightenment* (New York: Oxford University, 2013), 17. Also, for efforts to unite Asian art history and Buddhist studies, see Robert H. Sharf and Elizabeth Horton Sharf, eds., *Living Images: Japanese Buddhist Icons in Context* (Stanford, CA: Stanford University Press, 2002).

17. Discussed in Stephen Dodd, "History in the Making: The Negotiation of History and Fiction in Tanizaki Jun'ichirō's *Shunkinshō*," *Japan Review* 24 (2012), 154. According to Haruo Shirane, "The new disciplinary configurations, derived in large part from the German model, radically altered the premodern literary canon, leaving out texts in such fields as history, philosophy, religion, and political science, which had hitherto been an integral part of literary learning." Introduction to *Inventing the Classics: Modernity, National Identity, and Japanese Literature*, ed. Haruo Shirane and Tomi Suzuki (Stanford, CA: Stanford University Press, 2000), 7.

18. Setouchi Jakujō (1922–), a nun and a novelist, is perhaps an exception.

19. The special issue *Kokubungaku: Kaishaku to kanshō—Tokushū, kin gendai sakka to bukkyō bungaku* 55, no. 12 (December 1990) features articles on *Kin gendai sakka to bukkyō bungaku*. In addition, in this journal, critics discuss the reception of Buddhism by, for instance, Kawabata Yasunari, Tanizaki Jun'ichirō, Sakaguchi Ango, Minakami Tsutomu, Kamura Isota, Hayashi Fumiko, Takamura Kōtarō, Miyazawa Kenji, and Miki Rofū. *Kokubungaku: Kaishaku to kanshō* 56, no. 9 (1991) features Kawabata Yasunari—see Imamura Junko, "Kawabata Yasunari to bukkyō," 139–43; *Kokubungaku: Kaishaku to kanshō* 57, no. 2 (1992) features Tanizaki Jun'ichirō—see Hasegawa Izumi, "Tanizaki Jun'ichirō's shūkyōkan," 38–42; *Kokubungaku: Kaishaku to kanshō* 58, no. 2 (1993) features Sakaguchi Ango—see Takeuchi Kiyomi, "Sakaguchi Ango to bukkyō," 37–42; *Kokubungaku: Kaishaku to kanshō* 61, no. 2 (1996) features Minakami Tsutomu—see Uchida Asao, "Minakami Tsutomu no bukkyō," 23–27; *Kokubungaku: Kaishaku to kanshō* 63, no. 2 (1998) features Hayashi Fumiko—see Enomoto Takashi, "Hayashi Fumiko no shūkyōkan," 56–60; *Kokubungaku: Kaishaku to kanshō* 63, no. 9 (1998) features Takamura Kōtarō—see Fundō Junsaku, "Kōtarō to bukkyō," 34–40;

Kokubungaku: Kaishaku to kanshō 65, no. 4 (2000) features Kasai Zenzō and Kamura Isota—see articles written on Kamura Isota's works, 138–166; *Kokubungaku: Kaishaku to kanshō* 65, no. 2 (2000) features Miyazawa Kenji—see Satō Yasumasa, "Miyazawa Kenji to bukkyō," 20–26; *Kokubungaku: Kaishaku to kanshō* 68, no. 11 (2003) features Miki Rofū—see Fukushima Motoharu, "Miki Rofū to taishō seimei shugi," 18–23. Critics have also discussed briefly the Buddhist influence on Akutagawa Ryūnosuke (see, for instance, Maeda Jun, "Bukkyō: Kodoku jigoku ni hajimaru jiko keishōka no kokoromi," in *Akutagawa Ryūnosuke: Sono chiteki kūkan, Kobungaku: Kaishaku to Kanshō, bessatsu,* ed. Sekiguchi Yasuyoshi [Tokyo: Shibundō, 2004], 53–60); Higuchi Ichiyō (see, for instance, Sugisaki Toshio, "Higuchi Ichiyō to bukkyō," *Bungaku gogaku* 130 [1991]: 1–15); Izumi Kyōka (see, for instance, Tanikawa Keiichi, "Izumi Kyōka: Tasei no kioku," in *Kindai bungaku to bukkyō,* vol. 10 of *Iwanami kōza Nihon bungaku to bukkyō,* ed. Konno Tōru, Satake Akihiro, and Ueda Shizuteru [Tokyo: Iwanami Shoten, 1995], 169–91); Okamoto Kanoko (see, for instance, Oda Yoshisuke, "Okamoto Kanoko," in Konno Tōru et al., *Kindai bungaku to bukkyō,* 193–212; and Mineshima Hideo, "Bukkyō to bungaku no aida: Okamoto Kanoko *Shōjo ruten* o megutte," in *Gendai shisō,* vol. 3 of *Gendai nihon to bukkyō,* ed. Kobayashi Takasuke, Furuta Shōkin, Mineshima Hideo, and Yoshida Kyūichi [Tokyo: Heibonsha, 2000], 276–92); Hiratsuka Raichō (see, for instance, Shimada Akiko, "Hiratsuka Raichō no shisō to bukkyō," in Kobayashi Takasuke et al., *Gendai shisō,* 225–41); Mishima Yukio (see, for instance, Okamoto Katsuhito, "Mishima Yukio no bungaku to bukkyō: *Hōjō no umi o chūshin ni,*" in Kobayashi Takasuke et al., *Gendai shisō,* 308–27); and Nakazato Kaizan (see, for instance, Suzuki Sadami, "Nakazato Kaizan no bukkyō shisō o megutte," in Kobayashi Takasuke et al., *Gendai shisō,* 259–75).

20. Canon in this context refers to the collection of Buddhist sutras and commentaries compiled, read, and used by Buddhist studies scholars and Buddhist clergy. In modern Japan, various *tripiṭaka,* or collections of Buddhist scriptures, were compiled, including *Taishō Tripiṭaka.* Haruo Shirane, referring to Pierre Bourdieu's notion of production, states: "Canon formation is thus concerned not only with the immediate producers of the work—the authors, the scribes, the printers, etc.—but also with those agents and institutions (such as commentators, patrons, temples, schools, museums, publishing houses) that produce or *re*-produce the value of the text and that create the consumers and audiences capable of recognizing and desiring that value. Key questions, then are, how, by whom, and for what purposes this value is generated, maintained, and transmitted." *Inventing the Classics,* 2–3.

21. Scholars in the West have studied contemporary Christian novels of Japan. See, for instance, Philip Gabriel, *Spirit Matters: The Transcendent in Modern Japanese Literature* (Honolulu: University of Hawai'i Press, 2006); John Breen and Mark Williams, *Japan and Christianity: Impacts and Responses* (New York: Palgrave Macmillan, 1996); Sean Somers, "Passion Plays by Proxy: The Paschal Face as Interculturality in the Works of Endō Shūsaku and Mishima Yukio," in *Through a Glass Darkly: Suffering, the Sacred, and the Sublime in Literature and Theory,* ed. Holly Faith Nelson, Lynn R.

Szabo, and Jens Zimmermann (Waterloo, ON: Wilfred Laurier University Press, 2010), 329–48; Rebecca Suter, *Holy Ghosts: The Christian Century in Modern Japanese Fiction* (Honolulu: University of Hawai'i Press, 2015); and Massimiliano Tomasi, *The Dilemma of Faith in Modern Japanese Literature* (London: Routledge, 2018).

22. There is an edited volume exploring Japanese Buddhism and literature in English, but the articles included in the book focus on the medieval and early modern periods. See James H. Sanford, William R. LaFleur, and Masatoshi Nagatomi, eds., *Flowing Traces: Buddhism in the Literary and Visual Arts of Japan* (Princeton, NJ: Princeton University Press, 1992). Elisabetta Porcu analyzes modern Japanese culture, which includes literature, through the lens of the Pure Land Buddhist tradition; see *Pure Land Buddhism in Modern Japanese Culture* (Leiden: Brill, 2008). It is worth noting that the Association for Japanese Literary Studies (AJLS) chose "Religion and Spirituality in Japanese Literature" as the theme of its twenty-third annual meeting in 2014, which included a panel titled "Revisiting *Yogācāra*: Rendition and Interpretation of *Yuishiki* in Modern Japanese Literary Discourses," organized by Ikuho Amano. For the AJLS's twenty-third annual meeting, see Massimiliano Tomasi, ed., "Spirituality in Japanese Literature," *Proceedings of the Association for Japanese Literary Studies* 16 (2015).

23. Watsuji Tetsurō, *Zoku ninhon seishinshi kenkyū* (Tokyo: Iwanami Shoten, 1935), quoted in Kenri Bunshū, *Kindai bungaku to bukkyō no shūhen* (Higashine, Japan: Han'nyakutsu, 1986), 11.

24. See Kawabata Yasunari, *Japan, the Beautiful and Myself* [*Utsukushii nihon no watakushi*], trans. Edward G. Seidensticker (Tokyo: Kōdansha, 1991).

25. Umehara Takeshi, "Nihonjin no biishiki: Shi no bigaku," in *Kokubungaku: Kaishaku to kyōzai no kenkyū* 15, no. 8 (June 1970): 8–16.

26. See Nishida Masayoshi, *Mujō no bungaku: Nihonteki mujō bikan no keifu* (Tokyo: Hanawa Shobō, 1982). Nishida also discusses the relationship between the notion of impermanence and Japanese literature in *Mujōkan no keifu* (Tokyo: Ōfūsha, 1976) and *Shishōsetsu sai hakken* (Tokyo: Ōfūsha, 1973). Kobayashi Tomoaki discusses representations of impermanence in ancient and medieval Japanese literature; see *Mujōkan no bungaku* (Tokyo: Kōbundō, 1976). For a classic work on the Japanese notion of impermanence, see Karaki Junzō, *Mujō* (Tokyo: Chikuma Shobō, 1964). There are Japanese monographs which explore literature and religion in modern Japan by single authors, but these works do not focus on Buddhism. See, for instance, Kuyama Yasushi, *Kindai nihon no bungaku to shūkyō* (Tokyo: Sōbunsha, 1966) and Sugisaki Toshio, *Kindai bungaku to shūkyō* (Tokyo: Sōbunsha, 1991).

27. For a discussion of Itō's study in English, see, for instance, Keiko Kockum, *Ito Sei: Self-Analysis and the Modern Japanese Novel* (Stockholm: Stockholm University Press, 1994). Kamei Katsuichirō is another literary critic who considered the place of Buddhism in modern Japanese literature.

28. Itō Sei, *Shōsetsu no ninshiki* (Tokyo: Iwanami Bunko, 2006), 210–11, 214–15, 224.

29. Itō, 224–33.

30. Itō, 238–40, 243–47, 251–52.
31. Itō, 241–43.
32. Kenri, *Kindai bungaku to bukkyō no shūhen*, 23–24.
33. Kenri, *Kindai bungaku to bukkyō no shūhen*, 51–54. Kenri also uses the resulting hierarchy to determine which literature is genuinely or authentically Buddhist. For his detailed discussion, see "Kindai nihon no bungaku to bukkyō," in Konno Tōru et al., *Kindai bungaku to bukkyō*, 29–54.
34. Yoshio Sugimoto, *An Introduction to Japanese Society* (Melbourne: Cambridge University Press, 2008), 147.
35. See, for instance, Sako Jun'ichirō, "Shinran no shisō to kindai bungaku," in *Bukkyō shisō to nihon bungaku*, vol. 2 of *Bukkyō bungaku kōza*, ed. Itō Hiroyuki, Imanari Genjō, and Yamada Shōzen (Tokyo: Benseisha, 1995), 205–29; Ishikawa Kyōchō, "Nichiren no shisō to kindai bungaku," Itō Hiroyuki et al., *Bukkyō shisō*, 230–54; Nakajima Kunihiko, "Zen to kindai bungaku: Sōseki to sono shūhen o chūshin ni," in Itō Hiroyuki et al., *Bukkyō shisō*, 255–80. A chronological table in which historical Buddhist novels/dramas are listed can be found in Shimura Kunihiro, ed., "Kin gendai bukkyō bungaku nenpyō," in "Tokushū: Kin gendai sakka to bukkyō bungaku," special issue, *Kokubungaku: Kaishaku to kanshō—Tokushū, kin gendai sakka to bukkyō bungaku* 55, no. 12 (December, 1990): 150–57.
36. In 1999, Kokusai Nihon Bunka Kenkyū Center (International Research Center for Japanese Studies) published the symposium proceedings titled *Sōritsu jusshūnen kinen kokusai symposium: Nihon ni okeru shūkyō to bungaku* (Religion and literature in Japan), which includes Origas's article. In 2005, Chiba University published a report called *Religion in Japanese Modern Literature*. See Takitō Mitsuyoshi, ed., "Nihon kindai bungaku to shūkyō," *Chiba daigaku shakai bunka kagaku kenkyū hōkokusho*, vol. 120 (Chiba, Japan: Chiba Daigaku, 2005).
37. For the translation of *Chikumagawa no suketchi*, see Shimazaki Tōson, *Chikuma River Sketches*, trans., William E. Naff (Honolulu: University of Hawai'i Press, 1991).
38. For a translation of "Saigo no ikku," see David Dilworth and J. Thomas Rimer, eds., *The Historical Fiction of Mori Ōgai* (Honolulu: University of Hawai'i Press, 1991), 209–22. For a study of "Saigo no ikku," see, for instance, Doris G. Bargen, "Not Just Words: Shogunal Politics and the Daijōsai in Mori Ōgai's 'Saigo no ikku,'" *Monumenta Nipponica* 67, no. 1 (2012): 1–27.
39. Jean-Jacques Origas, "Iki jigoku, soshite hana: Meiji jidai no sanbun ni arawareta shūkyō to bungaku no kakawariai, kōsatsu to kasetsu," in *Sōritsu jusshūnen kinen kokusai symposium: Nihon ni okeru shūkyō to bungaku*, ed. Kokusai Nihon Bunka Kenkyū Center (Kyoto: Kokusai Nihon Bunka Kenkyū Center, 1999), 120–22. Origas makes two more observations. First, enlightenment thinkers (such as Fukuzawa Yukichi, Nakae Chōmin, and Nishi Amane) and religious thinkers (such as Uchimura Kanzō, Uemura Masahisa, Furukawa Rōsen, and Kiyozawa Manshi) must be placed on the same level when studying modern Japanese language and literature because they all contributed to it. Specifically, these religious leaders related a religious belief

to personal history, i.e., wrote autobiographical stories. Second, Origas observes the surge of religious interest among the second generation of modern Japanese writers, the period broadly defined as the 1880s and 1890s, and finds religious sensibilities either directly or indirectly expressed in the works of Tsubouchi Shōyō, Futabatei Shimei, Kōda Rohan, and Mori Ōgai.

40. Hata Kōhei, "Bukkyō to sengo bungaku: Bungaku toshiteno bukkyō hyōgen," in Itō Hiroyuki et al., *Bukkyō shisō*, 316–21.

41. Donald W. Mitchell, *Buddhism: Introducing the Buddhist Experience* (New York: Oxford University Press, 2002), 33.

42. Mitchell, 39.

43. *Saṃyutta-nikāya*, quoted in Mitchell, 60.

44. Paul Williams, *Mahāyāna Buddhism: The Doctrinal Foundations* (London: Routledge, 1989), 2.

45. Mitchell, 39.

46. Mitchell, *Buddhism*, 97–98, 355, 360.

47. Mitchell, 99–112.

48. For instance, for a study of doctrinal and sectarian development of medieval Pure Land Buddhism, see Mark L. Blum, *The Origins and Development of Pure Land Buddhism* (New York: Oxford University Press, 2002); for the medieval development of Shin Buddhism and Honganji, see James C. Dobbins, *Jōdo Shinshū: Shin Buddhism in Medieval Japan* (Honolulu: University of Hawai'i Press, 2002); for a study of the sectarian development of Sōtōshū, see William M. Bodiford, *Sōtō Zen in Medieval Japan* (Honolulu: University of Hawai'i Press, 1993); for a discussion of early modern Sōtō Zen, see Duncan R. Williams, *The Other Side of Zen: A Social History of Sōtō Zen Buddhism in Tokugawa Japan* (Princeton, NJ: Princeton University Press, 2005); and for a study of Nichiren and his successors, see Jacqueline I. Stone, *Original Enlightenment and the Transformation of Medieval Japanese Buddhism* (Honolulu: University of Hawai'i Press, 1999).

49. Nam-lin Hur, *Death and Social Order in Tokugawa Japan: Buddhism, Anti-Christianity, and the Danka System* (Cambridge, MA: Harvard University Press, 2007), 16.

50. Hur, 108. Also, for a discussion of the development of funerary Buddhism in Japan, see Jacqueline I. Stone and Mariko Namba Walter, eds., *Death and the Afterlife in Japanese Buddhism* (Honolulu: University of Hawai'i Press, 2008).

51. Sueki Fumihiko, "Introduction to the Symposium on Modernity and Buddhism," trans. Anton Luis Sevilla, *Eastern Buddhist*, n.s., 43, no. 1/2 (2012), 17.

52. Today, scholars generally agree that defining Kamakura New Buddhism as the central development of medieval Japanese Buddhism is a modern discourse. For the reexamination of Kamakura Buddhism, see, for instance, Fumihiko Sueki, "A Reexamination of the *Kenmitsu Taisei* Theory," *Japanese Journal of Religious Studies* 23, no. 3/4 (1996): 449–66; Kenji Matsuo, "What is Kamakura New Buddhism? Official Monks and Reclusive Monks," *Japanese Journal of Religious Studies* 24, no. 1/2 (1997): 179–89.

53. Thomas A. Tweed, *The American Encounter with Buddhism, 1844–1912: Victorian Culture and the Limits of Dissent* (Chapel Hill: University of North Carolina, 2000), xxxiv.

54. Thomas A. Tweed, "Tracing Modernity's Flows: Buddhist Currents in the Pacific World," *Eastern Buddhist*, n.s., 43, no. 1/2: (2012): 39–40.

55. David L. McMahan provides an overview of Buddhist modernism, which he defines as "a cocreation of Asians, Europeans, and Americans" and as "forms of Buddhism that have emerged out of an engagement with the dominant cultural and intellectual forces of modernity." *The Making of Buddhist Modernism* (New York: Oxford University Press, 2008), 6. Winton Higgins defines Buddhist modernism as "an increasingly fraught mix of ancestral Buddhism and modern discursive practices, [which] initially arose to deflect Western colonialism's Christianising mission in Asia, and provided a bridge for missionary Buddhism's entry into the West." "The Coming of Secular Buddhism: A Synoptic View," *Journal of Global Buddhism* 13 (2012): 111.

56. The author wishes to thank Charles Hallisey for introducing Dadi's book and Dennis Hirota for arranging a meeting with Hallisey.

57. Iftikhar Dadi, *Modernism and the Art of Muslim South Asia* (Chapel Hill: University of North Carolina, 2010), 12.

58. Andreas Huyssen, "Geographies of Modernism in a Globalizing World," *New German Critique* 100 (Winter 2007): 194, quoted in Dadi, 1–2.

59. Dadi, 13.

60. Dadi states that modern South Asian Muslim subjectivity included "fragments from Persianate humanism, Hindu and Buddhist mythology, the orientalist construction of the discipline of Islamic art, colonial governmentality, nineteenth-century theological and modernist reform, modern pan-Islamism, twentieth-century metropolitan and transnational artistic modernism, mid-twentieth-century nationalism and developmentalism, and contemporary debates on race, gender, and globalization" (2).

61. Dadi, 11.

62. Dadi, 27. Derryl N. MacLean points out six characteristics of cosmopolitanism by referring to the study of Steven Vertovec and Robin Cohen: "a global condition of socio-cultural interpenetrations, a Kantian philosophy of the universal citizen, a political project founded on transnational institutions such as civil society, a political project founded on the notion of citizens with multiple identities, an internalised orientation towards global engagement and a kind of multicultural competence or practice." Introduction to *Cosmopolitanisms in Muslim Contexts: Perspectives from the Past*, ed. Derryl N. MacLean and Sikeena Karmali Ahmed (Edinburgh: Edinburgh University, 2013), 3. Kai Kresse, in his study of Islam in the western Indian Ocean, defines cosmopolitanism as "openness to the world," "significant experience of the world," and "the skill of dealing flexibly with the world." "Interrogating 'Cosmopolitanism' in an Indian Ocean Setting: Thinking through Mombasa on the Swahili Coast," in *Cosmopolitanisms in Muslim Contexts*, 33.

63. Sōseki created more than two thousand haiku and adored *nanga* paintings. See Ienaga Saburō, *Nihon shisōshi ni okeru hitei no ronri no hattatsu* (Tokyo: Shinsensha, 1969), 325–26, 329–30. Both Katai and Shiga praised works by Ihara Saikaku, known as "the greatest fiction writer of the Edo period," to borrow Haruo Shirane's words (*Early Modern Japanese Literature*, 45).

64. *Nanga* defined by Shirane, *Early Modern Japanese Literature*, 383.

65. *Yōkyoku* defined in Alan Campbell and David S. Noble, eds., *Japan: An Illustrated Encyclopedia* (Tokyo: Kōdansha International, 1993), 1:1669.

66. During the 1960s and 70s, Japanese intellectuals began discussing categories of aesthetics unique to Japan. They defined the medieval Japanese sensibilities of beauty in terms of the feeling for impermanence, which was associated with Buddhism, and changes in natural scenery, such as the scattering of cherry blossoms or fall foliage. For a critique of the modern discourse on Japanese aesthetics, see Marra, *Essays on Japan*, 356–58.

67. Akegarasu Haya, "Rōsō," *Seishinkai* 8, no. 1 (1908): 48–52.

68. See Matsuda Shōichi, *Akegarasu Haya: Yoto tomoni yo o koen*, (Kanazawa: Hokkoku Shinbunsha, 1998), 2:198–250.

69. Dadi, *Modernism*, 5.

70. Irmela Hijiya-Kirschnereit, *Rituals of Self-Revelation: Shishōsetsu as Literary Genre and Socio-cultural Phenomenon* (Cambridge, MA: Harvard University, 1996), 3.

71. A number of Japanese scholars have studied *shishōsetsu*. For the present state of scholarship, see, for instance, *Shishōsetsu kenkyū ronbun mokuroku from 1960*, compiled by Hibi Yoshitaka. http://park18.wakwak.com/~hibi/html/in_bib_m.htm.

72. *Mono no aware* defined by Varley, *Japanese Culture*, 60–61.

73. Hijiya-Kirschnereit, *Rituals of Self-Revelation*, 191.

74. Fowler, *Rhetoric of Confession*, 66.

75. Fowler, 13–14.

76. Tomi Suzuki, *Narrating the Self: Fictions of Japanese Modernity* (Stanford, CA: Stanford University Press, 1996), 3.

77. Hirosawa Takayuki, "Bukkyō jutsugo no gainen ni tsuite: Hikaku shisō ni okeru hōhōron o megutte," *Gendai mikkyō* 16 (2003), 156.

78. Robert E. Buswell Jr. and Robert M. Gimello, introduction to *Paths to Liberation: The Mārga and Its Transformations in Buddhist Thought*, ed. Robert E. Buswell Jr. and Robert M. Gimello (Honolulu: University of Hawai'i Press, 1992), 2–3.

79. Buswell and Gimello, 10.

80. William Harmless, *Mystics* (New York: Oxford University, 2008), 206–7.

81. Steve Odin, *Artistic Detachment in Japan and the West: Psychic Distance in Comparative Aesthetics* (Honolulu: University of Hawai'i Press, 2001), 19–21.

82. Michael Marra critiques Odin's approach to defining aesthetic concepts of Japan: "However, once the author [Odin] turns his attention to Japan, and particularly to [the notion of] *yūgen*, he immediately falls into the trap of taking for granted the existence of an alleged 'classical aesthetics of Japan,' without ever considering the

possibility of a modernist genealogy for the construction of such classical aesthetics." *Essays on Japan*, 19–20.

83. Jingjing Ye, "Okakura Tenshin no cha no hon ni kansuru ichi kōsatsu," *Hikaku nihongaku kyōiku kenkyū center kenkyū nenpō* 12 (2016): 25–31.

84. Taoka Masahiro, "Nitobe Inazō no dōtoku ni okeru kyōikugakuteki igi," *Hokkaidō daigaku daigakuin kyōikugaku kenkyū kiyō* 126 (2016): 157–60.

85. Shishida Fumiaki, "Some Questions Accompanying the Acculturation of Japanese Martial Arts," *Sports kagaku kenkyū* 5 (2008): 199–200. For a brief discussion of *dō* associated with the spirit of Japan and its criticism, see Roger J. Davies and Osamu Ikeno, eds., *The Japanese Mind: Understanding Contemporary Japanese Culture* (North Clarendon, VT: Tuttle, 2002), 71–78.

86. Suzuki Sadami, *Nihon no bungaku o kangaeru* (Tokyo: Kadokawa Shoten, 1994), 141–42. Concerning the Taishō literary writers' perspective on life, Suzuki refers to Takami Jun, "Jun bungaku to bunshi" in *Takami Jun Zenshū* vol. 13 (Tokyo: Keisō Shobō, 1971).

87. Peter Skilling, introduction to *Buddhist Narrative in Asia and Beyond*, ed. Peter Skilling and Justin McDaniel (Bangkok: Chulalongkorn University, 2013), 1:ix, xii.

88. Linda Covill, trans., *Handsome Nanda* by Ashvaghosha (New York: New York University Press, 2007), quoted in Skilling, 1:ix.

89. LaFleur, *Karma of Words*, 7–8.

90. Haruo Shirane, *The Bridge of Dreams: A Poetics of "The Tale of Genji"* (Stanford, CA: Stanford University Press, 1987), xvi.

91. Bruce Hindmarsh, "Religious Conversion as Narrative and Autobiography," in *The Oxford Handbook of Religious Conversion*, ed. Lewis R. Rambo and Charles E. Farhadian (New York: Oxford University Press, 2014), 3, https://www.oxfordhandbooks.com/view/10.1093/oxfordhb/9780195338522.001.0001/oxfordhb-9780195338522-e-015.

92. Charles Hallisey and Anne Hansen, "Narrative, Sub-ethics, and the Moral Life: Some Evidence from Theravāda Buddhism," *Journal of Religious Ethics* 24, no. 2 (1996): 308.

93. Paṭācārā's story summarized by Hallisey and Hansen, 319.

94. Hallisey and Hansen, 322.

95. Hallisey and Hansen, 322–23.

96. Richard K. Payne, "The Path from Metaphor to Narrative: Gampopa's Jewel Ornament of Liberation," *Pacific World*, 3rd ser., no. 16 (2014): 30.

97. Payne finds the mode of the romance narrative—that is, "a drama of self-identification symbolized by the hero's transcendence of the world of experience, his victory over it, and his final liberation from it"—represented by the anecdote of Christ's resurrection also fits the description of the Buddha's life. "Fractal Journeys: Narrative Structure of the Path and of Tantric Practice," *Pacific World*, 3rd ser., no. 14 (2012): 278–79. In this article, Payne quotes Hayden White's study. See Hayden White, *Metahistory: The Historical Imagination in Nineteenth-Century Europe* (Baltimore: Johns Hopkins University Press, 1973), 8. Payne observes that in the experience of

Christianity and other Western religions, narrative tends to follow the pattern of "unity, fall, and redemption," going backward in time for a protagonist to seek perfect unity in the past ("Fractal Journeys," 293nn14–15). Also see Richard K. Payne, "Individuation and Awakening: Romantic Narrative and the Psychological Interpretation of Buddhism," in *Buddhism and Psychotherapy across Cultures: Essays on Theories and Practices*, ed. Mark Unno (Boston: Wisdom, 2006), 17–30. Northrop Frye finds a U-shaped narrative structure in all the stories in the Bible, for instance, a man "loses the tree and water of life at the beginning of Genesis and gets them back at the end of Revelation," and according to the Book of Judges, "the apostasy [is] followed by a descent into disaster and bondage, which in turn is followed by repentance, then by a rise through deliverance to a point more or less on the level from which the descent began." *The Great Code*, 169.

98. Payne, "Fractal Journeys," 279–80.

99. Payne, 287.

100. Scholars have pointed out different path schemes within Buddhism, depending on tradition and the degree of individual experience. In Theravada Buddhism, an ideal goal can be defined as "purity" and "calmness." See Grace G. Burford, "Theravada Buddhist Soteriology and the Paradox of Desire," in *Paths to Liberation: The Mārga and Its Transformations in Buddhist Thought*, ed. Robert E. Buswell Jr. and Robert M. Gimello (Honolulu: University of Hawai'i Press, 1992), 40–41. In Mahayna Buddhism, the "knowledge of the paths" is identified as gaining "direct realization of emptiness." See Donald S. Lopez Jr., "Paths Terminable and Interminable," in *Paths to Liberation*, 150. Further, Jared R. Lindahl points out different approaches that a practitioner can take after deconstructing a "narrative self"—"the default, deluded self that operates by telling stories about the way the world and the self is"—through which a "resultant self"—which is no longer related to "the phenomenal world through the false stories of the narrative self"—emerges. "Self-Transformation according to Buddhist Stages of the Path Literature," *Pacific World*, 3rd ser., no. 14 (2012): 233–34.

Chapter 2

1. Miyazawa Masayori, "Natsume Sōseki to bukkyō: Toku ni tariki jōdomon tono kankei, part 1," *Nihon Bukkyō* 42 (1977): 42–43; Ara Masahito, *Sōseki kenkyū nenpyō* (Tokyo: Shūeisha, 1984), 132, 853–54, 876–87. For a translation of *Hōjōki*, see, for instance, Yasuhiko Moriguchi and David Jenkins, *Hōjōki: Visions of a Torn World* (Berkeley: Stone Bridge Press, 1996). Concerning the quality of Sōseki's translation, Donald Keene states, "His English style is flowery, rather too ornate for modern tastes, but his lips are rare." *Dawn to the West: Japanese Literature of the Modern Era, Fiction* (New York: Holt, Rinehart and Winston, 1984), 308.

2. Mizukawa Takao, "Natsume Sōseki and Shin Buddhism," trans. Ken'ichi Yokogawa and Michihiro Ama, *Eastern Buddhist*, n.s., 38, no. 1/2 (2007): 147–48.

3. Mizukawa, 148.
4. Mizukawa, 147–48.
5. Mizukawa, 163.
6. Marvin Marcus summarizes Sōseki's experience in London as follows: "The young man came to see himself as a stranger in a strange land. He lived alone in a succession of London boardinghouses, reading book after book and making elaborate notes in a crabbed scrawl. There was only sporadic communication with his wife. Rather than take university courses, he settled for a weekly tutorial with a somewhat eccentric Shakespearean scholar. He obsessed over money and how to stretch the little that was available—much of it spent in the local bookstores. As he refined his understanding of English literature, Kinnosuke cultivated a profound distaste for its society and people." *Reflections in a Glass Door: Memory and Melancholy in the Personal Writing of Natsume Sōseki* (Honolulu: University of Hawai'i Press, 2009), 18.
7. Natsume Sōseki, "Danpen," *Sōseki Zenshū* (Tokyo: Iwanami Shoten, 1966–1967), 13:98 (hereafter cited as *SZ*), quoted in Karatani Kōjin, *Sōsekiron shūsei* (Tokyo: Daisan Bunmeisha, 1992), 70.
8. Marcus, *Reflections*, 203.
9. For a discussion of *Theory of Literature* in English, see Michael K. Bourdaghs, Atsuko Ueda, and Joseph A. Murphy, eds. *Theory of Literature and Other Critical Writings: Natsume Sōseki* (New York: Columbia University Press, 2010).
10. Scholars have performed psychoanalytic readings of *Ten Nights of Dreams*. See, for instance, Marcus, 10, 210.
11. Mizukawa, "Natsume Sōseki and Shin Buddhism," 153–54. For Mizukawa's discussion of Sōseki and Buddhism, see *Sōseki to bukkyō: Sokuten kyoshi e no michi* (Tokyo: Heibonsha, 2002).
12. Author's translation, modeled on the translation of *I Am a Cat* by Katsue Shibata and Motonari Kai: "I die. I die and receive peace. Peace cannot be had without dying. Save us, merciful Buddha! Save us, merciful Buddha! Gracious blessings, Gracious blessings." *I Am a Cat* (Tokyo: Kenkyūsha, 1969), 431. Aiko Itō and Graeme Wilson translate the passage this way: "I am dying, Egypt, dying. Through death I'm drifting slowly into peace. Only by dying can this divine quiescence be attained. May one rest in peace! I am thankful, I am thankful. Thankful, thankful, thankful." *I Am a Cat* (North Clarendon, VT: Tuttle, 2002), 470.
13. *Gubijinsō*, *SZ*, 3:17; author's translation.
14. Miyazawa, "Natsume Sōseki part 1," 56–57, quoted in Mizukawa, "Natsume Sōseki and Shin Buddhism," 155. For the English translation of *jakujōri*, see Luis O. Gómez, *The Land of Bliss: The Paradise of the Buddha of Measureless Light, Sanskrit and Chinese Versions of the Sukhāvatīvyūha Sutras* (Honolulu: University of Hawai'i Press, 1996), 158.
15. According to Katsuya Hiromoto, in 1896 Takahama Kyoshi and Sōseki visited the Dōgo hot spring resort in Matsuyama, where Kyoshi composed the *shinsentai* poems which depicted otherworldly subjects. "The Quiet Joy of Peace and Harmony:

Kyoshi Takahama's Life and Literature," *Hiyoshi Review of English Studies* 53 (2008): 31–74.

16. Miyazawa, "Natsume Sōseki part 1," 48, quoted and translated in Mizukawa, "Natsume Sōseki and Shin Buddhism," 150.

17. Mizukawa, 150–51; Miyazawa, "Natsume Sōseki to bukkyō, part 1," 42, 50.

18. Masaki Akira, "Taishō seimeishugi to bukkyō," in *Taishō seimeishugi to gendai*, ed. Suzuki Sadami (Tokyo: Kawade Shobō Shinsha, 1995), 147–48. The term neurasthenia (*shinkei suijaku*) became popular among modern Japanese intellectuals, even though symptoms of depression had already been observed before Japan's modern experience. For a discussion of *shinkei suijaku*, see Christopher L. Hill, "The Naturalist Novel and the Boundaries of Japanese Literature," *Proceedings of the Association for Japanese Literary Studies* 9 (2008): 71–75.

19. Ara, *Sōseki kenkyū nenpyō*, 158–59.

20. For a discussion of Shaku Sōen and the representation of Japanese Buddhism in the World's Parliament of Religions, see, for instance, Judith Snodgrass, *Presenting Japanese Buddhism to the West: Orientalism, Occidentalism, and the Columbian Exposition* (Chapel Hill: University of North Carolina Press, 2003); James E. Ketelaar, *Of Heretics and Martyrs in Meiji Japan: Buddhism and Its Persecution* (Princeton, NJ: Princeton University Press, 1990).

21. Janine Tasca Sawada, *Practical Pursuits: Religion, Politics, and Personal Cultivation in Nineteenth-Century Japan* (Honolulu: University of Hawai'i Press, 2004), 153–54, 189. Kasai Zenzō, a notable writer of autobiographical fiction, also practiced sitting in meditation at Engakuji in 1910. For him, the goal of literary art was to create a world of religion and faith. See Nishida Masayoshi, *Mujōkan no denshō* (Tokyo: Ōfūsha, 1976), 442–43.

22. Ama Toshimaro, "The Eyes of Pure Objectiveness: Natsume Sōseki's Search for the Way," trans. Michihiro Ama, *Eastern Buddhist*, n.s., 38, no. 1/2 (2007): 124–25.

23. Ara, *Sōseki kenkyū nenpyō*, 158–59.

24. *SZ*, 16:269, quoted and translated in Ama Toshimaro, "Eyes of Pure Objectiveness," 125–26.

25. *Omoidasu koto nado*, *SZ*, 8:312; author's translation.

26. For a definition of the *shōhin* category, see Marcus, *Reflections*, 9, 209.

27. Sōseki writes, "I did not even feel I was awaking from sleep. Nor did I feel I was emerging from darkness into light. I simply could not think. It felt like going to and returning from a mysterious world which can only be hinted at by expressions such as 'the faint fluttering of an insect,' 'a receding sound in the distance,' 'shadows of a fading memory,' and 'reminiscences of the past.' My chest felt heavy so I tried rolling my head to my right. That was when I saw red blood at the bottom of a bucket. Neither time nor space existed for the thirty minutes during which I was dead. How trivial death is, I thought while listening to my wife's explanation of what had happened. I then suddenly sensed the shining differences between life and death—that there is no negotiating between them. Why am I so dominated by these two aspects of my one

being? Although there might be some relationship between life and death—and I was unsure of what that might be—when I considered crossing the intersection between life and death, I became speechless and in a haze. Life and death is a set phrase that we use daily. It expresses contrast such as fast and slow, small and large, and hot and cold. Contemporary psychologists say that life and death are part of such a category of contrasts. But if the two completely different phases of life and death capture me one after other, how can I compare them on the same level?" *Omoidasu koto nado*, *SZ*, 8:313–14; author's translation.

28. *Omoidasu koto nado*, *SZ*, 8:320.

29. *Omoidasu koto nado*, *SZ*, 8:320; author's translation. Maria Flutsch translates it as follows: "I have died once. I have experienced that reality with my ordinary imagination." *Recollections* (London: Sōseki Museum in London, 2009), 63. In the source language, it reads *yowa ichido shinda. sōshite shinda jijitsu o heizeikarano sōzō tōrini keikenshita.* 余は一度死んだ。そうして死んだ事実を平生からの想像通りに経験した。

30. Maria Flutsch, "Time, Death and the Empire: Natsume Sōseki's *Omoidasu koto nado (Remembrances)*," *Japanese Studies* 23, no. 3 (2003): 241.

31. *Omoidasu koto nado*, *SZ*, 8:291; author's translation.

32. *Omoidasu koto nado*, *SZ*, 8:325–26; author's translation.

33. Maria Flutsch analyzes "Recollections" in terms of Sōseki's experience of nature, time, and death, and considers the text to be a "powerful critique of the dominant political discourses of his day." "Time, Death and the Empire," 239. According to Flutsch, Sōseki initiated "intense activism" after the publication of "Recollections." He criticized the policies of the Ministry of Education and the government suppression of academic freedom. Flutsch, 249.

34. Mark Johnston, *Surviving Death* (Princeton, NJ: Princeton University Press, 2010), 14.

35. Johnston, 14.

36. "A letter addressed to Hayashihara Kōzō, dated November 14, 1914," *SZ*, 15:414–15, quoted and translated in Mizukawa, "Natsume Sōseki and Shin Buddhism," 168–69. The translation is slightly changed. Sōseki's remarks of death in later life also include the following: (1) "I haven't considered life after death very carefully. However, although my body will probably disappear because of the nature of things, I don't want to believe that the spiritual side of me will disappear with it. Having said that, I can't accept the idea that my spirit hovers around in space, as those who study psychic phenomena seem to believe. At any rate, I feel that from the moment of my death, everything about me will no longer exist." Quoted in Imamura Hitoshi, *Shinran to gakuteki seishin* (Tokyo: Iwanami Shoten, 2010), 240; author's translation. (2) "Consciousness is not everything [that exists]. Even after the termination of consciousness, I will still exist. There is eternal life to my spirit. Death is the termination of consciousness and it is the auspicious state where my spirit finally goes into the absolute realm." Quoted in Ama Toshimaro, *Shūkyō no shinsō: Seinaru mono eno shōdō* (Tokyo: Chikuma Shobō, 1995), 214; author's translation. (3) "I feel that what is

called death is sweeter than life, and the thought strikes me that it is the highest state to which a man can aspire." Natsume Sōseki, *Inside My Glass Doors*, trans. Sammy Tsunematsu (Rutland, VT: Tuttle, 2002), 22–23. (4) "I am not saying we do not die. Everyone says we must eventually do so. Further, spiritualists and Maeterlinck say they do not consider individualism or individuals to continue after death. All I would like to state is that only after death do we enter the absolute realm, and when comparing the absolute world with the relative world, I sense something sacred . . ." Quoted and translated in Mizukawa, "Natsume Sōseki and Shin Buddhism," 169–70.

37. Ueda Shizuteru, "Sōseki and Buddhism: Reflections on His Later Works, part 1," trans. Jan Van Bragt, *Eastern Buddhist*, n.s., 29, no. 2 (1996): 195.

38. Ienaga, *Nihon shisōshi*, 325–29.

39. Ama Toshimaro, "Eyes of Pure Objectiveness," 136.

40. "Tomizawa Keidō ate shokan," *SZ*, 15:604–5, quoted and translated in Ama Toshimaro, 136.

41. "Tentōroku," *SZ*, 11:469, quoted and translated in Ama Toshimaro, 136–37. In Japanese, Sōseki says "*Zhaozhou no hisomi ni narau.*" The expression "*hisomi ni narau*" derives from *Zhuangzi*. Also, according to Matsuoka Yuzuru, when a student asked him about the implication of Buddhist enlightenment (*satori*), Sōseki was said to reply, "*Satori* probably refers to the capacity to freely control one's instincts while following them. In order to gain this, training (*shugyō*) is needed. Although this looks rather evasive at first, I think that the effect brought about by this will demonstrate the best way of living nobly." Matsuoka Yuzuru, *Ahh, Sōseki sanbō* (Tokyo: Asahi Shinbunsha, 1967), 150; quoted and translated in Ama Toshimaro, 134.

42. According to Kitayama Masamichi, Sōseki valued Zen because it helped him define a sense of selfhood in modern Japan in relation to the formation of the modern ego through which one has to deal with various problems of Meiji Japan. See "Sōseki to Zen," *Daijōzen* 46, no. 11 (1996): 16, quoted in Ama Toshimaro, *Shūkyō no shinsō*, 202.

43. Ienaga, *Nihon shisōshi*, 325–29; Ueda Shizuteru, "Sōseki and Buddhism: Reflections on His Later Works, part 2," trans. Jan Van Bragt, *Eastern Buddhist*, n.s., 30, no. 1 (1997): 41–42.

44. Imanishi Jun'kichi, "Sōseki to Bukkyō," in Kobayashi Takasuke et al., *Gendai shisō*, 224.

45. Mizukawa, "Natsume Sōseki and Shin Buddhism," 162–63.

46. Mizukawa points out that among the lecturers whom Sōseki recommended to the president of the South Manchuria Railway Company, Nanjō Bun'yū, then dean of Shinshū University, was found along with Shaku Sōen, under whom Sōseki had sat in Zen meditation (162).

47. "Nikki oyobi dampen," *SZ*, 13:772, quoted and translated in Mizukawa, 172.

48. Sōseki was believed to have said, "We, as rational beings, cannot think of God that is transcendent, and we do not need it if we examine ourselves immanently. However, if one wishes to identify the absolute value of awakening or the ultimate experience of having spiritual enlightenment as God or Buddha, that will be fine."

Matsuoka Yuzuru, *Ahh Sōseki sanbō*, 147–48, quoted and translated in Ama, "Eyes of Pure Objectiveness," 139.

49. Ketelaar, *Of Heretics and Martyrs*, 182.

50. According to Ōkouchi Shōji, Katai first wrote about insecure romantic relationships as depicted in *The Quilt*, and then treated the same theme while expressing Mahayana Buddhist soteriology as seen in *Remaining Snow*. Ōkouchi finds Pure Land Buddhist elements in Katai's later novels, such as *Time Goes By* (*Tokiwa sugiyuku*, 1916) and *One Hundred Nights* (*Momoyo*, 1927), and considers them to be Katai's effort to overcome "Oriental nihilism." "Kindai bungaku to bukkyō," in "Tokushū: Kin gendai sakka to bukkyō bungaku," special issue, *Kokubungaku: Kaishaku to kanshō* 55, no. 12 (December, 1990): 30. Through a chronological study of Katai's life and works, Kobayashi Ichirō demonstrates that later in life Katai became interested in Buddhism, attempted to reconnect self and others, and expressed a sense of impermanence and the sorrow of aging in his historical novels. *Shizenshugi sakka Tayama Katai, Nihon no sakka*, vol. 43 (Tokyo: Shintensha, 1982), 194–97, 247–48. Kenneth Henshall holds a similar view: Katai contemplated man's relationship with nature; studied the works of Joris-Karl Huysmans, who had come to value religious meditation after moving away from Zola's group; and adopted a "theological approach" with the help of a Buddhist priest who was Katai's brother-in-law. *The Quilt and Other Stories by Tayama Katai* (Tokyo: Tokyo University Press, 1981), 30. These studies are meticulous and detailed, and tend to categorize Katai's fiction based on the trajectory of the naturalist movement. These critics recognize Katai's Buddhist connection only in his later works.

51. *Hometown* (*Furusato*, 1899), an autobiographical work, offers a detailed account of the poverty and hardship Katai experienced during his childhood without a father. See Tayama Katai, "Furusato," *Teihon Katai Zenshū* (Kyoto: Rinsen Shoten, 1993–1995), 14:3–118 (hereafter cited as *TKZ*).

52. Kobayashi Ichirō, *Shizenshugi sakka Tayama Katai*, 5, 12–13, 25–39; Miyauchi Shunsuke, *Tayama Katai ronkō* (Tokyo: Sōbunsha, 2003), 44.

53. Katai began writing fiction without a personal style. In 1889, Katai created his first work, *An Autumn Evening* (*Aki no yūbe*), a "tragic love story," Hijiya-Kirschnereit, *Rituals of Self-Revelation*, 32. In 1891, Katai visited Ozaki Kōyō (1867–1903) and joined his literary group, Ken'yūsha. Through Kōyō, Katai met Emi Suiin (1869–1934), who helped him publish a short story titled *The Melon Field* (*Uribatake*, 1891), which was written in a style similar to Ihara Saikaku's style. In the following year, Katai wrote *Autumn in the Temple* (*Tera no aki*, 1892), a work seemingly influenced by Kōda Rohan's *The Elegant Buddha* (*Fūryūbutsu*, 1889). These works suggest the lack of originality in Katai's earlier work. Kobayashi Ichirō, *Shizenshugi sakka Tayama Katai*, 39–44. Like his contemporary writers, Katai was shocked by the suicide of Kitamura Tōkoku (1868–1894)—a leader of the romantic movement—and was influenced by the works of Kunikida Doppo (1871–1908), who shifted his emphasis from *shintaishi* poetry, new style poetry, to prose while exploring descriptions of nature. Hijiya-Kirschnereit, *Rituals of Self-Revelation*, 33.

54. Miyauchi, *Tayama Katai ronkō*, 46–47.

55. Hijiya-Kirschnereit, *Rituals of Self-Revelation*, 21–29.

56. The assessment of Katai's adoption of naturalism from Western literature varies. According to Hijiya-Kirschnereit, Katai's choice of European naturalist principles represents an "unconscious process" by which he attempted to revitalize the collective identity of Japanese literati vis-à-vis nature and objectivity. Hijiya-Kirschnereit, 39. Indra Levy, however, holds a different view: Katai's adoption of naturalism demonstrates a strategic effort to differentiate himself from the literary circles of Japan, which had rejected him, and to show his ability to discover the universal truth in Western naturalist literature to his contemporary writers. Katai, therefore, did not simply aim to recover the traditional notion of the unity between subject and object, which had been implied by the word *shizen*, by introducing Western naturalism to the Japanese literary establishment and linking it to *shizen*. *Sirens of the Western Shore: The Westernesque Femme Fatale, Translation, and Vernacular Style in Modern Japanese Literature* (New York: Columbia University Press, 2010), 114–16. According to Edward Fowler, "Naturalism taught Katai only what he wanted to hear." It advised him to record "the truth" and ignore narrative contrivance. Katai valued "unmediated presentation over mediated representation" and considered the former act to be a faithful description of the writer's own experience. Writing, therefore, became "an experiment in self-portraiture, and the author became his own hero." *Rhetoric of Confession*, 108.

57. Tomi Suzuki, *Narrating the Self*, 92. For a discussion of literary criticism between naturalists and Shirakaba writers, see, for instance, Maya Mortimer, *Meeting the Sensei: The Role of the Master in Shirakaba Writers* (Leiden: Brill, 2000), 105–6, and J. Thomas Rimer, "Kurata Hyakuzō and *The Origins of Love and Understanding*," in *Culture and Identity: Japanese Intellectuals during the Interwar Years*, ed. J. Thomas Rimer (Princeton, NJ: Princeton University Press, 1990), 30.

58. Other events that had negative impacts on Katai's life include the following: Katai dissociated from the journal *Bunshō Sekai*, which had published naturalist writings; the journal *Shinchō* gossiped about Katai's private life; Shimazaki Tōson's departure to France dispirited Katai; and the High Treason Incident of 1910 caused him to rethink the direction of his work. See Kobayashi Ichirō, *Shizenshugi sakka Tayama Katai*, 169–72, 174, 176.

59. For a discussion of Huysmans's efforts to evaluate the religious culture of France during the Middle Ages, see Elizabeth Emery, "J.-K. Huysmans, Medievalist," *Modern Language Studies* 30, no. 2 (2000): 119–31.

60. Summaries of these sutras are taken from Hanayama Shōyū, ed., *An Introduction to the Buddhist Canon* (Tokyo: Bukkyō Dendō Kyōkai, 1984), 36, 46, 74. For a translation of the *Avataṃsaka Sutra*, see Thomas Cleary, trans., *The Flower Ornament Scripture: A Translation of the Avataṃsaka Sutra* (Boston: Shambhala, 1993); for a partial translation of the *Nirvana Sutra*, see Mark Blum, trans., *The Nirvana Sutra*, vol. 1 (Berkeley, CA: Bukkyō Dendō Kyōkai America, 2013); and for a translation of the *Laṅkāvatāra Sutra*, see Daisetsu Teitarō Suzuki, trans., *The Laṅkāvatāra Sutra:*

An Epitomized Version (Rhinebeck, NY: Monkfish, 2014), or Bill Porter, trans., *The Laṅkāvatāra Sutra: Translation and Commentary* (Berkeley, CA: Counterpoint, 2013).

61. Kobayashi Ichirō, *Shizenshugi sakka Tayama Katai*, 176–81, 184, 189, 203–4. In March 1916, Katai published a short essay titled "The Unity of a Self and Other" (*jita no yūgō*) to discuss his realization of himself being part of others.

62. Katai's travel passion reflects a literary tradition of Japan. Poets, such as Saigyō and Bashō, often traveled. Medieval travel literature and traditional Japanese diaries include many poems.

63. Kenneth G. Henshall, *In Search of Nature: The Japanese Writer Tayama Katai (1872–1930)* (Leiden: Global Oriental, 2012), 192.

64. Katai discusses his realization of the working of time in *Time Goes By* (*Toki wa sugiyuku*, 1916).

65. Henshall, *In Search of Nature*, 207–8.

66. "Jita no yūgō," *TKZ*, 26:612–13; author's translation

67. "Naturalism kara Buddhism e," *TKZ*, 26:619–20.

68. "Naturalism kara Buddhism e," *TKZ*, 26:620–21. Katai might have supported a worldview held by the medieval Japanese, who had considered the problem of love affairs to be "unwholesome karma being carried over from their previous lives, and therefore, nothing can be done about the love." Muramatsu Takeshi, *Shi no nihon bungakushi* (Tokyo: Shinchōsha, 1975), 135; author's translation.

69. "Naturalism kara Buddhism e," *TKZ*, 26:622–23; author's translation.

70. "Naturalism kara Buddhism e," *TKZ*, 26:623–24; author's translation.

71. "Shōsetsu shinron," *TKZ*, 15:190–93, 197–98.

72. The notion and practice of *shikan* (C. *zhiguan*) is discussed by Zhiyi, the founder of Chinese Tiantai Buddhism in *Mohe zhiguan*. See, for instance, Paul L. Swanson, *Foundations of T'ien-T'ai Philosophy: The Flowering of the Two Truths Theory in Chinese Buddhism* (Berkeley, CA: Asian Humanities Press, 1989), 117–20.

73. "Shōsetsu shinron," *TKZ*, 15:201–2.

74. "Shōsetsu shinron," *TKZ*, 15:218; author's translation.

75. "Hōjōki ni arawaretaru genpei no seisui," *TKZ*, 15:297–303; "Ura no shiokai ni miidashitaru shizen," *TKZ*, 15:304–11.

76. Hijiya-Kirschnereit, *Rituals of Self-Revelation*, 39.

77. Henshall, *In Search of Nature*, 213.

78. Kobayashi Ichirō, *Shizenshugi sakka Tayama Katai*, 278. Katai's posthumous Dharma name is *Kōjuin seiyo zansetsu katai koji*.

79. Kōno Toshirō, "Shiga Naoya nenpu," in *Gunzō, Nihon no sakka vol. 9: Shiga Naoya*, ed. Sasaki Yukitsuna (Tokyo: Shōgakkan, 1991), 335.

80. Shiga remained in Uchimura Kanzō's non-denominational Christian group largely because of Uchimura's personality. Unlike other Christian ministers who exaggerated their beliefs just to win adherents, Shiga had found Uchimura's faith sincere. William Sibley, *The Shiga Hero* (Chicago: University of Chicago Press, 1979), 28. Shiga could not accept Christianity partly because of Uchimura's definition of sexual

misconduct: for a married man, having sex with his wife was acceptable, but for a single man, any kind of sexual behavior, including sleeping with his fiancée, was unacceptable. *Shiga Naoya Zenshū* (Tokyo: Iwanami Shoten, 1998–2001), 7:301–2 (hereafter cited as *SNZ*). According to Honda Shūgo, Shiga misunderstood Uchimura, who was seemingly urging the audience to refrain from fornication. *Shiga Naoya* (Tokyo: Iwanami Shinsho, 1990), 1:15–16, 55. Shiga maintained a close relationship with Uchimura even after he left the group.

81. "Sofu, 1956," *SNZ*, 4:598–99; "Zuihitsu Sofu, 1955," *SNZ*, 8:449. In a short autobiographical story titled "A Certain Man and the Death of His Sister" (*Aru otoko, sono ane no shi*), Shiga describes how seriously his grandfather studied Buddhism. For instance, he would get up at two or three o'clock in the morning, read Buddhist texts until dawn, and practice Buddhist calligraphy.

82. Diary dated April 5, 1904, *SNZ*, 10:63; author's translation.

83. "Yanagi no mingei undō, 1960" and "Mingei zukan ni yosete, 1960," *SNZ*, 8:293–94.

84. "Nentō shokan, 1952," *SNZ*, 7:474; author's translation.

85. "Kanjin Mōgo, 1950," *SNZ*, 7:461–62. Translated by Francis Mathy, *Shiga Naoya* (New York: Twayne, 1974), 144.

86. Mathy, *Shiga Naoya*, 95.

87. For discussions of "Confused Head" and "Han's Crime," see Mathy, 49–51, 127–30, and Sibley, *The Shiga Hero*, 52–55, 63–66.

88. Sibley, 33.

89. "Sōsaku yodan, 1928," *SNZ*, 8:5–6. "Wonder" (*fushigi*) is another term Shiga employed to describe inconceivable events. In "Kuma" (1939), when riding on a bus with his children, the narrator by chance sees a dog that strayed from his place a week earlier. With the help of others, he is able to catch it, but he cannot think of this incident as mere chance. Further, Shiga often admitted to the power of revelation, as he was able to predict an immediate future event, for instance, by means of dreams. Shiga was irrational in these aspects, but he simply trusted man's supernatural potentiality and separated the power of vision from superstition. "Zoku zoku sōsaku yodan, 1955," *SNZ*, 8:36–37. Aeba Takao analyzes the connection between dreams, consciousness, and nature in Shiga's work. For Shiga, dreams represent liberation, honesty, and even fear—as his dreams were often connected to crime. There is, however, an organic aspect to dreams, which reconnects nature and human beings, once divided by consciousness. Aided by artistic imagination, dreams can bring consciousness to the state of unity. "Shiga Naoya ron: Sono shizen to yume," *Bungakukai* 29, no. 8 (1975), 160.

90. Makoto Ueda, *Modern Japanese Writers and the Nature of Literature* (Stanford, CA: Stanford University Press, 1976), 88.

91. Sibley, *The Shiga Hero*, 8.

92. There were many causes for the confrontations between Shiga and his father. Because Shiga was born into an upper-class family, he was able to pursue a literary

career, of which his father disapproved, without struggling to make ends meet. Other elements of confrontation include "Naoya's protest over the pollution caused by a copper mine his family was associated with; his affair with one of the family maids and his determination to marry her; and finally his marriage in 1914 without his father's consent to a cousin of Mushanokōji." Roy Starrs, *An Artless Art: The Zen Aesthetic of Shiga Naoya* (New York: Routledge, 1998), 13. For a discussion of *Reconciliation*, see Tomi Suzuki, *Narrating the Self*, 113–23.

93. Honda Shūgo, *Shiga Naoya*, 1:193.

94. "Tokitō Nobuyuki, 1914," (*An'ya kōro sōko*, 23) *SNZ*, 6:327–28. Quoted by Honda Shūgo, *Shiga Naoya*, 1:189; author's translation.

95. English title, *Ten Abiding Stages of the Mind According to the Secret Maṇḍala*, from Ryūichi Abé, *The Weaving of Mantra: Kūkai and the Construction of Esoteric Buddhist Discourse* (New York: Columbia University Press, 1999), 14.

96. Ueda Shizuteru and Yanagida Seizan, *Jūgyūzu: Jiko no genshōgaku* (Tokyo: Chikuma Shobō, 1982), 4, 177. For an explanation of *The Ten Oxherding Pictures* in English, see, for instance, Yamada Mumon, *Lectures on the Ten Oxherding Pictures*, trans. Victor Sōgen Hori (Honolulu: University of Hawai'i Press, 2004).

97. Nanyan Guo, *Refining Nature in Modern Japanese Literature: The Life and Art of Shiga Naoya* (Lanham, MD: Lexington Books, 2014), 48.

98. Quoted and translated in Mathy, *Shiga Naoya*, 162.

99. "Zauhō Jō, 1926," *SNZ*, 7:72; "Watashi to Tōyō bijutsu, 1952," *SNZ*, 7:85. Shiga's viewing of Western arts represents the Shirakaba group's practice. According to Maya Mortimer, "the Shirakaba group looked to Western literature as an alternative to the bleak atmosphere at home. This escapist tendency shifted from literature to art immediately after Kōtoku's arrest [a.k.a., *Taigyaku jiken*, the High Treason Incident of 1910]. Art seemed even more impregnable than literature against depressing times and in fact, it proved to be a wise move." *Meeting the Sensei*, 64.

100. Rubinstein, *Religion and the Muse*, 142.

101. Rubinstein, 143.

102. Rubinstein, 145.

103. "Idol toshiteno geijutsu, 1908" (unpublished essay), *SNZ*, 9:266–67.

104. Guo, *Refining Nature*, 46–47.

105. Guo, 48.

106. "Geijutsuka bayari, 1958," *SNZ*, 8:459.

107. Quoted and translated in Makoto Ueda, *Modern Japanese Writers*, 89.

108. "Waga seikatsu shinjō, 1949," *SNZ*, 7:424–25; author's translation.

109. Saburō Morishita, "Good Works and the Question of Self-Presentation in Tenrikyō," *Nova Religio: The Journal of Alternative and Emergent Religions* 9, no. 2 (2005): 35.

110. Helen Hardacre, *Shintō and the State, 1868–1988* (Princeton, NJ: Princeton University Press, 1989), 71.

111. "Tenrikyō kikan zasshi e no henji, 1937," *SNZ*, 8:383–84; author's translation.
112. "Inamura zatsudan, 1948," *SNZ*, 8:84–85. Note that Shiga grew up in a family which denied fortune-telling but valued Confucian ethics. "Waga seikatsu shinjō, 1949," *SNZ*, 7:419–20.
113. "Kanjin mōgo, 1950," *SNZ*, 7:457–58.
114. "Shinpenki, 1937," *SNZ*, 7:49.
115. "Izumi," *TKZ*, 15:416–17.

Chapter 3

1. "Mohō to Dokuritsu," *SZ*, 16:420; author's translation.
2. Translated in Ueda Shizuteru, "Sōseki and Buddhism, part 1," 184.
3. Translated in Janine Beichman, *Masaoka Shiki: His Life and Works* (Boston: Cheng & Tsui, 2002), 110.
4. Beichman, 54, 108–9.
5. Ōno Akihiko, *Natsume Sōseki to Suzuki Daisetsu: Text kōironteki kōsatsu* (Tokyo: Surugadai Shuppansha, 2014), 22.
6. Odin, *Artistic Detachment*, 16–17.
7. Odin, 20.
8. Thomas Cleary, trans., *Rational Zen: The Mind of Dōgen Zenji* (Boston: Shambhala, 1995), 45–46.
9. Odin, *Artistic Detachment*, 19–21.
10. Odin, 243–44.
11. Masao Abe and Christopher Ives, trans., *An Inquiry into the Good* (New Haven, CT: Yale University Press, 1990), 3.
12. Abe and Ives, *An Inquiry into the Good*, 39.
13. Nishida Kitarō, "Ippansha no jikakuteki taikei," *Nishida Kitarō Zenshū* (Tokyo: Iwanami Shoten, 1965), 5:182; author's translation.
14. *Suzuki Daisetsu Zenshū* (Tokyo: Iwanami Shoten, 1968), 5:15–16, quoted in Suemura Masayo, "Suzuki Daisetsu ni okeru nyo no rikai: Zen to shinshū," *Hikaku shisō kenkyū* 38 (2011): 26.
15. Sharf, "Buddhist Modernism," 231, 243, 246. For a critique of Zen interpreted by Nishida and Suzuki, see Bernard Faure, *Chan Insights and Oversights: An Epistemological Critique of the Chan Tradition* (Princeton, NJ: Princeton University Press, 1993), 52–88.
16. Ogihara Keiko, "Natsume Sōseki to Nishida Kitarō ni okeru tōyō to seiyō: 'Kōjin' to 'Zen no kenkyū,'" *Kyūshū joshi daigaku kiyō* 43, no. 1 (2006): 65, 68–69. Also, for a discussion of James's influence on Sōseki and Nishida, see Kazashi Nobuo, "James kara Sōseki to Nishida e: En'un no genshōgaku, futatsu no Metamorphoses," *Tetsugaku* 48 (1997): 82–96.
17. Abe and Ives, *An Inquiry into the Good*, 77.

18. Beongcheon Yu trans., *The Wayfarer* (New York: Perigee Books, 1982), 292. Yuha Paku also discusses Sōseki's great interest in Numanami Takeo's book titled *Hajimete kakushin shietaru zenjitsuzai*, which was influenced by Nishida's idea of pure experience. Yuha Paku, "Nihon kindai bungaku to nashonaru aidentiti" (PhD diss., Waseda University, 2003), 180.

19. Yu, *Wayfarer*, 313.

20. "Nikki oyobi dampen," *SZ*, 13:774, quoted and translated in Ama Toshimaro, "Eyes of Pure Objectiveness," 132.

21. Robert E. Carter, *The Kyoto School: An Introduction* (Albany: State University of New York Press, 2013), 45. See also Suzuki Daisetsu, "Bukkyō no taii," *Suzuki Daisetsu Zenshū*, 7:32.

22. Kumakura Chiyuki, *Sōseki no henshin* (Tokyo: Chikuma Shobō, 2009), 183, 190.

23. Quoted in Komiya Toyotaka, "Kaisetsu," *SZ*, 6:610–11.

24. One day Kenzō thinks about himself very hard and hears a voice saying, "And what do you suppose you were really meant to do with your life? . . . I think you know. You know very well where you ought to be going—but you can't get there, can you? You're stuck." Edwin McClellan, trans., *Grass on the Wayside* (Rutland, VT: Tuttle, 1971), 158.

25. The word *tonjaku* in *Grass on the Wayside* appears in *SZ*, 6:295, 327, 329, 356, 379, 405, 419, 439, 482, 491, 508 (it actually appears twice on page 508). The difference between *tonjaku* and *tonchaku* is mentioned in Hōsō yōgo iinkai, ed., "Kotoba no yomi ni tsuite: 'NHK nihongo hatsuon akusento jiten kaitei ni atatte,'" *Hōsō kenkyū to kadai* (October 2013): 86–87. Japanese scholars such as Kyōgoku Kōichi and Satō Eisaku analyzed Sōseki's use of *rubi*, Japanese pronunciations of kanji characters. See Kyōgoku Kōichi, "Sōseki no jion kana zukai," in *Kindai nihongo no kenkyū: Hyōki to hyōgen* (N.p.: Tōensha, 1998). According to Satō, Sōseki was both intentional and unintentional in his use of *rubi*. Concerning *Grass on the Wayside*, Sōseki was disappointed by the printing company, which often misplaced *rubi*. See Satō Eisaku, "Sōseki jihitsu genkō no rubi saikō: *Michikusa* no rubi kara," *Ronshū* 7 (2011): 1–24.

26. McClellan, *Grass on the Wayside*, 28. English translations of *mutonjaku* or *tonjaku shinai* do not always convey the nuances of the state of being unconcerned. See, for instance, "Shimada seemed *unaware* of his host's bewilderment." McClellan, 74 (emphasis added).

27. According to the author's search for the kanji compound 頓着 through a web search engine called Aozora Search, Sōseki constantly gave kana syllables *tonjaku* to 頓着 in his works, which are found in Aozora Bunko, a Japanese digital library. This may indicate his habitual reading of 頓着. Other writers, such as Kunikida Doppo, Shimazaki Tōson, and Terada Torahiko, gave both readings, *tonjaku* and *tonchaku*, to 頓着 in their works. This suggests that they did not care about the reading of that kanji compound or that editors of their works randomly made *rubi* without thinking about the implications of the traditional kana reading, *tonjaku*.

28. Bessel A. van der Kolk and Onno van der Hart, "Pierre Janet and the Breakdown of Adaptation in Psychological Trauma," *American Journal of Psychiatry* (December, 1989): 1534.

29. Van der Kolk and Van der Hart, 1531–32; Bruce M. Ross, *Remembering the Personal Past: Descriptions of Autobiographical Memory* (New York: Oxford University Press, 1991), 147–48. Recent clinical treatments of post-traumatic stress disorder (PTSD) experienced by combat veterans and those who were subjected to domestic violence have proven narrative action to be effective in reintegrating patients to society. Judith Herman proposes a three-stage recovery: "establishment of safety," "remembrance and mourning," and "reconnection with ordinary life." *Trauma and Recovery: The Aftermath of Violence—from Domestic Abuse to Political Terror* (New York: Basic Books, 1997), 155. Herman finds the second phase, in particular, crucial for survivors. Recalling and verbalizing traumatic events is difficult, because survivors disrupt clinical treatment and conceal unbearable facts, alter their consciousness, or forget a story they have just written. They must, however, narrate their emotional responses each time; otherwise, telling a story is considered to be incomplete (177–78).

30. McClellan, *Grass on the Wayside*, 156.
31. McClellan, 62.
32. McClellan, 25–26.
33. McClellan, 69–71.
34. McClellan, 78, 102, 145.
35. McClellan, 108–9.
36. McClellan, 114–15.
37. Herman, *Trauma and Recovery*, 155.
38. McClellan, *Grass on the Wayside*, 158.
39. The phrase "*kanshaku o norikoeta hito*" is translated as "people who accepted the fact of their own naïveté or credulousness" (McClellan, 126), but this translation is inaccurate.
40. McClellan, 91.
41. McClellan, 169.
42. Francis Mathy, trans., *The Gate* (London: Peter Owen, 2006), 213.
43. Ueda Shizuteru, "Sōseki and Buddhism, part 1," 189.
44. McClellan, *Grass on the Wayside*, 34.
45. Ueda Shizuteru, "Sōseki and Buddhism, part 2," 32.
46. Ueda Shizuteru, "Sōseki and Buddhism, part 1," 195. Further, Ueda observes that in *Light and Darkness* Sōseki advanced the technique of writing that he gained by writing *Grass on the Wayside*. Ueda states that "it [*Light and Darkness*] goes on to depict the situation of the human interface as an impenetrable, complicated, opaque, and formless three dimensional but fluid body, wherein an indefinite number of 'self' and 'self' come into contact, bump into one another, and overlap in an everchanging mosaic of partnerships. And even a single 'self' and 'self' does not innerly constitute a true reciprocity: from both sides it is lived as a 'self and other,' and thereby the

unpredictability of the 'other' throws the relationship into disorder time after time." "Sōseki and Buddhism, part 2," 48–49.

47. "Shōsetsu to sahō," *TKZ*, 26:225; author's translation. Shimamura Hōgetsu, an advocate of naturalism, states, "Reality as it is (*aruga mama no genjitsu*) conveys the meaning of all existences, and is the world of [aesthetic] contemplation (*kanshō*). It suggests a life devoted to penetrating to the depths of all our senses. This state is called art." Quoted in Suzuki Sadami, *Nihon no bungaku o kangaeru*, 138; author's translation assisted by Ken'ichi Yokogawa.

48. Fowler, *Rhetoric of Confession*, xxvi.

49. Fowler, 41. For the "reportive" and "nonreportive" narrative styles, Fowler refers to the linguist S.-Y. Kuroda's definitions: "A narrative is reportive if related by a single-consciousness narrator who addresses a specific audience as if engaged in an act of communication; it is nonreportive if related by a multi-consciousness narrator whose utterances are not a part of actual linguistic performance" (30).

50. Fowler, 123.

51. Inagaki Tatsurō et al., eds. *Kindai bungaku hyōron takikei*, 10 vols. (Tokyo: Kadokawa Shoten, 1971–1975), 3:450, quoted and translated in Fowler, 123.

52. Shu Kuge, "Between Sight and Rhythm: Aspects of Modernity in Tayama Katai's 'Flat Depiction,'" in "Meiji Literature and the Artwork," ed. Miya Mizuta Lippit, special Issue, *Review of Japanese Culture and Society* 14 (December 2002): 26. Kuge further states, "The main goal of flat depiction is the acquisition of self-transparency through naturalization of writing. The irony is that Katai's exploration is indeed motivated by the fact that writing is essentially an 'unnatural' medium" (26).

53. Tomi Suzuki, *Narrating the Self*, 77.

54. Tomi Suzuki, 78–79.

55. Matthew Fraleigh, "Terms of Understanding: The Shōsetsu according to Tayama Katai," *Monumenta Nipponica* 58, no. 1 (2003): 70.

56. "Shukan kyakkan no ben," *TKZ*, 26:566–67.

57. David L. McMahan, *The Making of Buddhist Modernism* (New York: Oxford University, 2008), 78.

58. McMahan, 80.

59. "Tokyo no sanjūnen," *TKZ*, 15:547.

60. Kenneth G. Henshall, trans., *Literary Life in Tokyo 1885–1915: Tayama Katai's Memoirs* (Leiden: Brill, 1987), 101; "Tokyo no sanjūnen," *TKZ*, 26:523–24.

61. Judit Árokay, "Discourse on Poetic Language in Early Modern Japan and the Awareness of Linguistic Change," in *Divided Languages? Diglossia, Translation, and the Rise of Modernity in Japan, China, and the Slavic World*, ed. Judit Árokay, Jadranka Gvozdanovic, and Darja Miyajima (Cham, Switzerland: Springer, 2014), 95–96.

62. Quoted in Kobayashi Ichirō, *Shizenshugi sakka Tayama Katai*, 147; author's translation. Sōseki, at the same time, recognized *The Quilt* as "quite a bit of work." According to Tomi Suzuki, "Sōseki, whose criticism of Katai should not be reduced to an opposition between facts and fiction, regarded all literary works, including that

of the so-called Naturalists, to be fabrications and observed that the descriptions of ordinary 'ugly facts' that writers such as Katai value are not necessarily valuable unless the reader is blinded by the ideological aura that had come to be associated with those facts. Sōseki criticized Katai and others for coming to believe that the ordinary, ugly reality that their fiction represented was the only objective reality, thereby suggesting that Katai himself unknowingly transformed his productive reference into a reproductive reference." *Narrating the Self,* 90.

63. "Aruita michi ga kotonatte ita," *TKZ*, 26:614–16.

64. Ama Toshimaro, "Eyes of Pure Objectiveness," 132–33. Sōseki's *Meian* has been translated by both Valdo H. Viglielmo, *Light and Darkness* (VT: Tuttle, 1972), and John Nathan, *Light and Dark* (New York: Columbia University Press, 2014).

65. "Sakusha no shukan," TKZ, 26:561; "Shukan kyakkan no ben," *TKZ*, 26:567.

66. "Shōsetsu sahō," *TKZ*, 26:220, 287; "Hanarete mintosuru kokoro," *TKZ*, 26:607.

67. "Hanarete mintosuru kokoro," *TKZ*, 26:607; author's translation.

68. Oscar Benl, "Naturalism in Japanese Literature," *Monumenta Nipponica* 9, no. 1/2 (1953), 24.

69. Tayama Katai, "Zansetsu," *TKZ*, 10:176–84.

70. Tayama Katai, "Zansetsu," *TKZ*, 10:194.

71. For Nichiren, reciting the *daimoku* embodies the Buddha's awakening and the possibility of attaining Buddhahood. For a discussion of Nichiren, see Jacqueline Stone, *Original Enlightenment*, 68.

72. Tayama Katai, "Zansetsu," *TKZ*, 10:202.

73. Tayama Katai, "Zansetsu," *TKZ*, 10:278. In the source language, these passages read, "*gedatsu wa gedatsu de attewa naranai*" and "*godō wa godō de attewa naranai,*" respectively.

74. Tayama Katai, "Zansetsu," *TKZ*, 10:276.

75. Tayama Katai, "Zansetsu," *TKZ*, 10:283–84; author's translation.

76. Mitchell, *Buddhism*, 353.

77. Mitchell, 359.

78. "Chōhen shōsetsu no kenkyū," *TKZ*, 26:469; author's translation.

79. Nanyan Guo, *Refining Nature*, 13–14. Also see John Tucker, "Japanese Views of Nature and the Environment," in *Nature across Culture: Views of Nature and the Environment in Non-Western Culture*, ed. Helaine Selin (New York: Springer Netherland, 2013), 161–83.

80. Fabio Rambelli, *Buddhist Materiality: A Cultural History of Objects in Japanese Buddhism* (Stanford, CA: Stanford University Press, 2007), 129–39. Further research, however, is needed to clarify when and how the word *busshō* was translated into English as "Buddha nature."

81. Yanabu Akira also states that "*nature* belongs to the side of the object, in contradistinction to the side of the subject implied by artifice, but the inherited meaning of shizen belongs to a world in which subject and object are unified or have yet to

be distinguished, so as to erase the subject-object opposition." *Hon'yakugo seiritsu jijō* (Tokyo: Iwanami Shinsho, 1982), 133, quoted in Levy, *Sirens of the Western Shore*, 113. In medieval Japan, Buddhist priests used *jinen* in various ways. For instance, Saichō uses the term *jinen hongaku*, denoting ideas that "beings are inherently enlightened by nature" or "the defilements are expressions of original enlightenment just as they are" (Stone, *Original Enlightenment*, 68, 72). Dōgen writes, "[In *zazen*] body-mind are cast off naturally (*jinen*) and the original countenance (*honrai memmoku*) is realized." According to Steven Heine, "*Jinen* literally means 'in and of itself'; it can be used either in the philosophical sense of the unity and breadth of nature or in the ordinary sense of an automatic reaction." "Dōgen Cast off 'What': An Analysis of *Shinjin Datsuraku*," *Journal of the International Association of Buddhist Studies* 9, no. 1 (1986): 68n9. Shinran uses *jinen* as *jinen hōni* to explain the "spontaneous working of [Amida Buddha's] Vow" through which a person who entrusts himself to Amida's compassion attains birth in the Pure Land. Dennis Hirota et al., trans., *The Collected Works of Shinran* (Kyoto: Jōdo Shinshū Hongwanji-ha, 1997), 2:191. In "Loneliness and the Dharma Body" (*Kodoku to hosshin*, 1922), Katai states that "the term *hosshin* [usually translated as 'Dharma Body'] and the phrase 'life of a bystander' point to the same thing. Humans are individuals but at the same time are complete, and necessarily subject to the law [which also implies the Dharma]. This law is natural and the fundamental power of life. It is the pivot around which the universe revolves. Another way of referring to it is 'thus come' [Tathagata]." Quoted in Nishida, *Mujōkan no denshō*, 418; author's translation.

82. Mathy, *The Gate*, 6.
83. *Mon*, *SZ*, 4:626.
84. McClellan, *Grass on the Wayside*, 40.
85. *Michikusa*, *SZ*, 6:357.
86. Tayama Katai, "Zansetsu," *TKZ*, 10:117; author's translation.
87. "Sōsaku yodan," *SNZ*, 8:11; "Zoku Sōsaku yodan," *SNZ*, 8:27.
88. Guo, *Refining Nature*, 136. Also, for a discussion of the literary influence on Shiga, see Guo, 132–37.
89. "Rizumu," *SNZ*, 7:8; author's translation. Tomi Suzuki also translates this passage and discusses the implications of Shiga's spiritual rhythm: "[G]iven that Shiga's artistic ideal was the spiritual communion achieved through the work of art, it is clear that the notion of spiritual rhythm or spiritual resonance also implies an ideal reading mode in which the reader enters into a communion with the author's spirit. This particular view of the *shōsetsu* contributed to and became part of the larger I-novel discourse." *Narrating the Self*, 98–99.
90. "Rizumu," *SNZ*, 7:10.
91. Makoto Ueda, *Modern Japanese Writers*, 98.
92. Quoted in Makoto Ueda, 98.
93. Fowler, *Rhetoric of Confession*, 247.
94. Guo, *Refining Nature*, 6–7.
95. "Kinosaki nite," Kōki, *SNZ*, 2:646–74.

96. Lane Dunlop, trans., *The Paper Door and Other Stories by Shiga Naoya* (New York: Columbia University Press, 2001), 62–63.

97. Sibley, *The Shiga Hero*, 204. "Kinosaki nite" has been translated by both Sibley and Dunlop. Concerning the English translation of this passage, the author feels Sibley's translation is better because of Sibley's choice of the word "pathos."

98. Dunlop, *Paper Door*, 64.

99. Dunlop, 64.

100. "Kinosaki nite," *SNZ*, 2:180.

101. Dunlop, *Paper Door*, 62.

102. Scholars point out the lack of attention given to the redefining of Buddhist practice in modern Japan. According to Isomae Jun'ichi and Ōtani Eiichi, in modern Japan, Buddhism developed as a belief-centered religion, overshadowing the importance of various forms of practice, including ritual practice. See Isomae Jun'ichi, *Kindai nihon shūkyō gonsetsu to sono keifu: Shūkyō, kokka, Shinto* (Tokyo: Iwanami Shoten, 2003); Ōtani Eiichi, *Kindai bukkyō toiu shiza* (Tokyo: Pericansha, 2012). Jeff Humphries discusses the relationship between Buddhism and literature in terms of practice in *Reading Emptiness: Buddhism and Literature* (Albany: State University of New York Press, 1999).

103. Fowler, *Rhetoric of Confession*, 238.

104. See Shimizu Seiichirō, *Shōmatsu ari no mama no ki* (Kyoto: Nagata Bunshodō, 1923). For a discussion of Shōmatsu, see Okamura Yasuo, "Nan tomo nai, nan tomo nai: Myōkōnin, sanuki no Shōmatsu ni okeru shūkyōteki sei," *Yamaguchi daigaku tetsugaku kenkyū* 13 (2006): 1–22.

Chapter 4

1. Karatani, *Origins of Modern Japanese Literature*, 76, 83.

2. Karatani, 79.

3. Karatani, 85–86. For a discussion of the samurai who became Christians, see Irwin Scheiner, *Christian Converts and Social Protest in Meiji Japan* (Ann Arbor, MI: University of Michigan Press, 2002).

4. Karatani, *Origins of Modern Japanese Literature*, 88.

5. Karatani, 85–88.

6. For a discussion of the hidden Christians and the impact of Catholicism on modern Japan, see Kevin M. Doak, ed., *Xavier's Legacies: Catholicism in Modern Japanese Culture* (Vancouver: University of British Columbia Press, 2011).

7. Björn Krondorfer, *Male Confessions: Intimate Revelations and the Religious Imagination* (Stanford, CA: Stanford University Press, 2010), 3.

8. Krondorfer, 7.

9. Krondorfer, 7.

10. Shōjun Bandō and Harold Steward, trans., *Tannishō: Passages Deploring Deviations of Faith* (Berkeley, CA: Numata Center for Buddhist Translation and Research, 1996), 10.

11. Ueda Yoshifumi and Dennis Hirota, *Shinran: An Introduction to His Thought* (Kyoto: Hongwanji International Center, 1989), 144–46; Alfred Bloom, *Shinran's Gospel of Pure Grace* (Ann Arbor, MI: Association for Asian Studies, 1999), 30–31.

12. Hirota et al., *Collected Works of Shinran*, 1:455.

13. For a discussion of the Foucauldian interpretation of Buddhist confession and monastic disciplinary practice, see Malcom Voyce, "Buddhist Confession: A Foucauldian Approach," *Macquarie Law WP 2009-1* (March 2009): 1–50.

14. Christine Marran, "*Zange*: Buddhism, Gender and Meiji Literary Confession," *Working Words: New Approaches to Japanese Studies*, Center for Japanese Studies, UC Berkeley (2012), 1–4, http://escholarship.org/uc/item/7qg8j2kg.

15. James C. Dobbins, *Letters of the Nun Eshinni: Images of Pure Land Buddhism in Medieval Japan* (Honolulu: University of Hawai'i Press, 2004), 101. The *Nyobonge* verse is:

"If you the believer, because of the fruition of past *karma*, are driven to make love to a woman,
Then I shall take on the body of a beautiful woman to be ravished by you.
Throughout your entire life I shall adorn you well,
And at death I shall lead you to birth in the paradise" (quoted in Dobbins, 101).

16. Daisetz Teitarō Suzuki, trans., *Shinran's Kyōgyōshinshō: The Collection of Passages Expounding the True Teaching, Living, Faith, and Realizing of the Pure Land*, ed. Center for Shin Buddhist Studies (New York: Oxford University Press, 2012), 160.

17. Minor L. Rogers and Ann T. Rogers, *Rennyo: The Second Founder of Shin Buddhism* (Berkeley, CA: Asian Humanities Press, 1991), 226–27. Square brackets in the original. For a discussion of Rennyo in English, see Stanley Weinstein, "Continuity and Change in the Thought of Rennyo," in *Rennyo and the Roots of Modern Japanese Buddhism*, ed. Mark L. Blum and Shin'ya Yasutomi, 49–58 (New York: Oxford University Press, 2006).

18. Uranishi Tsutomu, "Shinshū dōjō ni okeru sange (*kokuhaku*) bungaku no hassei," *Bukkyō bungaku* 18 (1994): 86–89.

19. Marran, "*Zange*," 5. Marran discusses a link between *zange* narratives, originating from the Buddhist tradition, and modern "I" narratives of Japan, such as *shishōsetsu*.

20. There are other kanji compounds that are read differently by Buddhists and Christians. For instance, *raihai* is the traditional and Buddhist reading of 礼拝 (to worship or pray), whereas *reihai* is the popular and Christian reading of it.

21. In an essay entitled "Self-Comfort beyond Ethics" (*Rinri ijōno an i*, 1902), Kiyozawa wrote, "it was not coincidence that Shinran who expressed his religious faith said, 'For me, I do not know what is right and what is wrong' [*jiko no shinnen o hyōbyaku serareta Shinran shōnin no onkuchi kara Shinran ni oitewa zen'aku no futatsu*

sōjite motte zonchi sezarunari to ōseraretawa kesshite gūzen dewa arimasenu]." *Kiyozawa Manshi Zenshū* (Tokyo: Iwanami Shoten, 2002–2003), 6:122 (hereafter cited as *KMZ*). Andō Shūichi, another leading follower of Kiyozawa, wrote about him, "in the past, I confessed my religious faith to my teacher [*yo katsute sensei no mae ni jiko no shinnen o hyōbyakusu*]." *Kiyozawa sensei shinkō zadan* (Kyoto: Heirakuji Shoten, 1933), 93.

22. Kashiwahara Yūsen, "Kiyozawa Manshi," in *Shapers of Japanese Buddhism* (Tokyo: Kōsei, 1994), 231–34; Terakawa Shunshō, *Kiyozawa Manshi ron*, rev. ed. (Kyoto: Bun'eidō, 2002), 44–45, 67.

23. Edwin McClellan, trans., *Kokoro* (Mineola, NY: Dover, 2006), 138.

24. McClellan, 149.

25. McClellan, 166.

26. For a discussion of General Nogi's suicide and Sōseki's writing, see Doris G. Bargen, *Suicidal Honor: General Nogi and the Writings of Mori Ōgai and Natsume Sōseki* (Honolulu: University of Hawai'i Press, 2006).

27. Elizabetta Porcu summarizes the connection between K and Kiyozawa discussed by Japanese scholars. For instance, like K, at his father's suggestion, Kiyozawa initially studied medicine in order to become a doctor. He was also adopted into a Shin Buddhist temple family by marrying the daughter of a resident priest. *Pure Land Buddhism*, 107. According to Fujii Jun, Sōseki was interested in Kiyozawa's Buddhist reform movement. "Kindai nihon no hikari to kage: Natsume Sōseki to Kiyozawa Manshi," *Bungaku* 2, no. 2 (2001): 169–81. Also, see Fujii Jun, "Sōseki to Manshi: Sono shūhen ni tsuite," *Gendai to Shinran* 5 (2004): 2–23.

28. See Mark L. Blum, "Shin Buddhism in the Meiji Period," in *Cultivating Spirituality: A Modern Shin Buddhist Anthology*, ed. Mark L. Blum and Robert F. Rhodes (Albany: State University of New York Press, 2011), 3.

29. Hashimoto Mineo, "Two Models of the Modernization of Japanese Buddhism: Kiyozawa Manshi and D. T. Suzuki," trans. Tatsuo Murakami, *Eastern Buddhist*, n.s., 35, no. 1/2 (2003), 29–30.

30. Nobuo Haneda, trans., *December Fan: The Buddhist Essays of Manshi Kiyozawa* (Los Angeles, Shinshu Center of America, 2014), 15.

31. Yasutomi Shin'ya, "The Way of Introspection: Kiyozawa Manshi's Methodology," trans. Robert F. Rhodes, *Eastern Buddhist*, n.s., 35, no. 1/2 (2003), 102.

32. Hashimoto, "Two Models," 30.

33. Kiyozawa's philosophy was inclusive of all religions. He avoided participating in other Buddhist leaders' anti-Christianity campaigns during the Meiji period. Gilbert Johnston, "Kiyozawa Manshi's Buddhist Faith and Its Relation to Modern Japanese Society" (PhD dissertation, Harvard University, 1972), 7.

34. See Blum, "Shin Buddhism," 23.

35. Terakawa, *Kiyozawa Manshi ron*, 80–87. For an introduction to Kiyozawa's life in English, see, for instance, Alfred Bloom, "Kiyozawa Manshi and the Path to the Revitalization of Buddhism," *Pacific World*, 3rd ser., no. 5 (2003), 21–24; and Alfred

Bloom, "Kiyozawa Manshi and the Revitalization of Buddhism," *Eastern Buddhist*, n.s., 35, no. 1/2 (2003): 1–5.

36. Yamamoto Nobuhiro, *Seishin shugi wa dareno shisō ka* (Kyoto: Hōzōkan, 2011), 74.

37. Yamamoto, 76–80.

38. Mark L. Blum, trans., "The Nature of My Faith," in *Cultivating Spirituality: A Modern Shin Buddhist Anthology*, ed. Mark L. Blum and Robert F. Rhodes (Albany: State University of New York Press, 2011), 95. *Waga Shinnen* was also translated by Kunji Tajima and Floyd Shacklock, as well as by Nobuo Haneda. See Kunji Tajima and Floyd Shacklock, trans., "My Faith," in *Selected Essays of Manshi Kiyozawa* (Kyoto: Bukkyō Bunka Society, 1936), 73–78; Nobuo Haneda, trans., "My Religious Conviction," in *December Fan: The Buddhist Essays of Manshi Kiyozawa* (Los Angeles: Shinshu Center of America, 2014), 49–55.

39. Uchimura Kanzō said, "I don't believe that the Bible reveals the truth because it is said to be true. I believe that the Bible reveals the truth because it embodies the truth. I study the Bible and do not blindly accept what it says" (author's translation). Likewise, Kiyozawa came to believe in the Shin Buddhist teaching not because he was a Shin priest, but because he was able to establish his spiritual standpoint through Shinran's teaching. Fukushima Kazuto, *Kindai nihon no Shinran* (Kyoto: Hōzōkan, 1973), 17–18.

40. Kiyozawa, "Meiji sanjūgonen tōyō nikki shō," *KMZ*, 8:441, quoted in Terakawa, *Kiyozawa Manshi ron*, 148; author's translation.

41. Terakawa, 257.

42. Blum, "Nature of My Faith," 95. Square brackets in the original translation; emphasis on "for me" is added.

43. Terakawa, *Kiyozawa Manshi ron*, 256.

44. Bandō and Steward, *Tannishō*, 21.

45. Ikeda Eishun, "Kindaiteki kaimei shichō to bukkyō," in *Ronshū nihon bukkyōshi*, vol. 8, *Meiji jidai*, ed. Ikeda Eishun (Tokyo: Yūzankaku, 1987), 46–47. Kiyozawa's approach to Shin Buddhism needs to be understood in conjunction with Fukuda Gyōkai's efforts in modern times to restore the Buddhist practice of keeping the precepts.

46. Faure, *Chan Insights and Oversights*, 57.

47. In the *Seishinkai* journals, many essays include the word *kokuhaku* or *hyōbyaku* in their titles. Just to name a few, Akira, "Waga shinnen no kokuhaku" [Confession of my religious faith], *Seishinkai* 3, no. 4 (1903): 50; a serialization of Akegarasu's essays titled "Hyōbyaku" starting from *Seishinkai* 4, no. 1 (1904): 45–46; Sasaki Eiichi, "Shinkō no kokuhaku" [Confession of my faith], *Seishinkai* 9, no. 3 (1909): 59–61; Endō Tomohiro, "Kokuhaku," *Seishinkai* 10, no. 1 (1911): 47–49; Ikejima Masaharu, "Kokuhaku kyūsai gōhō" [Confessing my salvation and karmic punishment], *Seishinkai* 12, no. 6 (1912): 45–49; and Soga Ryōjin, "Kokuhaku," *Seishinkai* 16, no. 10 (1916): 1.

48. Kiyozawa wrote, "Nowadays, voices calling for religion are heard everywhere and the practice of religious confession prevails. All of them are, however, insignificant, but a person like Chikazumi has listened to those voices and he, himself, confesses his religious experience." Preface to Chikazumi Jōkan, *Shinkō no yoreki*, 14th ed. (Tokyo: Kyūdō Hakkōsho, 1921), 1–3; author's translation.

49. Because of the recent study initiated by Iwata Fumiaki and others, Chikazumi Jōkan's life and work have become known. Their archival research has demonstrated that Chikazumi was as influential as Uchimura Kanzō and Ebina Danjō. See Iwata Fumiaki, "Hajimeni," in *Kindaika no nakano dentō shūkyō to seishin undō: Kijunten toshiteno Chikazumi Jōkan kenkyū*, ed. Iwata Fumiaki (Tokyo: Heisei nijūnendo Heisei sanjūnendo kagaku kenkyūhi hojokin kenkyū hōkokusho, 2012), i; Iwata Fumiaki, "Miki Kiyoshi to Takeuchi Yoshinori," in Iwata, *Kindaika no nakano dentō shūkyō to seishin undō*, 25; Iwata Fumiaki, "Chikazumi Jōkan to Kamura Isota," in Iwata, *Kindaika no nakano dentō shūkyō to seishin undō*, 119. Fujimura Misao (1886–1903), who took his own life at the Kegon Falls in Nikkō, also attended Chikazumi's lectures at some point. See Nakajima Takeshi, "Fujimura Misao no fukakai," *Chikuma* 498 (September 2012): 18–21.

50. Ōmi Toshihiro, "Tetsugaku kara taiken e: Chikazumi Jōkan no shūkyō shisō," in Iwata, *Kindaika no nakano dentō shūkyō to seishin undō*, 9–10.

51. Yoshiya Abe, "Religious Freedom under the Meiji Constitution," *Contemporary Religions in Japan* 11, no. 1/2 (1970): 30.

52. Ōmi, "Tetsugaku kara taiken e," 9–10.

53. Ōmi, 14.

54. Ōmi, 15–18.

55. Ōmi, 18; author's translation.

56. Dennis A. Foster, *Confession and Complicity in Narrative* (Cambridge, UK: Cambridge University Press, 1987), 12.

57. Foster, 12–13.

58. Yamamoto, *Seishin shugi*, 166.

59. Nishida Masayoshi, *Mujōkan no denshō*, 468–70, 662.

60. For a discussion of Akegarasu's influence on popular writers, see Miyamoto Matahisa, "Akegarasu Haya to Ishikawa ken no minshū bungaku," *Kanazawa daigaku kyōiku gakubu kiyō* 27 (1979): 97–111; Matsuda, *Akegarasu Haya*, 2:71–77.

61. Niwa Toshio, "Miyazawa Kenji," in Konno Tōru et al., *Kindai bungaku to bukkyō*, 113–16.

62. Bandō and Steward, *Tannishō*, 5. Translation slightly modified. For a discussion of the *Tannishō* by the Kōkōdō members, see Ōsawa Ayako, "Kōkōdō dōjin ni yoru tannishō dokkai to shinranzō," *Shūkyō kenkyū* 387 (2016): 27–50.

63. Mizushima Ken'ichi, *Kin gendai shinshū kyōgakushi kenkyū josetsu: Shinshū ōtaniha niokeru kaikaku undō no kiseki* (Kyoto: Hōzōkan, 2010), 199–203.

64. Quoted in Matsuda, *Akegarasu Haya*, 1:272; author's translation.

65. Matsuda, 1:273–74.

66. Matsuda, 1:281–82.
67. Krondorfer, *Male Confessions*, 11–12.
68. Akegarasu Haya, preface to "Kōsei no zengo," *Akegarasu Haya Zenshū* (Mattōchō, Japan: Ryōfū Gakusha, 1975–1977), 12:3 (hereafter cited as *AHZ*); author's translation.
69. Rimer, "Kurata Hyakuzō," 33.
70. "Kōsei no zengo," *AHZ*, 12:4; author's translation.
71. Krondorfer, *Male Confessions*, 135–36.
72. "Chōraku," *AHZ*, 22:15–16; author's translation.
73. For Kiyozawa's attitude toward tuberculosis, see "Kakketsu shita haibyōnin ni ataeru tegami," *KMZ*, 6:140–47. For a discussion of the spreading of tuberculosis in modern Japan, see William Johnston, *The Modern Epidemic: A History of Tuberculosis in Japan* (Cambridge, MA: Harvard University Press, 1995).
74. "Chōraku," *AHZ*, 22:18; author's translation.
75. "Chōraku," *AHZ*, 22:19; author's translation.
76. "Chōraku," *AHZ*, 22:32; author's translation.
77. "Chōraku," *AHZ*, 22:35; author's translation.
78. "Chōraku," *AHZ*, 22:45–46; author's translation.
79. "Kōsei no zengo," *AHZ*, 12:13; author's translation.
80. "Kōsei no zengo," *AHZ*, 12:14–15; author's translation.
81. Nishida Masayoshi, *Mujōkan no denshō*, 422–23.
82. Krondorfer states, "The pleasure of writing intimately about the male self compels many men to blame women for their woundedness, and it seems that they are chronically unaware of this pattern." *Male Confessions*, 63.
83. Anatole France, *Thais*, trans. Robert B. Douglas (Project Gutenberg E-book, 2006), http://www.gutenberg.org/files/2078/2078-h/2078-h.htm.
84. Friedrich Nietzsche, *Thus Spake Zarathustra*, http://www.readcentral.com/chapters/Friedrich-Nietzsche/Thus-Spake-Zarathustra-A-Book-for-All-and-None/003.
85. "Kōsei no zengo," *AHZ*, 12:17; author's translation.
86. Krondorfer, *Male Confessions*, 154.
87. In his last letter to Akegarasu, Kiyozawa asked him to send him English translations of the three Pure Land sutras, including the *Larger Sutra of Immeasurable Life*.
88. The narrator states, "Tada, Sasaki, and I began visiting you back in 1896 when you were living in Shirakawa village. Although you were a great scholar and we respected you, we often discussed how to guide you to taste the dynamic of Shin Buddhism. While living together in Tokyo, the three of us discussed Shin Buddhism with you. Ten years after your demise, however, rather than sharing your spirit with others, we ended up explaining and interpreting your vibrant teaching according to standard doctrine, which had been corrupted since the Tokugawa era, and reinvigorated the same old beliefs under the fashionable name of 'Kiyozawa.'" "Kōsei no zengo," *AHZ*, 12:7–8; author's translation.
89. "Kōsei no zengo," *AHZ*, 12:17, 29.

90. "Kōsei no zengo," *AHZ*, 12:29–30; author's translation.

91. "Kōsei no zengo," *AHZ*, 12:79–80. This essay previously appeared in *Seishinkai* 14, no. 2 (February 1914), quoted in Mizushima, *Kin gendai shinshū kyōgakushi*, 237–38; author's translation.

92. The *Larger Sutra of Immeasurable Life* states:

The Buddha said to Ananda: "Then, the Buddha Sovereign Monarch of the World said to the monk Treasure of Dharma [Bodhisattva Dharmakara]: 'You yourself will know how to follow the practice and how to adorn a Buddha-field.' The monk said to the buddha: 'The meaning of this is vast and profound, not within the range of my abilities. I only request that the World Honored One teach me extensively the practice by which all buddhas, tathagatas, purify their field. Once I have heard this explanation, I will practice according to your teachings, and I will fulfill the vows I have made.'" Gómez, *Land of Bliss*, 164–65.

93. Haneda, *December Fan*, 25.

94. Mizushima, *Kin gendai shinshū kyōgakushi*, 238–41.

95. Yamamoto, *Seishin shugi*, 176.

96. Matsuda, *Akegarasu Haya*, 1:17; author's translation.

97. Miyamoto Matahisa, "Taishōki no bukkyō to minshū bungaku: Akegarasu Haya to Kita Katsuji," *Kanazawa daigaku kyōiku gakubu kiyō* 26 (1978): 64–65, 67–68; Miyamoto Matahisa, "Akegarasu Haya," 98.

98. Soga Ryōjin, "Bōfu shiu," quoted in Mizushima, *Kin gendai shinshū kyōgakushi*, 72; author's translation.

99. Mizushima, 72.

Chapter 5

1. *Guardians of the Dharma Castle* was reprinted more than a hundred times during the late Taishō and early Shōwa periods. See Yoshihara Hiroto, "Matsuoka Yuzuru, hōjō o mamoru hitobito," in "Tokushū: Kin gendai sakka to bukkyō bungaku," special issue, *Kokubungaku: Kaishaku to kanshō* 55, no. 12 (December 1990): 118. The formation of new religious organizations began in the late nineteenth century and accelerated after the Russo-Japanese War and during/after World War I. After the Meiji Restoration, people were able to leave rural communities and move to cities where they sought new economic opportunities. However, they were met by various hardships. As they suffered poverty, illness, and alienation, they turned to religions of worldly benefit. The New Religions include Tenrikyō, which was founded by Nakayama Miki in 1838 and became an independent religious organization in 1908; Ōmotokyō, funded by Deguchi Nao and Deguchi Onisaburō in 1916 and previously known as Kōdō Ōmoto; Perfect Liberty, whose forerunner was established by Miki Tokuharu in 1924; and others. See Susumu Shimazono, *From Salvation to Spirituality: Popular Religious Movements in Modern Japan* (Melbourne: Trans Pacific Press, 2004), 3, 6, 7–8.

2. Unlike *Guardians*, *Bodaiju* was translated into English in 1966. The translator, however, Christianized the novel by using Christian terms when translating Buddhist words and concepts.

3. Stephen G. Covell, *Japanese Temple Buddhism: Worldliness in a Religion of Renunciation* (Honolulu: University of Hawai'i Press, 2005), 4.

4. Barbara Foley, *Telling the Truth: Theory and Practice of Documentary Fiction* (Ithaca, NY: Cornell University Press, 1986), 25–26. Historians, literary critics, and novelists seem to agree that the boundary between history and fiction is arbitrary. According to Michel de Certeau, neither fiction nor literature is unmediated: fiction is "the repressed other of historical discourse." Quoted in Hayden White, "Introduction: Historical Fiction, Fictional History, and Historical Reality," *Rethinking History* 9, nos. 2–3 (2005): 147. De Certeau also states, "'the real' as represented by historiography does not correspond to the 'real' that determines its production. It hides behind the picture of a past the present that produces and organizes it." *Heterologies: Discourse on the Other* (Minneapolis: University of Minnesota Press, 2010), 203. According to Linda Hutcheon, literature and history are both "linguistic constructs" derived from "verisimilitude," but neither their languages nor their structures are completely clear, because both literature and historiography are intertexual—writers weave the earlier works into their present writings, making the texts complex. *A Poetics of Postmodernism: History, Theory, Fiction* (New York: Routledge, 1998), 105. According to Hayden White, historiographical narratives are actually literary and "historical accounts cast in the form of a narrative may be as various as the *modes of emplotment* which literary critics have identified as constituting the different principles for structuring narratives in general." "Historical Pluralism," *Critical Inquiry* 12, no. 3 (1986): 487. At the same time, there are distinct features in the documentary novel that make it different from other types of novels. Foley states that the documentary novel "purports to represent reality by means of agreed-upon conventions of fictionality, while grafting onto its fictive pact some kind of additional claim to empirical validation." Foley, *Telling the Truth*, 25.

5. Harry E. Shaw, *The Forms of Historical Fiction* (Ithaca, NY: Cornell University Press, 1983), 23.

6. Foley, *Telling the Truth*, 36, 40–41.

7. Foley, 67.

8. Foley, 70. The use of the mimetic contract is not limited to the documentary novel. Concerning other genres of literature, Foley states, "I would suggest that the so-called major modes of fictional narrative—sometimes described as naturalism, realism, romance, and fantasy—are simply variations on the basic form of the mimetic contract" (68).

9. J. Thomas Rimer, "The Historical Literature of Mori Ōgai: An Introduction," in *The Historical Fiction of Mori Ōgai*, ed. David Dilworth and J. Thomas Rimer (Honolulu: University of Hawai'i Press, 1991), 7. Rimer writes that in "History as It Is and History Ignored" (*Rekishi sono mama to rekishi banare*, 1914), Ōgai creates two categories, "fictional pieces (*rekishi shōsetsu*) that deal with historical themes in an

artistic and psychological way" and "biographical narratives (*shiden*) that remain more closely related to the factual information unearthed on his characters by Ōgai" (6).

10. Rimer, 8.

11. David Dilworth, "The Significance of Ōgai's Historical Literature," in *The Historical Fiction of Mori Ōgai*, ed. David Dilworth and J. Thomas Rimer (Honolulu: University of Hawai'i Press, 1991), 15–16. According to Katsukura Toshikazu, after Ōgai's exploration of human values and the inner world through history and literature, Japanese writers made fiction somewhat independent of history and cultivated rich artistic expressions in the space where "history is ignored." *Rekishi shōsetsu no kūkan: Ōgai shōsetsu to sono nagare* (Osaka: Izumi Shoin, 2008), 32.

12. Sekiguchi Yasuyoshi, *Hyōden Matsuoka Yuzuru* (Tokyo: Ozawa Shoten, 1991), 48–50, 66–70, 85, 347–50.

13. Kume Masao is a writer who also considered writing autobiographical fiction to be a spiritual practice. In 1925, he wrote that literature was a means for him to attain self-realization and that the writing of autobiographical fiction led him to gain spiritual peace and philosophical assurance. See Keene, *Dawn to the West*, 511.

14. Sekiguchi, *Hyōden Matsuoka Yuzuru*, 135–38, 148. Fudeko later rectified the misconception by saying that Kume and Matsuoka did not compete with each other, and that it was Fudeko who chose Matsuoka to be her husband (148).

15. Sekiguchi, 155.

16. Between 1932 and 1935, Matsuoka helped publish various Buddhist journals and books, such as *Contemporary Buddhism* (*Gendai bukkyō*), founded by Takakusu Junjirō; *Truth* (*Shinri*); and Maeda Toshikane's collected works, *A Religious Man* (*Shūkyō teki ningen*). Sekiguchi, 242, 245.

17. In *The Life of Shakyamuni*, Matsuoka conducted research on Avaghoa's *Buddhacarita* (J. *Bussho gyōsan*) and highlighted Avaghoa's criticism of Brahmanism. In *The Story of Dunhuang*, Matsuoka characterized Aurel Stein's and Paul Pelliot's attempts to collect the Dunhuang manuscripts as colonial projects, while justifying Japanese Buddhist expeditions as an act of saving Chinese Buddhist treasures. See *Shakuson no shōgai* (Tokyo: Daitō Shuppansha, 1978) and *Tonkō monogatari* (Tokyo: Kōdansha, 1991).

18. Sekiguchi, 155, 242, 245, 342, 353–60. It is worth mentioning that a descendent of Sōseki's and Matsuoka's lived in the United States. Yōko Matsuoka McClain (1924–2011), who taught Japanese at the University of Oregon between 1964 and 1994, was one of Matsuoka's daughters. She became professor emeritus and published many articles and books in Japanese and English, including *Handbook of Modern Japanese Grammar*. She contributed to the introduction of Japanese literature and culture in America. See Susan Schmidt, "Yōko Matsuoka McClain," in "Deceased Asianists," *Asian Studies Newsletter* 57, no. 1 (Annual Conference Issue, 2012): 40.

19. Matsuoka published *The Collected Works of Sōseki's Calligraphy and Paintings* (*Sōseki iboku shū*, 1922–23) in five volumes; *Reminiscences of Sōseki* (*Sōseki no omoide*, 1929), based on Kyōko's account of Sōseki; *The Sōseki Album* (*Sōseki shashin chō*, 1929); *Sōseki, His Life and Literature* (*Sōseki, hito to sono bungaku*, 1942); *Sōseki's Chinese Poems*

(*Sōseki no kanshi*, 1946); *Sōseki's Royalties Record* (*Sōseki's inzei chō*, 1955); and *Sōseki's Study Room* (*Ahh, Sōseki sanbō*, 1967). Sekiguchi, *Hyōden Matsuoka Yuzuru*, 286.

20. Matsuoka Yuzuru, *Ahh, Sōseki sanbō*, 150, quoted and translated in Ama Toshimaro, "Eyes of Pure Objectiveness," 134 (translation slightly modified). *Shūkyōteki mondō* was reprinted in Matsuoka Yuzuru's monograph titled *Ahh, Sōseki sanbō*.

21. The dialogue between Sōseki and Matsuoka also includes Sōseki's attitude towards religion. According to Matsuoka, Sōseki said, "Although the concepts of self-power and Other power, which sound so Buddhist-like, seem to be very clear, people are easily misled. It is unnecessary to presume the existence of absolute figures in the first place; however, I think there will be no salvation unless one reaches the stage explained by these concepts. We, as rational beings, cannot think of a God that is transcendent and we do not need it if we examine ourselves immanently. However, if one wishes to identify the absolute value of awakening or the ultimate experience of having spiritual enlightenment as God or Buddha, that will be fine." Matsuoka, *Ahh, Sōseki sanbō*, 147–148, quoted and translated in Ama, 139.

22. In 1917, Iwanami Shoten, a start-up publisher in Tokyo, published the book, called *Shukke to sono deshi* in Japanese, and it became a long-standing best seller, as did Natsume Sōseki's *Kokoro*, which Iwanami had published in 1914. By 1970, the paperback publishers Iwanami Bunko and Kadokawa Bunko, had each printed more than fifty editions of *Shukke to sono deshi*. Suzuki Norihisa, "Kaidai," in *Shukke to sono deshi* (Tokyo: Iwanami Bunko, 2007), 303; Fukushima Kazuto, *Kindai nihon no Shinran*, 223. Terakawa Shunshō estimates that *Shukke to sono deshi* sold about two million copies. "Kurata Hyakuzō: Ningen Shinran no hakkensha," in *Kurata Hyakuzō no seishin sekai*, ed. Byakkōkai (Kyoto: Nagata Bunshōdō, 1990), 22.

23. Angela Yiu translates *Taishō kyōyō shugi* as "Taishō elite intellectual cultivation." "Atarashikimura: The Intellectual and Literary Contexts of Taishō Utopian Village," *Japan Review* 20 (2008): 205, 226n3.

24. Chiba Masaaki, "Kurata Hyakuzō no tōjō," in *Taishō shūkyō shōsetsu no ryūkō: Sono haikei to ima*, ed. Igarashi Shinji et al. (Tokyo: Ronsōsha, 2011), 25–34, 42–47. Tsukada Sayaka discusses the surge of religious literature in modern Japan while analyzing how Japanese writers used words such as "religion" and "faith." See "'Shūkyō' to 'shinkō': 'Shūkyō bungaku' no ryūkō o meguru futatsu no jutsugo," in *Bungaku sen kyūhyaku nijūichi nen zengo*, ed. Nishi waseda kindai bungaku no kai (Tokyo: Nishi waseda kindai bungaku no kai, 2004), 111–33. For a recent study of *Shukke to sono deshi* in English, see Michihiro Ama, "Shinran as 'Other': Revisiting Kurata Hyakuzō's *The Priest and His Disciples*," *Japanese Journal of Religious Studies* 43, no. 2 (2016): 253–74.

25. Fukushima, *Kindai nihon no Shinran*, 222; Chiba Kōichirō, "Kūzen no Shinran boom sōbyō," in *Taishō shūkyō shōsetsu no ryūkō: Sono haikei to ima*, ed. Igarashi Shinji et al. (Tokyo: Ronsōsha, 2011), 97–98. Also, for a discussion of popular perceptions of Shinran during the Taishō period, see Ōsawa Ayako, "Taishōki shinran ryūkō to shinranzō," *Bukkyō bunka gakkai kiyō* 27 (2019): 11–37. The revival of Shinran was

also noted even in the English language. According to an article in the journal *Eastern Buddhist* published in 1922, "A kind of Shinran revival is sweeping over Japan just at present, and it centers around his personality. Some years ago, about the time of the Japanese-Russian War, Nichiren, the founder of the Nichiren sect of Buddhism, was the chief figure of religious interest, especially among soldiers and nationalists. While the Nichiren creed is still a living power in certain quarters, it is now Shinran that is attracting the attention, chiefly of the intelligent classes of Japan." "Notes," *Eastern Buddhist*, o.s. 1, nos. 5/6 (1922): 395.

26. In *Shiteki hihan Shinran shinden,* Murata Tsutomu questions the historical accuracy in Shinran's legends. Two historians, Tanaka Yoshinari and Yatsushiro Kuniji, advocated the so-called "massacre theory," eliminating Shinran from Japanese history (*Shinran massatsuron*) because they found it impossible to prove Shinran's existence. For these modern Japanese historians, Shinran was one of the figures for whom there was a lack of historical evidence. Chiba Jōryū, *Jōdo Shinshū* (Tokyo: Natsumesha, 2005), 216. This type of positivist study was pioneered by Shigeno Yasutsugu, the so-called "doctor of obliteration," of Tokyo Imperial University. He held the position that "[w]here there is little or no historical evidence to prove that a person lived, it was more likely that that person had never existed." Kikumura Norihiko, *Shinran: His Life and Thought*, trans. Ken'ichi Yokogawa (Los Angeles: Nembutsu Press, 1972), 31.

27. Chiba Kōichirō, "Kūzen no Shinran boom sōbyō," 117–19.

28. See Kenri, "Kindai nihon no bungaku," 37–38; Sekiguchi, *Hyōden Matsuoka Yuzuru*, 113–17, 194–99; Yoshihara, "Matsuoka Yuzuru," 118–23. Hasegawa Nyozekan, however, saw *Guardians of the Dharma Castle* as the first documentary naturalist novel depicting a religious world (Sekiguchi, 196). "Home to Protect the Dharma" was originally published as *Hōjō o mamoru hitobito*, but in order to avoid confusion with the *Guardians of the Dharma Castle* (in Japanese the same title as *Hōjō o mamoru hitobito*) published later, Matsuoka changed the former title to *Gōhō no ie* (Sekiguchi, 117).

29. Sekiguchi points out that autobiographical elements decrease as the story continues—the third section is less autobiographical than the second section (188).

30. Sekiguchi, 191–92.

31. Matsuoka Yuzuru, *Hōjō o mamoru hitobito* (Kyoto: Hōzōkan, 1981–1982), 1:187–89.

32. Matsuoka, 1:317–19.

33. Terakawa, *Kiyozawa Manshi ron*, 80–81, 111.

34. Matsuoka, *Hōjō o mamoru hitobito*, 1:321; author's translation.

35. Matsuoka, 1:320, 329.

36. Matsuoka, 1:355; author's translation.

37. It is incorrect, however, to limit a character's model to one single historical figure. For instance, in addition to Daidō, another character, Hanabusa Bunshō, also represents part of Akegarasu's activities. Matsuoka, 3:176. At the same time, Daidō's depiction is an exaggeration of Akegarasu's personality.

38. Matsuoka, 2:152–55, 159–61, 191–200.

39. Matsuoka, 2:226–35; author's translation.
40. Matsuoka, 2:288.
41. Matsuoka, 3:5–7; author's translation.
42. Matsuoka, 3:20–23.
43. Matsuoka, 3:9, 39, 45–46, 50.
44. Matsuoka, 3:214–15, 220.
45. Matsuoka, 3:241–42; author's translation.
46. Matsuoka, 3:92, 254, 272–79, 286–90, 350, 388, 411–12.
47. Matsuoka, 3:416; author's translation.
48. Hasegawa Nyozekan, "Shūkyōteki anarchism," quoted in Sekiguchi, *Hyōden Matsuoka Yuzuru*, 196.
49. Sekiguchi, 87.
50. Matsuoka Yuzuru, "Hōjōki," quoted in Sekiguchi, 190; author's translation.
51. Matsuoka Yuzuru, "Shinkansho no chosha yori," quoted in Sekiguchi, 191–92.
52. John Raines, ed., *Marx on Religion* (Philadelphia: Temple University Press, 2002), 5–6.
53. Keene, *Dawn to the West*, 594, 598.
54. Raines, *Marx on Religion*, 5.
55. Yoshitomo Takeuchi, "The Role of Marxism in Japan," *Developing Economies* 5, no. 1 (December 1967), 739.
56. For a summary of the development of Japanese proletarian literature during the 1920s and 1930s, see Heather Bowen-Struyk and Norma Field, eds., *For Dignity, Justice, and Revolution: An Anthology of Japanese Proletarian Literature* (Chicago: University of Chicago Press, 2016), 3–10.
57. Foley, *Telling the Truth*, 40.
58. Matsuoka, *Hōjō o mamoru hitobito*, 1:118–20; author's translation.
59. Matsuoka, 2:296–97.
60. Foley, *Telling the Truth*, 144–45.
61. Fukushima Kazuto, *Daichi no bussha*, 102, quoted in Mizushima, *Kin gendai shinshū kyōgakushi*, 177.
62. Tada Kanae, "Negawakuba, waga sakuhi o katarashimeyo," *Seishinkai* 12, no. 11 (1914), quoted in Mizushima, 71; author's translation.
63. Matsuoka, *Hōjō o mamoru hitobito*, 2:291–92; author's translation.
64. Shigaraki Takamoro, "Kindai shinshū kyōdan no shakaiteki dōkō," in *Kindai shinshū kyōdanshi kenkyū*, ed. Shigaraki Takamaro (Kyoto: Hōzōkan, 1987), 26–27.
65. Matsuoka, *Hōjō o mamoru hitobito*, 2:28.
66. Tada Kanae, "Shinshū jiin seikatsu no kako genzai mirai," *Kyūsai* 8, no. 3 (1918): 25, 29; Sekiguchi, *Hyōden Matsuoka Yuzuru*, 114.
67. "Shinran shōnin roppyaku gojukkai daienki sanpaisha de nigiwai o miseta umekōji teishajō no ato," *Shūhō*, 6:343–45. See also http://www.ryukoku.ac.jp/about/pr/publications/67/09_ancient/index.htm.
68. "Dai enki hōyō junbi gaikyō," *Shūhō*, 6:259–61.

69. Foley, *Telling the Truth*, 145.

70. Foley states, "The historical novel of the nineteenth century takes as its referent a phase of the historical process; its documentary effect derives from the assertion of extratextual verification" (25).

71. Georg Lukács, *The Historical Novel* (New York: Humanities Press, 1965), 42. For a summary of Lukács's study, see Jerome de Groot, *The Historical Novel* (New York: Routledge, 2010), 24–29.

72. Matsuoka, *Hōjō o mamoru hitobito*, 3:17–19.

73. For a discussion of Honganji during the War States period in English, see Carol Richmond Tsang, *War and Faith: Ikkō Ikki in Late Muromachi Japan* (Cambridge, MA: Harvard University Press, 2007).

74. Sekiguchi, *Hyōden Matsuoka Yuzuru*, 352.

75. Matsuda, *Akegarasu Haya*, 2:64–67, 74.

76. Matsuoka's father passed away in 1933, about seven years after the publication of *Guardians*. Sekiguchi, *Hyōden Matsuoka Yuzuru*, 352, 354.

Chapter 6

1. Susan B. Klein, *Allegories of Desire: Esoteric Literary Commentaries of Medieval Japan* (Cambridge, MA: Harvard University Press, 2002), 15.

2. Mitchell, *Buddhism*, 39.

3. Paul Williams, *Mahāyāna Buddhism*, 70.

4. The Japanese words for *manojalpa* come from Nagao Gajin, *Shōdaijōron: Wayaku to chūkai* (Tokyo: Kōdansha, 1987), 2:5.

5. Taiki Motomura, "On *manojalpa* in the *Mahāyāna-sūtrālaṃkāra*," *Journal of Indian and Buddhist Studies* 59, no. 3 (2011): 1201. Also, for a discussion of *manojalpa*, see, for instance, Chikafumi Watanabe, "An Examination of Mind-Talk (manojalpa) in the *Mahāyānasaṃgraha*," *Journal of Indian and Buddhist Studies* 50, no. 2 (2002): 31–35.

6. For a brief summary of Buddhism and language, see, for instance, Carl Olson, *The Different Paths of Buddhism: A Narrative-Historical Introduction* (New Brunswick, NJ: Rutgers University Press, 2005), 37–38.

7. Thomas Blenman Hare, "Reading Writing Cooking: Kūkai's Interpretative Strategies," *Journal of Asian Studies* 49, no. 2 (1990): 256.

8. Klein, *Allegories of Desire*, 18–19.

9. LaFleur, *Karma of Words*, 17.

10. LaFleur, 17, 21, 23.

11. LaFleur, 69–71.

12. LaFleur, 24.

13. LaFleur, 154, 156–57.

14. Heine, "Tragedy and Salvation," 386.

15. *Kusamakura* is translated into English by Kazutomo Takahashi (1927), Alan Turney (2000), and Meredith McKinney (2008). Takahashi added "Inhuman Tour" as a subtitle, while Turney translated *Kusamakura* as *The Three-Cornered World*. In the present work, English translations of *Kusamakura* are taken from either Turney's or McKinney's rendition.

16. Odin, *Artistic Detachment*, 240.

17. Odin, 264–80.

18. Alan Turney, trans., *The Three-Cornered World* (Boston: Tuttle, 2000), 12.

19. The word *aware* is translated as "compassion" by Turney (138, 184) and "pity" or "pitying love" by McKinney; see Meredith McKinney, trans., *Kusamakura* (New York: Penguin Books, 2008), 108, 146.

20. Odin, *Artistic Detachment*, 240.

21. Concerning the word *yo*, a first-person pronoun, used in *Kusamakura*, Atsuko Sakaki states, "The pronoun indicates that the narrator is a male intellectual who both is able and chooses to write in literary Japanese. He sounds a bit snobbish, if not pompous for his age (he reveals near the beginning of the work that he is almost thirty years old), in addressing himself in this way, albeit only in writing. (*Yo* uses another first-person pronoun, *watashi*, in conversation, which sounds free of gender and class connotations, although it is, for that very reason, very much a mark of a modern education.) This hint of aloofness proves to match his personality, because, as we will see, he thinks more highly of himself than the rest of the characters in intellectual terms. People of different educational background, class, and gender do speak, but their speeches are first heard by him and then transcribed or represented by him for the reader. Indeed, *yo* assumes responsibilities appropriate for his perceived status." *Recontextualizing Texts: Narrative Performance in Modern Japanese Fiction* (Cambridge, MA: Harvard University Press, 1999), 99.

22. Turney, *Three-Cornered World*, 19, 24, 49.

23. Turney, 25.

24. Turney, 48.

25. See "Notes on Kusamakura," *SZ*, 2:921–40.

26. Turney, *Three-Cornered World*, 50.

27. McKinney, *Kusamakura*, 124–25.

28. Turney, *Three-Cornered World*, 44.

29. Turney, 79.

30. Turney, 134.

31. Kin'ya Tsuruta, "Sōseki's *Kusamakura*: A Journey to 'The Other Side,'" *Journal of Association of Teachers of Japanese* 22, no. 2 (1988): 178–79.

32. Neither Takahashi nor McKinny translates the sense of ambiguity associated with the term *ōjō*.

33. Tsuruta, "Sōseki's *Kusamakura*," 180, 186.

34. Gómez, *Land of Bliss*, 146.

35. Turney, *Three-Cornered World*, 138.

36. Turney, 161.

37. Turney, 161. Critics have considered the relationship between the protagonist and Onami to be heterosexual, but in his recent study Robert Tuck analyzes the effect of "literary cross-identification" and points out that the protagonist projects his homosexual desire onto Nami and sees her as a man who assumes a female identity. "Doubled Visions of Desire: Fujimura Misao, Kusamakura, and Homosocial Nostalgia," *Review of Japanese Culture and Society* 29 (2017): 79–91.

38. See, for instance, Michele Marra, "The Buddhist Mythmaking of Defilement: Sacred Courtesans in Medieval Japan," *Journal of Asian Studies* 52, no. 1 (1993): 49–65.

39. Michele Marra, *The Aesthetics of Discontent: Politics and Reclusion in Medieval Japanese Literature* (Honolulu: University of Hawai'i Press, 1991), 11, 49, 59.

40. Herbert E. Plutschow, *Tabisuru nihonjin* (Tokyo: Musashino Shoin, 1983), 21.

41. Mathy, *The Gate*, 176, 178–79.

42. Mathy, 186.

43. *Mon, SZ*, 4:844; author's translation

44. Mathy, *The Gate*, 196.

45. Mathy, 204–5.

46. Damian Flanagan, introduction to *The Gate*, trans. Francis Mathy (London: Peter Owen, 2006), x–xi.

47. Mathy, *The Gate*, 213.

48. Flanagan states that "*The Gate* should not be viewed as a depressing book on religious frustration but more as a perfectly constructed satire on a certain type of will-less person." Introduction to *The Gate*, xxv. The will-less Sōsuke escapes to a Zen temple where will is required for him to resolve riddles.

49. Mathy, *The Gate*, 5.

50. Ōtani Daigaku, ed., *Bukkyō ga unda nihongo* (Tokyo: Mainichi Shinbunsha, 2001), 109.

51. Kazuaki Tanahashi, ed., "Continuous Practice, Part One," in *Treasury of the True Dharma Eye: Zen Master Dōgen's Shōbō Genzō* (Boston: Shambhala, 2010), 1:368.

52. Kazuaki Tanahashi, "Rules for Zazen," in *Treasury of the True Dharma Eye: Zen Master Dōgen's Shōbō Genzō* (Boston: Shambhala, 2010), 2:579.

53. Kumakura, *Sōseki no henshin*, 285.

54. Kumakura, 11, 36.

55. Mathy, *The Gate*, 213.

56. Kumakura, *Sōseki no henshin*, 36. Sōsuke's clipping his nails also resonates with Gidō's words: "When you have become saturated from head to foot with the *kōan*, a new heaven and a new earth will suddenly open up before your eyes." Mathy, *The Gate*, 202. In the source language, "foot" is *tsumasaki*, which means the tip of a toe, but the kanji characters for *tsumasaki* 爪先 shows the combination of "nail" and "tip." By shaping his toenails, Sōsuke can be ready for the kōan practice.

57. Mathy, *The Gate*, 213.

58. Jacques Derrida, *Margins of Philosophy* (Chicago: University of Chicago Press, 1982), 13.
59. Buswell and Gimello, introduction to *Paths to Liberation*, 22.
60. Norman Waddell and Masao Abe, trans., *The Heart of Dōgen's Shōbōgenzō* (Albany: State University of New York Press, 2002), 47, 51, 54–55.
61. Hijiya-Kirschnereit, *Rituals of Self-Revelation*, 47.
62. Tomi Suzuki, *Narrating the Self*, 69.
63. Fowler, *Rhetoric of Confession*, 104.
64. Tomi Suzuki, *Narrating the Self*, 71.
65. Fowler, *Rhetoric of Confession*, 118. Referring to a Japanese scholar, Tosa Tōru, Fowler also mentions that *Futon*'s conclusions might have been modeled on Zola's *Therese Raquin*.
66. Henshall, *The Quilt*, 73.
67. Henshall, 95–96.
68. Karatani, *Origins of Modern Japanese Literature*, 76–80.
69. Henshall, *The Quilt*, 35.
70. For historical information about *gokurakusui*, see, for instance, www.denzuin.or.jp.
71. Henshall, *The Quilt*, 68.
72. Henshall, 84.
73. Henshall, 37. In fact, in his memoirs, Katai considered Yoshiko to be his Anna Mahr and himself to be Johannes. For a discussion of the impact of Hauptmann's *Lonely People* on *The Quilt*, see Hijiya-Kirschnereit, *Rituals of Self-Revelation*, 46–48; Fowler, *Rhetoric of Confession*, 117–18.
74. Henshall, *The Quilt*, 42.
75. Henshall, 76.
76. Henshall, 48.
77. Henshall, 70.
78. Henshall, 71.
79. Henshall, 50.
80. Henshall, 49.
81. Michael Wheeler, *Death and the Future Life in Victorian Literature and Theology* (Cambridge, UK: Cambridge University Press, 1990), 33. Alan Warren Friedman comments on the painting titled *The Death of the Prince Consort at Buckingham Palace*: "a close-up of the same moment showing only the loving family, the children of owing their existence to erotic acts performed in the depicted bed by the dying Albert and his grieving wife." *Fictional Death and the Modernist Enterprise* (Cambridge, UK: Cambridge University Press, 1995), 76.
82. Henshall, *The Quilt*, 55–56. During the 1960s, cultural critics of modern Japan created a "discourse on beauty" and equated the "feeling for impermanence" with the "feeling for the beauty of impermanence." According to Michael Marra, they created a misconception that an "aesthetic and a tradition of reclusion" had already

existed in medieval Japan, although it was an interpretation projected onto medieval Japan. *Essays on Japan*, 357–58.

83. Ama Toshimaro, *Why Are the Japanese Non-Religious? Japanese Spirituality: Being Non-Religious in a Religious Culture*, trans. Michihiro Ama (Lanham, MD: University Press of America, 2005), 56.

84. Odin, *Artistic Detachment*, 3. Michele Marra states that "Noringa's aesthetic theory, known as 'the ability to be moved by things' (*mono no aware*), is an extremely conscious political act that led him to fabricate a nativist tradition untouched by the 'vulgarities' of foreign dogma [such as the Buddhist doctrine and Neo-Confucian thought]." *Aesthetics of Discontent*, 2.

Chapter 7

1. William Harmless, *Mystics* (New York: Oxford University Press, 2008), 13.
2. Harmless, 263.
3. Harmless, 264.
4. For Tugendhat, the path of religion "leaves wishes as they are and undertakes instead a *transformation of the world* by means of a wishful projection." *Egocentricity and Mysticism: An Anthropological Study*, trans. Alexei Procyshyn and Mario Wenning (New York: Columbia University Press, 2016), 99.
5. Tugendhat, 93.
6. Tugendhat, 101.
7. Tugendhat, xxi.
8. Tugendhat, 118–19.
9. Kobayashi Ichirō, *Shizenshugi sakka Tayama Katai*, 12.
10. Payne, "Fractal Journeys," 290–91.
11. Tugendhat, *Egocentricity and Mysticism*, 102.
12. Tugendhat, 107.
13. Harmless, *Mystics*, 221.
14. Harmless, 207.
15. "Aru sō no kiseki," *TKZ*, 9:29; author's translation.
16. Bekki Kōshō, "Rekishi no yami ni hito o mitsumete: Taigyaku jiken to bukkyōsha tachi," *Shindō* 17 (1988): 132–49. For a discussion of Takagi Kenmyō in English, see Ama Toshimaro, "Towards a Shin Buddhist Social Ethics," trans. Robert F. Rhodes, *Eastern Buddhist*, n.s., 33, no. 2 (2001): 35–53; Paul L. Swanson, "Takagi Kenmyō and Buddhist Socialism: A Meiji Misfit and Martyr," in *Modern Buddhism in Japan*, ed. Makoto Hayashi, Eiichi Ōtani, and Paul L. Swanson (Nagoya: Nanzan University Press, 2014), 144–62. For a discussion of Uchiyama Gudō in English, see Fabio Rambelli, *Zen Anarchism: The Egalitarian Dharma of Uchiyama Gudō* (Honolulu: University of Hawai'i Press, 2014).

17. Agawa Hiroyuki, "Kaisetsu," in *An'ya kōro* (Tokyo: Iwanami Bunko, 2007), 2:335–39.
18. Fowler, *Rhetoric of Confession*, 229–30.
19. Sibley, *The Shiga Hero*, 70; Starrs, *An Artless Art*, 99.
20. Fowler, *Rhetoric of Confession*, 238. Fowler discusses the issues of first and third narratives in chapter 2 of his book.
21. Starrs, *An Artless Art*, 86–88; Mathy, *Shiga Naoya*, 83–84.
22. Mathy, *Shiga Naoya*, 84–85.
23. Mathy, 85–86.
24. Mathy, 86–88.
25. Mathy, 88–91.
26. Edwin McClellan, trans., *A Dark Night's Passing* (Tokyo: Kōdansha International, 1976), 172, 186–87.
27. McClellan, 390.
28. McClellan, 374–75.
29. McClellan, 400–1.
30. William Sibley states, "in the conclusion of *An'ya kōro* we shall see him firmly reject mankind's efforts to cheat death with what he now considers to be empty and coercive delusions of 'immortal' accomplishments and the whole notion of progress." *The Shiga Hero*, 112.
31. Sigmund Freud, *Writings on Art and Literature* (Stanford, CA: Stanford University Press, 1997), 201. The author was introduced to the Freudian notion of "uncanny" by Michael Dylan Foster's *Pandemonium and Parade: Japanese Monsters and the Culture of Yōkai* (Berkeley: University of California Press, 2009), 19.
32. Freud, *Writings on Art and Literature*, 211.
33. Starrs, *An Artless Art*, 99.
34. McClellan, *A Dark Night's Passing*, 150.
35. McClellan, 115.
36. For instance, at the very end of part 1 (chapter 7), "Night was about to end outside. As he [Kensaku] watched from the rickshaw, the early morning sun, so beautiful after the rain, rose gradually in the east, and he remembered a boat trip he once took about ten years before along the Japan Sea. It was autumn. He was standing on deck, waiting for the dawn to break. And there, behind Mt. Tsurugi already lightly covered with snow, the sun had slowly begun to rise." McClellan, 74. In the process of writing, Shiga constantly reenacted the beauty of nature he had observed in the past. Francis Mathy states, "Shiga was to make good use of such early experiences of nature in his later work, and though there was always a considerable time lapse between the actual experience and his account of it, the details of the scene are so deeply etched in his memory that he seems to be still observing them." *Shiga Naoya*, 143–44. The climactic scene on Mount Daisen in *A Dark Night's Passing* is another example, though Shiga's memory is inaccurate. Kensaku experiences union with nature at the fifth station, but

according to Gorai Shigeru, it should have been at the ninth. *Yama no shūkyō* (Tokyo: Kadokawa Bunko, 2008), 186.

37. Tomi Suzuki points out that some Japanese critics see Kensaku's experience as part of an "archetypal characteristic of Japanese literature: namely an emphasis on harmony and unity with nature through physical and emotional ties of *aware*, of affection and sympathy." They also see Shiga's works as examples of "literary continuity and cultural identity" between classical texts and the *shishōsetsu*. Suzuki, however, remains cautious of that view. *Narrating the Self,* 131.

38. Fowler, *Rhetoric of Confession*, 242.
39. McClellan, *A Dark Night's Passing*, 406.
40. McClellan, 408.
41. Fowler, *Rhetoric of Confession*, 245–46.
42. McClellan, *A Dark Night's Passing*, 408.
43. McClellan, 180.
44. McClellan, 380.
45. McClellan, 381, 383, 392.
46. McClellan, 358.
47. McClellan, 305.
48. McClellan, 306.
49. McClellan, 312.
50. Freud, *Writings on Art and Literature*, 222–26.
51. Freud, 227.
52. Michael Dylan Foster, *Pandemonium and Parade*, 14.

Chapter 8

1. Marvin Marcus, for instance, considers "the memento mori episode" to be "a mainstay of Sōseki's literary reminiscence." *Reflections in a Glass Door*, 71.
2. Friedman, *Fictional Death*, 117–18.
3. Victor Turner, *The Anthropology of Performance* (New York: PAJ Publications, 1988), 34–35.
4. Turner, 101.
5. Turner, 38.
6. Turner, 33.
7. Susan Ackerman, *When Heroes Love: The Ambiguity of Eros in the Stories of Gilgamesh and David* (New York: Columbia University Press, 2005), 93.
8. Ackerman, 94.
9. Bjørn Thomassen, "The Use and Meanings of Liminality," *International Political Anthropology* 2, no. 1 (2009): 5.
10. Thomassen, 21.
11. Jay Rubin, trans., *Sanshirō* (London: Penguin Books, 2009), 9.

12. Rubin, 48.
13. Rubin, 55.
14. *Hydriotaphia* reads, "To subsist in lasting monuments, to live in their productions, to exist in their names and predicament of chimeras, was large satisfaction unto old expectations, and made one part of their Elysiums. But all this is nothing in the metaphysicks of true belief. To live indeed, is to be again ourselves, which being not only an hope, but an evidence in noble believers, 'tis all one to lie in St. Innocent's church-yard, as in the sands of Egypt. Ready to be anything, in the ecstasy of being ever, and as content with six foot as the moles of Adrianus." Quoted in Rubin, 180. However, the Japanese translation of this passage quoted in *Sanshirō* is different in terms of source language. The translator is not known, nor whether Sōseki read it in English or Japanese—Tsubouchi Shōyō introduced *Hydriotaphia* as early as the 1900s, but it seems that the entire Japanese translation became available much later. Sasaki Akiko, "*Sanshirō* no hon'yaku: Fukanōsei no taiken," *Aichi shukutoku daigaku kokugo kokubun* 28 (2005): 134. Because the Japanese translation better provides the context in which Sanshirō encounters a child's funeral, it is worth translating the Japanese passage back into English. It reads as follows: "Since ancient times people have wished to sleep [for eternity] in tombs that will not decay, have their names continue to be remembered [after their death], or hope to be transformed into mulberry leaves and remain in this world. When such wishes are granted, they [feel as if they] are in Heaven. From the standpoint of a doctrine of true faith, however, these wishes are not satisfying and are merely fleeting [emotions]. To 'live' means returning again to the self, which has nothing to do with wishes and hopes, and if what is seen by the noble-minded and devout is true, to be buried in St. Innocent's graveyard is no different from being buried [anonymously] in the sands of Egypt. Those who take pleasure in a permanent self that is theirs alone see no difference in [being buried in] a narrow six-foot plot or entombed in the Mausoleum of Adrianus. Be prepared to allow all things to take their own course." Author's translation assisted by Ken'ichi Yokogawa.
15. Rubin, *Sanshirō*, 181.
16. Rubin, 45.
17. Rubin, 223.
18. Rubin, 224.
19. Norma Field, afterword to *And Then* (Ann Arbor, MI: University of Michigan Press, 1997), 268.
20. Jay Rubin, trans., *The Miner* (Stanford, CA: Stanford University Press, 1988), 27.
21. Rubin, 84.
22. Rubin, 91–92.
23. Jay Rubin translates "jumbō" as "jangle" but *The Awakening* maintains the source language as it is.
24. Rubin, 92.
25. Rubin, 92–93.

26. Rubin, 93–94.
27. Quoted in Ackerman, *When Heroes Love*, 103.
28. Ackerman, 103.
29. Rubin, *The Miner*, 147.
30. Rubin, 158.
31. Rubin, 159.
32. Katai was not, however, in a position to obtain information related to military strategy and army positions in a timely manner. See Tomoko Aoyama, "Japanese Literary Responses to the Russo-Japanese War," in *The Russo-Japanese War in Cultural Perspective, 1904–05*, ed. David Wells and Sandra Wilson (New York: St. Martin's Press, 1999), 66–67.
33. Munakata Kazushige, "Kaisetsu" and "Dainigun jūsei nikki," *TKZ*, 25:794. In *The Diary*, Katai writes, "When I look at the pocket diary . . ." (91), and "Don't forget that this is the diary of an individual" (153).
34. "Dainigun jūsei nikki," *TKZ*, 25:33; author's translation.
35. "Dainigun jūsei nikki," *TKZ*, 25:91–92; author's translation.
36. Slavoj Žižek, *The Sublime Object of Ideology* (London: Verso, 2008), 39. The author was introduced to Žižek's discussion of belief by Sōhō Machida's *Renegade Monk: Hōnen and Japanese Pure Land Buddhism* (Berkeley: University of California Press, 1999), 108–9.
37. Žižek, *Sublime Object of Ideology*, 42.
38. Žižek, 39.
39. Žižek, 35.
40. Žižek, 39. This identification demonstrates the effect of "retroaction" in a Lacanian context—that is, memory of a previous event is interpreted and reconstructed by a future event. Malcolm Bowie, *Lacan* (Cambridge, MA: Harvard University Press, 1991), 14, 180.
41. In *Thirty Years in Tokyo* (*Tokyo no sanjūnen*, 1917), Katai recalls Ozaki Kōyō's (1867–1903) funeral, which was conducted in a Buddhist style. He wrote *Thirty Years in Tokyo* much later, after publishing *The Diary*, but Kōyō's funeral took place in Japan before Katai went to China to observe the Russo-Japanese War. Katai recalls how lavish the ceremony was and how he disliked pathos and sorrow he felt from a large attendance. For Katai, the Buddhist funeral was old-fashioned and even perfunctory, yet he became sentimental and was moved by the sense of loneliness he felt. For a translation of *Tokyo no sanjūnen*, see Henshall, *Literary Life in Tokyo*. In 1908, a year after the publication of *The Quilt*, Katai attended Kunikida Doppo's funeral, which was also arranged in a Buddhist style, and expressed his condolences.
42. Naoko Shimazu, *Japanese Society at War: Death, Memory and the Russo-Japanese War* (New York: Cambridge University Press, 2009), 110.
43. Shimazu, 110.
44. "Dainigun jūsei nikki," *TKZ*, 25:149.
45. "Dainigun jūsei nikki," *TKZ*, 25:281; author's translation.

46. "Dainigun jūsei nikki," *TKZ*, 25:351; author's translation.

47. Bjørn Thomassen states, "liminality is followed by reintegration rituals that re-establish the order of the new personality as a part of the social order that he or she re-enters with a new role, stamped by the formative experience. This is a critical passage, but without reintegration, liminality is pure danger." "Use and Meanings of Liminality," 22.

48. Katai writes, "I started writing 'Life' from the 1st March [sic] 1908. Four or five days earlier Shimazaki's 'Spring' had started appearing in the 'Asahi,' so I realized I had to try all the harder. I knew that my literary position was at a critical point, in the sense that it was at an important yet dangerous stage. 'The Quilt' had created something of a literary sensation, and in the New Year I had put out 'One Soldier' and 'The House on the Bank,' which had both received good reviews. If I did not now put everything I could into my writing, who knows when such an opportunity might come my way again? Such were my thoughts at the time. . . . The material for 'Life' was something I had had in mind for several years. It was about people around me, so I didn't need to use any imagination, but on the other hand it was, for that very reason, difficult to write. I found it particularly difficult to write about my mother. But what else could I do? I resolved to write openly about everything." Henshall, *Literary Life in Tokyo*, 206–7.

49. Hur, *Death and Social Order in Tokugawa Japan*, 9, 343.

50. Hur, 344. Literary representation of contemporary Shinto funeral rites is found in Etō Jun, *Tsuma to Watashi* (Tokyo: Bungei Shunjū, 1999).

51. "Sei," *TKZ*, 1:181; author's translation.

52. "Sei," *TKZ*, 1:188.

53. "Sei," *TKZ*, 1:192–95.

54. "Sei," *TKZ*, 1:195–99.

55. Sara Cobb, "Liminal Spaces in Negotiation Process: A Case Study of the Process of Crossing Relational and Interpretive Thresholds," *Journal of Conflict Management* 1, no. 1 (2013): 27n5.

56. Shimazu, *Japanese Society at War*, 153–54.

57. "Higan sugimade," *SZ*, 5:7.

58. Kingo Ochiai and Sanford Goldstein, trans., *To the Spring Equinox and Beyond* (Rutland, VT: Tuttle, 1985), 179–80.

59. Ochiai and Goldstein, 181–82.

60. Ochiai and Goldstein, 190.

61. Medieval Japanese believed that children belonged to a sacred world. Festivals of *shichi go san*—7 years old, 5 years old, and 3 years old—were meant to periodically celebrate a child's surviving and to prepare him or her for the human world. Infantile death, therefore, suggests the child's return to the worlds of *kami* and Buddha. See William LaFleur, *Liquid Life: Abortion and Buddhism in Japan* (Princeton, NJ: Princeton University Press, 1992), 35.

62. Rogers and Rogers, *Rennyo*, 255.

63. "Nikki, Meiji yonjū yonen [1911]," *SZ*, 13:673–74.
64. Ochiai and Goldstein, *To the Spring Equinox and Beyond*, 324.
65. "Zoku shokanshū, Meiji yonjū gonen [1912]," *SZ*, 15:120, quoted in Miyazawa, "Natsume Sōseki to bukkyō, part 1," 59.
66. "Danpen, Meiji yonjū yonen [1911]," *SZ*, 13:688.

Conclusion

1. Fowler, *Rhetoric of Confession*, xviii. In a recently published work on Sōseki, John Nathan explores Sōseki's life and work. See *Sōseki: Modern Japan's Greatest Novelist* (New York: Columbia University Press, 2018).
2. Harmless, *Mystics*, 207.
3. David C. Stahl, *Trauma, Dissociation and Re-enacting in Japanese Literature and Film* (London: Routledge, 2017), 20.
4. F. K. Stanzel, *A Theory of Narrative* (New York: Cambridge University Press, 1984), 90–91, 98–99.
5. Robert Lyons Danly, *In the Shade of Spring Leaves: The Life and Writings of Higuchi Ichiyō, A Woman of Letters in Meiji Japan* (New York: W. W. Norton, 1981), vii.
6. Danly, vii.
7. Sugisaki Toshio, "Higuchi Ichiyō to bukkyō," 1–15.
8. *Takekurabe* has been translated into English four times, including Danly's translation. For the list of English translations, see Danly, *In the Shade of Spring Leaves*, 335.
9. W. M. Bickerton translates *Takekurabe* as *They Compare Heights*, while Edward Seidensticker translates it as *Growing Up*.
10. Danly, *In the Shade of Spring Leaves*, 285.
11. Danly, 254.
12. The story continues, "They call this part of town beyond the quarter 'in front of Daion Temple.' The name may sound a little saintly, but those who live in the area will tell you it's a lively place. Turn the corner at Mishima Shrine and you don't find any mansions, just tenements of ten or twenty houses, where eaves have long begun to sag and shutters only close halfway. It is not a spot for trade to flourish" (Danly, 254).
13. Fowler, *Rhetoric of Confession*, 291.
14. The translated title, *Coffinman: The Journal of a Buddhist Mortician*, is misleading, as *Nōkanfu Nikki* literally means "the diary of a mortician." Because of the wide circulation of the book, however, *Coffinman* is used.
15. See Michihiro Ama, "Transcending Death in *Departures* (*Okuribito*): A Case Study of Film, Literature, and Buddhism in Modern Japan," *Journal of Japanese and Korean Cinema* 2, no. 1 (December 2010): 35–50.
16. Aoki Shinmon, "Bunkobon no tame no atogaki," in *Nōkanfu Nikki* (Tokyo: Bungei Shunjū, 2009), 211.

17. Wayne Yokoyama, trans., *Coffinman: The Journal of a Buddhist Mortician* (Anaheim, CA: Buddhist Education Center, 2002), 10.

18. Yokoyama, 79.

19. Aoki, "Nōkanfu Nikki o arawashite," in *Nōkanfu Nikki*, 162.

20. John Updike, "Subconscious Tunnels: Haruki Murakami's Dreamlike New Novel," *New Yorker*, January 24, 2005, http://www.newyorker.com/magazine/2005/01/24/subconscious-tunnels.

21. "The 10 Best Books of 2005," *New York Times*, December 11, 2005, http://www.nytimes.com/2005/12/11/books/review/the-10-best-books-of-2005.html.

22. Gabriel, *Spirit Matters*, 123–30.

23. Quoted by Hirano Jun on the book jacket of *Zero no rakuen: Murakami Haruki to Bukkyō* (Tokyo: Rakkōsha, 2008). Murakami's grandfather was also a Buddhist priest. See Haruki Murakami, "The Art of Fiction No. 182," interview by John Wray, *Paris Review*, no. 170 (Summer 2004), http://www.theparisreview.org/interviews/2/the-art-of-fiction-no-182-haruki-murakami.

24. Haruki Murakami, "Always on the Side of the Egg," *Haaretz*, February 17, 2009, http://www.haaretz.com/life/arts-leisure/always-on-the-side-of-the-egg-1.270371.

25. Murakami Haruki, *Kafka on the Shore*, trans. Philip Gabriel (New York: Knopf E-book, 2005), chap. 34.

26. Murakami, chap. 49.

27. Murakami Haruki, *Wakai dokusha no tameno tanpen an'nai* (Tokyo: Bungei Shunjū Bunko, 2004), 37–38, quoted in Suzuki Takami, "Proust to Murakami Haruki: Jiga hyōgen aruiwa shutai no kakuritsu o megutte," *Fukuoka daigaku kenkyūbu ronshū* A 13, 4 (2014), 84; author's translation.

28. Suzuki Takami, 83.

29. Murakami, *Kafka on the Shore*, chap. 42.

Appendix 1

1. Bandō and Steward, *Tannishō*, 5.

2. Śūraṅgama Sūtra Translation Committee of the Buddhist Text Translation Society, trans., *The Śūraṅgama Sūtra* (N.P.: Buddhist Text Translation Society, 2009), 9.

3. Śūraṅgama Sūtra Translation Committee, 10.

4. Śūraṅgama Sūtra Translation Committee, 13.

5. Śūraṅgama Sūtra Translation Committee, 14.

6. Śūraṅgama Sūtra Translation Committee, 403.

7. Śūraṅgama Sūtra Translation Committee, 31.

8. Śūraṅgama Sūtra Translation Committee, 32.

9. Śūraṅgama Sūtra Translation Committee, 179.

10. Akegarasu included two more citations from the *Śūraṅgama Sūtra* which are not included in this translation because those passages have not yet been identified.

The first passage discusses base passions of sentient beings, including carnal desires, while the second passage states that the causes are the same for the sages and ordinary people to become enlightened.

11. Shimazaki Tōson, *Shinsei*, chaps. 24, 26, quoted by Akegarasu.

12. All citations of *Thais* in this section are taken from the Douglas translation available at http://www.gutenberg.org/files/2078/2078-h/2078-h.htm.

13. Citations of Nietzsche's text are taken from *Thus Speak Zarathustra*, Read Central, 2011. http://www.readcentral.com/chapters/Friedrich-Nietzsche/Thus-Spake-Zarathustra-A-Book-for-All-and-None/003.

14. Leo Tolstoy, "Father Sergius," in *Master and Man and Other Stories*, trans. Paul Foote (London: Penguin Books, 1977), 15.

15. Tolstoy, 33.
16. Tolstoy, 33–34.
17. Tolstoy, 46.
18. Tolstoy, 49.
19. Tolstoy, 52.
20. Tolstoy, 53.
21. Tolstoy, 54.
22. Tolstoy, 54–55.
23. Tolstoy, 55.
24. Tolstoy, 64.
25. Gómez, *Land of Bliss*, 163.
26. Gómez, 165.
27. Gómez, 164.

Appendix 2

1. *Naniwabushi*, also known as *rōkyoku*, refers to a form of traditional story-singing in Japan. According to Hiromi Hyōdō and Henry D. Smith II, *naniwabushi* was the "most popular form of mass entertainment in Japan throughout the first half of the twentieth century." "Singing Tales of the Gishi: Naniwabushi and the Forty-Seven Ronin in Late Meiji Japan," *Monumenta Nipponica* 61, no. 4 (2006): 459. *Chongare* is an early form of *naniwabushi*, performed on the street (468).

Bibliography

Collected Works

AHZ Akegarasu Haya. *Akegarasu Haya Zenshū*. 27 vols. Mattōchō, Japan: Ryōfū Gakusha, 1975–1977.
KMZ Kiyozawa Manshi. *Kiyozawa Manshi Zenshū*. 9 vols. Tokyo: Iwanami Shoten, 2002–2003.
SZ Natsume Sōseki. *Sōseki Zenshū*. 17 vols. Tokyo: Iwanami Shoten, 1966–1967.
SNZ Shiga Naoya. *Shiga Naoya Zenshū*. 22 vols. Tokyo: Iwanami Shoten, 1998–2001.
TKZ Tayama Katai. *Teihon Katai Zenshū*. 28 vols. Kyoto: Rinsen Shoten, 1993–1995.
YHJ Yukawa Hideki. *Yukawa Hideki Jisenshū*. 5 vols. Tokyo: Asahi Shinbunsha, 1971.

Note that for *Sōseki Zenshū* the 1960s version of Iwanami *Sōseki Zenshū* is referenced because it contains old forms of kanji characters, whereas in the 1990s version, they were replaced with new forms of kanji characters.

Abe, Masao, and Christopher Ives, trans. *An Inquiry into the Good*. New Haven, CT: Yale University Press, 1990.
Abe, Yoshiya. "Religious Freedom under the Meiji Constitution." *Contemporary Religions in Japan* 11, no. 1/2 (1970): 27–79.
Ackerman, Susan. *When Heroes Love: The Ambiguity of Eros in the Stories of Gilgamesh and David*. New York: Columbia University Press, 2005.
Aeba, Takao. "Shiga Naoya ron: Sono shizen to yume." *Bungakukai* 29, no. 8 (1975): 150–69.
Agawa, Hiroyuki. "Kaisetsu." In *An'ya kōro*. Vol. 2, 335–43. Tokyo: Iwanami Bunko, 2007.
Akegarasu, Haya. "Rōsō." *Seishinkai* 8, no. 1 (1908): 48–52.
Ama, Michihiro. "Shinran as 'Other': Revisiting Kurata Hyakuzō's *The Priest and His Disciples*." *Japanese Journal of Religious Studies* 43, no. 2 (2016): 253–74.
———. "Transcending Death in *Departures* (*Okuribito*): A Case Study of Film, Literature, and Buddhism in Modern Japan." *Journal of Japanese and Korean Cinema* 2, no. 1 (December 2010): 35–50.

Ama, Toshimaro. "The Eyes of Pure Objectiveness: Natsume Sōseki's Search for the Way." Translated by Michihiro Ama. *Eastern Buddhist*, n.s., 38, no. 1/2 (2007): 112–44.

———. *Shūkyō no shinsō: Seinaru mono eno shōdō*. Tokyo: Chikuma Shobō, 1995.

———. "Towards a Shin Buddhist Social Ethics." Translated by Robert F. Rhodes. *Eastern Buddhist*, n.s., 33, no. 2 (2001): 35–53.

———. *Why Are the Japanese Non-Religious? Japanese Spirituality: Being Non-Religious in a Religious Culture*. Translated by Michihiro Ama. Lanham, MD: University Press of America, 2005.

Andō, Shūichi. *Kiyozawa sensei shinkō zadan*. Kyoto: Heirakuji Shoten, 1933.

Aoki, Shinmon. *Nōkanfu Nikki*. Tokyo: Bungei Shunjū, 2009.

Aoyama, Tadakazu. *Kinsei bukkyō bungaku no kenkyū*. Tokyo: Ōfū, 1999.

Aoyama, Tomoko. "Japanese Literary Responses to the Russo-Japanese War." In *The Russo-Japanese War in Cultural Perspective, 1904–05*, edited by David Wells and Sandra Wilson, 60–85. New York: St. Martin's Press, 1999.

Ara, Masahito. *Sōseki kenkyū nenpyō*. Tokyo: Shūeisha, 1984.

Árokay, Judit. "Discourse on Poetic Language in Early Modern Japan and the Awareness of Linguistic Change." In *Divided Languages? Diglossia, Translation, and the Rise of Modernity in Japan, China, and the Slavic World*, edited by Judit Árokay, Jadranka Gvozdanovic, and Darja Miyajima, 89–103. Cham, Switzerland: Springer, 2014.

Bandō, Shōjun, and Harold Steward, trans. *Tannishō: Passages Deploring Deviations of Faith*. Berkeley, CA: Numata Center for Buddhist Translation and Research, 1996.

Bargen, Doris G. "Not Just Words: Shogunal Politics and the Daijōsai in Mori Ōgai's 'Saigo no ikku.'" *Monumenta Nipponica* 67, no. 1 (2012): 1–27.

———. *Suicidal Honor: General Nogi and the Writings of Mori Ōgai and Natsume Sōseki*. Honolulu: University of Hawai'i Press, 2006.

Beichman, Janine. *Masaoka Shiki: His Life and Works*. Boston: Cheng & Tsui, 2002.

Bekki, Kōshō. "Rekishi no yami ni hito o mitsumete: Taigyaku jiken to bukkyōsha tachi." *Shindō* 17 (1988): 132–49.

Benl, Oscar. "Naturalism in Japanese Literature." *Monumenta Nipponica* 9, no. 1/2 (1953): 1–33.

Biddle, Ward William. "The Authenticity of Natsume Sōseki." *Monumenta Nipponica* 28, no. 4 (1973): 391–426.

Bloom, Alfred. "Kiyozawa Manshi and the Path to the Revitalization of Buddhism." *Pacific World*, 3rd ser., no. 5 (2003): 19–34.

———. "Kiyozawa Manshi and the Revitalization of Buddhism." *Eastern Buddhist*, n.s., 35, no. 1/2 (2003): 1–5.

———. *Shinran's Gospel of Pure Grace*. Ann Arbor, MI: Association for Asian Studies, 1999.

Blum, Mark L., trans. "The Nature of My Faith." In *Cultivating Spirituality: A Modern Shin Buddhist Anthology*, edited by Mark L. Blum and Robert F. Rhodes. 93–98. Albany: State University of New York Press, 2011.

———, trans. *The Nirvana Sutra*. Vol. 1 of 4. Berkeley, CA: Bukkyō Dendō Kyōkai America, 2013.
———. *The Origins and Development of Pure Land Buddhism*. New York: Oxford University Press, 2002.
———. "Shin Buddhism in the Meiji Period." In *Cultivating Spirituality: A Modern Shin Buddhist Anthology*, edited by Mark L. Blum and Robert F. Rhodes, 1–52. Albany: State University of New York Press, 2011.
Bodiford, William M. *Sōtō Zen in Medieval Japan*. Honolulu: University of Hawai'i Press, 1993.
Bourdaghs, Michael K., Atsuko Ueda, and Joseph A. Murphy, eds. *Theory of Literature and Other Critical Writings: Natsume Sōseki*. New York: Columbia University Press, 2010.
Bowen-Struyk, Heather, and Norma Field, eds. *For Dignity, Justice, and Revolution: An Anthology of Japanese Proletarian Literature*. Chicago: University of Chicago Press, 2016.
Bowie, Malcolm. *Lacan*. Cambridge, MA: Harvard University Press, 1991.
Breen, John, and Mark Williams. *Japan and Christianity: Impacts and Responses*. New York: Palgrave Macmillan, 1996.
Burford, Grace G. "Theravada Buddhist Soteriology and the Paradox of Desire." In *Paths to Liberation: The Mārga and Its Transformations in Buddhist Thought*, edited by Robert E. Buswell Jr. and Robert M. Gimello, 37–61. Honolulu: University of Hawai'i Press, 1992.
Buswell, Robert E., Jr., and Robert M. Gimello. Introduction to *Paths to Liberation: The Mārga and Its Transformations in Buddhist Thought*, edited by Robert E. Buswell Jr. and Robert M. Gimello, 1–36. Honolulu: University of Hawai'i Press, 1992.
Buswell, Robert E., Jr., and Donald S. Lopez Jr., eds. *The Princeton Dictionary Buddhism*. Princeton, NJ: Princeton University Press, 2014.
Campbell, Alan, and David S. Noble, eds. *Japan: An Illustrated Encyclopedia*. 2 vols. Tokyo: Kōdansha International, 1993.
Carter, Robert E. *The Kyoto School: An Introduction*. Albany: State University of New York Press, 2013.
Chiba, Jōryū. *Jōdo Shinshū*. Tokyo: Natsumesha, 2005.
Chiba, Kōichirō. "Kūzen no Shinran boom sōbyō." In *Taishō shūkyō shōsetsu no ryūkō: Sono haikei to ima*, edited by Igarashi Shinji, Sano Masato, Chiba Kōichirō, and Chiba Masaaki, 97–131. Tokyo: Ronsōsha, 2011.
Chiba, Masaaki. "Kurata Hyakuzō no tōjō." In *Taishō shūkyō shōsetsu no ryūkō*, 23–56.
Chikazumi, Jōkan. *Shinkō no yoreki*. 14th ed. Tokyo: Kyūdō Hakkōsho, 1921.
Cleary, Thomas, trans. *The Flower Ornament Scripture: A Translation of the Avataṃsaka Sutra*. Boston: Shambhala, 1993.
———, trans. *Rational Zen: The Mind of Dōgen Zenji*. Boston: Shambhala, 1995.
Cobb, Sara. "Liminal Spaces in Negotiation Process: A Case Study of the Process of Crossing Relational and Interpretive Thresholds." *Journal of Conflict Management* 1, no. 1 (2013): 25–40.

Covell, Stephen G. *Japanese Temple Buddhism: Worldliness in a Religion of Renunciation*. Honolulu: University of Hawai'i Press, 2005.
Covill, Linda, trans. *Handsome Nanda* by Ashvaghosha. New York: New York University Press, 2007.
Culler, Jonathan. *Literary Theory: A Very Short Introduction*. New York: Oxford University Press, 2000.
Dadi, Iftikhar. *Modernism and the Art of Muslim South Asia*. Chapel Hill: University of North Carolina Press, 2010.
Danly, Robert Lyons. *In the Shade of Spring Leaves: The Life and Writings of Higuchi Ichiyō, A Woman of Letters in Meiji Japan*. New York: W. W. Norton, 1981.
Davies, Roger J., and Osamu Ikeno, eds. *The Japanese Mind: Understanding Contemporary Japanese Culture*. North Clarendon, VT: Tuttle, 2002.
de Certeau, Michel. *Heterologies: Discourse on the Other*. Translated by Brian Massumi. Minneapolis: University of Minnesota Press, 2010.
de Groot, Jerome. *The Historical Novel*. New York: Routledge, 2010.
Derrida, Jacques. *Margins of Philosophy*. Chicago: University of Chicago Press, 1982.
Dilworth, David. "The Significance of Ōgai's Historical Literature." In *The Historical Fiction of Mori Ōgai*, edited by David Dilworth and J. Thomas Rimer, 12–42. Honolulu: University of Hawai'i Press, 1991.
Doak, Kevin M., ed. *Xavier's Legacies: Catholicism in Modern Japanese Culture*. Vancouver: University of British Columbia Press, 2011.
Dobbins, James C. *Jōdo Shinshū: Shin Buddhism in Medieval Japan*. Honolulu: University of Hawai'i Press, 2002.
———. *Letters of the Nun Eshinni: Images of Pure Land Buddhism in Medieval Japan*. Honolulu: University of Hawai'i Press, 2004.
Dodd, Stephen. "History in the Making: The Negotiation of History and Fiction in Tanizaki Jun'ichirō's *Shunkinshō*." *Japan Review* 24 (2012): 151–68.
Dunlop, Lane, trans. *The Paper Door and Other Stories by Shiga Naoya*. New York: Columbia University Press, 2001.
Emery, Elizabeth. "J.-K. Huysmans, Medievalist." *Modern Language Studies* 30, no. 2 (2000): 119–31.
Etō, Jun. *Tsuma to Watashi*. Tokyo: Bungei Shunjū, 1999.
Faure, Bernard. *Chan Insights and Oversights: An Epistemological Critique of the Chan Tradition*. Princeton, NJ: Princeton University Press, 1993.
Field, Norma M. Afterword to *And Then*, 258–78. Ann Arbor, MI: University of Michigan Press, 1997.
Flanagan, Damian. Introduction to *The Gate*, by Natsume Sōseki, v–xxxii. Translated by Francis Mathy. London: Peter Owen, 2006.
Flutsch, Maria, trans. *Recollections*. London: Sōseki Museum in London, 2009.
———. "Time, Death and the Empire: Natsume Sōseki's *Omoidasu koto nado (Remembrances)*." *Japanese Studies* 23, no. 3 (2003): 239–50.
Foley, Barbara. *Telling the Truth: Theory and Practice of Documentary Fiction*. Ithaca, NY: Cornell University Press, 1986.

Foster, Dennis A. *Confession and Complicity in Narrative*. Cambridge, UK: Cambridge University Press, 1987.
Foster, Michael Dylan. *Pandemonium and Parade: Japanese Monsters and the Culture of Yōkai*. Berkeley: University of California Press, 2009.
Fowler, Edward. *The Rhetoric of Confession: Shishōsetsu in Early Twentieth-Century Japanese Fiction*. Berkeley: University of California Press, 1988.
Fraleigh, Matthew. "Terms of Understanding: The Shōsetsu according to Tayama Katai." *Monumenta Nipponica* 58, no. 1 (2003): 43–78.
France, Anatole. *Thais*. Translated by Robert B. Douglas. Project Gutenberg E-book, 2006. https://www.gutenberg.org/files/2078/2078-h/2078-h.htm.
Freud, Sigmund. *Writings on Art and Literature*. Stanford, CA: Stanford University Press, 1997.
Friedman, Alan Warren. *Fictional Death and the Modernist Enterprise*. Cambridge, UK: Cambridge University Press, 1995.
Frye, Northrop. *The Great Code: The Bible and Literature*. New York: Harcourt Brace Jovanovich, 1982.
Fujii, Jun. "Kindai nihon no hikari to kage: Natsume Sōseki to Kiyozawa Manshi." *Bungaku* 2, no. 2 (2001): 169–81.
———. "Sōseki to Manshi: Sono shūhen ni tsuite." *Gendai to Shinran* 5 (2004): 2–23.
Fukushima, Kazuto. *Kindai nihon no Shinran*. Kyoto: Hōzōkan, 1973.
Gabriel, Philip. *Spirit Matters: The Transcendent in Modern Japanese Literature*. Honolulu: University of Hawai'i Press, 2006.
Godzich, Wlad. Foreword to *Heterologies: Discourse on the Other*, by Michel de Certeau, 7–21. Translated by Brian Massumi. Minneapolis: University of Minnesota Press, 2010.
Gómez, Luis O. *The Land of Bliss: The Paradise of the Buddha of Measureless Light, Sanskrit and Chinese Versions of the Sukhāvatīvyūha Sutras*. Honolulu: University of Hawai'i Press, 1996.
Gorai, Shigeru. *Yama no shūkyō*. Tokyo: Kadokawa Bunko, 2008.
Graham, Masako Nakagawa. *The Autobiographical Narrative in Modern Japan: A Study of Kasai Zenzō, a Shi-shōsetsu Writer*. New York: Edwin Mellen, 2007.
Guo, Nanyan. *Refining Nature in Modern Japanese Literature: The Life and Art of Shiga Naoya*. Lanham, MD: Lexington Books, 2014.
Hallisey, Charles, and Anne Hansen. "Narrative, Sub-ethics, and the Moral Life: Some Evidence from Theravāda Buddhism." *Journal of Religious Ethics* 24, no. 2 (1996): 305–27.
Hanayama, Shōyū, ed. *An Introduction to the Buddhist Canon*. Tokyo: Bukkyō Dendō Kyōkai, 1984.
Haneda, Nobuo, trans. "My Religious Conviction." In *December Fan: The Buddhist Essays of Manshi Kiyozawa*, 49–55. Los Angeles: Shinshu Center of America, 2014.
Hardacre, Helen. *Shintō and the State, 1868–1988*. Princeton, NJ: Princeton University Press, 1989.

Hare, Thomas Blenman. "Reading Writing Cooking: Kūkai's Interpretative Strategies." *Journal of Asian Studies* 49, no. 2 (1990): 253–73.
Harmless, William. *Mystics.* New York: Oxford University Press, 2008.
Hashimoto, Mineo. "Two Models of the Modernization of Japanese Buddhism: Kiyozawa Manshi and D. T. Suzuki." Translated by Tatsuo Murakami. *Eastern Buddhist*, n.s., 35, no. 1/2 (2003): 6–41.
Hata, Kōhei. "Bukkyō to sengo bungaku: Bungaku toshiteno bukkyō hyōgen." In *Bukkyō shisō to nihon bungaku.* Vol. 2 of *Bukkyō bungaku kōza*, edited by Itō Hiroyuki, Imanari Genjō, and Yamada Shōzen, 303–29. Tokyo: Benseisha, 1995.
Heine, Steven. "Dōgen Casts Off 'What': An Analysis of *Shinjin Datsuraku*." *Journal of the International Association of Buddhist Studies* 9, no. 1 (1986): 53–70.
———. "Tragedy and Salvation in the Floating World: Chikamatsu's Double Suicide Drama as Millenarian Discourse." *Journal of Asian Studies* 50, no. 2 (1994): 367–93.
———. *The Zen Poetry of Dōgen: Verses from the Mountain of Eternal Peace.* Boston: Tuttle, 1997.
Henshall, Kenneth G., trans. *Country Teacher, A Novel by Tayama Katai.* Honolulu: University of Hawai'i Press, 1984.
———. *In Search of Nature: The Japanese Writer Tayama Katai (1872–1930).* Leiden: Global Oriental, 2012.
———, trans. *Literary Life in Tokyo, 1885–1915: Tayama Katai's Memoirs ("Thirty Years in Tokyo").* Leiden: Brill, 1987.
———, trans. *The Quilt and Other Stories by Tayama Katai.* Tokyo: Tokyo University Press, 1981.
Herman, Judith. *Trauma and Recovery: The Aftermath of Violence—from Domestic Abuse to Political Terror.* New York: Basic Books, 1997.
Higgins, Winton. "The Coming of Secular Buddhism: A Synoptic View." *Journal of Global Buddhism* 13 (2012): 109–26.
Hijiya-Kirschnereit, Irmela. *Rituals of Self-Revelation: Shishōsetsu as Literary Genre and Socio-cultural Phenomenon.* Cambridge, MA: Harvard University Press, 1996.
Hill, Christopher L. "The Naturalist Novel and the Boundaries of Japanese Literature." *Proceedings of the Association for Japanese Literary Studies* 9 (2008): 71–75.
Hindmarsh, Bruce. "Religious Conversion as Narrative and Autobiography." In *The Oxford Handbook of Religious Conversion*, edited by Lewis R. Rambo and Charles E. Farhadian, 369–400. New York: Oxford University Press, 2014. https://www.oxfordhandbooks.com/view/10.1093/oxfordhb/9780195338522.001.0001/oxfordhb-9780195338522-e-015.
Hirano, Jun. *Zero no rakuen: Murakami Haruki to Bukkyō.* Tokyo: Rakkōsha, 2008.
Hirayama, Jōji. "Naka Kansuke Daibadatta." *Kokubungaku: Kaishaku to kanshō* 55, no. 12 (December 1990): 124–28.
Hiromoto, Katsuya. "The Quiet Joy of Peace and Harmony: Kyoshi Takahama's Life and Literature." *Hiyoshi Review of English Studies* 53 (2008): 31–74.

Hirosawa, Takayuki. "Bukkyō jutsugo no gainen ni tsuite: Hikaku shisō ni okeru hōhōron o megutte." *Gendai mikkyō* 16 (2003): 155–75.
Hirota, Dennis, Hisao Inagaki, Michio Tokunaga, and Ryushin Uryuzu, trans. *The Collected Works of Shinran*. 2 vols. Kyoto: Jōdo Shinshū Hongwanji-ha, 1997.
Honda, Shūgo. *Shiga Naoya*. 2 vols. Tokyo: Iwanami Shinsho, 1990.
Hōsō yōgo iinkai, ed. "Kotoba no yomi ni tsuite: 'NHK nihongo hatsuon akusento jiten kaitei ni atatte.'" *Hōsō kenkyū to kadai* (October 2013): 74–87.
Humphries, Jeff. *Reading Emptiness: Buddhism and Literature*. Albany: State University of New York Press, 1999.
Hur, Nam-lin. *Death and Social Order in Tokugawa Japan: Buddhism, Anti-Christianity, and the Danka System*. Cambridge, MA: Harvard University Press, 2007.
Hutcheon, Linda. *A Poetics of Postmodernism: History, Theory, Fiction*. New York: Routledge, 1998.
Huyssen, Andreas. "Geographies of Modernism in a Globalizing World." *New German Critique* 100 (Winter 2007): 189–207.
Hyōdō, Hiromi, and Henry D. Smith II. "Singing Tales of the Gishi: Naniwabushi and the Forty-Seven Ronin in Late Meiji Japan." *Monumenta Nipponica* 61, no. 4 (2006): 459–519.
Ienaga, Saburō. *Nihon shisōshi ni okeru hitei no ronri no hattatsu*. Tokyo: Shinsensha, 1969.
Ikeda, Eishun. "Kindaiteki kaimei shichō to bukkyō." In *Ronshū nihon bukkyōshi*. Vol. 8, *Meiji jidai*, edited by Ikeda Eishun, 1–65. Tokyo: Yūzankaku, 1987.
Imamura, Hitoshi. *Shinran to gakuteki seishin*. Tokyo: Iwanami Shoten, 2010.
Imanishi, Jun'kichi. "Sōseki to Bukkyō." In *Gendai shisō, Bungaku to bukkyō*. Vol. 3 of *Gendai nihon to bukkyō*, edited by Kobayashi Takasuke, Furuta Shōkin, Mineshima Hideo, and Yoshida Kyūichi, 208–24. Tokyo: Heibonsha, 2000.
Ishikawa, Kyōchō. "Nichiren no shisō to kindai bungaku." In *Bukkyō shisō to nihon bungaku*, 230–54.
Isomae, Jun'ichi. *Kindai nihon shūkyō gonsetsu to sono keifu: Shūkyō, kokka, Shinto*. Tokyo: Iwanami Shoten, 2003.
Itō, Aiko, and Graeme Wilson, trans. *I Am a Cat*. North Clarendon, VT: Tuttle, 2002.
Itō, Sei. *Shōsetsu no ninshiki*. Tokyo: Iwanami Bunko, 2006.
Iwata, Fumiaki. "Hajimeni." In Iwata, *Kindaika no nakano dentō shūkyō to seishin undō*, i–v.
———, ed. *Kindaika no nakano dentō shūkyō to seishin undō: Kijunten toshiteno Chikazumi Jōkan kenkyū*. Tokyo: Heisei nijūnendo Heisei sanjūnendo kagaku kenkyūhi hojokin kenkyū hōkokusho, 2012.
———. "Miki Kiyoshi to Takeuchi Yoshinori." In Iwata, *Kindaika no nakano dentō shūkyō to seishin undō*, 22–27.
Iwata, Fumiaki, and Ōsawa Kōji. "Chikazumi Jōkan to Kamura Isota." In Iwata, *Kindaika no nakano dentō shūkyō to seishin undō*, 119–39.
Johnston, Gilbert. "Kiyozawa Manshi's Buddhist Faith and Its Relation to Modern Japanese Society." PhD dissertation, Harvard University, 1972.
Johnston, Mark. *Surviving Death*. Princeton, NJ: Princeton University Press, 2010.

Johnston, William. *The Modern Epidemic: A History of Tuberculosis in Japan*. Cambridge, MA: Harvard University Press, 1995.

Karaki, Junzō. *Mujō*. Tokyo: Chikuma Shobō, 1964.

Karatani, Kōjin. *Origins of Modern Japanese Literature*. Translated by Brett de Bary. Durham, NC: Duke University Press, 1993.

———. *Sōsekiron shūsei*. Tokyo: Daisan Bunmeisha, 1992.

Kashiwahara, Yūsen. "Kiyozawa Manshi." In *Shapers of Japanese Buddhism*, edited by Kashiwahara Yūsen, 230–40. Tokyo: Kōsei, 1994.

Katsukura, Toshikazu. *Rekishi shōsetsu no kūkan: Ōgai shōsetsu to sono nagare*. Ōsaka: Izumi Shoin, 2008.

Kawabata, Yasunari. *Japan, the Beautiful and Myself* [*Utsukushii nihon no watakushi*]. Translated by Edward G. Seidensticker. Tokyo: Kōdansha, 1991.

Kazashi, Nobuo. "James kara Sōseki to Nishida e: En'un no genshōgaku, futatsu no Metamorphoses." *Tetsugaku* 48 (1997): 82–96.

Keene, Donald. *Dawn to the West: Japanese Literature of the Modern Era, Fiction*. New York: Holt, Rinehart and Winston, 1984.

Kenri, Bunshū. *Kindai bungaku to bukkyō no shūhen*. Higashine, Japan: Han'nyakutsu, 1986.

———. "Kindai nihon no bungaku to bukkyō." In *Kindai bungaku to bukkyō*. Vol. 10 of *Iwanami kōza Nihon bungaku to bukkyō*, edited by Konno Tōru, Satake Akihiro, and Ueda Shizuteru, 29–54. Tokyo: Iwanami Shoten, 1995.

Ketelaar, James Edward. *Of Heretics and Martyrs in Meiji Japan: Buddhism and Its Persecution*. Princeton, NJ: Princeton University Press, 1990.

Kikumura, Norihiko. *Shinran: His Life and Thought*. Translated by Ken'ichi Yokogawa. Los Angeles: Nembutsu Press, 1972.

Kimbrough, R. Keller. *Preachers, Poets, Women, and the Way: Izumi Shikibu and the Buddhist Literature of Medieval Japan*. Ann Arbor, MI: University of Michigan Press, 2008.

Kitayama, Masamichi. "Sōseki to Zen." *Daijōzen* 46, no. 11 (1996): 3–85.

Klein, Susan B. *Allegories of Desire: Esoteric Literary Commentaries of Medieval Japan*. Cambridge, MA: Harvard University Press, 2002.

Kobayashi, Ichirō. *Shizenshugi sakka Tayama Katai, Nihon no sakka*. Vol. 43. Tokyo: Shintensha, 1982.

Kobayashi, Tomoaki. *Mujōkan no bungaku*. Tokyo: Kōbundō, 1976.

Kockum, Keiko. *Ito Sei: Self-Analysis and the Modern Japanese Novel*. Stockholm: Stockholm University Press, 1994.

Kominz, Laurence R. *The Stars Who Created Kabuki: Their Lives, Loves and Legacy*. New York: Kōdansha USA, 1997.

Komiya, Toyotaka. "Kaisetsu." In *Sōseki Zenshū*. Vol. 5. Tokyo: Iwanami Shoten, 1966.

———. "Kaisetsu." In *Sōseki Zenshū*. Vol. 6. Tokyo: Iwanami Shoten, 1966.

Kōno, Toshirō. "Shiga Naoya nenpu." In *Gunzō, Nihon no sakka vol. 9: Shiga Naoya*, edited by Sasaki Yukitsuna, 335–43. Tokyo: Shōgakkan, 1991.

Kresse, Kai. "Interrogating 'Cosmopolitanism' in an Indian Ocean Setting: Thinking through Mombasa on the Swahili Coast." In *Cosmopolitanisms in Muslim Contexts: Perspectives from the Past*, edited by Derryl N. MacLean and Sikeena Karmali Ahmed, 31–50. Edinburgh: Edinburgh University Press, 2013.
Krondorfer, Björn. *Male Confessions: Intimate Revelations and the Religious Imagination*. Stanford, CA: Stanford University Press, 2010.
Kuge, Shu. "Between Sight and Rhythm: Aspects of Modernity in Tayama Katai's 'Flat Depiction.'" In "Meiji Literature and the Artwork," edited by Miya Mizuta Lippit. Special Issue, *Review of Japanese Culture and Society* 14 (December 2002): 25–38.
Kumakura, Chiyuki. *Sōseki no henshin*. Tokyo: Chikuma Shobō, 2009.
Kuyama, Yasushi. *Kindai nihon no bungaku to shūkyō*. Tokyo: Sōbunsha, 1966.
Kyōgoku, Kōichi. "Sōseki no jion kana zukai." In *Kindai nihongo no kenkyū: Hyōki to hyōgen*. N.p.: Tōensha, 1998.
LaFleur, William R. *The Karma of Words: Buddhism and the Literary Arts in Medieval Japan*. Berkeley: University of California Press, 1986.
———. *Liquid Life: Abortion and Buddhism in Japan*. Princeton, NJ: Princeton University Press, 1992.
Levy, Indra. *Sirens of the Western Shore: The Westernesque Femme Fatale, Translation, and Vernacular Style in Modern Japanese Literature*. New York: Columbia University Press, 2010.
Lindahl, Jared R. "Self-Transformation according to Buddhist Stages of the Path Literature." *Pacific World*, 3rd ser., no. 14 (2012): 231–75.
Lopez, Donald S., Jr. "Paths Terminable and Interminable." In *Paths to Liberation: The Mārga and Its Transformations in Buddhist Thought*, edited by Robert E. Buswell Jr. and Robert M. Gimello, 147–92. Honolulu: University of Hawai'i Press, 2012.
Lukács, Georg. *The Historical Novel*. New York: Humanities Press, 1965.
Machida, Sōhō. *Renegade Monk: Hōnen and Japanese Pure Land Buddhism*. Berkeley: University of California Press, 1999.
MacLean, Derryl N. "Introduction: Cosmopolitanisms in Muslim Contexts." In *Cosmopolitanisms in Muslim Contexts*, 1–9.
Maeda, Jun. "Bukkyō: Kodoku jigoku ni hajimaru jiko keishōka no kokoromi." In *Akutagawa Ryūnosuke: Sono chiteki kūkan, Kobungaku: Kaishaku to Kanshō, bessatsu*, edited by Sekiguchi Yasuyoshi, 53–60, Tokyo: Shibundō, 2004.
Marcus, Marvin. *Reflections in a Glass Door: Memory and Melancholy in the Personal Writing of Natsume Sōseki*. Honolulu: University of Hawai'i Press, 2009.
Marilyn, Ivy. "Modernity." In *Critical Terms for the Study of Buddhism*, edited by Donald S. Lopez Jr., 311–31. Chicago: University of Chicago Press, 2005.
Marra, Michael. *Essays on Japan: Between Aesthetics and Literature*. Leiden: Brill, 2010.
Marra, Michele. *The Aesthetics of Discontent: Politics and Reclusion in Medieval Japanese Literature*. Honolulu: University of Hawai'i Press, 1991.
———. "The Buddhist Mythmaking of Defilement: Sacred Courtesans in Medieval Japan." *Journal of Asian Studies* 52, no. 1 (1993): 49–65.

Marran, Christine. "*Zange*: Buddhism, Gender and Meiji Literary Confession." *Working Words: New Approaches to Japanese Studies*. Center for Japanese Studies, UC Berkeley (2012): 1–15. https://escholarship.org/uc/item/7qg8j2kg.
Masaki, Akira. "Taishō seimeishugi to bukkyō." In *Taishō seimeishugi to gendai*, edited by Suzuki Sadami, 142–50. Tokyo: Kawade Shobō Shinsha, 1995.
Masunaga, Reihō, trans. *A Primer of Sōtō Zen: A Translation of Dōgen's Shōbōgenzō Zuimonki*. Honolulu: University of Hawai'i Press, 1975.
Mathy, Francis, trans. *The Gate*. London: Peter Owen, 2006.
———. *Shiga Naoya*. New York: Twayne, 1974.
Matsuda, Shōichi. *Akegarasu Haya: Yoto tomoni yo o koen*. 2 vols. Kanazawa: Hokkoku Shinbunsha, 1998.
Matsuo, Kenji. "What is Kamakura New Buddhism? Official Monks and Reclusive Monks." *Japanese Journal of Religious Studies* 24, no. 1/2 (1997): 179–89.
Matsuoka, Yuzuru. *Ahh, Sōseki sanbō*. Tokyo: Asahi Shinbunsha, 1967.
———. *Hōjō o mamoru hitobito*. 3 vols. Kyoto: Hōzōkan, 1981–1982. First published 1923–1926 by Dai ichi shobō (Tokyo).
———. *Shakuson no shōgai*. Tokyo: Daitō Shuppansha, 1978.
———. *Tonkō monogatari*. Tokyo: Kōdansha, 1991.
McClellan, Edwin, trans. *A Dark Night's Passing*. Tokyo: Kōdansha International, 1976.
———, trans. *Grass on the Wayside*. Rutland, VT: Tuttle, 1971.
———, trans. *Kokoro*. Mineola, NY: Dover, 2006.
McKinney, Meredith, trans. *Kusamakura*. New York: Penguin Books, 2008.
McMahan, David L. *The Making of Buddhist Modernism*. New York: Oxford University, 2008.
Mineshima, Hideo. "Bukkyō to bungaku no aida: Okamoto Kanoko *Shōjō ruten* o megutte." In *Gendai shisō, Bungaku to bukkyō*, 276–92.
Mitchell, Donald W. *Buddhism: Introducing the Buddhist Experience*. New York: Oxford University Press, 2002.
Miyamoto, Matahisa. "Akegarasu Haya to Ishikawa ken no minshū bungaku." *Kanazawa daigaku kyōiku gakubu kiyō* 27 (1979): 97–111.
———. "Taishōki no bukkyō to minshū bungaku: Akegarasu Haya to Kita Katsuji." *Kanazawa daigaku kyōiku gakubu kiyō* 26 (1978): 61–75.
Miyauchi, Shunsuke. *Tayama Katai ronkō*. Tokyo: Sōbunsha, 2003.
Miyazawa, Masayori. "Natsume Sōseki to bukkyō: Toku ni tariki jōdomon tono kankei, part 1." *Nihon Bukkyō* 42 (1977): 41–62.
———. "Natsume Sōseki to bukkyō: Toku ni tariki jōdomon tono kankei, part 2." *Nihon Bukkyō* 43 (1978): 32–56.
Mizukawa, Takao. "Natsume Sōseki and Shin Buddhism." Translated by Ken'ichi Yokogawa and Michihiro Ama. *Eastern Buddhist*, n.s., 38, no. 1/2 (2007): 145–79.
———. *Sōseki to bukkyō: Sokuten kyoshi e no michi*. Tokyo: Heibonsha, 2002.
Mizushima, Ken'ichi. *Kin gendai shinshū kyōgakushi kenkyū josetsu: Shinshū ōtaniha niokeru kaikaku undō no kiseki*. Kyoto: Hōzōkan, 2010.

Moriguchi, Yasuhiko, and David Jenkins. *Hōjōki: Visions of a Torn World*. Berkeley, CA: Stone Bridge Press, 1996.
Morioka, Heinz, and Miyoko Sasaki. *Rakugo: The Popular Narrative Art of Japan*. Cambridge, MA: Harvard University Press, 1990.
Morishita, Saburō. "Good Works and the Question of Self-Presentation in Tenrikyō." *Nova Religio: The Journal of Alternative and Emergent Religions* 9, no. 2 (2005): 33–49.
Mortimer, Maya. *Meeting the Sensei: The Role of the Master in Shirakaba Writers*. Leiden: Brill, 2000.
Motomura, Taiki. "On *manojalpa* in the *Mahāyāna-sūtrālaṃkāra*." *Journal of Indian and Buddhist Studies* 59, no. 3 (2011): 1198–204.
Murakami, Haruki. "Always on the Side of the Egg." *Haaretz*, February 17, 2009. http://www.haaretz.com/life/arts-leisure/always-on-the-side-of-the-egg-1.270371.
———. "The Art of Fiction No. 182." Interview by John Wray. *Paris Review*, no. 170 (Summer 2004). http://www.theparisreview.org/interviews/2/the-art-of-fiction-no-182-haruki-murakami.
———. *Kafka on the Shore*. Translated by Philip Gabriel. New York: Knopf E-book, 2005.
———. *Wakai dokusha no tameno tanpen an'nai*. Tokyo: Bungei Shunjū Bunko, 2004.
Muramatsu, Takeshi. *Shi no nihon bungakushi*. Tokyo: Shinchōsha, 1975.
Nagao, Gajin. *Shōdaijōron: Wayaku to chūkai*. 2 vols. Tokyo: Kōdansha, 1987.
Nakajima, Kunihiko. "Zen to kindai bungaku: Sōseki to sono shūhen o chūshin ni." In *Bukkyō shisō to nihon bungaku*, 255–80.
Nakajima, Takeshi. "Fujimura Misao no fukakai." *Chikuma* 498 (September 2012): 18–21.
Nathan, John, trans., *Light and Dark*. New York: Columbia University Press, 2014.
———. *Sōseki: Modern Japan's Greatest Novelist*. New York: Columbia University Press, 2018.
New York Times. "The 10 Best Books of 2005." December 11, 2005. http://www.nytimes.com/2005/12/11/books/review/the-10-best-books-of-2005.html.
Nietzsche, Friedrich. *Thus Spoke Zarathustra*. ReadCentral, 2011. http://www.readcentral.com/chapters/Friedrich-Nietzsche/Thus-Spake-Zarathustra-A-Book-for-All-and-None/003.
Nishida, Masayoshi. *Mujōkan no denshō*. Tokyo: Ōfūsha, 1976.
———. *Mujōkan no keifu*. Tokyo: Ōfūsha, 1976.
———. *Mujō no bungaku: Nihonteki mujō bikan no keifu*. Tokyo: Hanawa Shobō, 1982.
———. *Shishōsetsu sai hakken*. Tokyo. Ōfūsha, 1973.
Niwa, Toshio. "Miyazawa Kenji." In *Kindai bungaku to bukkyō*, 107–38.
"Notes." *Eastern Buddhist*, o.s., 1, nos. 5/6 (1922): 391–99.
Ochiai, Kingo, and Sanford Goldstein, trans. *To the Spring Equinox and Beyond*. Rutland, VT: Tuttle, 1985.
Oda, Yoshisuke. "Okamoto Kanoko." In *Kindai bungaku to bukkyō*, 193–212.

Odin, Steve. *Artistic Detachment in Japan and the West: Psychic Distance in Comparative Aesthetics*. Honolulu: University of Hawai'i Press, 2001.
Ogihara, Keiko. "Natsume Sōseki to Nishida Kitarō ni okeru tōyō to seiyō: 'Kōjin' to 'Zen no kenkyū.'" *Kyūshū joshi daigaku kiyō* 43, no. 1 (2006): 63–72.
Okamoto, Kanoko. "Bukkyō no shinkenkyū." In *Bukkyō no meizuihitsu*. Vol. 1, edited by Kokusho Kankōkai Henshūbu, 207–61. Tokyo: Kokusho Kankōkai, 2006.
Okamoto, Katsuhito. "Mishima Yukio no bungaku to bukkyō: *Hōjō no umi o chūshin ni*." In *Gendai shisō, Bungaku to bukkyō*, 308–27.
Okamura, Yasuo. "Nan tomo nai, nan tomo nai: Myōkōnin, sanuki no Shōmatsu ni okeru shūkyōteki sei." *Yamaguchi daigaku tetsugaku kenkyū* 13 (2006): 1–22.
Ōkouchi, Shōji. "Kindai bungaku to bukkyō." In "Tokushū: Kin gendai sakka to bukkyō bungaku." Special issue, *Kokubungaku: Kaishaku to kanshō—Tokushū, kin gendai sakka to bukkyō bungaku* 55, no. 12 (December 1990): 27–37.
Olson, Carl. *The Different Paths of Buddhism: A Narrative-Historical Introduction*. New Brunswick, NJ: Rutgers University Press, 2005.
Ōmi, Toshihiro. "Tetsugaku kara taiken e: Chikazumi Jōkan no shūkyō shisō." In Iwata, *Kindaika no nakano dentō shūkyō to seishin undō*, 7–21.
Ōno, Akihiko. *Natsume Sōseki to Suzuki Daisetsu: Text kōironteki kōsatsu*. Tokyo Surugadai Shuppansha, 2014.
Origas, Jean-Jacques. "Iki jigoku, soshite hana: Meiji jidai no sanbun ni arawareta shūkyō to bungaku no kakawariai, kōsatsu to kasetsu." In *Sōritsu jusshūnen kinen kokusai symposium: Nihon ni okeru shūkyō to bungaku*, edited by Kokusai Nihon Bunka Kenkyū Center, 117–29. Kyoto: Kokusai Nihon Bunka Kenkyū Center, 1999.
Ōsawa, Ayako. "Kōkōdō dōjin ni yoru tannishō dokkai to shinranzō." *Shūkyō kenkyū* 387 (2016): 27–50.
———. "Taishōki shinran ryūkō to shinranzō." *Bukkyō bunka gakkai kiyō* 27 (2019): 11–37.
Ōtani Daigaku, ed. *Bukkyō ga unda nihongo*. Tokyo: Mainichi Shinbunsha, 2001.
Ōtani, Eiichi. *Kindai bukkyō toiu shiza*. Tokyo: Pericansha, 2012.
Paku, Yuha. "Nihon kindai bungaku to nashonaru aidentiti." PhD diss., Waseda University, 2003.
Payne, Richard, K. "Fractal Journeys: Narrative Structure of the Path and of Tantric Practice." *Pacific World*, 3rd ser., no. 14 (2012): 277–97.
———. "Individuation and Awakening: Romantic Narrative and the Psychological Interpretation of Buddhism." In *Buddhism and Psychotherapy across Cultures: Essays on Theories and Practices*, edited by Mark Unno, 17–30. Boston: Wisdom Publications, 2006.
———. "The Path from Metaphor to Narrative: Gampopa's Jewel Ornament of Liberation." *Pacific World*, 3rd ser., no. 16 (2014): 29–48.
Plutschow, Herbert E. *Tabisuru nihonjin*. Tokyo: Musashino Shoin, 1983.
Porcu, Elisabetta. *Pure Land Buddhism in Modern Japanese Culture*. Leiden: Brill, 2008.

Porter, Bill, trans. *The Laṅkāvatāra Sutra: Translation and Commentary.* Berkeley, CA: Counterpoint, 2013.
Raines, John, ed. *Marx on Religion.* Philadelphia: Temple University Press, 2002.
Rambelli, Fabio. *Buddhist Materiality: A Cultural History of Objects in Japanese Buddhism.* Stanford, CA: Stanford University Press, 2007.
———. *Zen Anarchism: The Egalitarian Dharma of Uchiyama Gudō.* Honolulu: University of Hawai'i Press, 2014.
Ramirez-Christensen, Esperanza. *Emptiness and Temporality: Buddhism and Medieval Japanese Poetics.* Stanford, CA: Stanford University Press, 2008.
Rimer, J. Thomas. "The Historical Literature of Mori Ōgai: An Introduction." In *The Historical Fiction of Mori Ōgai*, 1–11.
———. "Kurata Hyakuzō and *The Origins of Love and Understanding.*" In *Culture and Identity: Japanese Intellectuals during the Interwar Years*, edited by J. Thomas Rimer: 22–36. Princeton, NJ: Princeton University Press, 1990.
Rogers, Minor L., and Ann T. Rogers. *Rennyo: The Second Founder of Shin Buddhism.* Berkeley, CA: Asian Humanities Press, 1991.
Ross, Bruce M. *Remembering the Personal Past: Descriptions of Autobiographical Memory.* New York: Oxford University Press, 1991.
Rubin, Jay, trans. *The Miner.* Stanford, CA: Stanford University Press, 1988.
———, trans. *Sanshirō.* London: Penguin Books, 2000.
Rubinstein, Ernest. *Religion and the Muse: The Vexed Relation between Religion and Western Literature.* Albany: State University of New York, 2007.
Sakaki, Atsuko. *Recontextualizing Texts: Narrative Performance in Modern Japanese Fiction.* Cambridge, MA: Harvard University Press, 1999.
Sako, Jun'ichirō. "Shinran no shisō to kindai bungaku." In *Bukkyō shisō to nihon bungaku*, 205–29.
Sanford, James H., William R. LaFleur, and Masatoshi Nagatomi, eds. *Flowing Traces: Buddhism in the Literary and Visual Arts of Japan.* Princeton, NJ: Princeton University Press, 1992.
Sasaki, Akiko. "*Sanshirō* no hon'yaku: Fukanōsei no taiken." *Aichi shukutoku daigaku kokugo kokubun* 28 (2005): 123–43.
Satō, Eisaku. "Sōseki jihitsu genkō no rubi saikō: *Michikusa* no rubi kara." *Ronshū* 7 (2011): 1–24.
Sawada, Janine Tasca. *Practical Pursuits: Religion, Politics, and Personal Cultivation in Nineteenth-Century Japan.* Honolulu: University of Hawai'i Press, 2004.
Scheiner, Irwin. *Christian Converts and Social Protest in Meiji Japan.* Ann Arbor, MI: University of Michigan Press, 2002.
Schmidt, Susan. "Yōko Matsuoka McClain." In "Deceased Asianists," *Asian Studies Newsletter* 57, no. 1 (Annual Conference Issue, 2012): 40.
Sekiguchi, Yasuyoshi. *Hyōden Matsuoka Yuzuru.* Tokyo: Ozawa Shoten, 1991.
Sharf, Robert H. "Buddhist Modernism and the Rhetoric of Meditative Experience." *Numen* 42 (1995): 228–83.

Sharf, Robert H., and Elizabeth Horton Sharf, eds. *Living Images: Japanese Buddhist Icons in Context*. Stanford, CA: Stanford University Press, 2002.
Shaw, Harry E. *The Forms of Historical Fiction*. Ithaca, NY: Cornell University Press, 1983.
Shibata, Katsue, and Motonari Kai, trans. *I Am a Cat*. Tokyo: Kenkyūsha, 1969.
Shigaraki, Takamaro. "Kindai shinshū kyōdan no shakaiteki dōkō." In *Kindai shinshū kyōdanshi kenkyū*, edited by Shigaraki Takamaro, 7–49. Kyoto: Hōzōkan, 1987.
Shimada, Akiko. "Hiratsuka Raichō no shisō to bukkyō." In *Gendai shisō, Bungaku to bukkyō*, 225–41.
Shimazaki, Tōson. *Chikuma River Sketches*. Translated by William E. Naff. Honolulu: University of Hawai'i Press, 1991.
Shimazono, Susumu. *From Salvation to Spirituality: Popular Religious Movements in Modern Japan*. Melbourne: Trans Pacific Press, 2004.
Shimazu, Naoko. *Japanese Society at War: Death, Memory and the Russo-Japanese War*. New York: Cambridge University Press, 2009.
Shimizu, Seiichirō. *Shōmatsu ari no mama no ki*. Kyoto: Nagata Bunshodō, 1923. First published 1889 by Gohōkan.
Shimura, Kunihiro, ed. "Kin gendai bukkyō bungaku nenpyō." In "Tokushū: Kin gendai sakka to bukkyō bungaku." Special issue, *Kokubungaku: Kaishaku to kanshō—Tokushū, kin gendai sakka to bukkyō bungaku* 55, no. 12 (December 1990): 150–57.
Shirane, Haruo. *The Bridge of Dreams: A Poetics of "The Tale of Genji."* Stanford, CA: Stanford University Press, 1987.
―――, ed. *Early Modern Japanese Literature: An Anthology, 1600–1900*. New York: Columbia University Press, 2002.
―――. Introduction to *Inventing the Classics: Modernity, National Identity, and Japanese Literature*, 4–17. Edited by Haruo Shirane and Tomi Suzuki. Stanford, CA: Stanford University Press, 2000.
Shishida, Fumiaki. "Some Questions Accompanying the Acculturation of Japanese Martial Arts." *Sports kagaku kenkyū* 5 (2008): 197–211.
Sibley, William. *The Shiga Hero*. Chicago: University of Chicago Press, 1979.
Skilling, Peter. Introduction to *Buddhist Narrative in Asia and Beyond*, ix–xvi. Edited by Peter Skilling and Justin McDaniel. 2 vols. Bangkok: Chulalongkorn University, 2013.
Snodgrass, Judith. *Presenting Japanese Buddhism to the West: Orientalism, Occidentalism, and the Columbia Exposition*. Chapel Hill: University of North Carolina Press, 2003.
Somers, Sean. "Passion Plays by Proxy: The Paschal Face as Interculturality in the Works of Endō Shusaku and Mishima Yukio." In *Through a Glass Darkly: Suffering, the Sacred, and the Sublime in Literature and Theory*, edited by Holly Faith Nelson, Lynn R. Szabo, and Jens Zimmermann, 329–48. Waterloo, ON: Wilfred Laurier University Press, 2010.
Stahl, David C. *Trauma, Dissociation and Re-enacting in Japanese Literature and Film*. London: Routledge, 2017.
Stanzel, F. K. *A Theory of Narrative*. New York: Cambridge University Press, 1984.

Starrs, Roy. *An Artless Art: The Zen Aesthetic of Shiga Naoya*. New York: Routledge, 1998.
Stone, Jacqueline I. *Original Enlightenment and the Transformation of Medieval Japanese Buddhism*. Honolulu: University of Hawai'i Press, 1999.
Stone, Jacqueline I., and Mariko Namba Walter, eds. *Death and the Afterlife in Japanese Buddhism*. Honolulu: University of Hawai'i Press, 2008.
Sueki, Fumihiko. "Introduction to the Symposium on Modernity and Buddhism." Translated by Anton Luis Sevilla. *Eastern Buddhist*, n.s., 43, no. 1/2 (2012): 7–23.
———. "A Reexamination of the Kenmitsu Taisei Theory." *Japanese Journal of Religious Studies* 23, no. 3/4 (1996): 449–66.
Suemura, Masayo. "Suzuki Daisetsu ni okeru nyo no rikai: Zen to shinshū." *Hikaku shisō kenkyū* 38 (2011): 22–29.
Sugimoto, Yoshio. *An Introduction to Japanese Society*. Melbourne: Cambridge University Press, 2008.
Sugisaki, Toshio. "Higuchi Ichiyō to bukkyō." *Bungaku gogaku* 130 (1991): 1–15.
———. *Kindai bungaku to shūkyō*. Tokyo: Sōbunsha, 1991.
Śūraṅgama Sūtra Translation Committee of the Buddhist Text Translation Society, trans. *The Śūraṅgama Sūtra*. N.p.: Buddhist Text Translation Society, 2009.
Suter, Rebecca. *Holy Ghosts: The Christian Century in Modern Japanese Fiction*. Honolulu: University of Hawai'i Press, 2015.
Suzuki, Daisetz Teitarō, trans. *The Laṅkāvatāra Sutra: An Epitomized Version*. Rhinebeck, NY: Monkfish, 2014. First published 1932 by Routledge and Kegan Paul (London).
———, trans. *Shinran's Kyōgyōshinshō: The Collection of Passages Expounding the True Teaching, Living, Faith, and Realizing of the Pure Land*. Edited by the Center for Shin Buddhist Studies. New York: Oxford University Press, 2012.
Suzuki, Norihisa. "Kaidai." In *Shukke to sono deshi*, 303–17. Tokyo: Iwanami Bunko, 2007.
Suzuki, Sadami. "Nakazato Kaizan no bukkyō shisō o megutte." In *Gendai shisō, Bungaku to bukkyō*, 259–75.
———. *Nihon no bungaku o kangaeru*. Tokyo: Kadokawa Shoten, 1994.
Suzuki, Takami. "Proust to Murakami Haruki: Jiga hyōgen aruiwa shutai no kakuritsu o megutte." *Fukuoka daigaku kenkyūbu ronshū* A 13, 4 (2014): 83–101.
Suzuki, Tomi. *Narrating the Self: Fictions of Japanese Modernity*. Stanford, CA: Stanford University Press, 1996.
Swanson, Paul L. *Foundations of T'ien-T'ai Philosophy: The Flowering of the Two Truths Theory in Chinese Buddhism*. Berkeley, CA: Asian Humanities Press, 1989.
———. "Takagi Kenmyō and Buddhist Socialism: A Meiji Misfit and Martyr." In *Modern Buddhism in Japan*, edited by Makoto Hayashi, Eiichi Ōtani, and Paul L. Swanson, 144–62. Nagoya: Nanzan University Press, 2014.
Tada, Kanae. "Shinshū jiin seikatsu no kako genzai mirai." *Kyūsai* 8, no. 3 (1918): 20–36.
Tajima, Kunji, and Floyd Shacklock, trans. "My Faith." In *Selected Essays of Manshi Kiyozawa*, 73–78. Kyoto: Bukkyō Bunka Society, 1936.
Takahashi, Kazutomo, trans. *Kusamakura*. Digireads.com, 2013. First published 1927 by Japan Times (Tokyo).

Takeda, Taijun. "Watashi ni totte shūkyō towa nanika: Shūkyōsha to bungakusha wa dōshi de aru." In *Bukkyō no meizuihitsu*. Vol. 2, edited by Kokusho Kankōkai Henshūbu, 215–28. Tokyo: Kokusho Kankōkai, 2006.
Takeuchi, Yoshitomo. "The Role of Marxism in Japan." *Developing Economies* 5, no. 1 (December 1967): 727–47.
Takitō, Mitsuyoshi, ed. "Nihon kindai bungaku to shūkyō." *Chiba daigaku shakai bunka kagaku kenkyū hōkokusho*. Vol. 120. Chiba, Japan: Chiba Daigaku, 2005.
Tanahashi, Kazuaki, ed. *Treasury of the True Dharma Eye: Zen Master Dōgen's Shōbō Genzō*. 2 vols. Boston: Shambhala, 2010.
Tanikawa, Keiichi. "Izumi Kyōka: Tasei no kioku." In *Kindai bungaku to bukkyō*, 169–91.
Taoka, Masahiro. "Nitobe Inazō no dōtoku ni okeru kyōikugakuteki igi." *Hokkaidō daigaku daigakuin kyōikugaku kenkyū kiyō* 126 (2016): 155–69.
Terakawa, Shunshō. *Kiyozawa Manshi ron*. Rev. ed. Kyoto: Bun'eidō, 2002.
———. "Kurata Hyakuzō: Ningen Shinran no hakkensha." In *Kurata Hyakuzō no seishin sekai*, edited by Byakkōkai, 17–41. Kyoto: Nagata Bunshōdō, 1990.
Thomassen, Bjørn. "The Use and Meanings of Liminality." *International Political Anthropology* 2, no. 1 (2009): 5–27.
Tolstoy, Leo. "Father Sergius." In *Master and Man and Other Stories*. Translated by Paul Foote. 13–66. London: Penguin Books, 1977.
Tomasi, Massimiliano. *The Dilemma of Faith in Modern Japanese Literature*. London: Routledge, 2018.
———, ed. "Spirituality in Japanese Literature." *Proceedings of the Association for Japanese Literary Studies* 16 (2015).
Tsang, Carol Richmond. *War and Faith: Ikkō Ikki in Late Muromachi Japan*. Cambridge, MA: Harvard University Press, 2007.
Tsukada, Sayaka. " 'Shūkyō' to 'shinkō': 'Shūkyō bungaku' no ryūkō o meguru futatsu no jutsugo." In *Bungaku sen kyūhyaku nijūichi nen zengo*, edited by Nishi waseda kindai bungaku no kai, 111–33. Tokyo: Nishi waseda kindai bungaku no kai, 2004.
Tsunematsu, Sammy I., trans. *Inside My Glass Doors*. Rutland, VT: Tuttle, 2002.
Tsuruta, Kin'ya. "Sōseki's *Kusamakura*: A Journey to 'The Other Side.' " *Journal of Association of Teachers of Japanese* 22, no. 2 (1988): 169–88.
Tuck, Robert. "Doubled Visions of Desire: Fujimura Misao, Kusamakura, and Homosocial Nostalgia." *Review of Japanese Culture and Society* 29 (2017): 79–91.
Tucker, John. "Japanese Views of Nature and the Environment." In *Nature Across Culture: Views of Nature and the Environment in Non-Western Cultures*, edited by Helaine Selin, 161–83. New York: Springer Netherlands, 2003.
Tugendhat, Ernst. *Egocentricity and Mysticism: An Anthropological Study*. Translated by Alexei Procyshyn and Mario Wenning. New York: Columbia University Press, 2016.
Turner, Victor. *The Anthropology of Performance*. New York: PAJ Publications, 1988.
Turney, Alan, trans. *The Three-Cornered World*. Boston: Tuttle, 2000.

Tweed, Thomas A. *The American Encounter with Buddhism, 1844–1912: Victorian Culture and the Limits of Dissent*. Chapel Hill: University of North Carolina Press, 2000.
———. "Tracing Modernity's Flows: Buddhist Currents in the Pacific World." *Eastern Buddhist*, n.s., 43, no. 1/2 (2012): 35–56.
Ueda, Makoto. *Modern Japanese Writers and the Nature of Literature*. Stanford, CA: Stanford University, 1976.
Ueda, Shizuteru. "Sōseki and Buddhism: Reflections on His Later Works, part 1." Translated by Jan Van Bragt. *Eastern Buddhist*, n.s., 29, no. 2 (1996): 172–206.
———. "Sōseki and Buddhism: Reflections on His Later Works, part 2." Translated by Jan Van Bragt. *Eastern Buddhist*, n.s., 30, no. 1 (1997): 32–52.
Ueda, Shizuteru, and Yanagida Seizan. *Jūgyūzu: Jiko no genshōgaku*. Tokyo: Chikuma Shobō, 1982.
Ueda, Yoshifumi, and Dennis Hirota. *Shinran: An Introduction to His Thought*. Kyoto: Hongwanji International Center, 1989.
Umehara, Takeshi. "Nihonjin no biishiki: Shi no bigaku." *Kokubungaku: Kaishaku to kyōzai no kenkyū* 15, no. 8 (June 1970): 8–16.
Updike, John. "Subconscious Tunnels: Haruki Murakami's Dreamlike New Novel." *New Yorker*, January 24, 2005. http://www.newyorker.com/magazine/2005/01/24/subconscious-tunnels.
Uranishi, Tsutomu. "Shinshū dōjō ni okeru sange (*kokuhaku*) bungaku no hassei." *Bukkyō bungaku* 18 (1994): 76–90.
van der Kolk, Bessel A., and Onno van der Hart. "Pierre Janet and the Breakdown of Adaptation in Psychological Trauma." *American Journal of Psychiatry* (December 1989): 1531–40.
Varley, Paul. *Japanese Culture*. 4th ed. Honolulu: University of Hawai'i Press, 2000.
Viglielmo, Valdo H., trans. *Light and Darkness*. Rutland, VT: Tuttle, 1972.
Voyce, Malcolm. "Buddhist Confession: A Foucauldian Approach." *Macquarie Law WP 2009–1* (March 2009): 1–50.
Waddell, Norman, and Masao Abe, trans. *The Heart of Dōgen's Shōbōgenzō*. Albany: State University of New York Press, 2002.
Watanabe, Chikafumi. "An Examination of Mind-Talk (manojalpa) in the *Mahāyāna-saṃgraha*." *Journal of Indian and Buddhist Studies* 50, no. 2 (2002): 31–35.
Watsuji, Tetsurō, *Zoku ninhon seishinshi kenkyū*. Tokyo: Iwanami Shoten, 1935.
Weinstein, Stanley. "Continuity and Change in the Thought of Rennyo." In *Rennyo and the Roots of Modern Japanese Buddhism*, edited by Mark L. Blum and Shin'ya Yasutomi, 49–58. New York: Oxford University Press, 2006.
Whalen-Bridge, John, and Gary Storhoff, eds. *The Emergence of Buddhist American Literature*. Albany: State University of New York Press, 2009.
Whalen-Bridge, John, Gary Storhoff, and Jan Willis, eds. *Writing as Enlightenment: Buddhist American Literature into the Twenty-First Century*. Albany: State University of New York Press, 2011.

Wheeler, Michael. *Death and the Future Life in Victorian Literature and Theology*. Cambridge, UK: Cambridge University Press, 1990.
White, Hayden. "Historical Pluralism." *Critical Inquiry* 12, no. 3 (1986): 480–93.
———. "Introduction: Historical Fiction, Fictional History, and Historical Reality." *Rethinking History* 9, nos. 2–3 (2005): 147–57.
———. *Metahistory: The Historical Imagination in Nineteenth-Century Europe*. Baltimore: Johns Hopkins University Press, 1973.
Williams, Duncan R. *The Other Side of Zen: A Social History of Sōtō Zen Buddhism in Tokugawa Japan*. Princeton, NJ: Princeton University Press, 2005.
Williams, Paul. *Mahāyāna Buddhism: The Doctrinal Foundations*. London: Routledge, 1989.
Winfield, Pamela D. *Icons and Iconoclasm in Japanese Buddhism: Kūkai and Dōgen on the Art of Enlightenment*. New York: Oxford University, 2013.
Yamada, Mumon. *Lectures on the Ten Oxherding Pictures*. Translated by Victor Sōgen Hori. Honolulu: University of Hawai'i Press, 2004.
Yamamoto, Nobuhiro. *Seishin shugi wa dareno shisō ka*. Kyoto: Hōzōkan, 2011.
Yanabu, Akira. *Hon'yakugo seiritsu jijō*. Tokyo: Iwanami Shinsho, 1982.
Yasutomi, Shin'ya. "The Way of Introspection: Kiyozawa Manshi's Methodology." Translated by Robert F. Rhodes. *Eastern Buddhist*, n.s., 35, no. 1/2 (2003): 102–14.
Ye, Jingjing. "Okakura Tenshin no cha no hon ni kansuru ichi kōsatsu." *Hikaku nihongaku kyōiku kenkyū center kenkyū nenpō* 12 (2016): 25–31.
Yiu, Angela. "Atarashikimura: The Intellectual and Literary Contexts of Taishō Utopian Village." *Japan Review* 20 (2008): 203–30.
Yokoyama, Wayne, trans. *Coffinman: The Journal of a Buddhist Mortician*. Anaheim, CA: Buddhist Education Center, 2002.
Yoshihara, Hiroto. "Matsuoka Yuzuru, hōjō o mamoru hitobito." In "Tokushū: Kin gendai sakka to bukkyō bungaku." Special issue, *Kokubungaku: Kaishaku to kanshō—Tokushū, kin gendai sakka to bukkyō bungaku* 55, no. 12 (December 1990): 118–23.
Yu, Beongcheon, trans. *The Wayfarer*. New York: Perigee Books, 1982.
Žižek, Slavoj. *The Sublime Object of Ideology*. London: Verso, 2008.

Index

aesthetic sensibility, 14, 28, 156, 169, 170, 217
Akegarasu Haya: 2, 25, 86, 90, 104, 128, 130; on Amida Buddha, 109, 112–18; on Christianity, 114–15; on confession, 103–19; early life, 103; and Kiyozawa Manshi, 103–4, 106–10, 113–15, 117, 225, 227–28, 235, 242, 244; personal fiction, 6; as poet-Buddhist priest, 104; on sexuality, 6, 90, 103, 107, 110, 113, 115, 231; on *Tannishō*, 104, 226, 231. *See also* death, Akegarasu Haya on; Jōdo Shinshū
  Texts: "After Returning to the Womb of the Buddha," 105, 115–16; *Before and after My Rebirth*, 6, 90, 105–8, 112, 114–19, 216–17, 225; "Even Evil Acts Are Embraced by Tathagata's Grace," 104; "Is This How I Am Going to Ruin Myself?" 105, 115; *The Ruin*, 105, 108–10, 232
akunin, 104, 117
Akutagawa Ryūnosuke, 16, 125, 264n7, 267n19
ālaya-vijñāna, 9
allegorical reading, 2, 7, 144, 147. *See also* Buddhist symbols

Amida Buddha: 8, 17, 20–21, 87, 91–95, 129, 131, 150, 155, 207, 210–11, 216; Akegarasu Haya on, 109, 112–18; by the grace of, 104–5, 113–15, 117–18, 137–39, 143, 230; Chikazumi Jōkan on, 102–3; Kiyozawa Manshi on, 91, 96–100; Natsume Sōseki on, 37–38, 42; as *oyasama*, 93; Shiga Naoya on, 52, 56
Analects of Confucius, 3, 152
Anezaki Masaharu, 44
Aoki Shinmon, 217, 219–20
  Text: *Coffinman: The Journal of a Buddhist Mortician*, 220, 312n14
ari no mama, 4–5, 61–65, 74, 76, 83, 87. *See also* Natsume Sōseki, Nishida Kitarō, Shiga Naoya, Suzuki Daisetsu, Tayama Katai
Arishima Takeo, 16
Ashio copper mine, 51, 197
Aśvaghoṣa, 29
author, narrator, and hero: assumption of singular identity, 73, 164; Edward Fowler on, 3, 73–74, 86, 185–86; interdependent of, 62, 86
autobiography, *see* I-novels
auto*hetero*biography, 72, 82. *See also* Natsume Sōseki

Bai Juyi (Hakurakuten), 29
Battle of Liaoyang, 200, 204
Bell, Clive, 56
biographical criticism, 19, 215
Bodhisattva, 20–21, 29, 55, 82, 156, 173, 228; Dharmākara, 92, 113, 117, 243–44
Buddha nature, 39, 80–81, 288n80. *See also* nature
Buddhist funerals: 7–8, 22, 31, 144, 191–93; in *The Diary of the Second Army Corps at War*, 200–3, 205; in *Life*, 205–9; as Matsuoka Yuzuru's, 126; in *The Miner*, 196–200; as Natsume Sōseki's, 36; in *Sanshirō*, 193–95; as Tayama Katai's, 50; in *To the Spring Equinox and Beyond*, 209–12. *See also* liminality, funerary Buddhism
Buddhist modernism, 23, 271n55
Buddhist practice: 23, 122, 148, 190, 290n102, 293n45; lay Buddhist practice, 2, 86; and literary pursuit, 12, 61, 86; "right view," 4–5, 61; Shin Buddhist practice, 6, 93, 211; as writing of personal fiction, 5
Buddhist sutras: 55, 93, 101, 226, 267n20; *Avataṃsaka Sutra*, 47, 218, 280n60; *Diamond Sutra*, 21; *Heart Sutra*, 21; *Laṅkāvatāra Sutra*, 47, 280n60; *Larger Sutra of Immeasurable Life*, 21, 38, 92, 107, 113, 117, 244, 295n87, 296n92; *Lotus Sutra*, 9, 21, 47, 49, 78, 104, 162; *Nirvana Sutra*, 47, 49, 101, 280n60; *Perfection of Wisdom Sutras*, 20–21; *Shorter Sukhāvatīvyūha Sutra*, 155; *Vimalakīrti Sutra*, 21. *See also* Mahayana Buddhism
Buddhist symbols, 7–8, 147, 149–50, 263n7. *See also* allegorical reading

bungaku: as *bukkyō bungaku*, 17, 118; as modern Japanese concept, 13–14. *See also shūkyō*
bush warbler: 161, and *Lotus Sutra*, 162
butsudō, 27–28. *See also dō*

cherry blossoms, 144, 272n66
Chikamatsu Monzaemon, 13, 150, 229
Chikazumi Jōkan: 90–92; on confession, 101–3. *See also* Jōdo Shinshū, Higashi Honganji
 Texts: *A Record of My Repentance*, 101; "The Lingering of My Faith," 100
Christianity: 3, 6, 19, 21–22, 25, 41, 43, 46, 91, 98, 127, 166, 170, 172, 264n2, 274n97; Akegarasu Haya on, 114–15, 227; Karatani Kōjin on, 89–90; Shiga Naoya on, 51, 281n80; Uchimura Kanzō on, 15, 25, 51, 89–90, 95
Confucianism and Neo-Confucianism, 3, 12, 24, 26, 39, 45, 57, 63, 98, 124, 284n112, 306n84
Confucius, 58
cosmic Buddhas, 20

danka system, 21–22, 206
Daochuo, 25
daruma doll, in *The Gate*, 147, 160
Dasheng qixin lun (*Daijō kishinron*), 9
Dazai Osamu, 16
death: 4, 7–8, 13, 15–17, 59, 61–63, 114, 150, 191, 206, 209, 215–17, 311n61; Akegarasu Haya on, 6, 9; in "At Kinosaki," 84–86; of author, 215; in *Before and after My Rebirth*, 107–13, 225, 227–28, 230, 232, 234–35, 237, 242–43; in *Coffinman*, 219–20; in *A Dark Night's Passing*, 180, 183–86, 188, 190; in *The Diary*

of the Second Army Corps at War, 201, 203–4; in *Guardians of the Dharma Castle*, 130, 133; the High Treason Incident, 176; in *Kafka on the Shore*, 222; Kiyozawa Manshi on, 90, 95, 97, 109–10, 113, 121; in *Life*, 205–9; liminality, 192–93; in *The Miner*, 199; in *The Miracle of a Buddhist Monk*, 173, 175–77; Murakami Haruki on, 221; Natsume Sōseki on, 35–43, 65–66, 125–26, 276n27 (see also *Shuzenji* crisis); Paṭācārā on, 30; in *The Quilt*, 167–69; in *The Ruin*, 109–10; in *Sanshirō*, 194–96; Shakyamuni Buddha on, 20; Shiga Naoya on, 50–54, 58; Tayama Katai on, 44, 49–50, 191; in *The Three-Cornered World*, 154–55, 157; in *To the Spring Equinox and Beyond*, 210–13

Derrida, Jacques, 162

Dharma body, 80–81, 93, 289n81

dō: as *budō*, 29; as *bushidō*, 28; as *butsudō*, 27–28; as *geidō*, 28. See also path

Dōgen: "Being-Time," 163; Kamakura Buddhism, 22; as literary category, 17–18; poetry, 11–13; *Shōbōgenzō*, 160; sitting in meditation, 28, 64, 160, 175

early modern Japanese literature, 1, 11–13, 150, 198

Eastern Buddhism, 22

Edo period (1603–1867): Buddhist organizations, 21, 93, 141, 227; culture and literature, 21, 24, 49–50, 76, 124, 198; hidden Christians, 90, 166; shogunate, 12, 166

eightfold path, 19, 28

Eisai or Yōsai, 22

Emperor Meiji, 96, 176, 206, 232

Emperor Shōwa, 141

Engakuji, 38–39, 43, 157, 181

esoteric Buddhism, 9, 13, 81, 149

Father Sergius, 114–15, 235, 237–41

Fenollosa, Ernest, 25

five aggregates, 20, 167

Foley, Barbara, 123, 134, 137. See also historical fiction

Freud, Sigmund, 183, 188–89

Fujiwara Shunzei, 12, 63

Fujiwara Teika, 12, 63

Fujiwara Tetsujō, 132

Fukuzawa Yukichi, 269n39

funerary Buddhism: as *danka* system, 21–22, 206; as rites of passage, 7, 191–92, 215. See also Buddhist funerals

Furukawa Rōsen, 269n39

Furukawa Zaibatsu, 51

futon: as allegory, 147, 160; as *The Quilt*, 7, 163–64, 168–69

Genshin, 26, 55–57, 182

gokurakusui, 166

haikai, 1, 13, 24, 64, 152

haiku, 63, 83, 110, 150, 152, 226, 272n63

Hasegawa Nyozekan, 133, 300n28

Hearn, Lafcadio, 25, 83

Heian period (794–1185), 12, 63, 156

Higashi Honganji, 90, 95, 97, 99, 101, 103–4, 117, 121–22, 127–29, 137–43, 176, 226, 231

High Treason Incident, 176, 280n58, 283n99

Higuchi Ichiyō, 9, 217

Text: "Child's Play," 218–19

historical fiction: 7, 121, 140; definition of, 123–24; Matsuoka Yuzuru on,

historical fiction *(continued)*
  124; Mori Ōgai on, 124. *See also*
  Foley, Barbara
Hōjō Tamio, 16
Hōjōki, 35, 49, 274n1
Hōnen, 18, 22, 26, 43, 93, 100, 140
Hori Tatsuo, 16
Huainanzi, 81
Huysmans, Joris-Karl, 47, 279n50

Ichikawa Danjūrō, 13
ie, household system, 18
Ikkyū, 17
Imakita Kōsen, 39
impermanence, 4, 13–15, 17, 20, 24, 26, 35, 44–45, 49–50, 148–49, 156, 166, 169, 185, 191, 196, 201–3, 211, 213, 215, 218, 220–21, 223, 235
I-novels *(shishōsetsu)*: Edward Fowler on, 3, 26; Irmela Hijiya-Kirschnereit on, 26; Tomi Suzuki on, 3, 27. *See also* personal fiction
Inoue Yasushi, 17
Ippen, 22
Ishiyama War, 141
Islamic modernism, 23–24
Itō Sei, 15–17
Izumi Kyōka, 9

jakujōri, in *The Poppy*, 37
jakumetsu: in *Sanshirō*, 195; in *The Three-Cornered World*, 156
James, William, 42, 65, 171
jiriki, 44, 87, 98
Jōdo Shinshū (Shin Buddhism): 121, 127, 140, 176, 218; Akegarasu Haya on, 25, 104–5, 117; Chikazumi Jōkan on, 103; in *Guardians of the Dharma Castle*, 131, 136, 139; Kiyozawa Manshi on, 25, 95, 97–98; Matsuoka Yuzuru on, 121; Natsume Sōseki on, 36, 43; as practice, 90; Rennyo on, 93–94; Shinran on, 6, 43, 92. *See also Before and after My Rebirth*
jōruri, 13, 24
Jūgyūzu, 55
jumbō, 196–200

Kagami Pond, in *The Three-Cornered World*, 154–57
Kajii Motojirō, 16
Kamakura period (1185–1333): 12, 25, 63; as a place, 38–39, 42; Kamakura New Buddhism, 4, 18, 22, 100, 270n52. *See also* Engakuji
Kamei Katsuichirō, 18, 268n27
Kamono Chōmei, 35, 49
Kamura Isota, 100, 263n7
Kanbayashi Akatsuki, 16
Kanō Jigorō, 29
Karatani Kōjin, 5, 89–90, 98, 119, 166
karmic punishment, 4, 158
Kasai Zenzō, 263n7
Kawabata Yasunari, 15, 266n19
Kawakami Bizan, 16
Kenri Bunshū, 17–18
Kinoshita Naoe, 18
kirishitanzaka, 166
Kitamura Tōkoku, 16
Kitano Genpō, 51
Kiyozawa Manshi: 2, 6, 8, 26, 90; on Amida Buddha, 91, 96–100; on confession, 87, 97–99; early life, 95; on *Kokoro*, 96; and Shinran, 95, 97, 99–100; on *Tannishō*, 99. *See also* death, Kiyozawa Manshi on; Jōdo Shinshū **Texts**: "The Nature of My Faith," 6, 90, 95, 97–99, 103, 216, 227; *A Record of Repentance during My Sickness*, 95; *Skeleton of a Philosophy of Religion*, 25
kōan, 39, 42–43, 149, 157–59, 161, 163, 181, 184, 304n56. *See also* Zen Buddhism

Kōda Rohan, 18
Kōkōdō, 97, 121, 128, 139, 142
Kōtoku Shūsui, 176
Krondorfer, Björn, 91, 107–8
Kūkai, 149
Kumagai Naoyoshi, 49–50
Kumakura Chiyuki, 160–61
Kume Masao: 125, 298n13; *The Wrecked Ship*, 125
Kuo-an Shih-yuan (J. Kakuan Shion), 55
Kurata Hyakuzō, 18, 44, 127
Kūya, 55, 57, 182
kyōgen kigo, 12

LaFleur, William R., 12, 149–50, 311n61
Laozi, 1, 28, 81
lay Buddhism: 2, 4–5, 17, 22, 31, 60, 64, 86, 100, 243; Natsume Sōseki, 39
Leach, Bernard H., 25
letters: as means of confession, 106; Rennyo's, 94, 211–13
Letters of Nun Eshinni, 127
liminality: 8, 192–93; as persona, 191, 201, 203, 208. *See also* funerary Buddhism
Lukács, Georg, 140

Madhyamaka school, 20, 147
Maeterlinck, Maurice, 58, 278n36
Mahayana Buddhism, 9, 20, 47, 49–50, 78–79, 148, 173. *See also* Buddhist sutras
Manchuria, 25, 159, 173, 180, 201, 219, 278n46
Man'yōshū, 12
Marx, Karl, on religion, 134
Marxism: Akegarasu on, 143; in *Guardians of the Dharma Castle*, 133–36; in Japan, 134

Masaoka Shiki: 16, 151; on *ari no mama*, 62–63; and Natsume Sōseki, 36, 38, 62
Matsuo Bashō, 1, 13, 64, 150, 152
Matsuoka Yuzuru: 2–3, 6, 9, 24–25; early life, 121, 124–25, 133; and Higashi Honganji, 121, 128, 142; historical fiction, 123–24 (*see also* Foley, Barbara); and Kume Masao, 125; and Natsume Sōseki, 8, 43, 125–26; on *sokuten kyoshi*, 126–27; and Tada Kanae, 139; Taishō religious boom, 6
Texts: "A Blowfish Buddhist Priest," 125; *Guardians of the Dharma Castle*, 6, 9, 121–43, 247–61; "Home to Protect the Dharma," 127–28, 139, 300n28; *The Life of Shakyamuni*, 126; *The Mona Lisa*, 125; *The Story of Dunhuang*, 126
Matsuura Tatsuo: and Kagawas, 75–76; and Tayama Katai, 45
medieval Japanese literature, 1, 24, 81, 149, 265n5
meditation: 12, 28, 65, 76, 148, 163, 172, 184, 228; as aesthetic meditation, 24, 49, 63, 149; *futon*, 7, 160; as mystical, 175; Natsume Sōseki on, 5, 35, 37–38, 42–43, 50, 59, 73, 86, 157
Meiji Japan: Buddhist leaders, 44; Emperor Meiji, 96, 176, 206, 232; Meiji government, 13, 22, 45, 89, 176, 201; Meiji Restoration, 51, 57, 89
Meiji period (1868–1912), 13–14, 19, 58, 93, 100, 206
memory: as narrative memory, 61, 67, 69, 213; Pierre Janet on, 67
Miki Kiyoshi, 100
Mineo Setsudō, 176
Mishima Yukio, 17

Mitsui Kōshi, 100
Miyazawa Kenji, 9, 18, 104, 219
modern Japanese literature: 1, 2, 191; Buddhist characterization of, 15, 17–19, 190; Buddhist imagery 2, 150, 163 (*see also* Buddhist symbols); boundary (disciplinary divide) of, 2, 6, 9, 13–14, 92, 118; Christian influence on, 5–6, 89–90; as discipline or as *bungaku*, 13–14, 265n16, 266n17
mondō, in *The Gate*, 7, 39, 147, 161–63
mono no aware, 26, 306n84
monogatari, 1, 12
Mori Ōgai, 15, 17–19, 45, 124, 200, 204. *See also* historical fiction
Motoori Norinaga, 169
Mount Akagi, 58
Mount Daisen, 54–55, 180–81, 183–87, 307n36
Mount Hiei, 1, 100
Mount Minobu, 78
Murakami Haruki, 217, 220–22
 Text: *Kafka on the Shore*, 221–22
Murakami Senshō, 51
Mushanokōji Saneatsu, 18, 51
myōkōnin, 93, 290n104
mysticism: and Buddhism, 7, 216; in *A Dark Night's Passing*, 179, 185–86; in *The Miracle of a Buddhist Monk*, 173, 175–77; Natsume Sōseki on, 40; as rational mysticism, 172–73; Tayama Katai on, 44

Nāgārjuna, 25, 147–48
Nakae Chōmin, 269n39
Nakano Shigeharu, 104
Nakayama Gishū, 6
Nakayama Miki, 57, 296n1
nanga, 24
Nanjō Bun'yū, 140, 278n46

Natsume Fudeko, 125, 298n14
Natsume Kyōko, 72, 125, 298n19
Natsume Sōseki: xi, 2, 15, 18, 35, 96, 106, 124–25, 143, 147, 150, 157, 159, 212, 222; on *ari no mama* and attainment of Buddhahood, 61–63; auto*hetero*biography, 72, 286n46; choice of kanji characters, 67, 160–61, 285n27; dead for thirty minutes, 39, 73; early life, 36–39; lay Buddhism, 38–39; and Matsuoka Yuzuru, 43, 126; and Natsume Kyōko, 72, 298n19; on nature, 76–77, 81–82; and Nishida Kitarō, 65; no-self, 77; path, 42–43, 66; Pure Land Buddhism, 38, 43–44; and Shiga Naoya, 8; and Tayama Katai, 8, 76–77, 81–82; Zen Buddhism and Zen priests, 36, 38–39, 42–43. *See also Shuzenji* crisis
 Texts: *The Gate*, 157–63; *Grass on the Wayside*, 66–73; *I Am a Cat*, 37; "Imitation and Independence," 43, 62; *Kokoro*, 96, 106; *Light and Darkness*, 42, 76–77, 286n46; *The Miner*, 196–200; *The Poppy*, 37–38; "Recollections," 39–40, 277n29; *Sanshirō*, 193–96; *Ten Nights of Dreams*, 37; *The Three-Cornered World*, 150–57; *To the Spring Equinox and Beyond*, 209–13
naturalism, western influence on Japan, 45–46
nature: beauty of nature, 4, 6, 15–16, 24, 45, 50, 54, 151, 185, 217; as mother nature, 8, 50, 54, 179–80; Natsume Sōseki on, 8, 76–77; Shiga Naoya on, 17, 50–57, 307n36; as *shizen* and *jinen*, 81–82; Tayama Katai on, 8, 45, 49, 74–76, 80–81; Western Romantics on, 75. *See also* Buddha nature

nenbutsu or *namu amida butsu*, 37–38, 52, 92–93, 109, 111, 116, 132, 149, 155, 207, 210–11, 226, 230, 243, 251, 256
Nichiren: 18, 22, 44; in *Kokoro*, 96; in *Remaining Snow*, 78; and Tayama Katai, 44
Nietzsche, Friedrich, 46, 112, 159, 234
Nishi Amane, 269n39
Nishi Honganji, 127, 140–41
Nishiari Bokusan, 51
Nishida Kitarō: 15, 266n16; on *ari no mama*, 64; lay Buddhism, 22; and Natsume Sōseki, 65; on pure experience, 64, 100
Text: *Inquiry into the Good*, 64, 127
Nishida Masayoshi, 15, 104, 106
Nishitani Keiji, 266n16
Nitobe Inazō, 28
Niwa Fumio, 16–18, 121
no-self: as a Buddhist concept, 41; Kiyozawa Manshi on, 100; Natsume Sōseki on, 44, 77
Noma Hiroshi, 18
non-dual, 4–5, 7–8, 77, 83, 149–50, 157, 190–93

Oda Nobunaga, 141
ōjō, in *The Three-Cornered World*, 7, 147, 151, 154–57
Okakura Tenshin, 28
Okamoto Kanoko, 9
Ophelia, 153–155
Origas, Jean-Jacques, 18–19
Osaragi Jirō, 18
Ōta Gyokumei, 45, 47, 50, 173
Otani University, 97–98, 140
other-power Buddhism, 17, 43–44, 48, 60, 96–98, 100, 231
Otto, Rudolf, 56
Ōuchi Seiran, 51
Ozaki Kazuo, 16

Ozaki Kōyō, 279n53, 310n41

Paphnutius, 112, 234
path: Akegarasu Haya's 6; as Buddhist notion, 2, 7, 19–21, 27–30, 63, 93, 138, 215, 217; Kiyozawa Manshi's, 6, 100; as literary device, 7, 30–31, 60, 63, 143, 171, 217; Matsuoka Yuzuru's, 6; Natsume Sōseki's, 42, 43; as passage, 8; Shiga Naoya's, 55; Tayama Katai's, 47–48; as travel, 157; Yukawa Hideki's, 1. See also *dō*
path literature: 5, 29, 31, 61, 143, 215, 219–20, 223; "At Kinosaki" as, 85; *Before and after My Rebirth* as, 115, 216; "Child's Play" as, 218; *Coffinman* as, 220; *A Dark Night's Passing* as, 178, 180, 216; *The Diary of the Second Army Corps at War* as, 201; *The Gate* as, 162, 216; *Grass on the Wayside* as, 61, 66–67, 69, 71, 72; *Guardians of the Dharma Castle* as, 122; *Kafka on the Shore* as, 222; *Life* as, 205–6; *The Miner* as, 197, 200; *The Miracle of a Buddhist Monk* as, 174, 216; as narrative structure of Buddhism, 2, 27, 30, 191; "The Nature of My Faith" as, 98, 216; *The Quilt* as, 166, 170; *Remaining Snow* as, 77–79, 216; *Sanshirō* as, 193, 195; *The Three-Cornered World* as, 151; *To the Spring Equinox and Beyond* as, 212–13
personal fiction: 2, 5–9, 26–27, 29, 50, 61–62, 73, 83–84, 86, 92, 118–19, 123, 128, 143, 171, 177–78, 191, 213, 215–17, 219–20, 233; definition of, 3; modernism, 5. See also I-novels, path, path literature
proletarian: literature, 219, 301n56; writers, 134
Pure Land: aesthetic dimension, 15, 151; Akegarasu Haya on, 25, 86, 104,

Pure Land *(continued)*
109, 226, 244, 251; birth in the Pure Land, 7, 13, 21, 90–94, 137, 141, 149, 155–56, 166, 211; *gokurakusui*, 166; Matsuoka Yuzuru on, 121; Natsume Sōseki on, 9, 35, 38, 42–44; Seven Pure Land Masters, 25; Shiga Naoya on, 51–52, 55–56; Shinran on 43, 92–93; symbol of, 7, 150, 154–56; Tada Kanae on, 137

rakugo, 13
refiguration, 29–30
Rennyo: 93–94; "Letter on White Ashes," 211–12
Rinzai sect, 39, 176
Russo-Japanese War, 8, 25, 46, 59, 117, 193, 200–1, 203, 296n1
Ryōkan, 17, 43

Saichō, 289n81
Saigyō, 1–2, 149–50
Saitō Mokichi, 104
Sakaino Kōyō, 139
sange or *zange*, 93–95, 101
Sasaki Gesshō, 98, 140, 226–27, 231
Satō Haruo, 18
Schelling, Friedrich W. J., 75
Seinan War, 45, 201
Seishin shugi, 87, 97, 130, 132, 137, 142
self-detachment, 4, 8, 31, 61, 75, 77, 186
self-power Buddhism, 17, 43–44, 48, 60, 90, 96, 98
self-realization: 2, 7, 24, 31, 41, 71, 107, 114–15, 122, 143, 157, 173, 176–77, 216; Akegarasu Haya's, 92, 117; Kiyozawa Manshi's, 98; Kume Masao's, 298n13; *myōkōnin*, 93; Natsume Sōseki's, 43, 67; Shiga Naoya's, 59, 84; Tayama Katai's, 47–48

self-transformation, 2, 7, 26, 31, 62, 76, 86, 119, 143, 147, 162, 171, 186, 215, 222
setsuwa, 12, 56
sexuality: 19, 82, 149; Akegarasu Haya on, 6, 90, 103, 107, 110, 113, 115, 231; Shinran on, 93; Tayama Katai on, 166
Shaku Sōen, 36, 39
Shakyamuni Buddha: 5, 20–21, 25, 44, 49, 58, 79–80, 101, 107, 126, 136–38, 230; Four Noble Truths, 19, 167; Siddhartha Gautama, 78, 114, 172–73, 242
Shandao, 25, 94
Shiga Naomichi, 51
Shiga Naoya: 2, 16–17, 35, 118–19, 132, 171, 177–79, 183, 185, 216; on *ari no mama*, 83; early life, 50–51; and Natsume Sōseki, 8; nature, 54–57; on Pure Land, 51–52, 55–56; and the Shiga hero, 54–55, 61, 84–86, 178, 185; spiritual rhythm, 83–84; on Tenrikyō, 57–58; and Yanagi Muneyoshi, 52
Texts: "At Kinosaki," 5, 54, 61, 83–86, 217; "Confused Head," 53; *A Dark Night's Passing*, 7, 54, 171, 173, 177–90, 216–17; "Han's Crime," 53; "Kuma," 282n89; "The Razor," 53–54; *Reconciliation*, 54
shikan, 49, 63, 281n72
Shimada Seijirō, 104
Shimaji Mokurai, 51
Shimaki Kensaku, 16
Shimazaki Tōson: 15, 18, 50, 76, 107; *New Life*, 111–12, 233–34
shinjin, 93
Shinran: and Akegarasu Haya, 25; and Aoki Shinmon, 219–20; in *Before and after My Rebirth*, 227, 231, 243; and Chikazumi Jōkan, 101; in *Coffinman*, 219–20; confession, 6, 93–94; defining the Seven Pure

Land Masters, 25; as founder of Shin Buddhism, 92–93; in *Guardians of the Dharma Castle*, 131, 136–37, 139–40, 142; Kamakura Buddhism, 22; and Kiyozawa Manshi, 95, 97, 99–100; and Kurata Hyakuzō, 44, 127; *Kyōgyōshinshō*, 125, 251; as literary category, 17–18; and Matsuoka Yuzuru, 128; and Natsume Sōseki, 43; Shinran boom, 127; in *To the Spring Equinox and Beyond*, 211

shinsentai poems, 38, 275n15

Shinto, 8, 13, 18–19, 57, 169–70, 218–19; Buddhist–Shinto funeral in *Life*, 205–9

Shinto shrines: 13, 170, 218–19; Daisen Shrine, 187; Hachiman, 169; Hibiya Great Shrine, 207; Yasukuni Shrine, 206, 209

Shirakaba-ha, 25, 46

shugendō, 13, 185

shūkyō: 59, 65, 126–27; as modern Japanese concept, 13, 35. See also *bungaku*

Shuzenji crisis, 36, 39–41, 44, 59, 73, 209. See also death, Natsume Sōseki on

sincerity, as discourse, 4, 26, 74, 76

skillful means, 12, 20–21, 29, 93, 156

Soga Ryōjin, 118

sokuten kyoshi, 8, 15, 17, 126–27

Song dynasty China, 153

spiritual other, 91, 100, 103

subtextual, 2, 72, 144, 162, 170

suffering, 5, 7, 12, 19–20, 28, 30–31, 50, 76, 79, 83, 98, 102, 112, 122, 134, 138–39, 143, 148, 163, 166–67, 175, 196, 212–13, 215, 218, 233, 243

śūnyatā, 20, 47, 147

supernatural: elements, 186; events, 189; experience, 117; powers, 177, 185, 188, 232, 238–39, 282n89

superstition, 136, 177, 179, 186, 188–89

Suzuki Daisetsu: on *ari no mama*, 64–65; lay Buddhism, 22, 100; on *sokuhi no ronri*, 66, 78

Tada Kanae, 128, 130, 137, 226

Taishō religious boom, 6

Taishō religious literature, 123–24, 127

Takagi Kenmyō, 176, 306n16

Takahama Kyoshi, 38, 275n15

Takayama Chogyū, 18, 44

Takeda Taijun, 9

Takeuchi Yoshinori, 100

The Tale of Genji, 1, 156, 221

Tanaka Chigaku, 44

Tanluan, 25

Tannishō: Akegarasu Haya on, 104, 226, 231; Kiyozawa Manshi on, 25, 99

tathāgatagarbha, 9, 80

Taoism, 3, 16, 28, 40

tariki, 44

Tayama Katai: xi, 2, 35, 63, 106, 143, 147, 150, 163, 171, 200; on *ari no mama*, 73–74; on Buddhism, 44–50; early life, 45–46; method of writing, 73–77; and Mori Ōgai, 200, 204; and Natsume Sōseki, 76–77, 81–82; on naturalism, 45–50, 76; subjectivity, 74–77, 79; *waka* influence on, 45, 75–76

Texts: *The Diary of the Second Army Corps at War*, 8, 46, 50, 191, 200–5, 217; "From Naturalism to Buddhism," 44, 48–49; *Life*, 8, 46, 191, 205–9, 216; *The Miracle of a Buddhist Monk*, 7, 50, 171, 173–77, 216; *The Quilt*, 7, 46, 73, 76–77, 106, 147, 150, 163–70, 171, 205, 217; *Remaining Snow*, 5, 50, 61, 73, 77–83, 106, 216

Temple Buddhism, 122–24, 128–29, 131, 133–34, 136, 138–39, 142–43

Tenrikyō, 3, 57–58, 186–89
three poisons, 12, 19
Tokyo Imperial University, 24–25, 36, 38, 95, 101, 125, 300n26
Tolstoy, Leo, 46, 107, 114, 127, 235, 242
tonjaku, 67, 285n27
Tonomura Shigeru, 16–18
trilogy: Akegarasu Haya's, 106; Natsume Sōseki's, 9, 37; Tayama Katai's, 46
Tsubouchi Shōyō, 18, 63
tuberculosis, 6, 85, 95–96, 108–9, 111, 131
Turner, Victor, 192–93, 199

Uchimura Kanzō, 15, 25, 51, 89, 95, 98, 281n80
Uchiyama Gudō, 176
Uemura Masahisa, 269n39
ukiyo, 12
Umehara Takeshi, 15
uncanny, 183–84, 188–89
united Buddhism, 4, 22, 44
Unshō, Vinaya master, 51

Vasubandhu, 25

waka, 1, 24, 45, 63, 75, 217
Watsuji Tetsurō, 14–15, 127
Wordsworth, William, 75, 152
World's Parliament of Religions in Chicago (1893), 25, 39

Yanagi Muneyoshi, 52, 127
Yanagita Kunio, 45
Yogācāra school, 20, 148
yōkyoku, 24
Yoshida Rōken, 45
yūgen, 28, 45, 50, 151, 272n82
Yukawa Hideki, 1, 8

Zarathustra, 112, 159, 234–35
Zeami, 64
Zen Buddhism: 28, 43, 50–51, 151, 170; *futon*, 160; Zen monks, 36, 39, 42, 153, 156–58, 181. *See also* Engakuji, kōan, lay Buddhism, Natsume Sōseki
Zhuangzi, 1, 3, 28, 152
Žižek, Slavoj, 202

www.ingramcontent.com/pod-product-compliance
Lightning Source LLC
Chambersburg PA
CBHW030127240426
43672CB00005B/49